RACE IN THE COLLEGE CLASSROOM

RACE

IN THE COLLEGE CLASSROOM:
PEDAGOGY AND POLITICS

EDITED BY BONNIE TUSMITH AND MAUREEN T. REDDY

RUTGERS UNIVERSITY PRESS
NEW BRUNSWICK, NEW JERSEY, AND LONDON

LIBRARY OF CONGRESS CATALOGING-IN-PUBLICATION DATA

Race in the college classroom : pedagogy and politics / edited by Bonnie TuSmith and Maureen T. Reddy.

p.   cm.

Includes bibliographical references.

ISBN 0-8135-3108-X (cloth : alk. paper)   — ISBN 0-8135-3109-8 (pbk. : alk. paper)

1. Discrimination in higher education—United States.   2. Minorities—Education (Higher)—United States.   3. Education, Higher—Political aspects—United States. I. Reddy, Maureen T.   II. TuSmith, Bonnie, 1951–

LC212.42.R33   2002

306.43—dc21

2001058685

British Cataloging-in-Publication information is available from the British Library.

Manufactured in the United States of America

CONTENTS

Acknowledgments   *ix*

INTRODUCTION: RACE IN THE COLLEGE CLASSROOM   *1*
   Maureen T. Reddy and Bonnie TuSmith

PART I   AUTHORITY AND (IL)LEGITIMACY   *5*

TWO VOICES FROM THE FRONT LINES:
A CONVERSATION ABOUT RACE IN THE CLASSROOM   *7*
   Karen Elias and Judith C. Jones

TEACHING IN FLORIDA: THE END OF AFFIRMATIVE ACTION
AND THE POLITICS OF RACE   *19*
   Sarika Chandra

A GHOST IN THE COLLABORATIVE MACHINE:
THE WHITE MALE TEACHER IN THE MULTICULTURAL CLASSROOM   *28*
   Peter Kerry Powers

DECENTERING WHITENESS: RESISTING RACISM
IN THE WOMEN'S STUDIES CLASSROOM   *40*
   Patti Duncan

SMASHING THE RULES OF RACIAL STANDING   *51*
   Maureen T. Reddy

WHEN THE POLITICAL IS PERSONAL: LIFE ON THE MULTIETHNIC MARGINS   *62*
   Jennifer Ho

THE ENTANGLEMENTS OF TEACHING *NAPPY HAIR*   *71*
   Rebecca Meacham

BEYOND BULL CONNER: TEACHING SLAVERY IN ALABAMA   *84*
   Fred Ashe

FEAR AND THE PROFESSORIAL CENTER   *96*
   Kevin Everod Quashie

PART 2   REWARDS AND PUNISHMENTS   *109*

OUT ON A LIMB: RACE AND THE EVALUATION OF FRONTLINE TEACHING   *112*
   Bonnie TuSmith

WHITENESS ON A WHITE CANVAS: TEACHING RACE
IN A PREDOMINANTLY WHITE UNIVERSITY   126
  Karyn D. McKinney

GIFT WRAPPED OR PAPER BAGGED?:
PACKAGING RACE FOR THE CLASSROOM   140
  Rajini Srikanth

THE QUESTION OF COMFORT: THE IMPACT OF RACE
ON/IN THE COLLEGE CLASSROOM   153
  Virginia Whatley Smith

FAR MORE THAN FRYBREAD: THE TENDER ISSUE OF RACE
IN TEACHING LITERATURE   167
  Roberta J. Hill

MENACED BY RESISTANCE: THE BLACK TEACHER
IN THE MAINLY WHITE SCHOOL/CLASSROOM   176
  Gîtahi Gîtîtî

STRATEGIES FOR SURVIVING RACE IN THE CLASSROOM   189
  Karen J. Leong

TRAPS, PITFALLS, AND OBSTACLES: CHALLENGES
TO CONFRONTING RACISM IN ACADEMIA   200
  Brenda Boudreau and Tami Eggleston

PART 3   TRANSFORMATIVE PRACTICES   211

CONFRONTING THE "SCREAMING BABOON":
NOTES ON RACE, LITERATURE, AND PEDAGOGY   213
  José L. Torres-Padilla

CENTERING THE MARGINS: A CHICANA IN THE ENGLISH CLASSROOM   226
  Norma E. Cantú

RACE, DISCOMFORT, AND LOVE IN A UNIVERSITY CLASSROOM   239
  Daniel P. Liston and Sirat Al Salim

MOONWALKING TECHNOSHAMANS AND THE SHIFTING MARGIN:
DECENTERING THE COLONIAL CLASSROOM   253
  Louis Owens

THE COLORBLIND CYBERCLASS: MYTH AND FACT   264
  Sharon Packer

SKINWALKING AND COLOR LINECROSSING:
TEACHING WRITING AGAINST RACISM   277
  Gary L. Lemons

RACING INTO THE ACADEMY: PEDAGOGY AND BLACK FACULTY   286
  A. Yemisi Jimoh and Charlene Johnson

BETWEEN A ROCK AND A HARD PLACE: TEACHING THE BIOLOGY
OF HUMAN VARIATION AND THE SOCIAL CONSTRUCTION OF RACE   *299*
  Joseph L. Graves Jr.

CONCLUSION: TEACHING TO MAKE A DIFFERENCE   *315*
  Bonnie TuSmith and Maureen T. Reddy

  Selected References   *319*
  Contributors   *323*

ACKNOWLEDGMENTS

This volume represents a truly collaborative project among many people beyond the twenty-nine who contributed essays, and so we would like to thank some of them here. First, we are grateful to the scores of people who responded to our call for papers with proposals and enthusiastic comments; we wish we could have used all the proposed essays, but of course space constraints made that impossible. We are deeply grateful to our wonderful editor at Rutgers, Leslie Mitchner, who immediately saw the value of this project, gave us many helpful suggestions that greatly improved the book, and encouraged us every step of the way. Thanks are due also to Jerry Bergevin, who helped with research, fixed numerous computer glitches, and pitched in with the bibliography and headnotes.

I (Bonnie) would like to thank colleagues in MELUS who have helped me process race-in-academia issues over the years; academic and community women of color (especially SOCI members) from whom I have learned a great deal about racial issues; the myriad of students who have struggled through their classroom discomfort and not given up; and former graduate students who have found their way into this collection (I appreciate your company). I am especially indebted to the contributors who, true to their commitment to the project, wrote and revised on an extremely tight schedule. I thank my sisters and mother for their love and support, and my husband Jerry for his generous assistance and encouragement. My greatest appreciation goes to my coeditor, Maureen Reddy. Maureen's brilliance, killer work ethic, and unwavering sense of justice made our collaboration a joyful undertaking. I feel fortunate to have worked in the company of all these wonderful people.

I (Maureen) would like to thank my research assistant, Kristen Gagne, who helped to draft the book proposal and handled an astonishing volume of mail with aplomb. Thanks also to my supportive colleagues in the Department of English at Rhode Island College, to the students who have been willing to struggle with issues of race in my classes, and to my dean, Richard Weiner. Various friends have helped me to think through the complexities of race over the years; I am especially grateful for the insights of Thomas Glave, Robert Lee,

Jane Lazarre, and Barbara Smith. I am thankful for all the help and support provided by my husband, Doug Best, from rescuing corrupted files to faxing to talking about the issues on which this book focuses. I want to thank my children for their good humor about living in a whirlwind of paper and tolerating a monomaniacal mother for several months, during which virtually every dinner conversation turned to the topic of race in the classroom. I especially appreciate both children's honesty and thoughtfulness on the issue of race. Finally, I am grateful to my coeditor, Bonnie TuSmith, for suggesting that we work on a project together and for remaining totally dedicated to producing a book of which we can both be very proud. Working with her has been a pleasure, and I have learned a lot from her in these past few months.

Maureen T. Reddy
Bonnie TuSmith

INTRODUCTION:

Race in the College Classroom

The essays in this collection come straight from the heart. Accepting the challenge to make a public statement on pedagogy and race, our contributors took the risk of investing themselves in these pieces. Every one of these essays speaks powerfully and directly about often-painful personal experiences in the classroom; every one of them also puts those experiences in a wider political context. While a significant portion of university and college faculty members manage to ignore race in their teaching, contributors to this collection consider this option undesirable, if not impossible. As socially committed educators we believe that teaching responsibly, in the humanities as well as in other academic disciplines, requires an honest and searching examination of race.[1] The history of the United States has been molded by race, with the discourse of race and racism too seldom examined in popular culture or in the academy. Indeed, race—which shapes all of our lives—is generally thought to be the special province of specific academic programs, which are themselves usually relegated to the margins of the academy and easily avoided by students as well as faculty members.

Some of our contributors teach courses that focus on race, but most do not. Instead, the majority teach traditionally titled courses—American literature, composition, introduction to sociology, literary theory, curriculum theories, biology, psychology and religion, introduction to political science—but recognize the centrality of race in all disciplines, including those that seem unrelated to racial issues. Like many talented and dedicated educators, both veterans and novices, our writers struggle with race in the classroom on a daily basis, a struggle that constitutes a crisis in higher education.

Despite the spurious public consensus among the white majority that racism is an artifact of the past and that people of color have benefited all too much from affirmative action, a visit to almost any college or university campus should swiftly suggest a different story. Most postsecondary institutions

are visibly white, whether one considers the student body, faculty, or administration. The only areas of campus life in which people of color achieve critical
mass are in the clerical and secretarial ranks and in service and maintenance
work. In both of these areas, people of color are overrepresented. For instance,
53,433 blacks were employed as service and maintenance workers in colleges
and universities in 1997, compared with 99,997 whites in the same positions—
numbers that are, of course, considerably out of proportion to the general population.[2] Far more whites were faculty members than were service and
maintenance or clerical and secretarial workers in that year, a situation precisely reversed for every other racial category tracked by *The Chronicle of
Higher Education*. Based on these statistics and judging by physical appearance alone, a student encountering a middle-aged white person on campus
could logically assume he or she is a professor; that same student encountering a middle-aged person of color could logically assume he or she is not a faculty member but a member of the support staff. The paucity of faculty of color
on most college campuses reinforces the racist tautology that several of our
contributors describe: professors are white, Dr. X is not white, therefore Dr. X
is not a professor.

Nevertheless, the great majority of faculty polled by the *Chronicle* in
1998–1999 (86.7 percent) asserted that faculty of color at their home institutions were treated fairly and only a small number (9.8 percent) reported campus racial conflict.[3] Although the *Chronicle* did not track responses by race, we
have to assume that the majority of those claiming fair treatment for faculty of
color are white, a conclusion bolstered by the interesting coincidence that
roughly 86.6 percent of all faculty are white.

Nationwide, the statistics on postsecondary education are bleak. In 1997,
the most recent year for which data are available, only 13.4 percent of all faculty were people of color, with the great majority of that tiny group clustered
in the non-tenurable ranks of instructors and lecturers.[4] Although blacks constitute roughly 12 percent of this country's population, only 4.9 percent of all
faculty are black. The statistics are even grimmer for Latinos and Latinas, who
represent approximately 9 percent of the U.S. population, but only 2.6 percent
of all faculty. Americans of Asian descent and American Indians are similarly
underrepresented in higher education. Further, many colleges and universities
have *no* tenured ethnic minority faculty. A 1999 *Business Week Online* article
titled "A Dearth of Minority Faculty" includes a table showing that twenty-three
of the nation's top sixty-one schools have zero tenured faculty of color, with

most of the remaining thirty-eight having just one or two each.[5] The student population tends to be just slightly less white than the faculty.[6] Whites dominate in all but a few postsecondary institutions—most of them historically black colleges and universities (HBCUs)—which often means that most classes of twenty to thirty students will have, at best, just one or two students of color, and many will be entirely white. These facts are worth bearing in mind when considering the issue of race in the college classroom, as they constitute the context in which our struggles continue.

Although the twenty-five essays collected here reflect so many shared concerns that any thematic arrangement may seem artificial, even arbitrary, for the sake of greater reading ease we have grouped them into three broad categories according to what seem to us the individual essays' most salient themes: authority and (il)legitimacy, rewards and punishments, and transformative practices. Some of our contributors have decades of teaching experience, while others are graduate students and new Ph.D.s just entering the profession. We teach in every region of the country and at many different types of institutions. Readers are sure to find some element of their own experience reflected here.

In publishing this volume, our central hope is to open a conversation about how race structures all of our classrooms and how we—individually and collectively—can dismantle that structure to make way for a new, nonracist academic environment. We see the work that our contributors and others are doing as part of the larger ongoing project of eradicating racism in society as a whole, and hope that the essays collected here spark conversations and actions that further this most important cause.

NOTES

1 We use the term "race" while fully aware that it is a social and political construction, not a biological reality. We have opted to dispense with the use of quotation marks around the term, solely in the interest of readability.

2 *Chronicle of Higher Education* Almanac, http://www.chronicle.merit.edu/weekly/almanac/2001/nation/0102802.htm.

3 http://www.chronicle.merit.edu/weekly/almanac/2001/nation/0102901.htm.

4 U.S. Department of Education, National Center for Education Statistics, 1997 Integrated Postsecondary Education Data System, "Fall Staff Survey" (IPEDS-S:1997), at http://nces.ed.gov/quicktables.

5 http://www.businessweek.com/1999/99_25/b3634130.htm?scriptFramed#top.

6 U.S. Department of Education, National Center for Education Statistics, 1997 Integrated Postsecondary Education Data System, "Fall Enrollment Survey" (IPEDS-EF:1997), at http://nces.ed.gov/quicktables.

AUTHORITY
AND (IL)LEGITIMACY

While scientists have concluded that humans constitute one race, in the United States people think and act as if we were made up of different and incompatible races. The most visible marker of this assumed difference is physical appearance—which often boils down to the color of a person's skin. In the American educational system, the notion that "white is right" belies the purported goals of democratic, egalitarian pedagogy. A professor's race, in addition to racial issues in both course content and classroom student configuration, has a direct impact on the outcome of a course. With the recognition of multiculturalism in recent years, studies on "diverse" classrooms are now available. However, such studies tend to focus on the increasingly mixed student populations that professors are likely to encounter in the classroom, while the professor's racial identity—a large part of his or her "subject position"—is rarely addressed. One possible reason for this oversight is that professors are presumed to be "white." Since white is normative and un-raced, the professor's race does not enter the picture.

Whiteness studies in the past decade have been challenging this unexamined assumption. If we relate to one another as if we were different races, the studies contend, then white is also a race. Privileging white skin over black, brown, red, or yellow is racist. With the ingrained mindset of equating whiteness with legitimate authority in the classroom, students tend to respond to nonwhite professors with a variety of inappropriate emotions. Several of our contributors point out that, as faculty of color, their very presence creates havoc in the classroom. Students demonstrate their confusion and resentment—emotions triggered by what psychologists call "cognitive dissonance" derived from their social conditioning—by engaging in passive-aggressive power struggles with the professor. With the complexities of race and racism, white feminist theories of the de-centered classroom provide no easy solutions for professors of color.

Professorial authority is an especially thorny issue in the multicultural classroom—in courses where race and ethnicity are necessarily foregrounded. As the essays in this volume attest, student discomfort with addressing racial issues found in course materials—whether in an ethnic novel, a documentary film, or a scientific study on the fallacy of race—often translates into challenging the instructor's authority in and out of the classroom. In a hierarchical structure based on race and gender, for example, the authority to teach African American studies moves in descending order from visibly black male to black female, then visibly white female to white male. An Asian American or Native American of either gender would be suspect. Students accept black instructors for this course since it is supposed to be black, and white instructors due to the continued assumption of white-skinned legitimacy in education. The nonblack, nonwhite professor is automatically illegitimate in such a course. The equation of an instructor's skin color with what she or he can legitimately teach is problematic. That a white professor is acceptable while a nonblack, nonwhite professor is not is equally problematic. The unspoken understanding that ethnically identified courses are best served by a proper race/ethnic match (although whites are often exempt from this requirement)—while nonethnic courses are best served by white faculty—is itself a statement of institutional racism.

KAREN ELIAS
JUDITH C. JONES

TWO VOICES FROM THE FRONT LINES:

A CONVERSATION ABOUT RACE IN THE CLASSROOM

PHOTO: IMAGERY, PHILADELPHIA, PA

JUDITH: You and I have had some wonderful conversations about our experiences teaching race in college classrooms, so I'm pleased that we have this opportunity to document some of our thinking on this matter, including an exploration of how the dynamics of race play out differently for a teacher of European heritage (you) and a teacher of African heritage (me).

KAREN: I've appreciated so much the opportunity to share our experiences. Before we get to the important differences you mention, it might be helpful to start with the context within which we work. As teachers in mainstream U.S. colleges, we've both found that when we introduce issues of race in our classrooms, we do so in predominantly white environments.

JUDITH: Yes. For example, at Philadelphia University where we are both now teaching, the learners are drawn for the most part from the white population in

KAREN ELIAS became deeply committed to bringing anti-racist work to the classroom after attending the 1981 National Women's Studies Association Conference, "Women Confront Racism." She has taught at Purdue University, SUNY Oswego, Lock Haven University, and, most recently, Philadelphia University.

JUDITH C. JONES has years of experience facilitating diversity work in and out of the classroom. She grew up in a black working class community in Philadelphia. Jones earned her Ph.D. in political science at Atlanta University; she has taught at Central State University, Pennsylvania State University, and Philadelphia University.

A white professor and a black professor teaching at the same predominantly white university, Elias and Jones have faced different challenges to their authority. Their essay, a dialogue on race and authority in the college classroom, focuses on their shared interest in a racially aware pedagogy.

and around Philadelphia. There are very few students of African heritage or other people of color in a typical classroom. And of course economic class is another important factor here. Using socioeconomic status as the standard, the majority of our students would be defined as "mainstream." But I've noticed an interesting difference. White students from women's studies programs bring an awareness of diversity that distinguishes them from white students without similar academic exposure.

KAREN: I find that most white students have had little contact with people of color prior to coming to college. When I ask Beverly Tatum's question, "How many of you grew up in neighborhoods where most of the people were from the same racial group as your own?" almost all of them raise their hands.[1] As a result, what little they know about people of color has been derived from media-generated stereotypes. But it's good to note, as we characterize "white students," that there are some important exceptions. I wonder if we could describe the typical learning environment by examining ways traditionally educated white students are likely to respond—at least at first—to race as a central topic of discussion.

JUDITH: When I first started teaching courses focused on diversity, I became immediately aware of what I now know is resistance. There was palpable resistance to talking about race.

KAREN: I remember one of my white students actually calling out in class at one point, "Don't go there!" Though their perspective is certainly not monolithic, white students are likely to inhabit a subject position that makes it hard for them to think and talk about race.

JUDITH: I agree. For example, I find this shows up in their use of language. I've noticed that it's difficult, sometimes impossible, for them to use the terms "black" and "white," especially "white." When they describe themselves, they say, I'm an American, I don't think about my heritage, I'm an individual, I'm middle class. In addition, certain topics are hot-button topics: reverse discrimination, affirmative action, white male rage. And since I am often the only person of African heritage in the room, there is an undercurrent of "this is not real, this is not going on, this is your thing."

KAREN: Yes. White students come to college having absorbed certain beliefs: that racism belongs to another time, that they themselves do not "see color" and that to notice color at all is to be racist. Given the ideology of individualism that's so pervasive in our culture, whites also resist the notion that we are anything other than autonomous individuals; the idea that we might be shaped by gender, race, and class dynamics is completely foreign. These beliefs have an unmistakable impact on our classrooms in that for white students especially, direct discussion of race is considered divisive, separating people who would otherwise be perfectly able to get along.

JUDITH: At one point this semester I showed the Prime Time video *True Colors*, which documents how color matters in the daily interactions of a white man and a black man who are similar in all respects except for their skin color.[2] They are sent out to explore housing and job opportunities in St. Louis, Missouri, and the video shows clearly how the black man is subjected, on a daily basis, to blatant discrimination. In the discussion following the video, one young white woman commented, "This may have happened 'way back then,' but this is not the way things are now. Today we're all allowed to do whatever we want." And another student said, "What we saw here was awful. But this isn't typical. The people who discriminated were just 'bad people.'"

KAREN: I get the same responses when I show this video. When faced with examples of racism, mainstream students will claim that either the incident is exceptional or the agent is exceptional. They are likely to have only superficial knowledge of the history of race relations and thus are unable to formulate a structural analysis. And because most of our students have little understanding of the institutional nature of oppression, they have a tendency to equate racism with an internal condition that shows up as individual acts of prejudice. It therefore becomes easy for them to claim that "reverse racism" victimizes whites as often as it does people of color.

JUDITH: In my course on race, class, and gender, we read an essay called "Something About the Subject Makes It Hard to Name" by Gloria Yamato, an African American woman who discusses various types of racist behavior by whites, as well as internalized racism.[3] At the end of her article, she makes suggestions about how whites can interrupt racist behavior and how people of color can interrupt internalized racism. During class when a Jewish male attempted to engage the group in a discussion of racist behaviors, a very vocal group of white students went into defense mode full blast. One young woman characterized the author as "ignorant" because she used colloquial language in the essay. And another young woman claimed Yamato was "biased" because she didn't offer suggestions to people of color for ways they could interrupt "their own racist behavior."

KAREN: It's so difficult to challenge this thinking. I know both of us assign Peggy McIntosh's essay "White Privilege and Male Privilege" as a way of bringing white skin privilege into consciousness.[4] But of course here we're calling into question another deeply embedded belief: that race belongs only to people of color. The notions that whites are raced and that race relations are our mutual responsibility fall outside the operative paradigm.[5] So these are the assumptions that pervade the classes we teach.

JUDITH: And these dynamics are further complicated by the subject positions we ourselves bring to the classroom. Being aware of my own subject position as an African American teacher means having to navigate relationships with mainstream white students for whom having an African American authority figure is a new, and therefore uncertain, experience. The uncertainty is intensified when the students learn that the usual classroom format is being jettisoned for a more experiential, learner-centered approach. Since this approach engenders a climate of safety, I have to be prepared to hear—to use Gloria Yamato's terms—"unaware/unintentional" and "unaware/self-righteous" racist comments and observations from mainstream white students as the semester goes on.[6]

KAREN: In my classes, unless the number of students of color begins to approximate that of the white students, the former will keep their heads down for fear of being targeted. In fact, introducing discussions of race may feel quite dangerous to them. The students of color are hesitant to reveal themselves in a learning situation where both the teacher and most of the other students are white. Can they trust that we will reflect their concerns or treat them with respect? It's an important question. And in spite of my best efforts to establish a climate of safety, one in which the students of color can begin to trust that their perspectives will be honored and they will not be called upon in class to "represent the race," the safety that should be present for them as a matter of course cannot, unfortunately, always be guaranteed.

JUDITH: I'm also wondering about the element of surprise. It would seem to complicate matters for you that you teach courses on writing, so your students don't come in to class thinking they're going to have to deal with something like race. Since I teach courses that focus explicitly on diversity, I have the advantage that the issue of race is on the table from the first day.

KAREN: I recall two years ago in my freshman writing seminar, some white students began vigorously denying the existence of racial profiling. I tried using these comments as springboards for further analysis, but I noticed that a young Afro-Caribbean woman was obviously disturbed. She met with me in private to say that she was having a hard time sitting through the class. "I hear enough of this in my daily life," she said. "I shouldn't have to put up with it here. And besides, I didn't sign up for this." She meant that since she had registered for a generic freshman writing seminar, she hadn't expected to have to deal with issues of race yet one more time in my class. One of my biggest fears is that despite my best intentions, the racist dynamics of the larger society will get replicated in the classroom. Her words had a profound impact on me.

JUDITH: My classes are, in a sense, structured by race as soon as I walk into the room. I use the first couple of classes to elicit demographic data from the students, so I know they come from social and educational environments that are devoid of African American authority representation. I remember one particular incident that exemplifies how my credibility as an authority figure is often handled. During one class, in response to my policy of encouraging students to share their work-life experiences, a white female student invited a young white male professional to class to give a presentation about his background in labor relations. Following his fifteen-minute talk her comment was, "We've learned so much more about this topic from you." Her comment literally denied the thirteen weeks I had spent teaching the class, and I can still recall the feeling of deep-seated rage that this evoked in me.

I've noticed something else when there is a critical mass of African American students in a class. In discussions about race, the African American students are very vocal, and often these become exchanges between them and me, with little or no participation from the white students. So it appears that, with a person of African heritage as the teacher, the African American students feel more empowered to express their views. On the other hand, I've noticed that white students resist my authority by projecting it onto a white person or by making sotto voce comments rather than engaging with me directly. I could generalize about these dynamics and say that the white students "go victim" around giving voice to their feelings and views.

KAREN: What you say here is so important. My white skin privilege clearly offers me a number of protections and benefits. Because I'm white, I don't have to face the kinds of assaults on my status as an authority figure that you experience. In addition, though racist comments are also painful for me to hear, they do not have the same corrosive effect on my person. And though my pedagogy evolves from a passionate commitment to social justice, specifically to antiracist work, I can always step out of the classroom into a setting that validates me because I'm white.

Of course, my insistence on raising these issues is still threatening. I try to remember, in the midst of so much student discomfort, that I'm attempting to model the ability to "shift locations," as bell hooks puts it. This means deconstructing and decentering "the standpoint of 'whiteness'" while at the same time learning to "'occupy the subject position of the other.'"[7] This is, ideally, how I would like to be able to use my subject position as a white person in the classroom.

JUDITH: I know that, for both of us, the content as well as the practices associated with the traditional classroom are unsatisfactory in addressing issues of race. In rethinking my own pedagogy, I found myself first wanting to understand the essentials: the fundamental things that we need to become aware of in examining race. In other words, what needs to be learned, and what needs to be deconstructed? If you could compile a list of responses to these two questions, what would you say?

KAREN: Keeping in mind that deconstruction and new learning sometimes occur simultaneously when examining race, here are some of the basics. Learners should be exposed to:

- some history of race relations in the United States to show that the constitutional rights we take for granted today had to be fought for and won;
- the realities of racism as it currently exists, and the ways racism can affect its targets;
- the multiple ways racism can be resisted by people of color as well as by whites;
- the fact that white people are raced;
- the realities of white skin privilege;
- narratives by people of color that focus on common "human" experiences;

— different ways of understanding diversity, to illustrate various positions that can be assumed on these issues and to point up the fact that the choices we make have implications;

— the "norms" governing U.S. social arrangements as a way of understanding how "difference" gets defined and measured in relation to these arbitrary standards;

— the fact that most of us occupy multiple subject positions and thus can use our experiences of being outside the norm to understand "the subject position of the other";

— the idea that "race" is socially constructed; and

— the fact that racism is institutionalized in U.S. society.

JUDITH: I love the way you have formulated what I'd like to call a racially aware pedagogy. The task is finding ways to engage students around these issues. In my classes I want to balance theoretical presentations with interactive, experiential activities and outside resources.[8] For example, to tackle the realities of racism as it exists currently in the United States, I show the videos *Color of Fear, The Way Home,* and as mentioned earlier, *True Colors.*[9] To address the history of race relations in the United States, I recently showed *A Force More Powerful,* a PBS special on nonviolent movements, which includes a well-done documentary about the Birmingham bus boycott.[10] This segment can also illustrate how racism can be resisted by people of color as well as by whites.

Another way I'm working to engage students is by introducing an activity called "show and tell" this semester.[11] Students bring in articles from newspapers, magazines, and the web, or they summarize incidents seen on television or at campus events that reflect issues related to race/ethnicity, gender, and class. My goal is to keep their awareness working between classes by encouraging them to notice how institutionalized oppression operates in everyday life. It is proving an effective way to interrupt the "color evasiveness" and "power evasiveness" practiced by mainstream white students.

Something you said earlier about not wanting to replicate the racist dynamics of the larger society in the classroom calls to mind another thing I've struggled with in relation to methods. I used to require students to participate in an activity called "the otherness experience." This activity had to be completed outside the classroom because I wanted the students to place themselves in situations where they could occupy the subject position of the other. Students of color invariably protested the assignment because I was asking them to replicate racial dynamics that were all too familiar in order to educate mainstream white students. I have changed that assignment and now require students to think about the rank and privileges connected with various aspects of their identity. They are asked to place themselves in a situation of their own choosing to observe how their status affects their feelings and influences their communication with others. This allows me to illustrate, as you frame it, the different ways of understanding diversity as well as the various positions that can be assumed on these issues. So I can interrupt the internalized racial oppression from students of color when they say they don't have any "power" or "rank" in U.S. society by having them notice the rank and privileges they have as heterosexuals and/or able-bodied people.

KAREN: As we talk, I'm appreciating the risk-taking required to develop a racially aware pedagogy. One of the most difficult questions for me is how to bring prejudice to light so that it can be dismantled, without reinflicting harm inside my own classroom. This year I've been trying out new ways of creating a space where students can learn to talk about race. One method is to allow them the safety of voicing their concerns anonymously while insisting on public accountability at the same time. Students submit written comments, then each picks one from the hat and reads it aloud. This seems to reveal concerns that might not have been voiced otherwise. For example, after we had read several works by African American women, students wrote comments implying that these narratives lacked "universal" significance. One student asked, "Why do almost all of the authors make race/gender the most important feature in their essay? Also, why doesn't this course focus on the common human experiences of people living in America?" This opened up enormous opportunities for discussion, allowing us to analyze ways the norms of our culture, which privilege those in power, are used to define acceptable "human" experience.

JUDITH: And I got a similar response from students when I showed the video *The Way Home.* This video features eight different racial/ethnic councils of women talking about issues such as controlling the land, becoming an American, finding identity, and fighting internalized oppression. Women of color comprise six of the eight councils. In their written reactions, students criticized the women of color for "whining and complaining" and "being oversensitive about their color." Other students admitted that they just could not relate to anything the women of color discussed. And I wondered if this inability to appreciate the "voices" of women of color was connected to unaware/unintentional racism.

KAREN: I'd like to address the question of "voice" you raise here. How, and to what extent, do we represent in our classes the voice that cries out for justice and demands accountability, knowing that mainstream students will do their best to shut it out or defend against it? I realize, in asking this question, that I've tried several approaches. It's become quite clear that it does not work (especially in a generic freshman seminar!) to represent this voice myself. So, wanting to find ways to address these issues more effectively, two years ago I shaped the course around a critique of power relations within an historical context. The fact that we focused on a time other than the present allowed students to absorb this material fairly well because it was less threatening. Similarly, to unify this year's course materials, I chose the theme "coming of age." Using a number of narratives by people of color to illustrate this theme allows me to make the point that the lives of people of color are not unidimensional but in fact are richly complex and, indeed, representative of the human experiences of people living in the United States. Admittedly, though I continue to address race as a central issue in my classes, the voice that cries out for justice has become more muted over time. Perhaps in recent years I've backed off, become less brave.

JUDITH: I hear how your struggle around being a vigorous advocate for social change and working with young people exactly where they are creates extraordinary tension. That's why I don't see your decision to "back off" as having anything to do with your courage. I appreciate how you recognized a need to be more flexible and creative, which I feel is absolutely necessary in order to continue teaching about race in the classroom.

Getting back to the issue of accountability, I'm mindful of another contribution from McIntosh's work on privilege, which is that mainstream students have "permission to escape" the necessity of being vigilant about the dynamics of racial relations.[12] I recall an assignment where the students were required to read an article by Robert B. Moore, "Racist Stereotyping in the English Language."[13] Some students asked, "What's the big deal about using the word 'blackmail'?" and others commented, "I never think about whether the attributes for 'white' reflect goodness, purity, innocence; these terms are harmless— I would not get upset about stuff like this." I decided to combine Moore's analytical insights into language with deconstruction of an excerpt from a recent HBO movie entitled *Dancing in September.*[14] The movie is about the presentation of black images on television. I used the film because the two main characters, an African American man and woman in positions of authority within the television industry, present two different perspectives on black representation on television. Of the students who completed the assignment, half were able to utilize Moore's analysis and the other half were at least able to identify the racist representations.

KAREN: Excellent. Despite the students' initial reaction, you didn't give up but persisted in trying to engage them around the issue of black representation in the language and the media. And the result was greater awareness of ways these supposedly "harmless" representations do in fact produce toxic effects.

Regarding white accountability, as the semester ends I'm trying to steel myself against hearing that a student has accused me on the course evaluation form of being "racist against white people." Though I define the term "racist" carefully, some students persist in believing that insistence on white accountability constitutes an expression of racism! In today's conservative climate, simply raising the issue of race can carry this risk. And unless one is fortunate enough to have a sympathetic administration or the benefit of tenure, one's job may actually be threatened.

JUDITH: Your comment reminds me of a recent situation at another mainstream university. A young woman of color, who was hired in a tenure track position in the English department, received the most horrific evaluations from the students, who castigated her multicultural perspective, methodology, and academic competence. She left the university at the end of the second semester.

KAREN: A sad story. It exemplifies the response many mainstream academic institutions have made over the past decade to the threat of multicultural (and feminist) activism. It's becoming more difficult to incorporate perspectives that are considered in any way "political." The radical critique claiming that all knowledge is informed by ideological assumptions seems to have vanished. Thus, we are left with definitions of good teaching that seem modeled on "the way it's always been done." These ideas become so pervasive that it takes an enormous effort to call them into question. And, as we see from the example of this young woman, they shape students' assumptions of what our classrooms should look like.

JUDITH: I have not experienced this type of negative reaction from student evaluations. And, once again, I believe it has to do with the centrality of race in the courses that I teach. Students enter the course understanding that race will be discussed. What has happened over the years is that students will write comments on their final examination papers expressing their reactions to the course. Some recent comments include, "Dr. Jones, this was the most terrifying, thought-provoking class that I've been in since I've been at [the] University"; "I will never forget the simulation, this course, or you"; "This was a great course. This course helped me to understand how I take my privilege for granted in certain groups. I would not have seen this before."

KAREN: Yes! Comments such as these are a tribute to the transformative potential of courses that focus on race—and to the way you teach as well! These are the words we need to keep close to our hearts as we keep on keeping on. At the same time, it might be important to acknowledge that this report from the front lines is not a "master narrative," designed to show how grappling with these incredible difficulties always allows one to come out victorious on the other side. As teachers who work not only to engage a body of material but also to raise awareness and promote social justice, we're opening ourselves to additional expectations, and disappointments. And because the same tactics of denial found in the classroom are often present in the institution itself, we're also opening ourselves to criticism from colleagues. I know I've been marginalized by faculty and administration simply because I wanted to share concerns about discussing race in the classroom. There's also the danger of doing this work in isolation, something that teaching in academia seems to promote.

JUDITH: Yes, I have also experienced feelings of isolation for the reasons you've pointed out. However, I think I come to this position because I'm teaching from the margin. What I've tried to do to redress this sense of isolation is develop relationships with other cultural workers who work outside the mainstream. For example, I belong to a support group that focuses on designing popular education events, which may include a two-hour workshop or a sixteen-week curriculum.[15] This group has been enormously important in helping me to remember that the work I do does make a difference.

KAREN: I really like the way you've transformed "being marginalized" to "teaching from the margin"! It makes such a difference to be able to see my position as something I've chosen rather than had imposed on me from the outside. And it's true that the support I get also comes from the margins. What a joy to be able to shift focus. Being ejected from the center now becomes an *opportunity*—to claim connection with a network of progressive cultural workers, whose commitment to breaking the silence around race in the interest of social justice lends strength and courage to our own.

NOTES

1 Beverly Daniel Tatum, *"Why Are All the Black Kids Sitting Together in the Cafeteria?" and Other Conversations about Race* (New York: Basic Books, 1997), 4.

2 *True Colors*, ABC News Prime Time Live, 18 minutes, Coronet/MTI Film & Video Inc., 1991, videocassette.

3 Gloria Yamato, "Something About the Subject Makes It Hard to Name," in *Race, Class, and Gender: An Anthology*, 4th ed., ed. Margaret L. Andersen and Patricia Hill Collins (Belmont, Calif.: Wadsworth, 2001), 90–94.

4 Peggy McIntosh, "White Privilege and Male Privilege: A Personal Account of Coming to See Correspondences Through Work in Women's Studies," in *Race, Class, and Gender*, 95–105.

5 Ruth Frankenberg refers to this paradigm as "a discourse of essential 'sameness' popularly referred to as 'color-blindness'—which I have chosen to name as a double move toward 'color evasiveness' and 'power evasiveness.'" See *White Women, Race Matters: The Social Construction of Whiteness* (Minneapolis: University of Minnesota Press, 1993), 14.

6 Yamato, "Something About the Subject," 91.

7 bell hooks, *Black Looks: Race and Representation* (Boston: South End Press, 1992), 177. hooks takes her quote from Gayatri Spivak, *The Post-Colonial Critic: Interviews, Strategies, Dialogues* (New York: Routledge, 1990).

8 Arnold and Amy Mindell, *Riding the Horse Backwards: Process Work in Theory and Practice* (New York: Penguin, 1992), 25–35. I have found the Mindells' work on different learning channels (i.e., auditory, visual, movement) to be useful in designing interactive activities for the classroom. See also Lawrence Roth, "Introducing Students to 'The Big Picture,'" *Journal of Management Education* 25, no.1 (February 2001): 21–31.

9 *The Color of Fear*, produced and directed by Lee Mun Wah, 90 min., Stir-Fry Productions, 1994, videocassette. *The Way Home*, produced and directed by Shakti Butler, 1 hr. 40 min., World Trust , 1998, videocassette.

10 *A Force More Powerful: A Century of Nonviolent Conflict*, produced and directed by Steve York, 3 hrs., WETA, 2000, videocassette.

11 Jessica M. Charbeneau, "Instructor's Manual and Test Bank," for *Race, Class, and Gender* (Belmont, Calif.: Wadsworth, 2001), 5.

12 McIntosh, "White Privilege and Male Privilege," 102–103.

13 Robert B. Moore, "Racist Stereotyping in the English Language," in *Race, Class and Gender*, 322–333.

14 *Dancing in September*, produced and directed by Reggie Rock Bythewood, 1 hr. 50 min., Weecan Films Production, 2001, videocassette.

15 *The Growing Divide: Inequality and the Roots of Economic Insecurity* (Boston, Mass.: United for a Fair Economy, May 2000), 6. See this publication for a definition of "popular education."

SARIKA CHANDRA

TEACHING IN FLORIDA:

THE END OF AFFIRMATIVE ACTION AND THE POLITICS OF RACE

PHOTO: JEFF RICE

STATE AND INSTITUTIONAL POLITICS

The 2000 presidential election has shown among other things that the state of Florida is a contested site for a number of political issues. The close vote in which candidates Albert Gore and George Bush both received almost equal numbers is a signal that Florida residents are evenly divided on political matters. In fact, the media often presents American political issues as two-sided and binary in nature. For example, near election time, a clear distinction is made between candidates (usually two) as to which side of the issues they support. The members of the electorate then have to decide the same for themselves by casting a vote for one or the other candidate. Affirmative action policies in Florida have also been debated in this binary nature since Governor Jeb Bush announced in 1999 his plans to stop admitting students to universities and colleges based on race, gender, and other protected categories. This announcement regarding affirmative action, and its subsequent end in 2000, have for the most part reduced conversations on this subject to simplistic terms and divided the state's residents into one of two camps: those who are against affirmative action and those who defend it. Dominant discourse often

SARIKA CHANDRA is a Ph.D. candidate in English at the University of Florida, where she teaches courses in American literature and culture. Her research interests include contemporary American travel writing, and ethnic and immigrant literatures. She is working on a dissertation on American travel and immigrant literatures.

In this essay, Chandra explores the impact of state policies and university programs on teaching multiethnic material. She analyzes the ways in which pedagogy must take into account the context of state and educational policies, the instructor's subject position, and students' personal experiences.

presents affirmative action as mostly benefiting African Americans—therefore setting up a binary opposition between black and white people. The new "One Florida" plan and university outreach programs are meant to ease oppositions but in fact do not. Rather they strongly reinforce oppositions between blacks and whites and create new ones among all racial groups.[1] The divisive and contested nature of Florida politics, especially racial politics, affects even my classroom at the University of Florida and creates similar tensions.

Like many other universities, the University of Florida has made an effort to recruit and retain students who show promise but are classified as "at risk," that is, those who are less likely to succeed in college. The university does not clarify why a particular student is designated "at risk." However, it is indeed very clear that the students who are so identified are minority (primarily African American) students. In 1997, the university instituted the Achievement in Mainstreaming (AIM) program for these students' first year of study. In the English Department, AIM students take designated sections of writing composed of half AIM students and half mainstream (primarily white) students. The department frequently assigns me to teach AIM courses, and starting in fall 2001, all of the writing courses will register AIM students. While this classroom structure is designed to help these students become mainstream students over a one-year period, it nevertheless places them in direct opposition to non-AIM students in my writing classrooms.

It is very clear from the official description of this program that AIM is the university's outreach strategy for recruiting and retaining minority students. Consider how the College of Liberal Arts and Sciences explains this program in its recent newsletter (the only available official description): "The AIM program assists in the university's efforts to increase student diversity by working closely with the Office of Admissions to admit a select group of incoming freshmen . . . The participation of underrepresented minority students has increased from 78.3 percent in 1997 to the current year's [1999] 93.1 percent."[2] At first glance, it may seem that the university effort in targeting minority students for admission is at odds with the end of affirmative action. However, outreach programs for minority students are becoming even more crucial after the end of affirmative action.

Corrie Martine, in her article "University Outreach and Affirmative Action," explains that similar recruitment and outreach efforts have become important to the University of California system precisely because the universities have to devise other kinds of programs to recruit and retain minority students in the absence of affirmative action.[3] As other states, such as Texas, suffer a backlash against affirmative action, the universities located there will also have to assess how to recruit and retain minority students.

The principles of the AIM program are similar to the One Florida initiative designed to replace affirmative action. According to the official state records, One Florida is supposed to help minority students by increasing funds for tutoring and outreach that will in turn help them achieve higher test scores and gain admission to universities. Both One Florida and AIM do not see the need to focus on the larger structural reasons that might explain why minority students do not gain access to higher education—reasons such as discrimination based on race and gender. Rather, they place the burden of achievement largely on the individual minority student by suggesting they do not have the ability to learn and are therefore more likely to drop out of college. Consider for instance Governor Bush's contention in his 1999 State of the State address. He says that the state is "rapidly moving toward two Floridas. It is not divided by the color of our skin, our race, our nationality but by our ability to acquire knowledge."[4] The governor ignores the fact that race is still a factor in gaining access to institutions of knowledge production. However, it is interesting to note that the rhetoric of the two Floridas fits comfortably into the binary nature of American politics, as well as of a divisive new global order that dictates a knowledge-based economy. It seems that Governor Bush uses the idea of this new knowledge-based economy as a reason to eliminate programs such as affirmative action.

The end of affirmative action, along with the discourse of the global economy with its emphasis on individual ability, resonates with some of the fundamental ways in which we think about education. As Randy Martin suggests in his introduction to *Chalk Lines: The Politics of Work in a Managed University,* "We tend to think that the student enters into a free-contract with us to learn. We do not systematically look at how the production of knowledge in our classrooms is contingent on the labor of students and how we should address this fact."[5] For example, the grading system places students in achievement categories ranged against each other. My AIM students also have to contend with the added complication of their placement in "at-risk" categories because of their race. It is very difficult for me to distinguish AIM students from non-AIM students based on learning ability and writing skills. I take issue with Governor Bush's suggestion that it is the ability to learn that divides Florida into two halves. My classroom is indeed divided into two halves—based not on the ability to acquire knowledge, but based on race and ethnicity.

CLASSROOM PRACTICES

The content of my writing courses (argumentative and expository writing) is multiethnic. I organize my courses around issues already familiar to my students such as schooling, the idea of freedom, and so forth, with emphasis on race and ethnicity so as to make them understand how their views on these matters must be thought of in relationship to larger political problems. Usually, the first-year students bring to my classes a way of reading that is visceral and based on feelings, rather than analytical. For example, a journal entry by one of my students in response to Jamaica Kincaid's story "Girl" reads: "This story shows that African American mothers place unfair expectations on their daughters. This is not always true because my mother never told me what to do."[6] I help students to think analytically by asking them to consider larger structural problems. In writing argumentative papers, my students often want to slide into a kind of thinking that reflects the binary nature of political debates. For example, one student wanted to write a one-sided essay defending affirmative action. After many conversations, she saw affirmative action programs in more complex ways. She understood that affirmative action policies have not gone far enough in addressing social injustices and how, in some sense, these policies have themselves remained racist in nature. Helping students move away from binary thinking to more complex arguments is a difficult process that is intimately connected with students' attitudes toward race and exacerbated by the university's AIM program as well as by the end of affirmative action.

My AIM students often assume a defensive posture because they are labeled as "at-risk." Consequently, they spend their energy trying to break out of this stereotype. One of my Latino AIM students explains to me: "I want to be seen as different from other Latinos," and "I want to prove the university wrong." Yet AIM students also tend to form friendships and alliances with each other, partly because they spend more time attending special classes and meetings together. This alliance puts them in a position to agree with and defend one another in the classroom against the non-AIM students. The AIM students regard the few non-AIM minority students as belonging to the white side. Those minority students who might agree with their white peers in the classroom on a particular issue are perceived by most AIM students as trying to be white and betraying their fellow minority classmates. Additionally, those white students who happen to agree with minority students are also regarded as suspect. Of course, this is not always the case, and there are always exceptions to these observations. But my AIM courses generally work in this manner. The split in the classroom is very even and contested.

This impulse to create two sides in the classroom can become volatile when the students are confronted with the messiness of racial politics. Problems arise when I ask students to think in complicated nonbinary ways. Let me present an example from the class. Early on in the semester, I had assigned Charles Murray's essay "The Coming White Underclass," primarily as a way to discuss how Murray uses racist arguments to suggest society is in a crisis because single white women have followed the example of single black women in having children, thus adding to the welfare state.[7] The class began with a heated discussion largely between the black and white students, who in both cases pointed to the article's racism. During this discussion one of the African American female students turned to an Asian American female, a non-AIM student who had not yet participated in this discussion and asked: "Where are you from?" I started to object to this question, but my Asian American student replied anyway and said "Taiwan." The African American student responded: "This is why you don't care to participate in this discussion, because this is an American issue." It took me two whole class periods to have a discussion about how assumptions based on appearance are risky. Everyone participated in the discussion and raised important issues and questions regarding assumptions about race we all make. I did not want to let this incident stand without sufficient discussion, because I did not want this line of divisive thinking to continue in my class.

This incident and its aftermath damaged my relationship with the African American student and her allies, because she did not want to appear prejudiced to her peers. She felt she had been caught in a moment of political incorrectness and was not able to see beyond it. At first, other AIM students were reluctant to disagree with her, but after having a discussion with the rest of the class they, along with most of my students, came to see that assumptions based on appearance are hasty and can be harmful. In spite of this, my African American student and a few other AIM students who agreed with her saw me as someone who had betrayed them. They saw me as siding with an Asian American student because I am Asian American myself. Embedded in this event are very complicated attitudes toward race and ethnicity.

The media portrays affirmative action in the United States as mainly a black and white issue. African Americans are represented as the main beneficiary of many of the social welfare programs. The most vehement public opposition to the end of affirmative action in Florida comes from African American groups. Essays by Earl Graves ("Florida's Trojan Horse") and Pearl Stewart ("NAACP Files Brief Against 'One Florida' Plan"), pointing to the adverse effects of eliminating affirmative action, have appeared in *Black Enterprise* and *Black Issues in Higher Education*.[8] Whereas, in Maria Padilla's article "Hispanics Stay Quiet on Affirmative Action," Hispanics do not have a long history with affirmative action and generally do not see themselves as beneficiaries of the program.[9] Since most of my AIM students are African American, the end of affirmative action is a volatile matter for them. They do not want to seem to be receiving undue rewards, yet they want to defend affirmative action for the discussion on structural discrimination it affords. In this manner, dominant discourses on affirmative action place African Americans in opposition to other minority groups, especially Asian Americans, who are presented to be hardworking and exemplary. Critics such as Bonnie TuSmith and Curtis Chang show that Asian Americans are used as model minorities. In her book *All My Relatives*, TuSmith argues that Asians as model minorities "are supposed to be self-effacing and compliant."[10] She further suggests that the concept of Asians as model minorities is used to denigrate African Americans who are seen as complainers. In "Streets of Gold: The Myth of the Model Minority," Curtis Chang maintains that Asian Americans are presented as intelligent and adept. They are stereotyped as good employees because they do not complain as much about unfair wages and working conditions, and, most importantly, they are grateful. In contrast, African Americans are often stereotyped as loud protestors who are predisposed to be on welfare. Chang states: "unlike blacks . . . Asian Americans have not vigorously asserted [their] ethnic identity . . . and the American public has demanded assimilation over ethnic pluralism."[11] Drawing upon mainstream magazines such as *Time* and *People*, Chang observes that Asian Americans have public "approval of how [they] have succeeded in the 'American Tradition.' Unlike the Blacks and the Hispanics, 'Puritan-like' Asian [Americans] disdain governmental assistance." Moreover, the media "consistently compares the crime-ridden image of other minorities with the picture of law-abiding Asian parents whose 'well-behaved kids' hit books and not the street."[12] Chang argues that whites see Asian Americans as "whiter" than blacks, but "not quite white enough."[13]

The idea that dominant discourse considers Asian Americans exemplary minorities finds its parallel in the ways my African American students reacted to my Asian American student. The readings in my course, which include Chang's work, help students reach a more nuanced understanding of racial issues. Nevertheless, pointing to gaps in their arguments can elicit negative responses from minority students, especially African Americans. By the fact of being labled "at-risk," most of my AIM students receive the message that they are deficient in skills and abilities such as writing and math; however, they are led to believe that they are experts in racial issues. Therefore they are more reluctant to revise their thinking. Academic scholarship by critics such as Gregory Jay and Terry Dean supports and helps to establish the idea that minority students are indeed experts in race-related issues. For example, Terry Dean, in "Multicultural Classrooms, Monocultural Teachers," speaks eloquently about the need for teachers to allow multicultural students to tell their story of marginality so everyone can learn from their experience.[14] Similarly, in "The End of 'American' Literature: Toward a Multicultural Practice," Jay argues: while "developing a multicultural curriculum with specific attention to black writers [. . .] my pedagogical location would offer me a tough but simple lesson: these students knew a lot more about racism—consciously and unconsciously than I did."[15] He uses this note in charting his own development in teaching multiethnic literature, and suggests that the students' experience of racism is more credible in a classroom than scholarship and literary works about racism. Both these critics maintain they learn about racial politics from teaching minority students.

My objection to expertise based solely on experience is made worse by the fact that my AIM students are labeled as lacking expertise in other areas. When I point to the gaps in their thinking, they perceive me as betraying them because they think I should be on their side, because I also must have had the experience of being discriminated against. This sense of betrayal places them in a defensive situation and is reflected in classroom discussions. Studs Terkel's "Stephen Cruz," a story about a Mexican American man who felt he could not call attention to his Mexican heritage if he was to achieve corporate success, elicited a negative reading by white and minority students alike.[16] They quickly suggested that Stephen Cruz should not abandon his heritage in order to gain promotions and placed the entire blame on the individual character. I asked the class to consider how the story invites us to see the ways in which white corporate culture demands that Cruz hide his Mexican background. Most of the students willing to engage with this point of view were white students. Most of the minority students still maintained that Cruz was betraying his culture.

Such sidedness often results from my students' need to appear politically correct or not prejudiced. Additionally, my own racial background adds to this problem. Since most of my minority students receive the message that their skills are not as sharp as those of their white counterparts, the minority students seem to want to learn from someone who at least looks American (either a white or a black person) and who can help them do better and defy the low expectations the AIM program places on them. One of my African American female students once told me in my office that I didn't have the authority or the experience to teach her. She wanted to know whether I had received my academic degrees in the United States because that would at least signal my assimilation into American thinking. By the end of the course, this student was surprised that she was able to learn about racial politics from me and was also able to revise her initial reaction to me. My racial background as neither white nor black creates the perception that I am an outsider to the United States and to the English language. Xin Lu Gale writes about her experience as an Asian woman teaching African American students in her article " 'The Stranger' in Communication: Race, Class and Conflict in a Basic Writing Class."[17] She says that her African American students were skeptical of her correcting their grammar and indoctrinating them in writing standardized English because she was neither white nor black.

Similarly, my students perceive me as an outsider not only because they consider me as part of those institutional practices that place them in at-risk categories, but also because they do not see me as part of the politics of race in the United States. My ability to teach racial issues, therefore, is hampered by a continuing binary opposition of white and black. Addressing such issues in the classroom can be volatile and uncomfortable. Moving students away from binary thinking is a complicated process that is further compounded by the two-sided nature of an American politics that places issues in oppositional black and white categories. The university outreach program, along with the end of affirmative action, only reinforces these oppositions in my classroom— white against nonwhite students, white students against a nonwhite teacher, African American students against Asian American students, and against Asian American teachers. Furthermore, these tensions help in creating the perception that categories such as African American, black, or white are cohesive and homogenous. Each of these headings is comprised of many different groups of people with a history of conflict amongst themselves that is usually glossed over when one seemingly unified racial and ethnic category is positioned against others.

NOTES

1 "One Florida Summary," *One Florida Initiative 2000*, www.myflorida.com/myflorida/government/learn/one_florida/floridaSummary.htm (March 13, 2001).

2 Dana Peterson, "AIM-ing for Student Success," *CLASnotes* 13, no. 9 (28 September 1999).

3 Corrie Martine, "University Outreach and Affirmative Action." *ADE Bulletin* No. 125 (Spring 2000): 57–58.

4 Jeb Bush, "State of the State Address." *State of the State Address 1999*, March 2, 1999.

5 Randy Martin, "Introduction," in *Chalk Lines: The Politics of Work in a Managed University*, ed. Randy Martin (Durham, N.C.: Duke University Press, 1998), 1–29.

6 Jamaica Kincaid, "Girl," in *Rereading America: Cultural Contexts for Critical Thinking and Writing*, 4th Edition, ed. Gary Columbo, et al. (Boston: Bedford Books, 1998), 418–420.

7 Charles Murray, "The Coming White Underclass," in *Rereading America*, 81–88.

8 Earl Graves, "Florida's Trojan Horse," *Black Enterprise* (May 2000): 13, and Pearl Stewart, "NAACP files brief against "One Florida" Plan," *Black Issues in Higher Education* 17, no. 24 (Jan. 18, 2001): 20.

9 Maria T. Padilla, "Hispanics Stay Quiet on Affirmative Action," *Orlando Sentinel* (January 22, 2000).

10 Bonnie TuSmith, *All My Relatives: Community in Contemporary Ethnic American Literatures* (Ann Arbor: University of Michigan Press, 1994), 33.

11 Curtis Chang, "The Streets of Gold: The Myth of the Model Minority," in *Rereading America*, 366–375, 370.

12 Chang, "Streets of Gold," 370.

13 Chang, "Streets of Gold," 372.

14 Terry Dean, "Multicultural Students, Monocultural Teachers," *College Composition and Communication* 40 (1989): 23–37.

15 Gregory Jay, "The End of 'American' Literature: Toward a Multicultural Practice," *College English* 53 (March 1991):264–281, 272.

16 Studs Terkel, "Stephen Cruz," in *Rereading America*, 326–330.

17 Xin Lu Gale, "'The Stranger' in Communication: Race, Class, and Conflict in a Basic Writing Class," *JAC: A Journal of Composition Theory* 17 (1997): 53–67.

A GHOST IN THE COLLABORATIVE MACHINE:

THE WHITE MALE TEACHER IN THE MULTICULTURAL CLASSROOM

PHOTO: TAMMY BRINKLEY

The first class I ever taught that focused on race and gender was composed entirely of women save for two men—another student and me. In many ways the class was a great success; students were enthusiastic and hardworking, and class discussions were lively. Late in the semester, one woman asked the male student how he had felt being the only man in the room. Another student snickered and pointed out that, after all, I was also male. To which the first student replied, "Oh yes. But don't you always kind of think of your teachers as sexless?"

Being called "sexless" hardly fits even reconstructed notions of masculinity, but at the time I was really quite pleased. Indeed, given that I had attempted to facilitate a decentered classroom discussion, the student's comment was a ringing endorsement. As a white male, I felt I was an "outsider" to the course material, and I mitigated the problem of my pedagogical authority by democratizing the classroom. In short, I tried to disappear.

There is something comforting about this effort to become a ghostly presence—influential, perhaps, but imperceptible. Many teachers see this pedagogical model as a desirable and even necessary method for teaching multicultural

PETER KERRY POWERS teaches multiethnic American literature at Messiah College. The author of *Recalling Religions,* on religion and memory in ethnic women's literature, Powers is working on a book about race, religion, and masculinity in American culture during the 1920s.

In this essay, Powers contends that the move toward a democratic classroom has some drawbacks: student self-expression and the diminution of professorial authority together can create as many problems as they solve, especially if naively implemented. Powers here describes his search for a middle ground.

subject matter. Luis Sfeir-Younis describes a "genuinely multicultural class," as one in which "both content and process are transformed in ways that reflect the interests, behavioral styles, and learning modes of a diverse student population. In a course in which class interactions are an integral part of the subject matter, diversity is welcomed, new knowledge is generated, and new ways of conceiving reality are integrated, which may help stretch the paradigm of the discipline."[1] On this account, the decentered classroom is the necessary form of multicultural education, reflecting in the heteroglossia of multiple student voices the multicultural perspectives of the subject matter itself.

Despite the relief that the decentered classroom provided my all-too-centered voice as a white male, I want to interrogate here the assumption that decentered classrooms necessarily lead to liberating learning experiences. Indeed, at the extreme, undertheorized notions of student expression and of the power of whiteness—to say nothing of the concrete realities of the classroom—can lead to classroom experiences that undermine rather than enhance the teaching of race, ethnicity, and gender. A liberatory education often depends upon teachers—even white male teachers—finding ways of using their authority constructively without at the same time returning to coercive forms of pedagogy that are themselves antiprogressive.

Let me say first that of course students must be involved in the production of knowledge, and that we shouldn't return to a banking model of education. Jane Tompkins's wariness of performance rightly suggests that only a spurious form of education occurs when we teach to display our competence.[2] For whatever purposes, teachers can and do bludgeon students with their scholarly expertise. However, I would like to extend this recognition by suggesting that students, too, can bludgeon others, even in the naive enthusiasm of their own expressiveness.

This observation runs against the grain of many assumptions concerning the democratized classroom. In one of the few essays directly concerned with a white teacher's legitimacy in the classroom, Thomas Gerschick outlines his efforts to minimize his own authority when teaching about the oppression of others:

> I . . . stressed my belief that different people have different experiences and as a result have different perspectives. These different perspectives reflect our different realities. Hence, I noted that in order for us to learn from one another, all perspectives must be acknowledged and understood. . . .
> Second, I tried not to play the role of "expert"; rather, I continually

stressed that we all had something to learn from each other. This action resulted in reducing the hierarchy of the classroom. It also alleviated any responsibility students might have thought I had to convey everything about the different forms of oppression. Moreover, it meant that they had the responsibility to contribute what they knew about the subject matter. . . .

Through the use of "other voices," my legitimacy became a less significant issue.[3]

Before interrogating the limitations, I applaud the generous instincts. As teachers we do learn from students. And students do learn from one another. Classrooms in which this did not occur would be oppressive, not to say dull. Indeed, Gerschick's class embodies all that is best in what Sfeir-Younis describes as the "truly multicultural class."

What worries me in Gerschick's description is that the salutary feel of these passages depends on a vague and generalized conception of students. Their voices can be acknowledged and their contributions and interests valued precisely because they seem to come out of nowhere rather than being located in specific histories and cultural contexts—this despite the general effort to acknowledge different histories. In actual practice, different horizons of experience clash, and they clash not least because of differing experiences and levels of access to power.

For instance, a few years ago I taught *Uncle Tom's Cabin* to an all-white, all-male, all-southern class. At one point I was discussing the political and moral evil of slavery and the social practices that sustained it. One student objected, arguing that since white Southern culture accepted slavery at the time, neither I nor Harriet Beecher Stowe could fairly judge the defenders of slavery. Although they looked bad from our perspective, this student reasoned, defenses of slavery merely expressed the deeply held and even unconscious cultural norms of that time and place. Therefore, as a cultural outsider, I should not judge. No other student raised a voice to disagree.

Now, like Gershick's students, my student surely had different experiences that had given him a different perspective, a perspective that suggests a "different reality." I think he quite clearly also had interests at stake. But to assume that this must simply be acknowledged and understood as an equal contribution to the development of knowledge concerning racism strikes me as an untenable leap of the imagination.

My temptation is to dismiss the problem as unique to a small, all-male, predominantly white school. However, I have experienced similar kinds of classroom conversations in a variety of classroom settings, in large universities where white students were a minority in the classroom and in the predominantly white liberal arts college where I now teach, a college where women are in the overwhelming majority. In these various contexts, students relying on their native experiences and realities are often ill-equipped to address the social, historical, and cultural complexities of racism in ways that will make the classroom an energetic space of pedagogical progressiveness. Indeed, given the predominance of racial and ethnic stereotyping in our national history, it is not clear that having six or seven people voice an ethnic stereotype in a small group will be less oppressive and coercive than if I voiced the same stereotype in one loud voice from the front of the class. Nor will a student feel more empowered by having twenty peers misconceive some aspect of his or her cultural history than if I misconceive that history during a lecture. An interesting array of voices speaking eloquently, but uncritically, from the systems of power that shape and enable their voices in the first place will not a community of learning make.

Thus, my early efforts to democratize the classroom were insufficient on at least three counts. First, the assumption seems to be that relations of power and oppression are institutionally embodied in the figure of the teacher, or, perhaps more broadly, in the curriculum and other features of the educational institution. But power and oppression function "democratically" as well, in dispersed forms of discourse and daily practice.[4] Racism can be manifested through pedagogical authority or institutional decision making, but it also functions insidiously in networks of everyday practice, discourse, and assumption. The teacher's role can be, in part, to question or critique those everyday practices out of which most students find their abilities to express themselves—an unnerving and difficult process to be sure, but one that can enable the classroom to be more democratized than it would be without such an intervention.

Second, I can't withdraw from my own being in the classroom. Where could I find a disembodied voice in which my whiteness or my maleness would not count? Cheryl Johnson has pointed out that as a black woman her embodiment, as well as the assumptions about black women that students bring to the classroom, affect her teaching situation. As a black woman working in the academy, she *can't* withdraw from her embodied presence and disappear.[5] I would suggest that none of us should try to do so. This is all the more the case because the fantasy of withdrawal into invisibility is the privilege of whiteness and one of its fundamental strategies of power. Drawing on Henry Giroux and

Richard Dyer, AnnLouise Keating notes that by "erasing its presence, 'whiteness' operates as the unacknowledged standard or norm against which all so-called 'minorities' are measured."[6] Given that "whiteness" has tended to operate powerfully through a strategy of invisibility, I remain cautious about a pedagogy that masks the presence and power of the white teacher in the classroom. On the one hand, such disappearance may simply displace the effects of whiteness to the conversations of the classroom, and on the other it may prevent the white teacher from adequately confronting the implications of his or her own whiteness as it actually operates in engagement with the text and in the operations of the classroom and institution.

The conception of the teacher as facilitator can be insufficient on a third count. It too easily assumes the student's native ability to grapple with texts, and understand their complexities and particularities, see the ways in which they are drawing from and arguing with particular traditions. However, if we are not clear that we are training students into particular ways of seeing and speaking—even if only to treat the voices of others with respect—their expressiveness is as likely to be an iteration of cultural assumptions they have never thought to question as it is to be a developed form of democratic politics. On this score, the invisibility of the white teacher can serve to reinforce dominant ideologies within American culture. Students who have not been trained to critique the culture in which they live may keep on living it, in all its most laudatory and pernicious forms.

Burns Cooper has noted that students' undeveloped approaches to literature can lead them to refuse engagement with different cultural visions rather than be educated by them. He writes of a class in which some of his Alaskan Native students rejected Wendy Rose because her depiction of Alaskans was "inaccurate," in which women students rejected Scott Momaday because he depicted a rape, and Christian students rejected Louise Erdrich because her work was "bawdy."[7] Cooper says his students accepted Native American literature that presented them with "very positive, heroic views of older times . . . and realistic depictions of well-publicized contemporary problems such as alcoholism and Fetal Alcohol syndrome."[8] Cooper calls this interpretive approach a form of fundamentalism, whether coming from the left or the right. Its essence is the refusal to engage the complexities of human culture as embodied in literary texts.[9]

Acknowledging these three insufficiencies, it now seems to me that the theory of expression that undergirded my earliest practices as a teacher relied upon a mistakenly abstract theory of the personal voice. As Giroux has suggested, "The emphasis on the personal as the fundamental aspect of the political often results in highlighting the personal through a form of 'confessional' politics that all but forgets how the political is constituted in social and cultural forms outside of one's own experience."[10] To argue by analogy, if Michael Awkward is correct in arguing that white critics can fall into self-serving critical postures when considering ethnic literature, I think we should assume that students can do so as well.[11] Expressiveness may merely describe my students' imprisonment to received cultural paradigms rather than a truly freeing practice earned, at least partially, through a teacher's intervention in their different realities. To the degree that they remain enmeshed within those paradigms, they can, even in the innocence of their own expression, use their expression to imprison others.

Here's another example. An upper division course I taught on ethnicity and American literature included students of various ethnicities, but no one who was an active member of a Jewish American community. Two students identified themselves as having some Jewish ancestry in the distant past. At one point in the course we read *Goodbye, Columbus* by Philip Roth and *The Pagan Rabbi* by Cynthia Ozick, two short story collections that I chose because the authors envision very different forms of Jewishness in the American context. Mostly, my students were enthusiastic about Roth's work, identifying with the struggle that Ozzie, the main character from "The Conversion of the Jews," was having with his religion, his parents, and his teachers. We spent a good deal of time talking about how Roth placed a Jewish accent on some fairly common adolescent and preadolescent experiences in the United States. Upon getting to Ozick, however, a rumbling voice of discontent began to bubble just beneath the surface of the class, evident in the frowns I saw and the snippets of conversation overheard as I walked into the room, and in the more hesitant and disjointed conversations that went on in small groups.

To some degree, my pedagogical strategies seemed to work quite well. Small groups discussed how Ozick and Roth represented Jewish American ethnicity similarly or differently. Students immediately recognized profound differences between the two, and began to ask me—and the two students with Jewish ancestry—for the "real" story on Jewish ethnicity. We spent a good deal of time talking about how there was no "real" story in the way they wanted a real story. The real story was that there are different ways of being Jewish in America, and we would have to evaluate their consequences and histories and similarities on a case-by-case basis. As a deconstructor of the notion of an essentialized Jewish difference, I was quite pleased with the initial developments of this particular exercise.

I was less ready for what began to happen next. Admitting that there were significantly different forms of Jewishness, all but one of the students moved on to categorize Roth's way of being Jewish as good, and Ozick's way of being Jewish as bad. In investigating this judgment, students immediately fell into ethnic stereotyping. Roth was good because he was universal; Ozick was bad because she was particular. Roth was good because his language was immediately accessible, Ozick was bad because her syntax and her use of Yiddish were alienating. Roth was good because he wanted to speak to and with "everybody"; Ozick was bad because she wanted to be separate and exclusive. In short, Roth was good because he wanted to assimilate and erase a Jewish particularity, and Ozick was bad because she didn't value being "plain American." These kinds of judgments were quite plainly ethnophobic—made by students with various ethnic identifications—and verged on being anti-Semitic. As one student put it hesitantly, but with refreshing forthrightness, "I don't know if I should say this, but somehow I think that Ozick is *too Jewish.*"

This formulation reveals both the value and the limitation of expressiveness in the classroom. On the one hand, the student's openness helped locate the class regarding the texts and issues at hand. This openness was gained, I think, partly through my extensive use of small groups as well as my efforts to present strong counterarguments to my own at various points in the class through handouts, videos, and my knowledge of critical discussions. On the other hand, the participatory nature of the class discussion actually reinforced the anti-Semitic rationalizations of the Enlightenment by which it was O.K. to be Jewish, but only if this religio-cultural difference was kept at home where it would not disturb the "commonsense" operations of the rational public sphere. As Richard Rubinstein has pointed out in *After Auschwitz*, the logic of this formulation is the logic of the Holocaust.[12] An uncritical emphasis on expressiveness as an end does nothing to address the incipient anti-Semitism implicit in my student's evaluation of Ozick as excessively Jewish.

I would argue further that an uncritical emphasis on the decentered classroom tends to exacerbate this problem. If I structure my class in such a way that student expression is paramount to the success of the class as a whole and to the success of individual students, it is easy to see that students can come to place a higher value on literatures that help them do well and to prefer those things with which they most readily identify—that is, the literature with which they already feel an easy sense of familiarity. Thus, an uncritical emphasis on student expression *necessarily* means that students will see Roth as "better" than Ozick precisely because students are better able to express themselves about him. Many students will identify with Roth precisely because Roth values and conceives of himself as a contemporary liberal and cosmopolitan individual; he makes it easier for most students to express themselves because he speaks their language. Ozick's voice irritated many students, and they could not speak about her as well because she is far more alien in her insistence on the uniqueness and difference of Jewish thought and practice. Such experiences merely underscore a banal truth of undergraduate education, if not of reading as a general enterprise: students prefer those visions with which they can most readily and easily identify. In the same course we ran into similar problems reading Gloria Anzaldúa and Rudolfo Anaya. Students disliked Anzaldúa because she was "too angry with white people" and was an "angry feminist"—this last judgment made by many despite the class being made up entirely of women. Students tended to prefer Anaya because the protagonist in *Bless Me, Ultima* had experiences that students could "relate to," though none of them had been a young Chicano boy growing up in the Southwest. Perhaps this is because Anaya's book works with the conventions of the bildungsroman and with the masculine attraction to a feminized landscape, familiar conventions of Western literature, to say nothing of the fact that the challenge to Anglo supremacy in Anaya is less direct and confrontational than in Anzaldúa. In a recent course, I ran into the same problem in discussing Eric Walrond and Langston Hughes. Students found Walrond's use of Caribbean dialects annoying, a sign that he wasn't as good a writer as Hughes. Moreover, his understanding of the workings of race were more difficult for students to engage because—working from a Caribbean background—Walrond did not conform to the paradigmatic black/white divide that they saw and understood in Langston Hughes.

Although many essays on teaching multiethnic literature take on the problematic white student who cannot relate to a teacher or to a particular work, preferences for familiarity occur across the racial/ethnic spectrum. For instance, I once taught a course on James Baldwin to a class that was about evenly divided between African American and European American students. None of the students, however, was openly gay. Many students, black and white alike, were more than a little queasy about Baldwin's frank depictions of homoeroticism. Discussion was sometimes awkward—more than one long silence filled in with embarrassed laughter. Two different students came to me privately and said that they had stopped reading certain sections of Baldwin's work because they found the eroticism disturbing and contrary to their moral and religious upbringing. One African American student put it this way: "He's good with the race stuff, but I wish he would leave the sex stuff alone." Left entirely to the democratic interests of the class, I think it's unlikely that we would have even read *Giovanni's Room* or *Just Above My Head.*

This points to a final issue in the learning process that is, perhaps, too little incorporated into pedagogical theories that emphasize a democratized learning process. Learning is an often exhilarating and even transcendent experience, as we begin to see new horizons and experience the world in new ways. Equally true, however, is that such exhilaration and transformation are usually accompanied by—and perhaps only made possible through—the painful process of leaving things behind. Indeed my own engagement with ethnic literature required a serious revision of my undergraduate notions of high modernist writers such as Eliot and Pound—a revision that left me uncertain of how to speak about these kinds of literature at all, to say nothing of newfound hesitations about how to begin to speak about the literature of racial and ethnic others.

Such inability to express myself without hesitations and stumblings was, in a sense, a necessary failure, since such failures mark a struggle with things more difficult than the familiar world about which I could express myself so readily. My students who grapple with Baldwin's blackness or his homosexuality, with Walrond's Caribbean imagination or with Ozick's Judaism, are afforded a moment of important self-discovery: that of their own particularity, their own contingency, even their own incompetence in articulating their relationship to a new and different world.

In response, a teacher need not return to a banking model of education critiqued by Freire.[13] Rather, I would suggest that the simple either/or dichotomy—either collaborative/liberatory learning or banking/authoritarian teaching—ought to be displaced in favor of a much more complex, creative, and realistic figure, one that allows for both interventionist and reticent teaching strategies. My current favorite metaphors are those of the coach, the mentor, and, sometimes, the artist. The best of such figures know when to keep silent and let the players play the game. They also know when to push and drive a team beyond what it imagines as its point of endurance. Like the artist whose training and instincts must guide her when engaged in the moment of creation, the teacher must draw upon her expertise, her experience, and knowledge of individual students in order to create a classroom environment in which transformative learning is possible.

Such a view of teaching calls for a more precarious and dangerous practice than either that of the teacher as ghost or teacher as banker. Indeed, it seems to me that in such a position the teacher is always at risk of not intervening appropriately, and thus leaving students short of their potential at a particular moment or of intervening excessively and short-circuiting the necessary processes by which learning occurs.

No prescription ensures that this balance can be achieved. In my own experience I have found that teaching about race and ethnicity through literature continually makes me seek that balance. I have described various situations in which intervention has seemed necessary. On the other hand, teaching about race and ethnicity also induces the sense of particularity that helps prevent a return to an authoritarian style of teaching. The very fact that I am teaching the texts that I do constantly brings home to me my own fleshy particularity as a white male. As I read a passage from James Baldwin or Zora Neale Hurston and hear their language, their syntax, their vision burbling up from out of me, with the air from my lungs, the vibrations and pulsing of my body, I am made acutely aware of my own white and male particularity, my own historical, cultural, and material being. In short, I experience myself as different. I am certainly unable to disappear as the unacknowledged ghost in the collaborative machine. Rather, where my students are frustrated with their inability to engage a particular work, I have to try and train them into new ways of seeing and speaking—which must also be a training into new ways of being. Where my students iterate racist or sexist assumptions concerning American culture, my students' engagement with other voices—including my own—can lead them to understand their uniqueness as historical and social individuals rather than as representatives of "the norm," however they may have initially construed that norm. Ironically, then, teaching ethnic literature often requires me to exercise more authority in the classroom rather than less, even though this authority must be exercised from a decentered position of particularity. This sense of my own particularity does not guarantee, but at least encourages, a sense of humility about my authority and competence—a humility that should discourage me from bludgeoning my students in a return to the banking model of education.

In similar ways, reading, discussion, and lecture can decenter my students, reveal their own contingency and their own historical particularity. In class they must risk the confusion and disorientation that occur when the assumptions and indeed the sense of self upon which their expressiveness has relied are decomposed or overturned. But it is through such struggle and even loss that new knowledge and possibilities for living are gained. In one course, I had students write a journal on the first day of class answering the question, "Are you ethnic?" At the end of the course I had the students write a short essay on how their conceptions of ethnicity had changed, if they had. Several students wrote about moving from seeing themselves as just "plain American" to an understanding of how being white constituted a particular rather than a "normal" American experience, and that even within the designation "white" there were various experiences based on religious, class, national, and other kinds of differences. By contrast, a Korean American student—one of three students who began the class with a developed sense of ethnic identity—indicated that she was surprised when reading literature from Jewish Americans and Chicanos to discover a wide array of common interests and experiences, things she had previously conceived of as unique to herself and other Korean Americans. I take stories such as these as successes since they are the stories of students who are discovering how to articulate their relationship to their own histories and also the histories of others. To echo Giroux, they are learning to hear their personal voices in the social, cultural, and political structures that have framed their experience. I also take this assignment as a useful deployment of "expression" since it asks students to articulate how their own voices have begun to evolve, and may need to continue to be transformed, rather than simply reifying expression as an end in itself. These new selves are rightly understood as liberated selves, whose expression may serve to liberate others.

NOTES

This essay was completed with the assistance of a fellowship for Arts Commentary from the Pennsylvania Council on the Arts.

1 Luis F. Sfeir-Younis, "Reflections on the Teaching of Multicultural Courses," in *Multicultural Teaching in the University*, ed. David Schoem, Linda Frankel, Ximena Zuniga, and Edith Lewis (Westport, Conn.: Praeger, 1993), 71.

2 Jane Tompkins, "Pedagogy of the Distressed," *College English* 52, no. 6 (1990), 653–660.

3 Thomas J. Gerschick, "Should and Can a White, Heterosexual, Middle-Class Man Teach Students About Social Inequality and Oppression? One Person's Experience and Reflections," in *Multicultural Teaching in the University*, 204.

4 Michel Foucault, "Truth and Power," in *Power/Knowledge: Selected Interviews and Other Writings, 1972–1977*, ed. Colin Gordon, trans. Colin Gordon, Leo Marshall, John Mepham, Kate Soper (New York: Pantheon, 1977), 109–133.

5 Cheryl L. Johnson, "Participatory Rhetoric and the Teacher as Racial/Gendered Subject," *College English* 56, no. 4 (1994):409–419.

6 AnnLouise Keating, "Interrogating 'Whiteness,' (De)Constructing 'Race'," *College English* 57, no. 8 (1995), 905.

7 Burns Cooper, "White Men Can't Teach," *SAIL* 6, no. 1 (1994), 17.

8 Burns Cooper, "White Men," 17.

9 Burns Cooper, "White Men," 20–21.

10 Henry Giroux, *Living Dangerously; Multiculturalism and the Politics of Difference* (New York: Peter Lang,1993), 73.

11 Michael Awkward, "Negotiations of Power: White Critics, Black Texts, and the Self-Referential Impulse," *American Literary History* 2, no. 4 (1990), 581–606.

12 Richard Rubinstein, *After Auschwitz: History, Theology, and Contemporary Judaism* (New York: Bobbs-Merrill Company, Inc, 1966; reprinted, Baltimore: Johns Hopkins University Press, 1996), 83–102.

13 Paulo Freire, *Pedagogy of the Oppressed*, trans. Myra Bergman Ramos (New York: Continuum, 1989).

PATTI DUNCAN

DECENTERING WHITENESS:

RESISTING RACISM IN THE WOMEN'S STUDIES CLASSROOM

PHOTO: MISTY McELROY

"GO BACK TO WHERE YOU BELONG"

Recently, near the beginning of the term at my university, I taught an upper-level women's studies seminar entitled Asian American Women's Studies, versions of which I've taught in the past at other universities.[1] On the agenda for one particular discussion was the topic of national belonging, especially Asian Pacific Americans' experiences of not belonging and of being made to feel like perpetual outsiders and guests in the United States, regardless of how long our families have lived here or how "American" we may feel. That day I planned to engage the students in a discussion of the function and daily effects of racism as they pertain to Asian Pacific American women's lives and experiences. Before class, I walked a couple of city blocks to Portland's downtown post office. There, at a busy crosswalk, a young woman in a car turned in front of me and I waited for the light to change. Behind me, a young man, presumably a student at the same university, muttered to his companion, "Damn Asians in their fucking nice cars." I turned in time to see his friend nod

PATTI DUNCAN received her Ph.D. from Emory University and is an assistant professor of women's studies at Portland State University. Her current scholarship and activism focus on Asian Pacific American women's resistance to oppression, women of color and third world feminisms, and queer women's histories and movements.

In her essay, Duncan describes classroom experiences in which white students and students of color talk past one another and use conflicting racial discourses. She argues that white entitlement and white feelings of belonging within academe greatly affect how professors teach about race and contends that many professors behave as if white students are the primary concern.

in agreement. Both young men were white. The woman driver, turning with the right of way, was Asian American. "How dare those Asians come to *our* country, own expensive cars, and turn in front of *us*?" was what I heard in the tone of his question. Or, how dare those Asians take up any space in this— *our*—country?

The young man's remark, made flippantly to a fellow "insider," resounds with a sense of entitlement, a confidence in his own sense of belonging, and a hostility to any "foreign" elements, like the young Asian American woman presuming to drive her car in front of him (doesn't she know her place?), or the Asian American professor who turned to confront him on the street after overhearing his comment (he simply stared at me incredulously). After all, we're supposed to be passive, submissive, and above all, silent. Any departure from this scripted role for Asian Pacific American women is considered an affront to normalcy, and an insult to "true" (read: white) Americans. His attitude mirrors that of other white students in the university, especially those from dominant groups who often maintain a belief that the process of education is intended solely for their benefit. They subsequently express hostility for students of color (and others deviating in some way from the mythical norms of U.S. society, including women, working-class and poor students, differently abled students, older students, and lesbian, gay, bisexual, and transgender students). In addition, this young man's comment (and the assumptions underlying its articulation) highlights the specific hostility many non-Asian Americans reserve for Asian Americans, whom they see as benefiting from affirmative action and other government programs and resources, and stereotype as the "model minority."[2]

In class that day, I shared this experience with students in an attempt to provide a concrete example of what we had been reading and theorizing about. Asian American students in the class began sharing similar examples, and we discussed all of them carefully, examining the assumptions behind each one. Questions like "Where are you from?" and "How did you learn to speak such good English?" are the most common reminders that we—and others like us— do not belong, and that neither this space nor this tongue are considered "ours." Rather, we are visitors, allowed to share in the American dream and the English language as long as we remember not to overstep the boundaries of racist propriety. Several students shared experiences of being told, in not so many words, to "go back to where they belong," regardless of the fact that many of them are American citizens, born and raised here.

Students in the class were pushing quickly through the materials and ideas. Several of them stated that they felt excited about the opportunity to finally discuss something that related to their own lives, after sitting through countless classes that proceeded as though Asian Pacific Americans, and especially Asian American women, did not exist at all. But we were interrupted in this powerful moment by a white student's comments about the racism she, too, has experienced. Though we had spent a great deal of time in this class reading and discussing theories of race and racism, she categorized her feelings of exclusion and her experience as a "minority" in this particular classroom as "racism." Her attempt to recenter herself and her whiteness was met with silence and disappointment from other students, some of whom quietly retreated from the discussion. And I realized how often white students feel the need to recenter themselves, even in classes about race, racism, and the history, literature, and social movements of people of color.

It is this critical moment upon which I wish to focus in this essay, for this is a common moment, and a recurring one. I hope to provide some context for and analysis of this particular move—a move to recenter whiteness not in terms of interrogating and challenging white privilege, something that is often initiated by critical, antiracist white students, but rather to return things to the way they were (what is considered normalcy for many white people—namely, white supremacy). It is a fear of the destabilization of white supremacy, and hence white privilege, that keeps many white students in terror of discussing race and racism in the classroom, on any but the most superficial levels.

In countless ways, students of color—and other students considered "deviant" by dominant values and standards—are taught that they do not belong in American higher education. In both explicit and subtle ways, these students receive certain messages about their place in the academy. For example, theorist bell hooks comments on the ways in which she was "terrorized" as a student of color during graduate school through racist and sexist messages intended to humiliate and demoralize her.[3] Writer and artist Kyo Maclear explores the ways in which she was silenced as a student, often due to the fact that there was no one "like her" represented in the curriculum.[4] When she did speak, she was generally either not heard or objectified and made to feel "like a freak sideshow whose stories are used to satiate curiosity, or worse, uphold the myth of inclusion." What she learned, she writes, is that for many students of color, "the notion of the classroom as a 'safe' space is a dangerous illusion." Finally, Joanna Kadi, in her essay "Stupidity 'Deconstructed,'" describes her internalization of such messages and her subsequent belief that she must simply be "stupid" and unqualified.[5] Privileged people, she argues, misuse words and distort reality to create a space—the academy—that excludes all of the "misfits." More importantly, such institutions socialize us to believe that we are not even worthy of gaining entry, often succeeding in separating "us" from "them." What I argue here is that these two processes—the messages students of color receive about "not belonging" in educational institutions, and the recentering of white students at all junctures in educational processes—are intricately tied together.

"I'M MORE OPPRESSED THAN YOU ARE": TACTICS WHITE PEOPLE USE TO DIVERT OR UNDERMINE DISCUSSIONS OF RACISM

Last year, in an upper-level women's studies class I taught called Women of Color in U.S. Society, I was amazed by the number of white students taking the class who seemed surprised that we were to spend so much time discussing women of color. Although the title of the course was clear, they still expected to be discussing white women as the cultural norm. In such classes, when I attempt to push students to center and explore the histories, writings, and experiences of women of color, the women of color students in the class often feel empowered to speak up. Some of them tell me that this is the first and only class for them in which this has been possible. However, there are white students who inevitably seem threatened by the empowerment and centering of people of color, and they often begin pointing out the ways in which they too are oppressed, either by focusing on how they are in the minority in this particular instance or by beginning to list the ways in which they are oppressed as a German American or a person of Italian descent, for example. One white student wrote in her journal entry for the class that she felt "hurt" and "angry" after reading Gloria Anzaldúa's introduction to her anthology *Making Face, Making Soul/Haciendo Caras: Creative and Critical Perspectives by Feminists of Color*, in which Anzaldúa calls on white people to be accountable for their white privilege and racism.[6] This student explained that racism is over and people of color should stop making such a big deal of it. She wrote, "I feel robbed of my heritage," noting that her European American ethnicity was not being taken seriously in this class. Here I do not argue that these students have not experienced oppression, or that various groups of

European Americans have not been discriminated against, but simply that there is a curious—and racist—phenomenon that occurs when white students find themselves decentered in discourses of race, racism, and white privilege in this country.

Another tactic white students often employ is that of simple digression. When issues of race and white privilege are introduced in class discussions and readings, I am always amazed by how quickly some students move to bring up other topics—not to tie them to a discussion of race and racism, but simply to divert attention away from their own whiteness and white privilege. Sometimes they de-emphasize race and racism and choose instead to focus on some other category of identity and social stratification, preferably one which marks them as clearly and unarguably oppressed. One white queer student consistently redirected class discussions to emphasize issues of sexuality and her own oppression as a lesbian, not to make critical connections between and among these parts of our identities and lives, but to shut down the discussion of racism and white privilege, including concrete experiences of racism. Another working-class white woman, after reading Peggy McIntosh's article "White Privilege and Male Privilege," wrote in a response essay, "Class is the *real* issue, not race. Growing up poor, I have never had white privilege or any kind of privilege." I welcomed her attempts to complicate our understandings of whiteness and white privilege by pointing out the ways in which white people occupy different positions in society. However, I was again dismayed by white students' consistent efforts to recenter themselves and to dismiss any notion of white privilege or accountability in their own lives.

As Michael Omi and Howard Winant argue, and as I have witnessed in the classes I teach, discussions of race take on peculiar "crises of meaning" in the classroom where white students and students of color talk past one another, employing conflicting racial discourses.[7] Citing Bob Blauner, Omi and Winant suggest that white students generally tend to argue that racism is a thing of the past, while also considering any mention of race as racist. According to this ideology, "colorblindness" is the only way to be "antiracist," and necessitates a disavowal of any racial discourse.[8] And Gloria Yamato, also commenting on discussions of race, argues that whenever the subject of racism arises, many white students want to focus on the racism of people of color and on themselves as victims of racism—what she views as a diversionary tactic to take pressure off themselves and other white people.[9] In contrast, many students of color root racism in power, arguing that race and racism permeate history and everyday experience on multiple levels. They often connect readings about race and racism to their own daily experiences, attempting to bridge the dichotomy so prevalent in the academy between theory and practice. Such students of color also often have a great deal to say about strategies of resistance to racism, so rarely discussed in the academy.

Meanwhile, white teachers (and some teachers of color) spend so much time worrying about how to make the white students in their classrooms feel comfortable and "safe" speaking about race and racism that it is often the students of color, again, whose identities and words end up elided, negated, or otherwise invalidated. Racism, of course, is present on at least three levels within the university setting. First, at the level of curriculum, students of color not only find themselves presented with little or no reading materials and other resources by or about people of color, but they also encounter both explicit and subtle racist themes in what they do study. Thus, they often find themselves misrepresented or completely excluded from the curriculum. When issues related to race are introduced in classes, they often rely upon additive, tokenistic frameworks that contribute to a climate in which actual people of color are singled out and further objectified and exoticized.

Among the faculty, administration, and fellow student body at the majority of institutions of higher education, students of color find few people like themselves and thus have difficulty locating role models, mentors, and even friends with whom to share common experiences, often resulting in a profound sense of isolation. In terms of locating support from other students, there are additional barriers. Students of color are generally underrepresented in higher education, and often pitted against one another and forced to compete for limited resources. White students often view them as affirmative action cases and refuse to treat them as serious colleagues, and white faculty may view students of color in this light as well. Mary Romero quotes one student, who said: "Being the only students or the only one of two students of color was difficult, particularly in an environment that attributed my achievements to affirmative action and where faculty interest was a response to my ethnicity and a need to affirm their liberalism."[10] Finally, within the larger social and political context, students of color encounter invisibility, erasure, stereotyping, violence, economic disenfranchisement, and other forms of racism and oppression. Thus it should come as no surprise that even at the level of classroom interaction, students of color are victimized by racist comments and assumptions made by professors and other students.

Why are the safety and comfort of white students almost always made a priority, even by some faculty of color? What are our course objectives, in teaching about race? What are the implications of the constant recentering of whiteness in the classroom, on the part of both white students and teachers? How can we reach white students to teach them about race—especially accountability and white privilege—without simply recentering them (and whiteness) to the exclusion and detriment of students of color? What are the risks of this radical pedagogy? What can we gain from using it? And what can students of color gain from professors willing to interrupt racism, despite the difficulties and risks involved in doing so? Of course, we as faculty occupy different social locations, too. As faculty of color, our footholds within the academy are much more tenuous, and our status less secure. We can choose to play the role of gatekeeper, enjoying status as tokens. Or we can use this position to try to transform some of the more oppressive elements of the university and create contexts for radical, liberatory pedagogy. White faculty can be allies, but they must take accountability, and interrogate their own status as white people in a racist, white supremacist environment. Otherwise, they replicate the fear and elisions of so many of their students, who would rather turn away than confront racism head-on.

What I argue here is that my opening example, and the themes of entitlement and belonging within the university, especially where racial and other identities are concerned, have everything do to do with how we teach about race. The majority of the university functions as though white students exist at the center of all pedagogical processes, and many professors continue to teach as though this is true. Even worse, some faculty members of color also teach this way. In other words, the assumption is made that white students are the true "subjects" of the learning experience, while students of color are expected to diversify the classroom and university space, enabling white students to receive a more "multicultural" and diverse experience. When, on the job market, search committee after search committee asked me how I would make my white students comfortable in my classes about race, and when my teaching assistants worry over how to make sure the white students feel "safe" in our classrooms, I know they are teaching primarily to the white members of each classroom.[11] Such questions and concerns make it clear who the focus of the education process is for these educators. When my teaching colleagues worry that too much discussion about race and racism in our classes will alienate the students, I know they are speaking primarily about the white students in our classrooms and conflating students with whiteness. What I also know is that students of color (and many white students) often do not feel safe in the classes they take, especially when professors fail to interrupt racist and other offensive remarks or to create a context in which racism and other systems of oppression, including sexism and homophobia, can be adequately addressed. While it is important to teach white students (as well as students privileged in other ways) to critically interrogate privilege, it is also crucial to decenter them in our teaching. Not doing so simply reinforces assumptions on the part of white students that even classes like Women of Color in U.S. Society are really about them.

SUBVERTING RACIAL DISCOURSES IN THE CLASSROOM

To truly teach about race and racism in meaningful, antiracist ways, we as faculty must acknowledge and engage our own social locations. Doing so means being always aware and attempting to understand the complexities of our own power in student-teacher interactions. Also, we should attempt to recognize the experiences and social locations of our students. As Adrienne Rich suggests, the concept of "coeducation" is misleading not only in terms of gender inequalities in the classroom (and outside, which inevitably shape students' experiences), but also in terms of racial inequalities and other inequalities premised on class, sexual orientation, age, and ability.[12] Coeducation is a misnomer because students and faculty of color do not have the privilege of ever forgetting that we live in a racist society. There can be no adequate teaching of race without consistent awareness of students' experiences in this racist society. Sometimes this may also mean making oneself aware of the racial stratification in one's own department or institution. Women of color in the academy are often expected to perform social reproductive labor to maintain departmental activities, while we are rarely acknowledged or compensated for doing so. Students of color often encounter problematic expectations from faculty members and other students, and are rarely provided with departmental support and services to ensure their survival in the academy.

In our classrooms, it is imperative that we critically examine our own curricula, including assignments and materials, and also language use and daily classroom interactions. It is also crucial to socially locate the texts and readings we assign. By tokenizing authors of color, faculty members may actually encourage the tokenization of students, too. While it may be easier or more familiar to rely on tokenistic, additive approaches to teaching, it is clear that such approaches simply reinforce racism and other forms of oppression in classroom interactions. For example, many women's studies instructors continue to rely on syllabi comprised of weekly topics or units, such as "women's health" and "women and work," in which race, class, and sexuality are often relegated to separate weekly topics. In such formats, writings and issues of women of color are often covered during the day or week entitled "race," and similarly, queer women's experiences are addressed in the unit called "sexuality." Such a format assumes that all other topics (reproductive politics, family, domestic violence, media representations, etc.) are really about white, middle-class heterosexual women, and that women of color have nothing to say about such issues. Also, words like "race" and "sexuality" are often conflated with those groups most marginalized by relations of power, whereby "race" is conflated with women of color, for example, and sexuality is conflated with lesbian, bisexual, and transgender women. Such a method overlooks the fact that white people also occupy racial positions in this society, and that whiteness, too, must be critically interrogated for its many meanings and cultural practices. Finally, many instructors who attempt to teach about race and racism often find themselves beginning each class with whiteness and the experiences of white people. Challenging this practice destabilizes the notion that whiteness is and should be the norm.

Race and racism are difficult, sometimes painful topics in the classroom, for both students and faculty. In my own classes, I have found it useful to establish ground rules early in the term, during which I ask students to discuss their own needs for creating a relatively safe space. Many students are able to articulate at this time the practices that make them uncomfortable and unsafe, and we work as a group to balance sensitivity and awareness of our differences with academic, intellectual freedom in the classroom. At the same time, I recognize that the classroom has rarely been safe for students of color, and I work to create a context for discussing race and racism through readings, films, discussion, and classroom exercises. I have also found it necessary to teach and model appropriate, sensitive ways of interrupting racist remarks and other oppressive comments in class. We can employ overt and subtle techniques for interrupting racism, and our strategies will vary according to our own identities, experiences, disciplines, and pedagogical concerns. In my experience, however, interrupting racism is generally easier to do in classes that rely on nonadditive approaches to the understanding of race, where experiences and writings of people of color are adequately contextualized. Decentering whiteness and white people has been central to my own practice. For example, not only do I attempt to teach about the rich, varied histories and social experiences of people of color, but I also teach *to* students of color, as much as any other students in the room.

Transformation in classrooms must occur at all levels, and involves examining and reshaping curricula, being attentive to social locations and contexts, and working to create as safe a space as possible for antiracist interpersonal communication in the classroom. I have encountered many students and faculty members who shy away from discussions about race and racism because these topics make them feel uncomfortable. However, racism is *not* comfortable, and certainly never has been for people of color. Confronting racism, teaching about race, and developing teaching strategies that are explicitly antiracist may not feel comfortable or familiar to many instructors who have grown accustomed to the centering of whiteness, white experiences, and white subjectivity in their classrooms, in the university, and in society in general. However, it will be through such work that we will eventually find ourselves teaching about race in relation to theoretical frameworks and to daily, lived experience for all students.

NOTES

1 I currently teach at Portland State University, a large, urban public university in Portland, Oregon. Students of color make up approximately 25 percent of the student population, with Asian Pacific American students comprising the largest group of students of color.

2 The myth of the model minority assumes that Asians possess certain innate cultural traits and values that make us opportunistic, even dangerous, to U.S. society. It sends the message that Asian Americans have "made it," usually as a result of these unscrupulous, inscrutable Asian values. At the same time, this stereotype, describing Asians as the *model* minority in the United States, pits Asian Americans against other groups of people of color, as it places the blame for not making it squarely on the shoulders of people of color. Indeed, it ignores the fact that many Asians in the United States, especially immigrant women, recent immigrants from Southeast Asia, and the growing number of homeless Asian Americans, are not surviving economically, politically, and socially and face increasing levels of discrimination and hate violence. Finally, the myth of the model minority, as Shirley Hune suggests, often results in the further neglect of Asian Pacific American students in higher education, as they are seen as not needing academic assistance or guidance. See Hune, *Asian Pacific American Women in Higher Education: Claiming Visibility and Voice* (Washington, D.C.: Association of American Colleges and Universities, 1998).

3 bell hooks, "Black and Female: Reflections on Graduate School," in *Talking Back: Thinking Feminist, Thinking Black* (Boston: South End Press, 1989), 55–61.

4 Kyo Maclear, "Not in So Many Words: Translating Silence Across 'Difference,'" *Fireweed: A Feminist Quarterly of Writing, Politics, Art, and Culture*, no. 44/45 (Summer 1994), 6–11.

5 Joanna Kadi, "Stupidity 'Deconstructed,'" in *Is Academic Feminism Dead? Theory in Practice*, ed. The Social Justice Group at the Center for Advanced Feminist Studies, University of Minnesota (New York: New York University Press, 200), 327–346.

6 Gloria Anzaldúa, *Making Face, Making Soul/Haciendo Caras: Creative and Critical Perspectives by Women of Color* (San Francisco: Aunt Lute Foundation Books, 1990).

7 Michael Omi and Howard Winant, *Racial Formation in the United States from the 1960s to the 1990s* (New York: Routledge, 1994).

8 Of course, those who maintain the belief that "colorblindness" = antiracism fail to recognize that there is already a central racial discourse in the United States, namely white supremacy. Thus, by refusing to speak of race at all, proponents of colorblindness simply uphold and reinforce white supremacy, however unknowingly.

9 Gloria Yamato, "Racism: Something About the Subject Makes It Hard to Name," in *Race, Class, and Gender in the United States: An Integrated Study*, fourth edition, ed. Paula Rothenberg (New York: St. Martin's Press, 1998), 150–154. I've also heard white people say that they wish we could do away with terms like "race" and "racism," because these words are simply not "useful" anymore. Their sentiments provoke concern and anxiety for me, as I realize that what they really wish for is an end to any discussion of their own accountability or collusion with racism.

10 Mary Romero, "Learning to Think and Teach about Race and Gender Despite Graduate School: Obstacles Women of Color Graduate Students Face in Sociology," in *Is Academic Feminism Dead?*, 283–310.

11 My colleague Patti Sakurai discusses her experience on the job market and the recurring question regarding the comfort and safety of white students in her essay "That's Dr. Sakurai to You: Reflections on Race and Gender Along the Academic Front," presentation at the Women's Studies Colloquium Series on Race and Gender, Portland State University, March 7, 2001. She wonders, "Were white candidates asked the same question?" and writes, "In only one interview in my three years on the job market was any concern expressed or a question asked about my intended interactions with students of color . . . The educational priorities at many of these institutions and for whose benefit they viewed multiculturalism and diversity were quite painfully clear" (12).

12 Adrienne Rich, "Taking Women Students Seriously," in *On Lies, Secrets and Silence: Selected Prose* (New York: W. W. Norton and Company, 1979), 237–245.

SMASHING THE RULES OF RACIAL STANDING

SECOND RULE:
Not only are blacks' complaints discounted, but black victims of racism are less effective witnesses than are whites, who are members of the oppressor class. This phenomenon reflects a widespread assumption that blacks, unlike whites, cannot be objective on racial issues and will favor their own no matter what.

—Derrick Bell, "The Rules of Racial Standing" [1]

After giving a powerful talk on antiracist pedagogy, with a particular focus on teaching students to read whiteness as a raced category in literary texts, a prominent white feminist scholar was asked how she deals with her own conferred white authority in the classroom. Her reply—"Oh, I use it. I think we have to use whatever we have against racism"—met laughter and scattered applause, indicating audience approval. The disjunction between this assertion and her talk's trenchant critique of white dominance was shocking, yet the scholar, along with most of her audience, seemed untroubled by the logical and ethical problems inherent in her position. Although Audre Lorde's adage that the master's tools will never dismantle the master's house is not always true, it seems apt in relation to white authority in the classroom. That is, a professor who "uses" this conferred—as opposed to earned and examined—authority reinscribes racism through her self-presentation regardless of the content of her course; the master's tools thus rebuild the master's house of white supremacy even as the overtly antiracist intent of the course materials

---

MAUREEN T. REDDY is a professor of English and women's studies at Rhode Island College. Her other books include *Crossing the Color Line: Race, Parenting, and Culture* and *Everyday Acts Against Racism*. She is working on a book on race and popular fiction.

This essay considers strategies for dealing with the presumption of authority attending on whiteness and for decentering whiteness in the classroom. Reddy reports here on the mixed results she has achieved with several such strategies.

dismantles that house, with the long-term net effect being maintenance of the racial status quo.

By not confronting and then explicitly rejecting her students' unarticulated but nonetheless discernible assessment of her as an authority on race by virtue of her whiteness, this scholar further bolsters the existing racial hierarchy; to think about it in a slightly different way, the professor relies upon the established rules of racial standing. In *Faces at the Bottom of the Well: The Permanence of Racism*, critical race theorist and law professor Derrick Bell details five rules of racial standing, the social and cultural assumptions that govern how testimony on race is understood—and far more frequently, unheard or misunderstood—in the court of U.S. public opinion. Although Bell attends only to the black/white binary that structures racial relations in the United States, several of his rules apply to interactions between whites and all people of color. His second rule, part of which stands as an epigraph to this essay, has especially broad applicability. When targets of racism—a category that includes all people of color—speak of their experiences with racism, their testimony often meets disbelief. The majority of whites dismiss it as "special pleading" that is distorted, entirely subjective, and of no value in understanding the world. With just two exceptions—overt, unabashed racists, such as acknowledged members of white supremacy groups, and whites who are known to be in intimate relationships with people of color—whites who testify publicly on the subject of racism are perceived as objective and therefore believable by other whites. This contrasting treatment has its roots in, and also helps to reproduce, some of the meanings of whiteness to whites, including authority and intelligence. Paradoxically, both vocal white supremacists and antiracist whites intimately involved with people of color are socially coded as not really white, as lacking authority because they are caught in an outmoded or entirely alien understanding of racism.

According to majority white opinion, we live in a post-racist society. Racism is widely—whitely—perceived as an historical artifact, not as the powerful shaper of all of our lives it actually continues to be. This view of racism as nasty but finished, except for aberrational outbreaks by unrepentant white supremacists, is constructed as the truth by successful, conservative politicians and repeatedly reinforced by all kinds of cultural institutions, including ostensibly "liberal" media. In "Teaching Resistance," bell hooks points out that one way that mass media reproduce white supremacist ways of thinking is by making white people who have no personal contact with people of color nonetheless come to feel that they "know" blacks through the distorted images presented on television. hooks persuasively traces a variety of ways in which this television-based knowledge reinforces white supremacy.[2] For instance, she describes a pattern in mid-1990s television programs in which a black character charges racism but is shown to be wrong—sometimes misguided, sometimes calculatedly making false accusations—by the rest of the show, with the viewer "bombarded with evidence that shows this [racism] to be a trumped-up charge. . . . The message that television sends then is that the problem of racism lies with black people—that it exists in our minds and imaginations."[3] This pattern strikes me as a particularly insidious demonstration of Derrick Bell's second rule of racial standing, as the authority figures whose testimony such programs upholds are always white, even when absent from the program itself. Usually such problem-and-resolution programs present a white character to refute directly the black character's assessment of racism, but in some instances no white character articulates the "true" situation of nonracism; instead, the authority invoked is the invisible whiteness responsible for the program (the director, producer, and writer) and thus indistinguishable from white public opinion. One powerful reinforcement of racism and white supremacy is in television's bolstering of white authority in relation to all subjects, but particularly race itself. White viewers, then, are endlessly interpellated as authority figures themselves, most compellingly when there is no individual white character to stand as the authority on race, because then that authority is diffused across the constructed-as-white viewing public.[4] Television, like other mass media, consistently reinforces the old saying "if you're white, you're right."

Mainstream television's investment in continuing white dominance may seem a long way from an avowedly antiracist white woman professor's classroom, but both in fact operate similarly when that professor chooses to "use" white authority rather than attempt to undo it. While Bell's second rule of racial standing may appear to assume a situation close to those in the television programs hooks describes, with white denials of racism overriding black complaints of racism, in fact the rule extends also to whites who testify against racism. Although white complaints about racism are less likely to be heard than are white denials of racism, white complaints are considerably more likely to get attention than are those of people of color. Teaching responsibly about race necessarily includes making that usually invisible (to whites) and unremarked (by whites) dynamic visible in order to revise the rules of racial standing in the classroom.

Students—especially but not exclusively white students—arrive in our college classrooms with predictable cultural baggage.[5] Prepared by virtually every element of the society in which we live, they come ready to accept white authority, intelligence, and rightness while discounting the views and experiences of people of color. Encountering a professor who teaches against racism, which includes uncovering the secret history and disguised workings of white supremacy, most students respond in fairly predictable ways, from mild discomfort to silent disagreement to outspoken fury. Overtly hostile responses to antiracist course content may be less common in courses whose titles announce a focus on what students recognize as race (African American Literature) than in courses that seem to them race-neutral (Gothic and Sensation Fiction). Apart from the comparatively few students who really want to raise hell and deliberately register for courses in which they expect to fight the professor, most students who scoff at antiracism will self-select out of courses they surmise will focus on race. I am certain, too, that white professors face fewer direct challenges than do professors of color, whatever the course context. That lower level of hostility and challenge translates into a classroom environment in which it is easier for the professor to work and consequently for students to feel confident in the professor's ability to maintain the class's respectful attention. The presumption of authority attending on whiteness, and only on whiteness, also insures that white professors' course evaluations will be superior to those of professors of color in similar courses, which in turn leads to an easier time getting tenure, promotions, and the many perks doled out by institutions such as released time for research, merit pay, and the like.

White professors who conceive of ourselves as antiracist must acknowledge our duty to eradicate white privilege in the classroom, in relation to ourselves as well as to our students, both for the immediate purpose of ameliorating the inequities faced by our colleagues of color and for the long-term purpose of ending racism in society. The point may be obvious, but figuring out how to act on that duty presents huge challenges. We may see ourselves as rightful authorities in our classrooms—as indeed most of us probably are—and consequently have a hard time distinguishing between the authority our students grant us on illegitimate, racist grounds and the authority they grant us on legitimate grounds, such as our preparation in our fields. Divesting ourselves of all authority, were that even possible, would be counterproductive, surely. Where to draw the line between legitimate and illegitimate authority? And how to begin?

I want to try to answer those questions by reflecting on some of my own teaching experiences. When I was in graduate school in the early 1980s, my female colleagues and I often talked about our marginal positions and the problems we all faced in establishing ourselves as figures of authority for our students. As graduate students, as women, as young (we were all in our twenties), we were seen differently than were other teachers in our department. We all identified ourselves as feminist, yet the central themes of feminist discussions of pedagogy at the time—decentering classroom authority, for instance, and working for a more democratic classroom environment—seemed laughably beside the point. After all, it appeared to us that we had no authority to decenter; instead, we worried about convincing students that we were legitimate presences at the front of the room. We would have welcomed what we saw as the luxury of interrogating conferred authority instead of spending our time trying to persuade students that they should listen to us at all. Thinking about these conversations now, I am struck by how consistently we defined ourselves by what we lacked and never, in my recollection, attempted to address what we had. We were all white, but never once did it occur to us to discuss the ways in which our whiteness also affected our classroom positions, granting us the kind of illegitimate authority we saw our male counterparts enjoying based on gender. Yet we all conceived of ourselves as race-aware, even as antiracist; some of us—including me—lived in families that were not all white and thus confronted at least some issues of race every day.

White transparency is old news. That we could not or would not see our own whiteness and the myriad advantages it conferred on us in our classrooms is thus unsurprising. However, to complicate matters further, I do recall thinking about my own position as a raced one even then, but only in the context of one particular course, a writing course structured around black American literature. As near as I can remember, what concerned me as I planned that course was not the authority granted me as a white person in a racist society, but again lack of authority. This was still the era of identity politics, and I remember worrying about how to justify myself as a white teacher of black literature. I even recall having fantasies of students confronting me about my whiteness and challenging me to explain myself. I didn't know whether I could defend my "right" to teach this literature, and spent a lot of time before the term began thinking about what I was doing, why I was doing it, whether I should switch themes, and so on. As it turned out, no such challenges were forthcoming. Students—a few black, most white, one American Indian—said absolutely nothing about my whiteness, although I did begin the course by talking about that whiteness or, more accurately, my not-blackness in a kind of preemptive strike against the fantasized critiques that never materialized.

I have my preparation notes from that first class meeting, and they seem to me now more like notes for an entire term. Judging from those notes, I gave a lengthy lecture that covered an astounding range of historical material, presumably as background to the literature we would be reading. I think I conceived of this lecture as a way of establishing the seriousness of the course content and its legitimacy as a subject of study, while also conveying my own preparation in the field; looking back now with a critical eye, I see that my real purpose was to distance myself as an object of interrogation by foregrounding "academic" material, casting black literature into the mode of literary study then dominant. While this purpose may seem innocuous, perhaps even necessary given the historical context, in the event my course ended up following a white model based on a white way of being in the academic world: cool, distanced, defining "serious" as unemotional, controlled, wholly calm and rational. There was no room in that course for real pain, real anger, real growth. Nobody, including me, got hurt, at least not about race. At the end of the course, my students gave me great evaluations.

Several of the students from that course stayed in touch with me for some time, most memorably a young white woman who was struggling during our term together with the possible consequences of revealing her lesbianism to her professors and fellow students. She was partly closeted, partly out, and couldn't decide where exactly she wanted to be. Toward the end of the course, she came out to the class during a discussion of Barbara Smith's essay "Toward a Black Feminist Criticism," which reads *Sula* as a lesbian novel.[6] In a letter to me a few years later, she told me she felt empowered to speak in my class because I had become openly angry at some students' thinly disguised homophobia and had confronted several students about it during class. She said that what she most appreciated was my anger and my "willingness to take the heat by not asserting [my] own heterosexuality."

I kept that letter filed away with other correspondence from former students until I was prompted to reread it nearly ten years later after looking at the student evaluations from an introductory course in African and African American studies that I had built around revolutionary movements. The evaluations were wholly laudatory, with many appreciative comments, but one theme running through them shocked me into entirely changing the way I taught. Repeatedly, students remarked on how much they liked class discussions and how comfortable they felt because I always deflected potentially explosive moments. The course "successfully avoided the emotional aspects of the material," as one representative comment had it.[7] I thought I had grown and developed as a teacher since my graduate student days, but these comments showed one significant way in which I had not, as they were virtually indistinguishable from the evaluations from that first black American literature course I taught. The difference was that in the first course I had worried about my authority to teach, whereas in the more recent course I took that authority for granted. The results, however, were the same, but this time around I knew enough to be disturbed rather than flattered.

My former student's letter helped me to understand what had gone wrong. She felt affirmed by the course, I now saw, because I deliberately made the classroom an unsafe space for homophobia and was not at all concerned with making heterosexuals feel comfortable. Further, my authority did not derive from my own normative position, which I consciously concealed from the students. That concealment made it difficult, perhaps even impossible, for straight students to bond with me around our shared sexuality. In the later course, in contrast, I was concerned on some level with making white students feel comfortable, at least insofar as I tried to protect them—but really me—from the possible consequences of their own unconscious racism by avoiding "the emotional aspects of the material." My authority, in their eyes anyhow, derived from my whiteness, a fact I only apprehended once the course was over and some of them referred to my whiteness in positive terms on the course evaluations. My white students apparently had bonded with me through our shared whiteness, a situation so common that my students of color had not remarked on it nor evidently held it against me, judging from their positive comments on evaluations. My classroom, in both cases, was a white-defined and occupied space, with a few students of color in it. Although the course content and design were antiracist, the classroom dynamic was not, as student assumptions about white authority were not effectively undermined. Unintentionally, unthinkingly, I had employed the master's tools and had thus helped to maintain the master's house.

Figuring out how to undo that white bonding and to reject illegitimately granted authority was then, and remains, challenging. Concealing my whiteness as I had tried to conceal my heterosexuality was not an option, so directly addressing the issue of authority and whiteness in class seemed a

likely place to begin. The semester following the damningly positive evaluations of my African and African American studies course, I taught a black
American literature course and an introductory women's studies course. I
structured both syllabi so that we spent the opening week entirely on background and method, considering how we would approach the material, what
the historical contexts for each course were, how to judge sources' authenticity and reliability, and by what rules of engagement class discussion would
operate. I required that we all follow a particular procedure in class, which
included explaining how we "knew" what we "knew" each time we made an
assertion. What were our sources of information? Why did we think those
sources were reliable? How did one establish oneself as an "authority" on a
particular topic, especially one so fraught as race? This procedure worked far
better in the women's studies course than in the literature course, partly
because I designed the former so that the difference between women as
objects of study and women as subjects of study was foregrounded throughout, which made interrogating our own assumptions about women's lives—
including assumptions about race—always immediately relevant. In both
courses, however, discussion was often awkward and tension-filled; students,
especially white students, frequently chafed against the demand that they
explain every statement. At a number of points during the term, students
(both black and white) in my literature course appealed in exasperation to the
idea of "common sense": they thought what they thought because it was obviously common sense, I should stop pretending there was no such thing, and
we should all get on with the business of discussing Richard Wright's *Black
Boy* or whatever the day's text was. I persevered, however, despite obvious
student discomfort and annoyance as well as numerous temptations to abandon my plan.

That term was the beginning of more mixed student evaluations for me.
Ever since then, at least a few students each semester remark on the final evaluations that I am not open to all opinions (true) and that I sometimes made
them feel uncomfortable when they expressed their ideas (good!). In courses
whose titles do not foreground race, I can expect complaints that the class
spent "too much time on race." For instance, no matter how much time I devote
in introductory women's studies courses to developing a critical analysis of the
term "woman" and to feminism's fraught racial history, I can depend on at least
one student expressing the belief on the evaluation that the course should be
about women, not women of color, as if those are distinct categories. Interest-

ingly, however, student comments on my "knowledge of the course subject"—
the first category in my department's standard course evaluations—remain uniformly positive, with only a tiny minority of students checking anything but the
"excellent" box and all the written remarks in that category complimentary,
even from students who also say they disliked the course. I suspect this pattern
reflects continuing social investment in white authority, which sticks like fly-
paper regardless of my efforts to get it off me in my courses. Remaining alert
to the persistence of white authority requires an ongoing, committed effort,
because authority based exclusively on whiteness is a default position, like
normative whiteness itself. Put a white person at the front of a classroom or
lecture hall and she will look like a figure of authority to most of the people sitting at the desks. She has to fight harder to shake that perception than does a
person of color to gain it.

I recently had two disturbing reminders about white authority in my
classes, each of which forced me to examine again both my self presentation
and classroom racial dynamics. The first happened in a course on women,
crime, and representation during a student-led discussion of Eleanor Taylor
Bland's *See No Evil*, a black-authored crime novel featuring a black female
police detective as the main character. Several students—Latina, black, and
white—said they greatly preferred this book to one we had read by Valerie
Wilson Wesley because Bland's character did not dwell on racism. In fact, said
one white student approvingly, "I kept forgetting Marti was black and just
thought of her as a detective." An unraced detective? Didn't that actually mean
a white detective? With the exception of one white woman, the students
stonewalled me during this discussion, reverting again and again to the in-
supportable claim that absence of race did not suggest whiteness. It just meant
that the book's focus was on crime, not on race. I tried another tack: since
Marti never thinks of race and racism in the book, must we then characterize
it as a fantasy, since no person of color in contemporary U.S. society can get
through a day, never mind the weeks the novel spans, without being forced to
think about race? Silence, then some grudging agreement from students of
color but continuing resistance from white students. We spent the next class
period on issues of authority and race, including race as a subject most white
people would like to avoid. Eventually, the class concluded that they liked the
Bland novel precisely because it was escapist in terms of race, which I considered a major step forward from their initial position. Whereas most students
began by confusing a fantasy of colorblindness for reality, the majority came to

acknowledge that their desire to escape race had made them susceptible to that particular fantasy. We were then able to talk about popular fiction's appeal to widely shared fantasies, moving from there to a wide-ranging discussion about the possible impact on writers of color of white desires to avoid thinking about race and racism. Several students pointed out that one effect must be to make it far more difficult for writers of color than for white writers to find publishers for genre fiction (science fiction, fantasy, crime, romance). This and similar comments led us back to the issue of authority: whose word counts, whose desires are taken seriously, whose worldview prevails.

The second incident happened in a seminar on gothic and sensation fiction, again in a student-led discussion, this time on Jewelle Gomez's *The Gilda Stories*. One white male student began his presentation by remarking that when he realized the book was about "a black lesbian vampire, I expected some vile, pornographic text, but by halfway through the book, I thought of Gilda as nearly normal." I was stunned briefly into silence, wondering what had made him feel that this class was a safe place to make such a statement and how I had contributed to creating an atmosphere in which "normal" could remain equated with not-black, not-lesbian (I'll leave not-vampire aside for now). No other student challenged him, leaving that responsibility to me. Was "vile pornography" the first thing that came to mind when he heard of Bram Stoker's Dracula, a white heterosexual vampire? Nervous laughter from the rest of the all-white class. I pointed out that we had read a fair number of texts that could indeed be considered pornographic, such as Mathew Lewis's *The Monk*, which lingers voyeuristically over the rape of a drugged woman, among other incidents, but that no one in the class had until that moment said the word "pornography." Why? What difference about *The Gilda Stories* caused this change in perspective? The main character's lesbianism? Unlikely, since we had already read one text about a lesbian vampire—Sheridan LeFanu's *Carmilla*—without any such reaction. The main character's blackness? The author's blackness? The author's lesbianism? Some combination of these factors? In the ensuing discussion, the white male students' apparent confidence in their right to determine what counted as literature, what as pornography, and their confidence in their own authority on issues of race and sexuality were palpable presences in the classroom. Obviously, I had not done enough during the term to undercut that confidence or to require us all to examine our authority to speak on any topic. Sadly, it was too late in the term for me to have much impact on these students' confidence in their own rightness.

Both of these incidents required me to recognize anew the truth that when white authority is not constantly foregrounded and interrogated in the classroom, it sneaks back into silent, invisible prominence. It is not possible to "use" conferred authority to undermine racism; from a student perspective, there is no discernible difference between a professor who is deliberately using that authority in the cause of antiracism and one who simply accepts that authority as her right. It does not follow that because I know that my authority to teach gothic and sensation fiction or crime fiction rests on my scholarly preparation, and not on my whiteness, that my students also know that. Indeed, I would argue that most students do not even think about questioning white professors' scholarly preparation because the professors' whiteness stands as a visible marker of authority.

Until these two incidents, my courses had been comfortable for most of the students and for me. These incidents reminded me that the last thing I want is for my classes to be comfortable or safe. I want them to be uncomfortable and dangerous, for my students and for me, because when they are not, they are merely rooms in the master's house, not places where real learning happens. We have to smash the rules of racial standing over and over again, as they reproduce themselves whenever and wherever they are not under direct attack.

NOTES

1 Derrick Bell, *Faces at the Bottom of the Well: The Permanence of Racism* (New York: Basic Books, 1992), 113.

2 bell hooks, "Teaching Resistance," in *Killing Rage, Ending Racism* (New York: Henry Holt, 1995), 112.

3 hooks, "Teaching Resistance," 112.

4 I am using Louis Althusser's terms deliberately here, as Althusser's analysis of how we are interpellated as subjects in ideology seems to me the most useful way of thinking about how whiteness is reproduced.

5 Throughout this essay, I refer mainly to U.S.-born or -raised students, although with the U.S. media's international hegemony, even students born and raised in quite different cultural environments are increasingly likely to have internalized the same racial matrix as U.S. students.

6 Barbara Smith, "Toward a Black Feminist Criticism," in *The Truth That Never Hurts* (New Brunswick, N.J.: Rutgers University Press, 1998).

7 I discuss this course in more detail in *Crossing the Color Line: Race, Parenting, and Culture* (New Brunswick, N.J.: Rutgers University Press, 1994), 138–141.

WHEN THE POLITICAL IS PERSONAL:

LIFE ON THE MULTIETHNIC MARGINS

My favorite and most memorable teaching evaluation contained a critique from a student who wrote that my teaching methodology reflected too much of a "female-centered perspective."[1] The comment, while designed to cast aspersions on my character and capabilities as an instructor, seemed to me a quite fitting compliment. My student, having internalized a normative model of classroom legitimacy which equates maleness with power, was obviously dismayed at my lack of a male perspective and hence authority. My delight in his comment (and I know it was a man who wrote this particular evaluation) arises from my challenge to his worldview.[2] In my classroom, this student was exposed to an alternative voice and vision, one that stemmed from my experience and training as a female instructor who could offer a "female-centered perspective." For at least one semester, I succeeded in conveying to him that I was a woman in a position of power; he may not have liked it, but by the very nature of his evaluation, he was forced to concede that I did indeed hold authority in the classroom. And when my race is factored into this equation, my very body becomes a challenge to the white male authorities that many students assume as the model for classroom legitimacy.

JENNIFER HO teaches Asian American literature at Mount Holyoke College. She is finishing her Ph.D. at Boston University; her dissertation looks at the intersections of food and ethnic identity formation in Asian American literature and popular culture.

Ho's essay examines classroom politics as they intersect with the personal. She analyzes her feelings of displacement and marginalization as she works to articulate a "home" for herself in the academy.

The opening lines of a Pat Parker poem read: "The first thing you do is to forget that I'm Black. / Second, you must never forget that I'm Black." This paradox of interracial dialogue faced by black Americans is also a problem that many people of color experience in their daily lives.[3] The dilemma that Parker describes, to both forget and remember her visible racial difference, is one that I encounter every time I step into a predominantly white classroom. Teaching multiethnic literature is never simple. Unlike William Shakespeare's plays or Emily Dickinson's poetry, works described as "multicultural" or "multiethnic" contain an embedded sense of identity politics—these are works by and usually about a nonwhite "other," and they are meant to speak for the experiences of people of color in the United States. Teaching multiethnic texts, especially to predominantly white college students, can be a challenge because the literature often serves as a representative of, for example, black, Jewish, Chinese American, Chicano, or Kiowa life: students' interpretations of these works inform their perception of these ethnic communities. And just as these texts oftentimes stand in, for better or worse, as the voice of these various ethnic Americans, the instructor's identity and area of expertise also becomes another text for students to interpret alongside the multiethnic literature they are reading.

Teaching as a faculty of color at a predominantly white institution, I have realized that it is not only my scholarship but my very body that students learn from in the classroom: I am marked by my professional credentials and by my race, age, and gender. Students use me as a filter for understanding the literature; they see me as their resident expert for multiethnic texts or women's writing, and at times they become resistant when they believe my politics to be interfering with the purity of the literature. In other words, they accuse me of turning my personal experiences into a political agenda by the sheer nature of the multiethnic works on my syllabus. When Eileen Julien was accused of teaching an "ideological" course on Western Literary Traditions after 1500—an assumption made because she, as a black woman, came with certain "baggage"—she astutely notes that "a good many students in Western Literary Traditions . . . have not yet realized that they too are racialized, that race in this hemisphere is not black baggage but, rather, American baggage."[4] Like Julien, it is assumed that I, an Asian American woman, must be carrying around baggage that my students have yet to recognize as the unclaimed luggage of their own historical past and present.

Classroom politics necessarily always intersect with the personal. As Carol Hanisch's well-known feminist mantra reads, "the personal is political."[5]

But what happens when the political—in my case the commitment to research-ing and teaching multiethnic literature—becomes personal, colored by my experiences as a woman who identifies among multiple cultural trajectories such as Chinese, American, and Jamaican? How do students respond to my authority when I am positioned by virtue of my status, ABD doctoral candidate, on the margins of academia, almost faculty yet still a student? How does my visible racial background, Asian, shape the discourse of the literature I teach? As Ruth Spacks writes in her essay "The (In)Visibility of the Person(al) in Academe": "given the cultural work that many of us are doing, we need to understand who we are as historical, political, social, and cultural beings in order to gain a fuller sense of the complexity of the relationship between teacher, student, and text."[6] But the larger question I want to raise is, how do graduate students of color who are teaching in the college classroom build community among their students given the political nature of their person?

In order to answer these questions, I want to reflect on a course I taught one spring semester a few years ago at Boston University. This class was not one I was initially scheduled to teach; instead, one week before the start of the spring semester, I was told that the original professor assigned to the course had broken his leg. Since I had been his teaching assistant once upon a time, the department asked me to teach this introductory course on fiction. I would need to keep at least three of the texts on his syllabus since it would take the bookstore a few weeks to fill my new order, so the course reflected a hybrid of texts that he had selected and works that I chose, given my research interests in multiethnic American literature and feminist theory. Thus, the students who walked into the class expecting to see an older, white male professor instead encountered a young, visibly Asian looking woman, and upon receiving their syllabus they realized that Thomas Hardy's *Tess of the D'Urbervilles* and Franz Kafka's *The Trial* would be replaced with Alice Walker's *The Color Purple* and Margaret Atwood's *The Handmaid's Tale.*

The demographics of the class were unlike any I had encountered before at Boston University, where previously most of my students had been white and female. This particular semester I had a roughly even number of men and women, and out of thirty students, ten visibly looked to be Asian or Asian American. None of the students were English majors, most were taking the course to fulfill a graduation requirement, and for at least three students, Eng-lish was not their primary or original language.[7] I describe the cultural makeup of this class because again, to cite Spacks, "we have multiple identities that cross language, cultural, racial, religious, and other boundaries, as do the students we teach."[8] From the moment I distributed the syllabus for the course, my students were going to learn from not only the texts and my teaching but from their interactions with me and with each other.

In many ways, this class was one of the best and one of the worst that I taught, or at least, the range of reactions that both I and the texts received during the course of the semester ranged from one end of the critical spectrum to the other. But specifically I want to address three points that relate to the themes of this essay: the political as personal and pedagogy and community in the multiethnic literature classroom:

— My authority was openly and consistently challenged in class by a group of five male students who were led by one particularly vociferous young man. Four of these men, including their ringleader, were Caucasian, and the other student was Asian American.

— My evaluations were split into two types: students who found the class to be engaging, interesting, and one of the best that they had ever taken at Boston University, and students who were critical of my teaching either because my course was dominated by women writers, focused too much on issues of oppression and marginalization, or because I allegedly used the class to forward my politically correct feminist agenda of promoting works that addressed racism and sexism at the expense of "other" literature.

— During my office hours I developed a relationship with several of my Asian American students, who sought me out to talk about both classroom issues and other concerns such as summer employment, future graduate school and career choices, and personal struggles with their ethnic identity.

In the first scenario, the group of male students all sat together in the middle of the class, and at least two of them were very charismatic, engaging, and talkative, and actively participated in class discussion in many fruitful ways. However, they also felt free to challenge my authority, disagreeing in many vehement and sometimes counterproductive ways about my interpretations of the texts. Discussing Chinua Achebe's *Things Fall Apart*, these students felt that the village life Achebe describes was simply uncivilized and wrong, not understanding the principle of cultural relativism or his critique of colonialism. They dismissed Jane Austen's *Persuasion* as a literary "soap opera," a novel that only "girls" could appreciate because it was filled with marriage plots and gossip. And before we even began discussion of Michael

Ondaatje's *The English Patient*, the ringleader of this group informed me that they (the group of male students) had all agreed that they did not like the novel and found reading it to be a waste of their time. Although I was eventually able to persuade them to re-evaluate all of their previous statements (except where Austen was concerned), their constant challenge of my authority in class was draining, and I'm sure that they felt comfortable in vocalizing their dissent because as a young, female, Asian American graduate student I held no automatic authority for them based on my age, gender, academic rank, and race.

Which leads me to my second point, my student evaluations. As per custom, these evaluations were anonymous, although I'm sure that some of these same male students who challenged me in class also challenged my teaching methods on paper. As with their constant classroom critique of the literature or my attempts to have them look at these works from a different perspective, many students could only read the literature through the lens of my visible identity. For these students, because I am a woman I therefore included an inordinate amount of works by women on the syllabus and interpreted the texts in a manner that reflected my feminist leanings. And because I am a person of color, I forced them to read works by an overwhelming number of non-white writers that dealt with issues of racism and oppression.

The reality of my course, however, was that there were exactly three novels and four short stories by men and three novels and four short stories by women; only three of the novels were by writers of color, and one of the works that they objected to the most, Achebe's novel, had been selected by my predecessor, not by me. I often wonder what their reaction to *Things Fall Apart* would have been had the previous professor continued with the class. Would they have accused him of a race-based agenda? According to Julien, the answer would probably be no, as she relates how a white colleague "remark[ed] that he had no particular difficulty teaching African American literature to white students; he sensed moreover that his whiteness somehow legitimized the field for these students."[9] For Julien's colleague, his very body conveys legitimacy; to be white and male grants an automatic authority to any material. "Not only could white instructors teach virtually any subject," writes Julien, "but whiteness was the ultimate guarantor of impartiality and judicious reading."[10] And based on my own anecdotal evidence, it appears as if both my female and male white colleagues who teach multiethnic literature are not encountering the same type of resistance to their authority that I constantly encounter when I teach multiethnic literature to predominantly white students.

As for the feeling among some of my students that the class had been overwhelmed by a number of women writers, I had an exactly equal number of works by men and women on the syllabus. Therefore, my students' perception of inequality stems not from a realistic accounting but from the fact that female equality is so underrepresented that when it actually occurs it feels like domination instead of parity, or, as Peggy Ornstein relates of a middle-school teacher she interviewed for her work *Schoolgirls: Young Women, Self-Esteem, and the Confidence Gap:* "'boys perceive equality as a loss.'"[11] Furthermore, it would appear that the gender disparity that my students perceived arose as an effect of my own presence as a female authority figure, as my "female-centered perspective" skewed the gender orientation of the classroom environment.

For both the male students who challenged my authority in class and the student evaluators who felt that my political agenda interfered with their education, there was a problem separating my visible identity from my research expertise. Clearly if I had been a Shakespeare scholar and had included works of the Renaissance period on my syllabus, I would not be accused as an Anglophile. However, because my own race and gender became visible in both my body and in the texts, I became subject to the authority/authenticity paradox that many instructors of color face when teaching multiethnic literature. On the one hand, my students relied on my identity as a person of color to translate the novels by Alice Walker, Chinua Achebe, and Michael Ondaatje, granting me automatic authority because of my authenticity as a racial minority. Yet in my evaluations some students discredited my authority because of this same authenticity. In other words, how could I provide an objective and informed reading of *The Color Purple* when I was a woman of color? I think that some of my students believed that I was teaching from the gut rather than from the mind; for them, my intellectual authority was subverted by my authenticity as a woman of color teaching multiethnic literature, even though they consistently depended on me to answer their questions about the cultural and ethnic signifiers that they did not fully understand in these texts. Despite whether the students viewed my racial identity as an asset or a liability, in either event they did not recognize that I was teaching these texts not simply because of my identity politics but because multiethnic literature and feminist theory are my areas of specialization. For them, my gender and race obscured their recognition of my academic expertise.

My third point, the relationships I developed with a group of my Asian American students during office hours, relays the converse of the problem I have just articulated. Rather than seeing my race and gender as hindering my ability to teach, these students saw my identity as an entrance for them outside the classroom to discuss both the literature in the course and academic and personal concerns unrelated to the class. Because they saw the personal reflected in the content of the syllabus, I believe it led them to feel more comfortable in approaching me outside of class to talk about their own private concerns, to identify with me as a fellow Asian American. Although these same students could have also written critically about the course and my political agenda, I believe that for the ones I got to know in a very in-depth and personal way, my course finally allowed them to see themselves reflected in literature and to understand that the work in the classroom did not have to remain separate from their private concerns: the personal could be political.

Which brings me back to the question I raised earlier about building community—what type of community did I achieve in this classroom and what lessons, if any, did I learn from teaching this course? If community is defined as a united and single-minded group of individuals, then I did not achieve community with this group of students. However, according to the *Oxford English Dictionary*, the third definition of community, "social intercourse, fellowship, communion," are all elements which do apply to this group, because my class did form a community of students trying to understand the texts, me, each other, and themselves in a spirit of social intercourse and, at times, fellowship and communion.[12] The fact that they felt comfortable disagreeing with both me and with one another shows their involvement with the issues I raised—even if I wished, at times, that their challenging of the texts were not always veiled challenges to my authority.

However, I do not want to leave readers with the impression that my students did not support me. On the contrary, the students in the class often countered remarks made by the rowdy group of male studentss, so that I was not always in a position of defending both the literature and myself. For example, many of the women in the class took offense to their assessment of *Persuasion* as just a "chick's book," and opposed their sexist arguments with passages that showed Austen's deeper engagement with the issues of her time, ones that extended beyond the drawing room. And when the ringleader of this group of men dismissed the quality of *The English Patient*, several students rose to defend its value, citing specific lines from the novel that they found moving and insightful. In this way, my students formed a community of thoughtful critics, actively engaged in discussion of the texts. And what I learned from teaching this course was that I could use the tension in the class and my position as a woman of color teaching multiethnic literature to push my students to really interrogate their beliefs and assumptions about communities of color and multiethnic literature. The success of this class did not lie in my being able to convert all my neo-conservative students into future NAACP members; the class was successful because my very presence as a female Chinese American graduate student challenged their notion of who qualified as an authority figure in the classroom.

And for the nonwhite students in this class, particularly the Asian American students with whom I had built a relationship during my office hours, I believe that it was precisely due to my marginalized position—my race, gender, age, and academic rank—that these students felt comfortable confiding in me. I was unlike the model of the older, white, male professor that they had so often been confronted with in the classroom. David Palumbo-Liu, in the conclusion to his essay "Historical Permutations of the Place of Race," writes: "The politics of multiculturalization involves a rethinking of every participant's personal place."[13] If I am to remain dedicated to teaching multiethnic literature, I must re-examine my personal place and understand the impact of my subject position for both my white and my nonwhite students. I must learn to embrace this intersection of the personal and political as an integral component to my students' education.

Finally, I believe that graduate students who are immersed in the task of reading and thinking critically about multiethnic literature both live and work on the margins of the texts they examine. Quite literally, their thinking is recorded in the textual margins of the books that they read; borders become the place where the work of their minds become recorded and synthesized. So often the idea of marginalization implies inferiority, but I want to rethink and reclaim the borders and margins of the text as a place for deep intellectual thought and rigorous teaching. It is because I identify as a marginalized person that my students in this class became challenged by myself and the literature. By living and working on the textual and academic margins of the mainstream, I can observe the work in the middle and provide an alternative voice for students, challenging them to read not only between the lines but on the edges.

NOTES

This essay was originally presented in an abbreviated form at the 15th Annual MELUS (Society for the Study of the Multi-Ethnic Literature of the United States) conference in Knoxville, Tennessee, at the graduate student caucus panel "The Multiethnic Classroom and the Community," March 1, 2001.

1 This quotation was taken directly from an anonymous student evaluation based on a composition course that I taught at Boston University: English 104: Expository Composition I, spring semester 2000.

2 Although all student evaluations at Boston University are anonymous, in the case of this particular student his evaluation contained many specific references to meetings we had had in my office, so that I knew the exact identity of the student from the details in his comments.

3 Pat Parker, "For the white person who wants to know how to be my friend," in *Making Face, Making Soul Haciendo Caras: Creative and Critical Perspectives by Feminists of Color*, ed. Gloria Anzaldúa (San Francisco: Aunt Lute Books, 1990), 297.

4 Eileen Julien, "Visible Woman: Or, a Semester Among the Great Books," *Profession* (1999): 227.

5 Carol Hanisch, "The Personal is Political," in *Feminist Revolution: Redstockings of the Women's Liberation Movement*, ed. Kathie Sarachild (New York: Random House, 1978), 204–205.

6 Ruth Spacks, "The (In)Visibility of the Person(al) in Academe," *College English* 59, no. 1 (1997): 10.

7 I know this to be true of at least three of my students because each of them came to see me during office hours to express concerns about their writing, revealing that their apprehensions came in part from the fact that English was not their primary language.

8 Spacks, "(In)visibility," 16.

9 Julien, "Visible Woman," 233.

10 Julien, "Visible Woman," 233.

11 Peggy Ornstein, *Schoolgirls: Young Women, Self-Esteem, and the Confidence Gap* (New York: Anchor Books, 2000), 255.

12 *Oxford English Dictionary*, Second Edition (Oxford: Clarendon Press, 1989), 582.

13 David Palumbo-Liu, "Historical Permutations of the Place of Race," *PMLA* 111, no. 5 (October 1996): 1078.

THE ENTANGLEMENTS OF TEACHING *NAPPY HAIR*

PHOTO: CHUCK RYBACK

In 1998, Ruth Sherman, a white third-grade teacher in Brooklyn, taught Caro-livia Herron's illustrated book *Nappy Hair*. Published in 1997, the award-winning picture book is illustrated by Joe Cepeda and tells the story of Brenda, whose family teases her for having the "nappiest hair in the world."[1] Using the oral tradition of call and response, the story is narrated by Uncle Mordecai, who says, "Ashamed? I'm not ashamed, I'm proud" of Brenda's hair and other stigmatized elements of African American culture.[2] Uncle Mordecai compares the willfulness of Brenda's hair—which defies straightening combs and relax-ers—to the resilience of Africans who survived slavery, and says, "This nap come riding express . . . across the ocean from Africa . . . Danced right on through all the wimp hair . . . Wouldn't stop, wouldn't mix, wouldn't slow down for nobody."[3]

When Sherman read this book to her mostly black and Hispanic students at PS 75, she did so to teach the kids about "self-esteem and pride."[4] By all accounts, her students loved the book, which is why she made photocopies for them. Months later, a parent found these photocopies in her child's folder and

REBECCA MEACHAM is pursuing a Ph.D. in English at the University of Cincin-nati, specializing in fiction writing and ethnic American literatures. Her dissertation combines her own short fiction with analyses of contemporary African American short stories. Her study of Amiri Baraka's Black Arts poetry is forthcoming in *Archetypal Criticism*.

Meacham assesses her teaching and scholarship as a white woman dealing with various nonwhite experiences. She analyzes her experience teaching a course with volatile subject matter. At the end of the semester her students exhibit an equanimity and complacency that disturbs the instructor.

interpreted the title as a racial slur. The parent met with Sherman—asking where the teacher kept her "white hood"—then photocopied the photocopies for members of the community.[5] The next day, Sherman was called from a morning lesson to a school meeting in the auditorium, and there, fifty parents, most of whom did not have children in her class, reportedly interrogated and threatened her.[6] In the media coverage of the story, it was never reported why the administration chose this forum to confront the issue. It was, however, widely reported that Sherman has straight blond hair. She was sent home by the superintendent and never saw her class again.

Although the school supported Sherman and her use of the book, she transferred schools and the controversy continued to make headlines. African American writers like Clarence Page and Jill Nelson roundly criticized the parents who had protested the book, emphasizing the importance of what grew inside, and not atop, the heads of young African Americans.[7] Numerous articles included the comments of Isoke T. Nia, the African American director of research at the Teacher's College at Columbia, who said, "These are the things that blacks say in their home, and this book is bringing it to the public. I'm surprised, astonished and appalled."[8] *Nappy Hair*'s author, Carolivia Herron, registered her own shock: "I love my own nappy hair and the stories my uncle used to tell about it . . . I had no idea it would be political."[9] While Herron said she "admired what [Sherman] desired to do," she added that the teacher didn't "know about that pain, that ache that preceded her into the room."[10]

That pain, that ache, that preceded Sherman into the room is essential to understanding the controversies raised by *Nappy Hair*. It is an ache that I, a young white teacher like Sherman, have never felt, and likely never will. However, in a multicultural classroom, it is an ache felt acutely by many of my students, and this controversy casts into relief a number of issues for teachers of multiethnic literatures. Seeking a way to address these issues, I designed a composition course at the University of Cincinnati around the theme of images in children's media, and for two of the four assigned essays, my course focused on Herron's book and its impact. In selecting this topic, I intended not only to generate subjects for argumentative papers, but also to politicize my role as a white scholar and teacher in the field of multiethnic literatures. At the same time, I wondered how forefronting "race" would affect individual students as well as our classroom community. Although the course ended long ago, my experience teaching *Nappy Hair* continues to raise some age-old questions: To what extent does a "teacher of conflicts" build or divide the classroom community? To what extent should or does a teacher's background relate to his or her materials? And if, as so many critics have noted, Anglo Americans are often blind to their subject positions—are, in fact, blind to whiteness as a color or racial marker—how can teachers like Sherman and myself, and our white students, ever begin to see?

Now, I have to admit that even saying the words "nappy hair" makes me uncomfortable. Thus, it might be prudent to explain why this controversy attracted my attention. As a female in my early thirties, I have struggled with projecting authority during my teaching career because I've generally been close in age to many of my students. Yet when it comes to assuming authority over the materials of my field, I also feel challenged by my subject position: a white woman discussing various nonwhite experiences. Despite the fact that I've conducted research in Harlem and have taught a wide range of multicultural materials, at times I wonder if my students question my "cultural authority." At the same time, I also wonder when they don't. While it is easy to assert the familiar argument—that a color or culture does not guarantee knowledge—I wonder if my whiteness creates blind spots in my scholarship, an issue raised by feminist critic Peggy McIntosh, among others.[11]

THE CONFLICTS OF TEACHING
AND TEACHING THE CONFLICTS

In fact, I still remember the moment, early in my scholarship, when I first unpacked what McIntosh terms "the knapsack of white privilege" and was stunned at all that spilled out. Although in my undergraduate training I had begun the process of unpacking, after college I attended an MFA program in fiction writing, and such programs are often highly New Critical and traditionally canonical in their emphases. When African American short story writer Jewell Parker Rhodes comments that, "never [in my post-secondary education] was I assigned an exercise or given a story example that included a person of color," she could be speaking of my experiences.[12] In this way, my academic identity has become multiple: I'm now both a creative writer and a doctoral candidate in English, and a white person studying ethnic American literatures. As a result, I'm constantly hearing a dialogue, which is often more like an argument, between these various communities.

The conflicts between my academic communities led me to the subject matter for my composition course. Teaching the conflicts, in fact, was something

I'd done for a long time. In 1992, the year I began teaching, Gerald Graff published *Beyond the Culture Wars: How Teaching the Conflicts Can Revitalize American Education*, and I took Graff literally. Soon, every composition course I taught focused on social conflict, points-of-view, and the processes of debate. For example, if I was teaching an "obedience to authority" unit, I would compile a packet on the 1970 Kent State Shootings and have students engage in a "town debate," role-playing the parts of National Guardsmen, protesting students, and administrators. For units on "gender roles," students read about date rape not only from the point of view of the female victims, but also from the vantage point of males who felt victimized by the system. However, until the *Nappy Hair* unit, I had never put issues of "race" to my students. Perhaps this was because I had been teaching on largely white, midwestern campuses, where students of color were rare. More likely, though, my reluctance to center "race" related to my liminality—and uncertainty—as a teacher of conflicts. After all, by encouraging students to argue, the teacher of conflicts risks a loss of classroom community—indeed, there is a fine line between faction and fracture. Until recently, the conflicts I selected had straddled this line: about issues of campus radicalism or sexist advertising, students might become impassioned, but generally not inflamed. In addition, students were required to support their ideas with source material and develop opinions into essays, which tempered the heat of verbal exchange with the cool detachment of writing. In this forum I could stir things up, steer discussion, and solicit a diversity of opinions, all while maintaining a sense of class unity. In centering "race" as a teachable conflict, however, I stood to endanger, and possibly rupture, the classroom community. Everyone in the classroom would be personally invested; everyone in the classroom, including me, would be "raced." If teaching this book had already fractured the PS 75 community and sent one teacher packing, what might happen in my class?

Developing a course from the *Nappy Hair* controversy would also necessitate a change in my usual classroom position. In my previous classes, I had largely allowed students to argue as I played the moderator: I stood on my desk and shouted over shouts when white male students dominated discussions; I set up listservs on the web to solicit opinions that had been silenced during class. As a moderator, my subject position was marginal, or so I thought, to the conflicts I created. What mattered was that I enabled students to justify their ideas in a way that addressed the opinions of others. In my mind, the teacher was a facilitator, and my political identity was separate, irrelevant and, I worried, dangerous to articulate.

THE INVISIBILITY OF WHITENESS IN THE CLASSROOM

Of course, even when teachers don't articulate politics, politics articulates them; as Graff writes, "Politics lies in what is taken for granted as going without saying."[13] However, politics is something Anglo American teachers often believe they can suppress, or selectively enact, in a classroom situation. As Lori Schroeder Haslem, a professor of Early English Literature, writes in a recent *Profession* article, "I believe that . . . a great deal would be lost if I made my own views too clear to the class. Students' values and assumptions simply cannot be surfaced if the teacher's are too obvious. So the single value I want to communicate foremost in the classroom is tolerance of and even more an intellectual curiosity about . . . other's opinions and values."[14] In this manner, Haslem seems able to make her political status and personal values "invisible" and play the moderator, creating an open environment for communal exchange.

But what happens when, as Eileen Julien asks, despite a teacher's best efforts to suppress her values, students instead attack her politics? After a semester at the helm of a western literary traditions course, wherein Julien was the only African American in the room, this professor of comparative literatures sensed a hostility she believed was connected to student perceptions of her subject position. She writes, "To be black and a woman, as I am, and to know African literatures in addition . . . somehow renders my American–Western identity suspect and jeopardizes thoroughly my ability to read and interpret this so-called West."[15] It is difficult, if not impossible, for a teacher like Julien to remove her political values from classroom discussions when, because of her "visible racial–gender status," students automatically assume she espouses a political agenda. However, in contrast to Julien's inevitable classroom visibility, Haslem can choose to enact invisibility. Thus, the choice to be "apolitical" as a teacher, to suppress one's values or to articulate them, can be packed into the knapsack of white-skin privilege. Invisibility also confers authority over subject matter, for as Julien writes, "whiteness—in addition to providing a certain comfort to students, a sense of shared identity—gives teachers the benefit of the doubt and tends to lend greater credibility to their readings and interpretations, even when they are not specialists."[16]

Yet both the point and the paradox of invisibility is that it can't be seen: to illuminate its presence, one must already be looking for an absence. One must also be able to delineate this absence—to become visible, the Invisible Man of horror films had to walk through flour, be splashed with paint, or wrap himself in bandages. At the very least, visibility requires the perception of contours. Thus, to illuminate a teacher's Anglo American subject position, as I tried to do, I would have to frame Ruth Sherman's whiteness as well as my own. At the same time, I would have to sensitize my mostly white students to, as Julien writes, "the ways in which their own status informed their readings."[17]

THE ENTANGLEMENTS OF TEACHING *NAPPY HAIR*

I wish I could say that I'd worked all of this out before planning my course on "Nappy Hair." But at that time, I worried about how the topic would highlight the visibility of my African American students, who might be discomfited by a book directed at their racial and bodily experiences. As a result, I was primarily concerned with maintaining the classroom community. I invented discussion "rescue plans"—how to defuse potentially volatile confrontations during class discussions, and how to redirect any instincts my non–African American students might have to ask their African American peers about "the black experience." However, in my quest to build a classroom community, I overlooked how I might delineate my white students' specific ethnic communities, or how I might capture that Invisible Man.

Instead, in an effort to settle the inevitable tension between classroom conflict and cohesion, I focused on two things: course structure and source material. English 101 at University College, an open admissions campus at the University of Cincinnati, requires proficiency in analytical and argumentative writing, with attention to critical sources. It is also UC's most diverse campus, with students of various ages, ethnicities, and socioeconomic backgrounds. On the first day of class, I observed the ethnic composition of the course: four perceptibly African American students and eight Anglo American students. I asked my students if they were aware of *Nappy Hair* and told them the conflict would constitute much of our later discussion of images in children's media, our course theme. For the next four weeks, we worked on this theme. First, to hone their skills of image analysis, students wrote a mini-essay on an advertisement of their choice, then a full-length essay on a children's book or movie. Our supplemental articles concerned long-standing issues in mediated children's imagery: Disney's Arabian characters in *Aladdin*, the use of color to connote villainy, and the implications of femininity in *Cinderella*. Following these essays, students would write an in-class position paper and a solution paper on the *Nappy Hair* controversies. Using this course design, I hoped to build community and critical skills early on, then elicit strong arguments and counterarguments, and conclude with a paper designed to solve the problems raised at PS 75. With every essay assignment, the classroom community operated on the micro level in collaborative peer review groups.

By mid-term, my students had a good rapport with each other, and our classroom environment was diversely opinionated but pleasant. It was time for *Nappy Hair.* To prepare the class for my pedagogical staple, the "town debate," I had planned to represent through sources and role-playing four points of view, in this order: Ruth Sherman's and the third graders; the school administrators; African American fans of the book, including the writer; and the outraged parents of PS 75. Before we began the unit, I'd copied articles on the situation, editorials by African American writers, and reader reviews from bookseller web sites, but I could not find sources to adequately represent the angry parents' point of view. All of my print sources either vilified the parents or celebrated the book. Regardless, I had to start the unit that day, and so that my students had access to the book for their own writing, I set out to make a few extra photocopies.

But then a funny thing happened on the way from the copy machine. Looking down at the stark black and white pages of *Nappy Hair* I was about to distribute, I was transformed into a parent looking through my third-grader's school folder. And just as suddenly, I was enraged. What had appeared nuanced, animated, and cheerful in color became the worst of racial caricatures in a photocopy. It was no longer Brenda cartwheeling across the page; it was Topsy. Her eyeballs were white, her hair was huge, her skin was pitch black. How could Ruth Sherman *not* have seen this? How idealistic, young, or naïve—or blinded by her own whiteness—was she? Despite Sherman's good intentions, she must have realized, to paraphrase Herron, the pain and ache these images would activate. Now that I understood the parents, I became angry not only at Sherman for her oversight, but also at the African American columnists who'd lambasted the parents. The columnists had faulted the parents for looking only at photocopies and not at the whole book. But the columnists had looked only at the whole book. Had they seen these photocopies?

At that moment, the blundering good intentions of Ruth Sherman's photocopies resonated with my experience as a white teacher of black literatures. I wondered if I, too, had ever, with the best of intentions, inadvertently committed an act of minstrelsy. I also wondered if I was about to do so now. And, in reference to Eileen Julien's comments, I worried that if I had somehow reinscribed white racism, my mostly white classes would never notice and just blindly accept my authority—or, worse yet, reinscribe my error. With minutes until class, the least I could do was subvert the schedule I had planned. My students would first see the book through the eyes of the parents, as photocopies. And they would be angered.

It was remarkably easy to accomplish an instant dislike for the book among all of my students. First, I explained the controversy and held up the book in all its color and said, "This is what Ruth Sherman taught, and we'll see more of this next class," flipping the pages. Next, I passed around the photocopies, saying, "And this is what the parents saw." Then, illuminating my presence as a white teacher, I told them of my copy room discovery and that these copies—not Sherman's good intentions—were the crux of the controversy. This is where *we* start. I told them, "Imagine you are a third-grader's parent, just discovering these photocopies in your child's folder." Then, they spent twenty minutes as "parents," free-writing about how the photocopies made them feel. Nobody felt good.

Still, Carolivia Herron and those who taught her book had wanted readers, particularly African American readers, to feel good. She had wanted to validate and revalue the experiences of a particular community. So, in the next class period, I changed our hypothetical community from that of parents to that of students. I passed around juice and cookies, and told my students, "Now imagine you are third-graders, and I'm Ruth Sherman, and we're having story time." Using the photocopies, I asked volunteers to read the responses as I read the Uncle Mordecai's calls and held up the pictures. As I awkwardly read Uncle Mordecai's words in black dialect, my whiteness was clearly contoured. Yet as we read, my anger and my students' anger from the previous class seemed to dissipate. The book was fun to perform together, and it seemed that as a class, we experienced a small and tentative joy. Afterwards, we ended class with a free-writing exercise that compared and contrasted the experience of seeing the copies with hearing the book read aloud. Although I asked them to consider the fact that I, a white teacher, had read them this book called *Nappy Hair*, this question was not addressed. Indeed, none of my students chose to focus their writing on issues of whiteness throughout the remainder of the course.

What they did focus on was both predictable and surprising. After reading the book aloud, I assigned critical sources that concerned the controversy's immediate context. While we began the next class in a town debate format—with students using sources to role-play the parts of parents, administrators, Sherman, Herron, and so forth—these categories soon destabilized and students talked freely. Despite my efforts to build a discussion based on role-playing and textual sources, students increasingly spoke from experience and emotion. Perhaps because of the community we had built for the first few weeks, my students remained respectful of each other throughout the discussion. This is not to say that the discussion was easy. In fact, on their end-of-term evaluations, many students expressed frustration at the views of their peers, and during our discussions, clearly registered their distress. At the same time one student would cede the floor, and a point, to a peer, another student would lay his head on his desk in total exasperation. Still, the debates seemed to toe the line between community faction and fracture. Classmates wanted to hear and to challenge one another's opinions. Fascinated by their autonomy, over the next few class periods I retreated into invisibility as a moderator.

I offer some typical discussion responses as voiced by individual students.[18] Edward, an African American student, sided with the black columnists we had read and announced that these parents needed to pay attention to the fact that fewer than one percent of PS 75 students read at their grade level.[19] Also decrying the parents were Stacy and many other Anglo students, who wondered why the parents were going through their children's folders months after the book had been taught. Despite her laughter during our class "juice and cookies" reading, Paula, an African American woman, stated she did not like Herron's work. She imagined a scenario wherein the book provided the words for children to tease a child with nappy hair. More distressing to her, though, was the brief mention of slavery, wherein Uncle Mordecai says, "Sold your mama for a nickel, sold your daddy for one thin dime."[20] Edward and Paula debated this point, with Edward asserting, "But that's what happened. That's the way it was," and Paula returning to her scenario of children teasing each other with exactly those words. Instead of the tool of community Herron intended, and the tool of self-esteem Sherman wished for, Paula saw the book as a tool of persecution. Meanwhile, some white students didn't see what the fuss was about, and advocated the teaching of the book in all types of schools in an effort to promote diversity. What, they wondered, was the big deal about a person's hair? As Johnny, a white student, said, "Differences make the world go round."

Students also listened intently to the comments of Natalie, an African American student who spoke entirely from her own lived experience and not the role-playing, hypothetical communities of our composition classroom. During discussion, she launched the ideas she would later develop in both her position and solution essays: "From the perspective of a full-haired African American woman who refuses to accept the word *nappy* to describe my beautiful hair, I personally feel the book shouldn't be in print." What most disturbed Natalie was the book's endorsement of nonstandard English because, as she wrote, "This makes the impression that most blacks are ignorant and not very educated." And just as Paula disdained Herron's discussion of slavery, writing, "These words may make children think that you can put a price on a human being," Natalie stated, "The selling of African Americans for the best bid isn't any African American's description of positive motivation." This is exactly the opposite reaction of many Anglo American students, who, with no heritage of oppression to speak of, easily endorsed the book as a celebration of heritage. As Johnny wrote: "We change so many things in our culture and take so many things for granted that I believe the teaching of this book would help people come in touch with the person that they should strive to be to make everyone who sacrificed for them proud."

Significantly, Johnny uses the words "we," "people," and "our," while Natalie and Paula particularize their experiences as African American women. Like the rest of my white students, Johnny never identifies his cultural location, and comfortably displays his whiteness as both normative and universal. Whereas Natalie sees the book as racist and recommends it never be taught, Johnny advocates that the book be taught without comment in every classroom in the United States. Yet both he and Natalie are making bids for a type of cultural authority. Also interesting is how, in Johnny's poorly conceived essay, he manages simultaneously to sympathize with the opinions voiced in class by Natalie and Paula, and to stereotype African Americans with his appreciation of their "baggy clothes." However self-contradictory Johnny's writing is, it represents an extreme, just as Natalie's essay represents an extreme. These viewpoints were the exceptions. Charged with solving the controversy of *Nappy Hair* at PS 75, after they'd experienced the fractious impact of the book on our classroom community, my students on the whole recommended teaching the book through a collaboration between the communities of teachers, students, parents, and administrators. Parallel to the structure of my 101 course, building this larger community, they imagined, would take place through dialogue and through writing.

For example, Stacy writes, "The only solution is for parents and teachers to become educated as to the other's agenda for the children's education, which means keeping open communication at all times," and to do this, she suggests that teachers could even lend the parents books to foster their reading to children. Similarly, Paula calls for teachers to "send home letters with some choices of what might be taught and ask for opinions in return." Nearly every student developed a solution based on precaution, sensitivity, knowledge, and feedback—on the creation of a forum to contain and settle conflicts before they might explode. Students also focused on the permeability between classroom and neighborhood communities. Regardless of Ruth Sherman's whiteness, or the parents' blackness, my students had seen in class the discomfort of Paula and the frustrations of Johnny, and they had been distressed. Now, they desired the peace and the safety of a unified community.

CLASSROOM CONSENSUS:
AN UNSETTLING PEACE

In the remaining two weeks of the course, unity was restored as students collaboratively revised their essays. Working together to develop as a community of writers allowed them a soothing transition from the debate of conflict to its clear and written articulation. I was thrilled by the unexpected and unassigned essay one white male was inspired to write on tolerance, citing Martin Luther King, Jr. and Cornel West. As a class, we shared a palpable sense of relief: for myself, a relief that students could disagree about personal issues yet continue to work together; for my students, relief that the debates were over and they had passed the class. Later, when I looked over my anonymous student evaluations, I was further relieved to find that no one had felt bullied, excluded, or singled out as a result of my teaching of *Nappy Hair* and its controversies. Unlike Ruth Sherman, I had retained my position at the head of the class, and my students had departed feeling productive and safe. Everything was at peace. Except to me, it was like the calm in the horror movies, right before the Invisible Man creeps in.

The calm was eerie because many of my white students still perceived the controversy as something that had affected others and not them. Somehow, most white students remained impermeable to a conflict that, to them, seemed impersonal. As one wrote in her evaluation, "I feel some people took it way too personal . . . like it was an attack on them personally." This student, like many others, felt her own identity was left intact while all the "otherness" of role-playing and discussion was projected onto someone else. Identifying with Sherman, many Anglo students had reacted strongly against the parents' charge of racism; identifying with the parents, many African American students had reacted against Herron's seemingly racist stereotypes. And in my effort to retain a sense of classroom community, I had conflated the reactionary with the enlightened.

While teaching this conflict seemed risky, in retrospect it seems I didn't risk enough. In the weeks we spent debating, I should have shifted my focus on classroom community to individual students, challenging each writer's intellectual complacency with more complicated questions. For in trying to be sensitive to African American students, I never pushed Paula or Natalie to write about why they so disliked a book written, according to Herron, for women like them. Would it have mattered if they'd first seen the book on a bookshelf, instead of in English 101? Was it a generational issue—the fact that Herron and the book's supporters are self-identified "60s people"—or did my students just dislike the book?[21] At the same time, I never challenged Johnny's imperialist language, or asked why so many of my white students blithely spoke of "diversity" and other people's "heritage." How did they possess, as the multicultural critic Gregory Jay puts it, "the luxury to be tolerant and liberal"?[22] Perhaps, as Jay advises, I should have rattled the structure of their superiority by incorporating a historical context and more overtly "putting the race of white people . . . before the class as a subject for critique."[23] Instead, because I selectively made visible my whiteness as a teacher while discussing the highly visible blackness of the *Nappy Hair* debate, I never quite illuminated the power and presence of whiteness. Though our classroom community remained intact, most students still lacked self-awareness as racial, generational, communal, and individual subjects. In the end, I was a teacher of conflicts left in a strangely unsettling peace.

NOTES

1 Carolivia Herron, *Nappy Hair* (New York: Alfred A. Knopf, 1997), 15.
2 Herron, *Nappy Hair*, 10.
3 Herron, *Nappy Hair*, 24.

4 Michele Norris, "*Nappy Hair* Flap," ABCNEWS.com, December 4, 1998.

5 Liz Leyden, "N.Y. Teacher Runs Into a Racial Divide," *Washington Post*, December 3, 1998, sec. A3.

6 Leyden, "NY Teacher," A3.

7 Nelson, quoted in Norris, "*Nappy Hair* Flap," 2. See also Clarence Page, "Nappy Hair Isn't that Important," *Toledo Blade*, December 28, 1998, sec. 1–11.

8 "Nappy Hair! Oh, my! Almost as Silly as 'Niggardly'!" www.adversity.net/special/nappy _hair.htm, November to December 1998.

9 Leyden, "NY Teacher," A3.

10 Dinitia Smith, "Furor Over Book Brings Pain and Pride to Its Author," *New York Times*, November 25, 1998, sec. A24.

11 Peggy McIntosh, "White Privilege and Male Privilege: A Personal Account of Coming to See Correspondences through Work in Women's Studies," *Gender Basics: Feminist Perspectives on Women and Men*, ed. Anne Minas (Belmont, Calif.: Wadsworth, 1993), 30–39.

12 Jewell Parker Rhodes, *Free Within Ourselves: Fiction Lessons for Black Authors* (New York: Doubleday, 1999), ii.

13 Gerald Graff, *Beyond the Culture Wars: How Teaching The Conflicts Can Revitalize American Education* (New York: W. W. Norton, 1992), 124.

14 Lori Schroeder Haslem, "Is Teaching the Literature of Western Culture Inconsistent with Valuing Diversity?" *Profession* (1998): 126.

15 Eileen Julien, "Visible Woman; or, A Semester among the Great Books," *Profession* (1999): 232.

16 Julien, "Visible Woman," 232.

17 Julien, "Visible Woman," 232.

18 All remarks, via essays or class discussion, occurred between October and December, 1999, and will henceforth remain uncited.

19 Norris, "*Nappy Hair* Flap," 3.

20 Herron, *Nappy Hair*, 22.

21 Leyden, " *Nappy Hair* Flap," A3. This issue is also discussed in Page, "Nappy Hair," 1–11.

22 Gregory Jay, "Taking Multiculturalism Personally: Ethnos and Ethos in the Classroom," *American Literary History* 6.4 (Winter 1994), 626.

23 Jay, "Taking Multiculturalism Personally," 624.

FRED ASHE

BEYOND BULL CONNER:
TEACHING SLAVERY IN ALABAMA

PHOTO: BRAD DALY

At a conference ten years ago, in conversation with a colleague from some-where else, I described my white English students at Birmingham-Southern College, Alabama, as racially self-conscious.

"Hm," she said. "Don't you mean *un*conscious?"

My initial response was that, no, I meant self-conscious. Hyperconscious. Obsessed. I believed this about my students for at least my first few years on the faculty at BSC, a small, 90–95 percent white liberal arts college with the highest academic profile and the highest tuition in the state.[1] I had inherited an upper-level major course that I called Slavery and the African American Tradi-tion, and early in my career I taught it annually. I had entered into it excited but anxious about my authority as a white teacher—in particular about how I would be received by black students. What impressed me through the first few runs of the course, though, was how racial self-consciousness—guilt, fear, resentment, desire—played havoc with my white students, in class discussion and in their journals and during my office hours.

Yet what I notice now, as I read back through the pink-sheet evaluations from all of my sections of the course, is how minor a role race plays in the stu-

FRED ASHE is an associate professor of English at Birmingham-Southern College. His specialty is American literature, and his research interests include African American literature, family memoir, and urban homelessness.

Ashe's essay traces his realization across time that his white students, whom he initially saw as racially conscious, are not racially *self*-conscious at all. He expresses discomfort and concern with this avoidance of whiteness among students and considers ways to disrupt it.

dents' comments. Slavery alumni as an aggregate, it seems, appreciate my openness to interpretations and are split over whether I lecture too much or sanction too much pathless class discussion. They are quite clear, if miles from consensus, about which books they love and which are damnable wastes of their time. They rarely mention race. So now I'm wondering just how much of the self-consciousness that I had been ascribing to my students belongs in fact to me.

There's no question that I'm hypersensitive to cracks about Alabama. I grew up here, in the northwest corner of the state, and even though I lived in the Midwest during high school and college, I came back south to Nashville for graduate study, and I always assumed I'd end up in Alabama. The time away served mainly to make me defensive about my home state—especially its racial reputation. When I was a boy my father commanded me never to say "nigger" and I've considered myself a race liberal ever since. As such, of course, I'm embarrassed for Alabama all the time. We still carry some pretty sorry traces of our past—state flags, bombing trials, marriage bans (we voted only 60 percent last November to remove an unenforced ban on interracial marriage from the state constitution). But we are changing, and I find myself concerned that people understand this. Birmingham has a black government now and a superior civil rights institute and genuinely integrated public spaces. I get a little greedy, in a perverse way, for bad racial publicity from outside the Deep South: Howard Beach, Bensonhurst, Simi Valley, Cincinnati.

For a white southerner purporting to teach black texts, how appropriate can this raced pride of place be? As I age, I'm more aware of the potential for patronizing and stereotyping inherent in white liberalism. If I think hard enough, and I usually do, I can come to suspect my motives for pretty much anything. As for teaching African American literature at Birmingham-Southern College, what is driving me? How pure is my scholarly take? What am I really accomplishing with my students, and what needs am I responding to in myself?

And why does the class's appeal seem to be waning? In the last four years I have offered Slavery and the African American Tradition only once. The course caps at twenty-five, and enrollments the first five times I taught it ranged from twenty to twenty-six, with anywhere from one to five of those students being black. Last spring the enrollment was fourteen, including thirteen white students and one Asian American. I do not teach it this year, and it is not on the books for the two following.

CHARGES

I was not trained in African American literature. But when the American-ist at Birmingham-Southern announced in late spring 1992 that he was taking a position back home in Wisconsin, and I was bumped up from adjunct work to a one-year position, I eagerly assumed a course he had developed that he called Literature of Slavery. Without knowing the literature, I was drawn to what I fig-ured would be the issues. My dissertation had looked at protest writing, includ-ing a chapter on Eldridge Cleaver's *Soul on Ice*. I had been taken with the re-emergence of race in American pop culture in the late 1980s, films like *Do the Right Thing* and *Boyz N the Hood*, groups like Public Enemy and N.W.A. Finally, and not to be discounted, I needed a niche if I meant to convert my one-year position into a tenure track.

I first offered the course that fall. I studied history over the summer, and then lifted my predecessor's reading list wholesale. I offer it here, cut and pasted from that first syllabus:

> Henry Louis Gates, ed., *The Classic Slave Narratives*
> Harriet Wilson, *Our Nig; or Sketches from the Life of a Free Black* (1859)
> Herman Melville, *Benito Cereno* (1856)
> Zora Neale Hurston, *Their Eyes Were Watching God* (1937)
> Alex Haley, *The Autobiography of Malcolm X* (1965)
> Toni Morrison, *Beloved* (1987)
> Charles Johnson, *Middle Passage* (1990)
> Assorted essays to be distributed in class

From the *Slave Narratives* anthology we read Frederick Douglass's *Narrative of the Life* (1845) and Harriet Jacobs's *Incidents in the Life of a Slave Girl* (1861). In the course pack I included essays and excerpts from Henry David Thoreau, Booker T. Washington, W.E.B. Du Bois, James Baldwin, William Sty-ron, and Eldridge Cleaver (most of these were suggested by my predecessor as well). I put as many histories of slavery as I could find on reserve at the library.

I renamed the course Slavery and the African American Tradition, in part to justify the readings not explicitly concerned with slavery, and in part out of uneasiness over possible implications of the previous name. I drafted a course description, mindful of my departmental obligation to teach the historical development of a literary tradition (it fulfills the "breadth" requirement for our major):

Scholar Henry Louis Gates Jr., contends that "the narratives of ex-slaves are, for the literary critic, the very foundation upon which most subsequent Afro-American fictional and nonfictional narrative forms are based." In this course we will operate according to that proposition, first studying slave narratives and the nineteenth-century black American experience as it was embodied in written form. Next we will examine the ways in which this tradition has shaped later fiction, essays, and autobiographies by African American writers. I encourage you throughout to be alert to the ways that issues in the course relate to contemporary American race relations, as well as to the practice of literature in general.

For that first edition of the course, I discovered and tried to teach a number of patterns in the literature: the theme of literacy as freedom; the distinctions between male and female narratives; the Exodus motif; the journey from south to north (leading later in the tradition to returns south); uses of masking; the unmasking of religious pretense; the role of storytelling; the importance of community; the value of voice. I fell in love with Douglass and *Benito Cereno* and Hurston and *Belóved,* and many of the students did too. I did have a white student tell me that her Christian beliefs were so offended by *The Autobiography of Malcolm X* that she had to stop reading 180 pages in (I had her write a short paper detailing and documenting her objections). I had another white student tell me that *The Autobiography of Malcolm X* changed his life.

Mostly we talked about the books, but once or twice a week I would put us in a circle and solicit group discussion of the bigger issues. I'd usually toss out one or two of the questions I had put on the assignment sheet for their journals, such as,

> Describe your experiences with another race in high school.
>
> Describe the racial situation at Birmingham-Southern College.
>
> Discuss your feelings and your thoughts (do they differ?) about the public display of particular racially charged symbols, such as rebel flags or "X" hats.
>
> Do you agree with the logic behind affirmative action? Is there such a thing as reverse discrimination?
>
> Describe your experience with and feelings about the word "nigger." Is there a comparable epithet for white people?
>
> Does race ever figure into your dreams? Explain.

I had twenty-two students in that first class, five of them black. We had lively discussions. I remember one session in particular: we had been talking about racial misconceptions, and a white student admitted to the group that as a child she had been afraid to swim in a pool with black people, afraid their color would wash off on her. She did not know where this idea came from nor how she outgrew it. A black student responded that she had grown up assuming white people's skin was colder than hers, and that she had persisted in this belief until once she hugged her friend in high school. It was a powerful class session. I felt like Oprah.

But class discussions sometimes created discomfort too. This was truer the second time I taught the course, when the enrollment rose to twenty-six while the number of black students dropped to three, making their minority status even more conspicuous. I began to notice how white students would cut their eyes toward black classmates when making a point—sometimes apologetically and sometimes not, but never without a concern for how they were being received. I noticed longer silences, and a striking divide between the emotions expressed in student journals and those voiced in class. One of my better students, white, told me in my office mid-semester that she left class sick to her stomach most days. I emailed her recently and got her to elaborate, retrospectively, on what she had felt those days. Here's part of her reply:

> I remember one very striking, articulate girl . . . comment[ing] once that she felt that every time she DID talk, that she was representing the entire black race to the white kids in the class. And, in a very real way, for me at least, she was. I know so few black people. We live in such a self-segregated society, that I rarely have opportunities to meet them. BSC was no different. So, this was one of the only times I actually had the chance to hear opinions "from a black person." And it made me uneasy. I think that it was more about me discovering that I really was a racist that scared me the most. . . . that was a very real, very big fear. I wanted (and still do struggle with this) to be this open-minded, tolerant, see-past-skin-color person, but in reality, I think I am more nervous of a homeless black man near me on the street than a homeless white man. Your class made us face up to not only what our parents and grandparents' generations did, but to what we felt. And that was not always a place I wanted to go.[2]

These last two sentences are a perfect formulation of what I would like to accomplish as a teacher in this life. But in practice, the journal-discussion sessions were starting to make me nervous. I didn't feel like I was managing conflict well; I found myself overly concerned with trying to assure that no one was offended. In a mixed-race circle this was stressful enough, but my comfort level did not improve as the mix became more one-sided. Whether it was a natural result of college demographics or a response to some reputation the class had picked up without my knowing, fewer black students seemed to register for it each year. After that second section I taught a couple runs of the course with one or two black students, and then this past spring there were zero. And zero was the number of explicit journal discussions we had.

We discussed plenty, however. The moment that stands out for me from that class came in response to a handout that I had been using for years, excerpting a 1908 fifth-grade textbook on Alabama history that a friend of mine had dug out of his grandmother's attic. The author is given as Joel Campbell DuBose, M.A. I always appoint a student to read the first paragraph of Chapter XXI, "The Negroes," which concludes,

> Whatever may have been the evils of slavery, contact with white masters and their families has been the most civilizing and uplifting influence that ever came to the negroes in all the ages. Booker Washington has said: "We went into slavery pagans, we came out Christians; we went into slavery a piece of property, we came out American citizens; we went into slavery without a language, we came out speaking the proud Anglo-Saxon tongue.[3]

Students are generally amazed or amused by this (and I am astounded every time I read it at the idea that Booker T. Washington might actually have said that Africans had no language). We spend a little time identifying the author's rhetorical strategies—not a tough chore—and one day last spring I was pointing out DuBose's citation of a "safe" black authority to make his point when one of my students said something like, "You know, I'm glad to hear a black person saying this. Because sometimes I wonder if they really know just how good they've got it here."

In this case, my colleague from the conference was right: this person could have stood to be more racially self-conscious about how he would be received. I suspect he felt no need to consider his words, since no black people were around to hear them. And I suppose it is my job to raise his consciousness. In retrospect, I can think of all sorts of ways that I could have turned this exchange to educational effect. But at the time I simply felt self-conscious. I probably politely brought the class back to the issue of rhetorical strategies, I don't recall. All I remember is a small sick feeling, and a sharp sense of the artifice of my presenting this material to these students at that moment.

CONVICTION

My most confident conviction about race in America is this: race is a myth, but it is a myth with profound consequences in the real world. Our race inevitably impacts our responses to literary and cultural texts. For all the variety among individuals and for all the other factors that determine the ways we read, there are aspects of the black experience in America that whites will never really know, and vice versa. What matters is not that we convince anyone of the superiority of our own responses, but that we come to recognize and acknowledge the feelings and presuppositions we bring to the text; we become familiar with each other's feelings; and we learn to trust at least that each other's feelings are sincere. Maybe this way we can become a little less inflexible in our readings, which is another way of saying that maybe we can become more tolerant.

Of course, this begs the question of whether whites should teach African American texts at all, a topic that has not lacked for discussion these last thirty years. Those who say "yes" often label the opposing view as essentialist and then frame it as an absurdity: only blacks can teach black texts, only women can teach female texts, only white southern men can teach Faulkner, and so forth. I'm no essentialist. I have a Ph.D. in American literature, of which African American writing is an important part. I am paid to help undergraduates uncover the ways that texts work, and I think I do a good job of this over a wide range of material.

But I am also a postmodernist, and I know that the position of the observer partially determines the content and quality of any observation. I know that my position is roughly that of a safe white man in America. I am forty, married, with a son about to turn three. I am tenured. We live in Homewood, the closest in of the "over-the-mountain" (upscale, white) Birmingham suburbs, which we chose in part because it has the most integrated of the affluent public school systems.[4] I spent only three years of my schooling in a significantly integrated school (grades six through eight in Sheffield, Alabama), and the experience of integration is something I want for my child. Yet our neighborhood is almost entirely white. My parents taught me that racism was wrong. They also employed a series of black cleaning women whom we called by their first names. I am self-conscious about this, though I was not at the time.

Experientially, I doubt I have what Molefi Kete Asante calls "a proper orientation" for the teaching of black literature.[5] On the other hand, I can't imagine there really is such a thing as a proper orientation. I am more challenged by the charge that there is a kernel of the black experience I will never have access to, and that this is an interpretive deficiency I will always bring to the text. The question is whether that kernel is definitive, and to what extent do I compensate for my deficiency by indulging what Michael Awkward calls "the self-referential impulse"? In a widely read 1990 piece published in *American Literary History*, Awkward examines instances wherein a white critic's acknowledgement of his or her own "racial positionality" might mask "sinister . . . tyrannizing intentions." Isn other words, this gesture is not sufficient, but Awkward does see it as necessary. He quotes Houston Baker as saying, "the white critic 'who honestly engages his or her own autobiographical implication in a brutal past is as likely to provide such [compelling and informed] nuances as an Afro-American theorist.'"[6] I know I cannot give students everything that a black professor could give them, and if we could hire a black teacher of African American literature I would, I suppose, hand the course over. But until that happens, I can model for my students a love for and an openness to the literature. And I can model the self-referential impulse.

Of course, like the former student I quoted above, going into myself on these issues is not always something that I want to do. Catherine Stimpson, among others, has posited some of the underlying motives driving whites into this field, and her catalog does not make me particularly comfortable. According to Stimpson, some whites "use black literature" to "massag[e] guilt." Some use it for political capital (she specifies here scholars of Eldridge Cleaver, whose work she finds "bombastic, schematic, vicious to homosexuals, unfair to white women"). Still others "use black literature emotionally—for kicks, for a 'primitive' energy lost or missing from their own lives."[7] (I picture suburban white males—and not just teenagers—driving slow, memorizing murderous raps, bass booming through sealed S.U.V. windows.) Although I honestly do not believe any of these motives are primary for me, I recognize them all. I would be lying to myself if I denied my complicity in the racial dynamics of this country, and I think Stimpson here identifies a subset of those dynamics quite accurately.

I want to force my students to interrogate those dynamics within themselves as well—that is, to become more racially self-conscious, but with a degree of honesty that doesn't paralyze them. Almost all of them will be troubled by the racist abuses depicted in, say, Ralph Ellison's "Battle Royal" or Martin Luther King's "Letter from the Birmingham Jail." The thing is, black students often read themselves into these texts, where white students do not. It is easy to side against the sort of gross white racism presented in a film like *Mississippi Burning*, even here in Alabama where the past described is our own. The danger is that in projecting our idea of racism onto this rabid redneck Other, we become complacent or even self-righteous about our perceived color-blindness. On my journal assignment sheets, I always cite Shelby Steele's observation that no one he knows, himself included, is "capable of seeing color without making attributions, some of which may [be] negative."[8] I want my students, black and white, to be self-conscious about those attributions—not guilty, but self-aware.

Of course, I also want to raise their consciousness about the culture surrounding them. It is impossible in Birmingham to be unconscious of race as an issue, but I do believe that students at Birmingham-Southern are often unaware of the ways that racial history structures their immediate environment. I'm just beginning to grasp some of it myself. I don't think our white students, for instance, always notice that the preponderance of African Americans on campus work in food service or on the cleaning staff, and if they do notice they still don't see what history has to do with it. A lot of them buy into the unofficial campus counsel against "turning right at night" into the majority-black neighborhoods of West Birmingham (a left turn takes you quickly to the interstate). They don't recognize the economic and aesthetic diversity of these neighborhoods: Bush Hills, Graymont, Smithfield, College Hills, Elyton. White students tend to accept the imposing black iron fence that encloses our well-tended campus as a safeguard, which it undoubtedly is (it was constructed in response to the 1976 murder of a student who was kidnapped from a neighborhood grocery store).[9] They might not get that it also, inevitably, is a symbol, a sort of public relations tool.

I try to find other ways as well to shake up students' unexamined assumptions about race. In my composition courses or literature surveys, I generally find an opportunity to draw a continuum on the board, labeling one pole black and the other pole white. I then ask the students where, in cases of mixed "blood," the line should be drawn separating the two. I will place a line just to one side of the white pole, where American law has traditionally drawn it, and ask them why? In these classes I can usually find a reason to stand a student wearing a white shirt next to a student with "white" skin, and, if I happen to have any black students in the classroom, to place one of them next to someone in a black shirt. Are the terms descriptive, class? What cultural connotations does the language carry? What were you taught in high school that white symbolizes when it appears in literature? What about black? Is there any reason that white doesn't refer to ice, to coldness, and black to richness and fertility? What is the etymology of "denigrate"?

But these are set pieces, and I tend to toss them out like little firecrackers and then move us on back to the text—to Nathaniel Hawthorne's "The Minister's Black Veil" or Kate Chopin's "Desiree's Baby" or Ellison's "Battle Royal." What I have not done in a while is put my students in a circle to engage in a more sustained and much messier focus on how these issues operate within each of us. What I haven't done is volunteer to teach Slavery and the African American Tradition any time in the foreseeable future. I am uncertain about whether I will get back to it. Sometimes I see this sort of course as my professional calling. And other times I notice how I have used Henry Louis Gates to justify my virtual equation of slavery with the African American tradition, and Shelby Steele to discredit people's protestations of color-blindness, and I recall Joel Campbell DuBose, M.A., quoting Booker T. Washington to make his point about the civilizing influence of slavery. Am I just another white man with letters after his name, taking up the task of educating Alabama's youth about "the negroes"? Is it enough to be aware of that possibility? Is it enough to be radically less confident than DuBose that I have any idea what I'm talking about?

VERDICT

About nine months ago I was turning right out of my son Laughlin's downtown daycare center, and half a block later I pulled up to a stop sign at the same time the driver to my right pulled up to hers. She was a black woman in a large brown car. We both feinted, braked again, made exaggerated gestures of deference. Hers prevailed, and as I accelerated into the intersection I nodded to her and mouthed aloud, "thank you."

"Why you say thank you?" Laughlin asked. He was about two at the time.

"She was being nice, letting me go," I explained.

"I don't like brown people," he said.

Oh shit, I thought. Then, "You like 'Mond, don't you?"

"Yes."

"Uh huh. And you like Jalen, and you like Miss Jonita, don't you?"

"Yes."

"Who don't you like?"

I didn't get much more out of him than "those ladies." We think it had to do with some of the women who oversee the children in the late afternoons after his teachers have gone home. We assume that he was identifying them by their color without connecting that color to classmates or teachers whom he likes.

One night recently I came home from school a little late and Laughlin was crying on an easy chair, having been placed in a sort of makeshift timeout for disliking brown people. We know we can't punish him into having more appropriate feelings, and it did turn out that his mother was responding to some small act of defiance that went along with his comment. But it was also right about the time that the bombing trial was starting, and she may have been feeling especially sensitive. Just yesterday a jury here convicted Thomas Blanton of bombing the Sixteenth Street Baptist Church in 1963. The papers and the airwaves are filled with it.

Many afternoons I drive Laughlin home down Sixteenth Street. We pass the stately Civil Rights Institute, and he might ask if we can stop and play on the swings and monkey bars on its grounds. We pass the bright pansies of Kelly Ingram park, which has been made over into a memorial of Bull Conner's notorious overreaction to a children's march against city segregation. Once or twice I have walked my son through the park to show him the iron sculptures of shepherds emerging from a wall and of fire hoses mounted and aimed at the sidewalk. The dogs scare Laughlin. He likes fire hoses.

We also pass the eastern wall of the church itself, the wall from which a huge jagged hunk was blown that Sunday morning in 1963. Yesterday I was unable to resist trying to explain to Laughlin why that wall was famous. I told him about the bomb, and about the way the wall had been blown apart, and how four little girls had gone to be with the angels.

"Why?" he asked.

I stammered around for a minute trying to formulate something about misguided people and their feelings about color, but I could tell it didn't make a damn bit of sense to him.

NOTES

1 A Birmingham-Southern publication breaks down a recent representative incoming class (1998) of 308 students as follows: 91 percent White, 3 percent African American, 4 percent Asian-Pacific Islander, 0.7 percent Hispanic, 0.3 percent non-resident alien, and 1 percent American Indian. I am using "race" in this essay primarily in terms of black and white, which is what it almost always means in Alabama. I use the terms "black" and "white" self-consciously, as I hope to clarify later in the essay.

2 Nicole Bates, "RE: Too many BSC references in one week . . . " April 11, 2001, personal

email (April 19, 2001). I would like to thank Nicole for granting permission to use her words in this paper.

3 Joel Campbell DuBose, M.A., *Alabama History*, Revised Edition (Richmond, Va.: Johnson Publishing, 1913), 189. DuBose does not identify the source of the Washington quotation.

4 I phoned Homewood High to ask the racial makeup of the high school, and was informed in a return voicemail, "the racial makeup of the high school is 21 percent. We don't break it down into Asian or Hispanic or whatever. Just 21 percent."

5 Molefi Kete Asante, "Where Is the Professor Located?" *Perspectives* 31, no. 6 (1993), 19.

6 Michael Awkward, "Negotiations of Power: White Critics, Black Texts, and the Self-Referential Impulse," *American Literary History* 2, no. 4 (1990), 602, 582.

7 Catherine R. Stimpson, "Black Culture/White Teacher," *Where the Meanings Are: Feminism and Cultural Spaces* (New York: Routledge, 1988), 2, 1.

8 Shelby Steele, "I'm Black, You're White, Who's Innocent?: Race and Power in an Era of Blame," *The Content of Our Character: A New Vision of Race in America* (New York: Harper Perennial, 1990), 8.

9 Greg Garrison, "Citizenship by Example: Berte's 25 Years at BSC," *Birmingham News*, April 22, 2001, 26A. This article also discusses the current administration's resistance during the 1970s to public pressure on the College to leave what was perceived as a dangerous and run-down section of town.

PHOTO: DONN A. BOULANGER JR.

KEVIN EVEROD QUASHIE

FEAR AND THE PROFESSORIAL CENTER

In the African American studies classroom, the professorial center does not hold.[1] By this I mean that the normative centers or authorizing sites for an instructor, rather than being reliable, are instead conditional and sometimes contradictory. Such a claim can probably be made about any classroom context, as the classroom is a volatile and dynamic space that always has at least as many centers as there are people present. Nonetheless, there are particular and predictable dynamics that disturb the professorial center of the African American studies classroom, and it is to these that this essay speaks.

So the center does not hold; it is conditional, or contradictory, or both: conditional, because the center's presence and potency is informed by factors such as the racial/ethnic identities of the professor and the students, how easily one can read such identity markers, as well as what these social subject positions mean to all involved. The legitimacy of the instructor (as well as of the class) is subject to the familiar scrutiny that all classroom instructors encounter, as well as to particular questions of place and right that generate from the anxiety of race. Hence, the legitimacy that might otherwise characterize a classroom is less a given and more a contingent. Further, the conferring of legitimacy, more than being delayed, is sometimes impeded by

KEVIN EVEROD QUASHIE is an assistant professor of Afro-American Studies at Smith College. He is coeditor of the anthology *New Bones: Contemporary Black Writers in America* and is currently working on a book called *The Love Project: A Cultural Theory of Contemporary Black Women's Aesthetics.*

This essay explores the "disciplinary illegitimacy" he sees as haunting African American studies and those who work in that area. Quashie—who describes himself as black, queer, and young—searchingly interrogates fear as it characterizes the classroom.

contradictions between a professor's perceived subject and political positions, her embraced or inhabited ones, the classroom material, and the students' expectations.

This heightened tension is the originating moment in the African American studies classroom; its presence is perpetual rather than momentary, and it produces a context that textures and manages perhaps every other tension, dynamic, or interaction in the classroom. This compulsive attention to identity—the instructor's, the students', and the identities of the text's subjects—is facilitated by many macrofactors, including historical and national anxieties about race, and the difficulty and volatility of discussing race. But on a more particular level, the attention is directly related to the way that race, especially as classroom subject, compels everyone to self-assess, such that the classroom literally becomes its own "I" narrative. I have come to value this tendency toward self-assessment, especially because I think it reflects one of my pedagogical principles: every student should, no matter what subject, work to come to a relationship with the material. She, the student, should be dynamically and discordantly linked to the subject at hand, an agent in relationship to its complexity, beauty, and (in)comprehensibility.[2]

But I am also aware that the use of first-person can unwittingly contribute to the idea that "cultural" material is simplistic, as well as inadvertently invite casual, even superficial, engagement of such material. As students and instructors alike articulate their "local" knowledge, they also readily invoke pseudo-sociological perspectives and ignore the sophisticated challenges posed by the material. The text becomes part of a large swath of cultural memoir, its nuances surrendered to the ease of its surface; this ease yields a feel-good sensibility as each person's interpretation (or confessional) gains prestige. When this happens, both the text and the complicated history in which it and we are imbedded, are muted. Still, the real insidiousness is in the affirmation that such conditions give to the idea that real academic rigor is found in the hard sciences, not the soft ones that emphasize feeling, emotion, and personal history. The misuse of first-person can seemingly corroborate and collaborate with the academic illegitimacy that haunts many area studies disciplines.[3]

Furthermore, reliance on the first-person might also reassert the notion that only those who can speak in a similar voice as the text can have legitimate access to the body of knowledge. Hence, a pedagogical strategy that was intended to broaden the invitation to rigorous and careful consideration of cultural material instead limits access.

In all of these instances, the utility of first-person quickly erodes. For my own purposes, in conjunction with an appreciation for first-person, I choose to remain committed to a pedagogy that extends beyond the local. And still, these caveats reveal the peril that teaching cultural material can be and highlight some of the pervasive and unresolved convolutions that are present as student and teacher encounter the African American studies classroom.

Let me undo the claim that the center does not hold. I was, in some ways, being dramatic and declamatory in making that statement, especially because I liked the poetics and the signifying of the moment.[4] But let me restate, and be more precise: in the African American studies classroom the professorial center, that place of authorization and legitimacy, is multiple. Rather than one center, there are *centers*—interests that are competing, contradictory, contingent, and sometimes confounding; these centers are places from where the instructor can and has to access her authority, as well as places where students interpret and assess the instructor's authority.

I would not want my attention on the professorial center to imply that I am either arguing for a return to more Draconian models of teacher–student, ones that are perhaps no less volatile but that are more punitive in regard to acts of volatility; or that I am arguing against the interest in student-centered pedagogy or participatory learning techniques (which, amongst other things, aim to reduce the centrality of the professorial center). I am assuming here that there are also student centers in the classroom, places where students access their own authority and agency in the learning moment. I am instead trying to make clear that in any institution of higher learning, teaching is in part always about a professorial center, always in part a set of attempts to negotiate power and opportunity. This description is not summative of all that teaching is, or even of its most important aspects; but the description, especially this idea of a disturbed professorial center, is key to three qualities of teaching that I think are paramount: generosity, inclusivity, and risk.

I TEACH AT Smith College, a modest-sized private liberal arts women's institution, heavily endowed and one of the elite private colleges in the country. I am an assistant professor in Afro-American studies, male, queer, black, young (in comparison to my colleagues), and I teach cultural studies. I was hired while ABD as a replacement for a faculty member on fellowship; then as a visiting assistant professor when that fellowship stay extended; and am now in a tenure-track position. I was a first-generation college student, and attended state institutions that offered high-quality education (and in some cases, are well-considered in the disciplines that I was studying), but that are not prestigious by any means. I was born in St. Kitts in the Caribbean and am feminist.

This current spring semester, one of my two classes is twentieth-century African American literature. As was the case the year before, the class is large: eighty students this time (fifty-five last time), which indicates the growing interest in our discipline, as well as perhaps the interest in me as someone new to the campus (and how hyper-visible I sometimes am). As was also the case the year before, there is a greater proportion of students of color in the class (as can be immediately identified by visual cues as well as self-identificatory comments) than would be expected at Smith's campus, but this is not unusual for my discipline. There are nine black women in the class; and ten women who are Latina, Asian American, or indigenous. These include students who are or have identified as biracial, but could possibly exclude other students of color who are not "visible." There is a wide mix in terms of class rank, with almost equal numbers of first-years through seniors; and there are three students who are nontraditional in age, two graduate students from the one-year International American Studies Certificate program, and one high-school senior. In comparison to their predecessors, the students in the class come with varying levels of interest, familiarity, and expertise, though this year there is a larger proportion who are less familiar both with methods of literary inquiry as well as African American literature, history, or culture. Yet their interest in the class is high: there is the sense that the class will be fun or interesting (which is how many students across various identity indices have described it), as well as the regular comments that it is one of their best (and hardest) classes.

What remains unspoken is the fear, the anxiety: black students wondering how they will be perceived by me, by their white and non-black classmates; wondering if they will be expected to know certain things, wondering if they will measure up, anxious about their place in relationship to the material; other students of color wondering about similar questions, and wondering about falling between the gap that is the U.S. race binary; white students anxious about the same things, and wondering about how little they know, how much they know, how much they think they know, and especially about their relationship to the material. In small comments, or casual bits of office-hours conversation, I hear shadows of these anxieties, but though they are powerful and evocative, they remain largely unarticulated.[5]

Of course I have my own anxieties: I am worried about the casualness of how black culture is engaged, how superficially it is often imagined; I want them to like me, but also to think that I am good at what I do; I want to be challenging in ways that affirm my commitment to inclusivity and critical thinking; I want to be supportive of the black students, the other students of color, as well as the white students, and though aware that each group (though not necessarily each person who can be categorized in a group) may need and want to engage me in a different way, and that I may want to do the same, I am also conscientious of the professional ethos of being "equally" available. I have many other anxieties, but suffice to say that I begin the semester by expressing some of this in a manner that I think is open, a modeling of risk-taking: I use Pat Parker's poem "For the White Person Who Wants to Know How to Be My Friend," which gives all of us the opportunity to talk seriously yet somewhat humorously about race (in general, but also its common manifestation as a binary, and its presence in the classroom moment), as well as to read literature closely.

Without overkill, I talk throughout the semester about issues that express or reflect some of my anxieties; these discussions are usually brief, and often in relevance to a text or scene, a historical debate, or a campus event. For example, in announcing my department's presentation of the major, I introduce the announcement with a brief comment about the place of black studies in most of the academy, and the incredible service function that such departments perform, often without measurable recompense. I am not cajoling them; I am being very careful. I am informing them as well as attempting to narrate a larger picture of how complicated this study of African American literature is, how it extends beyond text and classroom. And they respond, with questions, various comments, or clarifications. It is a fine moment in our classroom, and I make the point that I believe the study of African American literature (or any other class in my discipline) is a complicated endeavor, so much so that it should be overwhelming. Overwhelming, but not deterring; "undeterringly overwhelming" is the lovely trope I use to make the point. I can sense their appreciation of my disposition for flair.

And then there is the grade anxiety, which is where much of my flair and their appreciation unravels (or at least where I unraveled): I am known somewhat as a rigorous grader, and it also bears mentioning that Smith, like most elite institutions, has identified grade inflation as an area for discussion and informal study.[6] Grading is one locus of professorial authority, and readily reveals the problems of such authority. For example, its punitive nature, as well as the unidirectional way that comments are usually made, undercut the fluidity of learning. A more severe problem is the ways that an assessment of a student's work (whether based on a particular product, or on her overall progress) can be confused with an assessment of person. But my concern here is less about grading as an act, one that many of us who teach are considerate about, and more about the anxiety that grading produces for students and instructors—anxieties which interact with the anxieties already noted in the African American studies classroom. So after a midterm on which many students did poorly, a midterm which was, in my estimation, reasonable, doable, and fair, I respond with a work ethic that inspires anxiety rather than relieves it. After the midterm I am afraid that I have failed to teach clearly; and when that particular fear subsides, I am afraid that students will be disappointed with and in me (for whatever reasons), and just what such disappointment could mean on evaluations, for example, to say nothing of my still-stellar reputation on campus. I talk with the class, and hear from them the comfortable things—that they ran out of time, that they were less capable of identifying form/style aspects of the texts (which was a significant part of the exam), that the exam was fair. But I hear nothing about their anxieties, and of course, I am not honest with them about mine. I devise a "work harder, be available more" strategy that includes making myself available before every class for twenty minutes for anyone who wants to follow up on the previous class's discussion; having extra office hours; composing a two-page document that goes over a variety of key points for each midterm question; severely reducing the percentage worth of the midterm; compiling a mini-packet (twenty-seven pages) on how to read literature; being even more structured in my class lecture; and supplementing each lecture with a two-page, single-spaced summary of key points.[7] I am in overdrive, and perhaps even overkill, but I want them to have what they need to do well; and of course, I am silently afraid.

THE RACIAL context and implications of how these students respond to the midterm and my interventions are telling: most students continue to work hard, maybe resolved to not doing as well as they might have wanted to do, maybe believing my interventions to be suitable for better progress (and surely some of these are students who are satisfied with their work). About twenty students individually visit me over a week of office hours to discuss their progress and status. They fall into two groups, invariably: a group about eleven students who begin with praise for the class, for me, for how much they are learning, as well as an assurance that this is not about the grade, and then quickly move to asking if they can take the class pass/fail. The second group sometimes also begin with those reassuring comments, but all of them quickly move to a more frustrated (though respectful) comment on how hard the class is, and then solicit suggestions toward improvement. This latter group is composed of back women (one of them is nontraditional), one white woman (also nontraditional), and one Asian American woman; we talk about their papers, the midterm, a shorter assignment, as well as upcoming readings. The former group is, except for one woman, all white; three of them are seniors; all of them traditional in age. I did not realize the starkness of this breakdown until later when I was trying to make sense of the fact that I was angry and hurt by the students who wanted to take the class pass/fail; in fact I felt violated, taken for granted; I resented what felt to me like their rejection of my hard efforts as well as their casual approach to the class, an interpretation that bears implications beyond the classroom moment. This somewhat unqualified anger became wider and deeper with more reflection, and the white women who want to (in my opinion) "cop out"—perhaps except for the seniors, whose predicaments I convinced myself were understandable—are exhibiting cultural and institutional racism at its best: their wanting to interact with and engage black culture without wanting to work, without wanting for this interaction to be challenging. This is a moment of not taking the literature or the culture or the people (or me!) seriously, a reckless and typical assumption of illegitimacy and frivolousness. And I am further resentful of the extra work I had put into three of the women's papers. I am resolved: they can take the class pass/fail, but they get nothing further from me.

Somewhere along the line, in my dishonest presentation of what are really generous and useful (as well as necessary and successful) interventions, I had forgotten to acknowledge my fears and then later, my pain. These refusals to speak truthfully made it impossible for me to see that they, these students, are afraid, even if their fears point attention to the privileges of institutionalized whiteness. And in my resentment, which is the result of my attending poorly to my own fears, I have became more hierarchical, more attached to my professorial center, which is from the beginning unreliable, contradictory, confounding; it is even more so now as I clamor for a center, a sense of legitimacy, something to salve and soothe my disturbances. It is my friend Edward, a white man, who gently critiques my heavy-handed interventions, and though he is somewhat careless in considering the racial dynamics he reminds me, as Edward often does, of what my commitments are: love, openness, generosity— all three in the most critical of senses.[8]

THIS IS ABOUT fear, and a response to fear that pushes the trigger in me to police the culture: being readily aware of the ways that my discipline, my people, and my person are woefully regarded, I have a strong desire to determine who enters "the culture" and how, and what is the proper deference. This urge to police the culture is not easy to dismiss, because ethically I cannot merely surrender and let all students access the discipline as they wish; that would be unprofessional, as well as unproductive. But there are fine and shifting lines between inviting students to cultivate a complicated and respectful (and hence difficult) relationship to the material; and impeding their ability to do so. These lines turn upon the idea of the professorial center, which is where both the invocation of openness and the dispensation of rightful access happens.[9]

This is about fear, and the contexts that make my fear possible. It is a "post" moment of cultural interaction, where difference is sexy and exciting, which means that the interest in and engagement of black cultural texts is not ever simple—not merely appreciation or celebration, but also not only appropriation or exoticization. It is, instead, some amalgamation of these, some modern cultural mix that at once delights and disgusts. These moments are complicated, but often are not considered to be anything more than their surface.[10] The critical edge slips away, and what makes these "post" conditions fear-inducing for me is the violence that can happen when a cultural text invokes and evokes race, but does not facilitate or encourage an interrogation of one's relationship to race and racism. And therein is my fear: the fear that they will mishandle the text, and perhaps even me.

It is Pema Chodoron's comment that makes me less anxious about fear: "fear is the natural reaction to moving closer to the truth."[11] Hers is not a suggestion that I become immobilized by or too comfortable with fear; instead, she says that fear points attention to something that is crucial, truth-like, necessary. The turning point, for me, comes with my honesty, my telling the students at the beginning of one class period a reflective and careful version of what I was struggling with, and reminding them of this one principle: that everyone already has, should have, is responsible for, the material; our specific places of entry, our specific struggles with and joys about the material may be different, but the cultural material belongs to everyone and no one; that having a relationship with the material of necessity means having a relationship to thinking about racism. I apologize for my anxiety, remind them that this, as is any educational endeavor, is a rigorous enterprise; and I articulate a renewed commitment to teaching. I stop there, field comments and questions, and proceed with the day's material.

I of course want to tell them about the problematic disposition that I think many of them, including students of color, bring to this particular classroom moment: many enter thinking (even saying) that it will be fun and interesting. And it should be: education should be pleasurable, as bell hooks argues.[12] But education is also hard, demanding, and the idea of pleasure, especially in context of the already superficial and casual perception of black culture, becomes a double bind. What frames of mind does this comment, "I am so excited to take this class; I think it will be fun," put any student in, and how do those frames constitute a disposition that is attentive to the challenge of the class? And what would it mean if students entered this class with a disposition similar to how many of them enter a physics class—not the dread, but the sense that the class will require regular and intense consideration, hours of reflection and thought and practice? I have no answers to these questions, but I am sure that my students all around could be a little more attuned to the challenge that African American studies require.

But I forego that comment especially because it feels too much like a disguised policing admonition, and instead, a few days later, make a more lovely comment, one that is outside of the "heavy" atmosphere that characterized my earlier apology: I begin class with a discussion (my comment, and then invitation for student input) about education as "the practice of freedom" and as self-knowledge.[13] We talk about learning as a process that requires that they learn about themselves, that they become greater agents in their lives than before they entered the class. I suggest that in such a context, success can only be measured and calibrated by themselves; I and others may provide comments and feedback that are useful, but the assessment, the rewards and the disappointments, are their own. I tell them that teaching's greatest reward for me is in being more graceful and more capable when I leave the room than when I came in, and no one but me can possibly define that.

THIS IS A MARK on water for me; it leaves a cautionary imprint. So, at the end, I come to this place: a place of believing that it is the negotiation of vulnerability that most disrupts and but also crystallizes my professorial center. This essay began with the various causes of and anxieties around an untenable center; and somehow my subjectivity became overdetermined by just what these anxieties could, and did, mean. So I am acknowledging again that for me, as it is for Parker Palmer, bell hooks, and Paolo Freire, learning is risk and openness; it changes between states of close and those of abandon. In trying to live through the centers of professorial authority—the ones afforded and denied me, as well as the ones obscured and complicated—I have to remember that helping each person in that room to find a relationship with the text is what I should do. I also have to remember that what is most useful about professorial authority is my ability to be comfortable with how such authority shifts, as well as being honest about how I feel and what I think these shifts mean. I cannot possibly want to encourage agency, if I am not willing to make the venture into vulnerability also my venture.

My challenge then is how to fill the professorial center with acts and examples of successful vulnerability—not unconsidered risk that fails to take adequate note of the human weight in the teaching moment, but risk that is about compassion and sensibility as well as about helping students to place and displace themselves. In practice, this commitment to vulnerability means becoming quite comfortable with intellectual production from sites of local knowledge, which is where fear resides, as well as considering the relationship between the local and its social and historical context. And I am realizing again the need to speak about fear as part of the learning process; the need to forego the ready-made professorial center in favor of one that is more complicated, and in some ways unreliable; the need to take and sometimes create opportunities to sensibly give attention to fear.

Of course, being a black gay man, and my discipline's status as "soft," makes such an undertaking possible but also complicates it (as does teaching at an all-women's institution). This is where my anxieties began: wanting to police the culture, to control the sense of rigor, to reflect a legitimate authority in the classroom. Perhaps instead I can authorize myself and my class with openness, and with risk-taking; perhaps I can be more honest, that while I am not willing to be without a professorial center, I am also unwilling to be afraid. Perhaps this is also about realizing the failings of my community: that is, part of my anxiety about race, about the casualness of how students engage and encounter race, is because there are few spaces in the community where students might be further challenged to think of race more rigorously. If there was a truly vibrant and collective engagement of race and privilege and culture and learning here (or anywhere), then perhaps I might feel less the intense and specific burden to police and assess, to dispense and to mark. But the community is as it is: sometimes capable, more times not. So I go on, working toward a balance between authority and openness. At the end, I have learned to remember that I am concerned about what my students' actions reveal about how seriously they take the material, black culture, or me—but also about how seriously they take *themselves*. And such concern is what inspires my attempt to foster a sense of agency. This and more toward achieving a practice where we, my students and I, can be both breathless and breathing.[14]

NOTES

1 I am grateful to Ruth Ellen Kocher for her coining this term for a recent panel at the National Association of Ethnic Studies Conference in New Orleans (March 2001). I am also grateful to Kocher and Vanessa Holford Diana for their comment on and engagement of beginning versions of this work. Finally, I would like to thank Edward Bartok-Baratta for conversations, Cypriane Williams and Sara Feldman for attentive and indispensable readings, Ann Arnett Ferguson for her insights late in the process of writing this essay, and Donn Boulanger for love.

2 The imagining of race as a self-reflexive construct is a central idea of cultural studies. See for example Toni Morrison's *Playing in the Dark: Whiteness and the Literary Imagination* (New York: Vintage, 1993), bell hooks's *Black Looks: Race and Representation* (Boston: South End, 1992), and Ann duCille's *Skin Trade* (Cambridge, Mass.: Harvard University Press, 1996). In specific reference to pedagogy, see Beverly Daniel Tatum's work, especially *"Why Are All the Black Kids Sitting Together in the Cafeteria?" and Other Conversations About Race* (New York: Basic Books, 1997), as well as two earlier essays, "Talking about Race, Learning about Racism: The Application of Racial Identity Development Theory in the Classroom," *Harvard Educational Review* 62 (1992) and "Teaching White Students about Racism: The Search for White Allies and the Restoration of Hope," *Teachers College Record* 95 (1994). Also see hooks' insightful *Teaching to Transgress: Education as the Practice of Freedom* (New York and London: Routledge, 1994) and Henry Giroux's *Disturbing Pleasures: Learning Popular Culture* (New York and London: Routledge, 1994). Finally, some feminist pedagogies also consider race as a self-reflexive meditation; see for example Frances A. Maher and Mark Kay Thompson Tetreault's *The Feminist Classroom* (New York: Basic Books, 1994).

3 Henry Louis Gates argues against casual and sociological engagement of black texts in his introduction to *Figures in Black: Words, Signs, and the "Racial" Self* (New York: Oxford University Press, 1987). Also see pages 15–42 of Robin D. G. Kelly's *Yo Mama's Disfunktional: Fighting the Culture Wars in Urban America* (Boston: Beacon, 1997). This matter of disciplinary legitimacy is engaged by hooks, *Teaching*, 16–17; 137–141; 191–199; and Maher and Tetreault, 1–24; 77–86. Also see Manning Marable's "Black Studies and the Racial Mountain," in *Dispatches from the Ebony Tower*, 1–28 and Nell Irvin Painter in "Black Studies, Black Professors, and the Struggles of Perception," *The Chronicle of Higher Education*, December 15, 2000; Review Section.

4 It plays off of the well-known William Butler Yeats line "Things fall apart, the center cannot hold" from the 1921 poem "The Second Coming," which has become the enunciation of postmodernity.

5 I also know that these anxieties are present from my teaching experiences prior to Smith, my conversations with students from the class the semester before, and my familiarity with work by Parker Palmer, especially *The Courage to Teach: Exploring the Inner Landscape of a Teacher's Life* (San Francisco: Jossey Bass, 1998), bell hooks, Beverly Tatum, and others.

6 The problem of grade inflation is manifest on all campuses, I imagine, though the most recent articles in *The Chronicle of Higher Education* have focused on elite institutions.

7 I took the initiative to compile the mini-packet when a student suggested that I put a text on literary forms on reserve. I initially hesitated, because many such texts often ignore particular aspects of form relevant to African American literary traditions, but I gave in, making the necessary caveats.

8 I am aware of and grateful for the way Parker Palmer has talked about fear in the second chapter of *The Courage to Teach*. I am also appreciative of Jane Tompkins' insights in "Pedagogy of the Distressed," *College English* 52 (1990): 653–660.

9 The idea (but not the nomenclature) of policing the culture is part of a great conversation between Stuart Hall, bell hooks, Cornel West, and others in Gina Dent's edited collection *Black Popular Culture* (New York: The New Press, 1998). Also see Kobena Mercer's *Welcome to the Jungle: New Positions in Black Cultural Studies* (New York: Routledge, 1994), especially 259–285.

10 The "post" refers to postmodernism, postcolonialism, and poststructuralism, as well as the critical, cultural, and popular contexts that these schools of thought attempt to frame: for example, the meaning of "now," the intersection of the internet and MTV, globalization and capitalism as empire, or heightened conversation about biracial and multiracial identity (in the context of a larger population of children of such identities). In the United States especially, the contemporary cultural condition is one where blackness is a present and sometimes even coveted commodity, even though this coveting has no essential link to antiracist self-consciousness.

11 Pema Chodoron, *When Things Fall Apart: Heart Advice for Difficult Times* (Boston and London: Shambhala, 2000), 1.

12 hooks, *Teaching*, 7. Giroux and Peter McLaren also make similar arguments.

13 "The practice of freedom" is the subtitle of hooks' *Teaching*.

14 It is also worth noting that the students' place in my imagination has shifted, and continues to shift, as some of them share their own reflective consideration of this class experience. I would not want to paint a portrait of them that renders static their own lovely volatility.

PART 2

REWARDS AND PUNISHMENTS

"Data from interviews with minority women teachers, surveys of professors, and evaluations by students indicated that the predominantly white classroom with a minority teacher was a contested terrain, and some students struggled to reproduce society's systems of inequality."[1] This brief statement from the abstract for a December 1999 journal article "When the 'Other' Is the Teacher: Implications of Teacher Diversity in Higher Education" supports the claims of faculty of color included in this volume. Unfortunately, as yet there is no full-scale study available to substantiate the largely anecdotal accounts of the effects of racism on teaching evaluations. Because extant studies on course evaluations have not accounted for race and racism in relation to either the instructor's subject position or course content, we believe that the essays in the present volume provide much-needed insight on the subject. When it comes to the responsibility of teaching race, the stakes are high.

Inevitably, addressing race in the classroom makes students—and at times professors—uncomfortable. While we can theorize that discomfort is an integral part of learning, when it comes time for course evaluations students often recall that they were made to feel uncomfortable. If a "good" course is equated with comfort, as less mature students often assume, then professors who cause discomfort are likely to receive lower ratings. If, in addition to addressing race in the classroom, the professor has "high" standards, gives weekly written assignments, teaches subjects that always include race and ethnicity, has an accent, looks "foreign," is visibly nonwhite, is a youngish and/or petite female—any or all of the above—then student evaluations of this professor are likely to be lower than the mean. The significance of this situation is that, according to one professor and former department chair, "In recent years, student evaluations included in faculty dossiers have become a vital element in promotion-and-tenure cases: one thoughtless or flippant comment can ruin a promising career."[2]

The use of standardized evaluations for courses that inherently trigger student discomfort is unjust if not discriminatory. In a persistently racist society, race is the bottom line when it comes to resistance from students. Professors who embody diversity or multiculturalism—any deviance from the Anglo-Saxon "norm"—are likely to take the brunt of student unease. A system for evaluating teaching that has not accounted for this crucial factor is, in fact, invalid and counterproductive. Furthermore, from the essays included here it is obvious that white faculty who teach race-related courses can also be "punished" through course evaluations. For one thing, students with white-skin privilege often expect white professors to reinforce that privilege by catering to their level of comfort. Thus, white professors whose pedagogy addresses racial issues would seem to be siding with the enemy. In addition, white male professors who teach African American or Native American literature, for example, risk being equated with the "oppressor" who is metaphorically labeled "the white man." Faculty teaching such courses who get consistently high evaluations must then suspect that their pedagogical approach is somehow faulty because they made the students too comfortable. The reliance on standardized course evaluations in these situations hardly determines the effectiveness of the course or the instructor. High ratings might simply show that the professor did not push hard enough.

The most difficult aspect of addressing racial issues in college courses is the sense of isolation the instructor is likely to experience. Considering how many colleagues on the faculty manage to avoid race in their teaching—rationalizing that it is not their problem—the minority of individuals who do accept the challenge are often marginalized. Colleagues and administrators who learn about conflict in a particular classroom frequently equate this with poor teaching. Because they themselves do not address difficult subjects like race and racism, they don't recognize classroom conflict as a potentially transformative praxis. To them, course ratings that are "lower than the mean" explain the classroom commotion they heard about. They pass on such assessments of their maverick colleague to the administrators who, in turn, can use the low scores against the professor when it comes to tenure, promotion, and merit reviews.

Assuming that those of us who address racial issues in our courses are not martyrs or masochists, why do we do this? The short answer is, we still believe in education—and true education requires an open and honest examination of race. Of course, faculty of color may not have the option of evading race. One contributor notes, for example, that students dropped his course in Spanish after they saw that the professor was black. Many of us continue our "front-line" teaching to help combat such ignorance. Our reward is to see young people begin to think and act for themselves—to no longer be intimidated by the taboo subject of race. Having experienced the potential for social change in our classrooms, we practice a pedagogy of hope.

NOTES

1 Lucila Vargas, "When the 'Other' Is the Teacher: Implications of Teacher Diversity in Higher Education," *Urban Review*, 31:4 (December 1999), 359–383.

2 Douglas Hill, "What Students Can Teach Professors: Reading Between the Lines of Evaluations," *Chronicle of Higher Education* (March 16, 2001), B5.

OUT ON A LIMB:

RACE AND THE EVALUATION OF FRONTLINE TEACHING

We are concerned that our colleagues all across the country appear to feel freer and more willing to discuss diversity and multicultural education if racism is omitted from the topic.

—Benjamin Bowser et al.,
Confronting Diversity Issues on Campus

The bad news is that teachers who present minority history and literature—or similar topics—almost uniformly face varying degrees of hostility, anger, and rejection: reactions unlike anything they have faced before.

—Thomas Trzyna and Martin Abbott,
"Grieving in the Ethnic Literature Classroom"

"You're really a lousy teacher; you're just using your color as an excuse." On the final day of a national convention for English teachers, a stranger sitting across the table—a white-haired, portly man with a sardonic grin—made this declaration as I was describing a classroom experience to a colleague. I stopped in mid-sentence. How should one respond to such a comment? How I did respond might surprise some people and I will return to this later. What the comment brought home to me is more to the point.

BONNIE TuSMITH is an associate professor of English at Northeastern University in Boston and President of MELUS, the national multiethnic literary society. Her publications include *All My Relatives: Community in Contemporary Ethnic American Literatures; Colorizing Literary Theory; Conversations with John Edgar Wideman;* and *American Family Album: 28 Contemporary Ethnic Stories.*

TuSmith argues that addressing racial issues in the classroom makes students uncomfortable. This discomfort is often reflected in negative end-of-term course evaluations. Especially when the instructor is a person of color, the X-factor of "race" renders the use of standardized student evaluations "one of the greatest threats to quality teaching."

The stranger's remark encapsulates two issues that I have been grappling with for years as an ethnic literature professor and a visibly Asian American woman. The first is how we evaluate teaching ("you're really a lousy teacher") and the second is how race operates in this evaluation ("you're using your color"). We do an abysmal job in assessing college teaching, I believe, due to our overreliance on standardized course evaluations. Many educators would agree with this assertion. However, too many educators and college administrators consistently ignore and adamantly resist the claim that, if we seriously consider the X-factor of race, the use of such evaluations poses one of the greatest threats to quality teaching.

The stranger actually did me a great service. His assumption helped me to make the connection between my teaching and my position as a visibly "colored" subject in a white-dominant society. As someone who considers teaching her calling and works hard at it, I have been baffled for years by end-of-term evaluations. Too often the gains made by individual students and the class as a whole—the ability to analyze a broad range of culturally diverse and frequently complex works of literature, for example—have not been reflected in these assessments. Reliance on numbered ratings and anonymous written comments on evaluation forms left out the context of the classroom experience. As Zora Neale Hurston and Alice Walker have reminded us, African American folk wisdom says not only to give the facts but to provide the understanding to go with them. This requires slowing down for a longer look.

According to the researchers cited in my second epigraph, student hostility is to be expected in race-related courses. Behind each student's evaluation of such courses is the unacknowledged emotional turmoil that he or she has undergone. Based on their three-year study of ethnic literature students at Seattle Pacific University, Trzyna and Abbott conclude, "Teaching about race, gender, poverty, and other social and cultural differences is fraught with obstacles, and high on the list of those obstacles is grief, that complex bundle of hostility, sorrow, denial, bargaining, and other feelings that can manifest itself in many forms, including student protests . . ." Students grieve over their loss of innocence, say the researchers, "over the death, perhaps, of [their] notions of the American dream." The emotions they undergo are "structurally identical" to what Elisabeth Kübler-Ross identified as the six stages of death and dying.[1]

Most students do not associate emotional turmoil with a "good" class. When evaluating a course in which they felt discomfort—even though, according to the Tyrzna and Abbott study, their discomfort was caused by the course content and subject matter—many students are likely to rate the course "below average." This rating says little about the quality of instruction and the learning that took place. Granted that discomfort is not the sole province of ethnic literature classrooms, my point is that it is not valid to judge a course by how comfortable the students felt. The fact that race-related courses are likely to trigger "grief" in students renders the uniform use of course evaluations problematic. In my experience, the system is open to abuse.

I have been teaching ethnic American literatures for the past dozen years. During campus interviews for my first tenure-track position I was told by every English department faculty member I met that they were aware of my "situation." They understood that my particular combination—a "minority" woman who teaches "minority" literature full-time to predominantly white students— meant that my course evaluations would be on the low side. "It won't count against you," they reassured me. These senior faculty members cited the example of my predecessor, an African American woman, whose experience had demonstrated that students do not love professors who teach material that makes them uncomfortable—especially when the professor is "colored." My future colleagues convinced me that they were well aware of such special circumstances. When it came time for my my tenure case, however, this knowledge had vanished. My above-average scores were no longer good enough; since my numbers were not among the highest in the department, the chairman said over the phone, the tenure committee did not recommend my going up for tenure. In this way, the student evaluations were used against me.

I share this story to invite serious consideration of what is going on in institutions of higher education today. In recent years, there have been national conferences on race, but these efforts barely scratched the surface of entrenched racial attitudes in institutions of higher learning. Part of the problem is that few academics openly acknowledge that there *is* a problem. It seems that whoever mentions the "R" word is "it" and, similar to the childhood game, the point is to avoid being tagged as "it." We also know that not dealing with a problem does not make it go away. In publicly discussing the connection between race and the evaluation of teaching, I set myself up to be "it." Colleagues can accuse me of playing the race card, as the stranger did. The issue is too important, however, for me to remain silent. As someone who continues to believe in higher education I must speak my mind: the use of standardized course evaluations promotes poor teaching.

The cynicism expressed by some colleagues when I have raised this issue astounds me. In discussing student evaluations I have received advice from "give them all A's" to "don't do the evaluations at all." The latter advice tended to come from high-ranking white male professors. In my experience, not allowing students to complete course evaluations has never been an option. First of all, simply refusing to distribute evaluations shows contempt for one's students and colleagues. Second, at institutions where I have served on the faculty no student evaluations also means no merit raise, no tenure, no promotion. How could anyone afford this?

The "give them all A's" proposition may have been said in jest, but I suspect that there is more truth to it than we teachers care to admit. Grade inflation has been a nationwide trend for years. The villains are not an underground network of revolutionaries posing as teachers to overthrow the U.S. government. However, the much-publicized 1983 report *A Nation at Risk: The Imperative for Educational Reform* used this analogy: "If an unfriendly foreign power had attempted to impose on America the mediocre educational performance that exists today, we might well have viewed it as an act of war. As it stands, we have allowed this to happen to ourselves."[2]

Grades no longer accurately reflect academic achievement, because many teachers have given up. Not all have given up for the same reason, of course, but how can one not be discouraged when teaching with integrity jeopardizes one's job? Too often, assigning the grade that a student has earned means that the teacher is vilified and cannot rely on the support of his or her institution. In my experience, assigning an "A–" to a graduate student often meant that he or she did not take a second course with me. A grade of "B+" actually resulted in the students' reporting me to the dean (as two students did in the first graduate course I taught). If A's are a foregone conclusion, then why grade at all?

Nationwide, educators have been making a similar point for years. For example, under the pseudonym of Peter Sacks, a journalist-turned-professor describes his "sandbox experiment" in the disturbing book *Generation X Goes to College* (1996). Here is Sacks's summary of his teaching experience:

> I undertook this Machiavellian step after my institution told me to get glowing student evaluations or I'd be out of a job. So I pandered and grade-inflated and got those glowing student evaluations, until I was awarded tenure. Then I quit, unable to endure the pandering and inflating any longer.[3]

In recent years, articles in the *Chronicle of Higher Education* have noted increasing student behavior problems in the classroom. "New Research Casts Doubt on Value of Student Evaluations of Professors," for example, cites studies claiming that "professors who want high ratings have learned that they must dumb down material, inflate grades, and keep students entertained." According to these studies, professors tend to "teach to the evaluations." It would seem obvious that this situation defeats the purpose of education. And yet, the majority of American colleges and universities utilizes such student ratings and considers them valid assessments of teaching performance.[4]

The fact that white male educators have been criticizing the use of course evaluations should refute the notion that all those who object to the system are weak teachers who use their color as an excuse. During the height of the PC debate, conservatives tried to claim the moral high ground as defenders of academic standards. According to Dinesh D'Souza, "illiberal education," which he defines as "an education in closed-mindedness and intolerance" perpetrated by a "tyranny of the minority," had replaced the previous curriculum that was more rigorous and benign.[5] And "multiculturalists"—namely, faculty of color and their supporters—are the cause of the decline. In this scenario the helpless victims of this hostile takeover are honest, hard-working students. In response, faculty of color have vigorously and successfully defended their subject matter and integrity against such unfair polemical attacks. Going relatively unnoticed, however, is the use to which teaching evaluations can be put by university administrators in such a politicized environment. According to Sacks, "Once employed as an innocuous tool for feedback about teaching, student surveys have evolved into surveillance and control devices for decisions about tenure and promotion."[6]

In the still-simmering culture wars debate, race is the X-factor. Based on substantial research as well as personal experience, I have concluded that the reliance on course evaluations—and the use to which they are put—compounds the hidden, persistent, and ignored problem of racial prejudice in the college classroom. In the published scholarship that connects multiculturalism and diversity with pedagogy, scholars are curiously reticent about race. As the first epigraph to this essay observes, academics nationwide are uncomfortable with the subject. The three "tenured radicals" who wrote the statement—two African American sociologists and a European American communications professor—constitute a handful of scholars who attempt to call the question. As they declare in the preface to their book: "We believe that in a race-conscious society, race, racism, and other ways to oppress people of color take primacy in framing discussions about diversity and the multicultural perspective."[7]

I am in complete agreement. That multiculturalism has been an educational movement for many years with minimal positive results is directly attributable to our personal discomfort with race. Avoidance in dealing with our racial prejudices—both in our racist actions toward others and in our internalization of racist beliefs—has only allowed the sore to fester. Defining "diversity" in terms of gender, class, sexual orientation, age, and physical ability (all serious issues, to be sure) has enabled academics and university administrators to circumvent the irreducible factor of racism in the United States. The stranger in my opening anecdote did not say that I was a poor teacher due to my gender or class; instead, he used what society sanctions as the easiest, most assailable marker of "minority" difference against me. In this and other potentially volatile scenarios, race is the bottom line. The three scholars have a point when they claim that, "if we can confront racism in diversity the other hurdles will be much lower."[8]

To accept these scholars' call to confront racism will mean engaging in intellectual combat. How will such open conflict affect our classroom teaching? I agree with Gerald Graff, who argues persuasively that our teaching can benefit from our most intense professional exchanges. He suggests "teaching the conflicts."[9] However, the conflicts that Graff discusses are those among colleagues outside of class. In the multicultural classroom, conflict often arises in the form of student hostility—toward the subject matter, toward each other, and at times toward the teacher. It is an obvious fact that faculty with more institutional power are better positioned to deal with such conflicts than those with less power. First, students are conditioned to equate professorial authority with the white male subject. They are inclined to credit the professor who fits this profile with being open-minded and fair, even in a very contentious classroom. Second, when their course evaluations are negative, such professors are better protected from the professional consequences.

When it comes to women of color faculty, however, too often it is an entirely different story. In many of our classrooms, conflict is unavoidable. Forefronting conflicts and openly "teaching" them, however, can play right into stereotypes about incompetent, unprofessional people of color. Suddenly, our courses are visible in the department—and they spell trouble. Student course evaluations are then used to corroborate this impression. An easy conclusion is that the "minority" colleague is an ineffective teacher, since she cannot control her class. A theory that rewards one group of practitioners can punish another; identical classroom strategies can elicit opposite results. The risks are simply not the same. This means that before ethnic women faculty subscribe to the latest wisdom in multicultural pedagogy, we should keep in mind that the theorist might not have taken our specific and multiple subjectivities into account.

The first undergraduate course I taught as a new tenured professor at a private urban university illustrates this point. At the start of the term, a white male student came into my contemporary literature class, took one look at me, and declared: "I'm against multiculturalism. I can see that I'll be against you all term." When I asked the student what he meant by multiculturalism and why he equated me with it, he simply stood his ground and said, "My father thought this way, my grandfather thought this way, and I'm not about to change!" At that moment a white female student marched up to my desk and said that she was paying good money to study American literature and I had no business including those "other" (meaning ethnic) writers. Had I allowed the conflicts raised by these students to dominate classroom discussion, the course might never have gotten off the ground.

The female student dropped my course. The male student stayed and I taught him to the best of my ability. I noted two points in his favor: he was articulate and he was not invested in being politically correct. Throughout the term, I pushed for in-depth class discussions and maintained a dialogue with each student on their weekly written assignments. By the end of the ten-week term the student wrote in a self-assessment:

> The one thing that I think will stick with me well after this quarter is over comes from Anna Lee Walters's "Apparitions." I never truly understood or realized the plight of the underclass in different cultures. Walters's description of Wanda's "physical abuse" by the shoe clerk made me realize how bad things can get. It made me realize some people need to put things on layaway just as there may be some people who need welfare and as a society we cannot and should not condemn these people for this. I now "see" that it is easy to be "one-sided" on issues when you're only told one side. Walters shows and tells me about "the other side" and it is this that I feel will stick with me perhaps for the rest of my life. . . .
>
> Overall I learned a great deal about acceptance and tolerance of other cultures as well as other cultures' literature. I don't know if that was a goal of Prof. TuSmith's when she chose the lit for this class. Nonetheless, I would just like her to know, regardless, that I feel I now have a better

understanding for cultures and the literature of cultures that I previously didn't know about or didn't care to know about. I am now much more accepting of things that are "different" from me and I thank Prof. TuSmith for this.

One remarkable thing about this testimonial is that the student came up with the details about layaway and welfare on his own. I did not privilege these social practices in class discussions nor did I remain in conflict with him throughout the term. I made sure that he read each assignment and pushed him to work in my class. My reward was that he began to think for himself.

Of course, not every hostile student of mine made such a turnaround within a few weeks. A Chicana student who gave me a hard time in my Latino/a literature course took two years before signing up for another course with me. Somehow her opinion of me had changed in her senior year. In one class session she even made the bold gesture of declaring to her white classmates (when they tried to gang up on me) that I was an excellent professor who was more than qualified to teach them African American literature. No one talked to her for the rest of the term. These classroom anecdotes indicate that conflict and confrontation could erupt at any moment in my classroom, and openly processing the issues is not a foolproof strategy when my race—in addition to the visible racial difference among my students—is a major source of conflict in the first place.

For those endowed with white male privilege and institutional power, teaching the conflicts might be an appropriate strategy to confront racism in the classroom. In fact, this would be the responsible thing to do. If more senior white faculty incorporated racial issues into their teaching, then racism can be addressed as part of the educational enterprise. This would model for students an honest and responsible way of working through the cultural baggage that they bring into the classroom. Moreover, this would alleviate some of the pressure currently sustained by faculty of color in the one or two diversity courses of a department or college. That pressure does build up in these courses is well documented by ethnic teachers and scholars.

In 1985, Johnnella Butler, an ethnic scholar in multicultural pedagogy, wrote: "The fear of being regarded by peers or by the professor as racist, sexist, or 'politically incorrect' can polarize a classroom. If the professor participates unconsciously in this fear and emotional self-protection, the classroom experience will degenerate to hopeless polarization, and even overt hostility."[10] Butler recommends "pressure-valve release" sessions to alleviate built-up tension in the classroom. These discussions work best, she asserts, "when the teacher directly acknowledges and calls attention to the tension in the class-room."[11] In a later essay on teaching about women of color, she reiterates the need for such sessions. Tension builds from the "rage, anger, or shame" that "Black and White students alike" feel in learning about the history of atrocities perpetrated against women of color in the United States. "Furthermore," she states, "all students may resent the upsetting of their neatly packaged under-standings of U.S. history and of their world."[12]

Butler's observations corroborate the grieving thesis. Given the very nature of a race- and gender-related course, classroom polarization can occur with the most aware and multiculturally adept of teachers. In terms of racial attitudes, a teacher who underestimates the classroom situation—or who has not examined his or her own racial prejudices—can easily contribute to the problem. I concur that effective teaching requires the ability to work through such tensions. Remarkably, however, this theorist, similar to others that I have consulted, never mentions the likely consequences of such intervention: namely, the negative course evaluations from students who equate pressure release sessions with a "bad" course due to the sessions' open acknowledg-ment that there was tension in the first place.

In an informative compilation of essays titled *Multicultural Teaching in the University* there is a question-and-answer section where thirteen contrib-utors are asked specific questions about multicultural teaching and conflict in the classroom. Of special note is the impressive effort that these teachers make to deal with classroom conflicts. For example, one respondent cites group eval-uation, self-evaluation, and feedback, and notes that "if unresolved feelings or unanswered questions remain, we sometimes devote a whole class session to the issues. . . ." Issues are also individually processed outside class, and then brought into the classroom for collective brainstorming. A second respondent relies on weekly reflection journals to process conflicts. As for rating the course, one respondent cites two written evaluations, plus "weekly or biweekly session evaluations . . . at the end of class periods." Another cites an "evalua-tion/feedback activity at the end of each session throughout the term for about ten minutes." This instructor also requires a written student evaluation and individual student conferences in mid-semester, as well as a final written eval-uation in addition to the one required by the university.[13]

Such self-reports indicate to me that teachers of multicultural material are often running scared. Some will go to any lengths to protect themselves from the dreaded formal student evaluations. While this is not a question of intentionally dumbing down their courses, the obvious question of time must be raised. With so much time and energy devoted to resolving conflicts and eliciting and assessing student reaction, when is the course material actually being taught? With only so much time allocated for each course—and, in my case, when a term is only nine or ten weeks long—something has to give. The multicultural teacher may find herself sacrificing every other assignment on the syllabus in order to process classroom dynamics. An initially rigorous agenda may end in minimal coverage of the subject matter. Thus, the instructor who focuses on teaching the conflicts could lose sight of his or her primary objective. Realistically, if students are required to evaluate the course on a weekly basis via journals, letters, or other written feedback, it is likely that they are not writing papers on the course content. That is, my students would be commenting on class dynamics and issues rather than engaging the literary work being studied. Students thus trained might be well-versed in processing conflicts, but they are ill prepared to read and write critiques of ethnic literature.

If avoiding conflict is irresponsible, then the same might be said of excessive attention to process. Constantly soliciting feedback can be another form of teaching to the evaluations. And yet, as I stated earlier, instructors are often left with little choice when they are held to their students' assessment of their teaching. When it comes to teaching courses with an ethnic American or Third World focus, instructors are doubly at risk. Even relatively secure full professors have discovered this through experience. After team-teaching a conflict-ridden course on Third World women, a geography professor at the University of Michigan concludes: "It is very difficult to sustain this kind of risk-fraught teaching without institutional attention and compensation. How should such efforts be rewarded? If this chapter helps to bring that question to prominence in academic discourse so that some positive institutional changes in costs, risks, and especially recognition are made, I will consider myself well rewarded."[14]

Then there is the endowed history professor at Harvard, whose stint in team-teaching "The Peopling of America" brought him student accusations of racial insensitivity. D'Souza reports:

> As for Stephan Thernstrom, he has decided, for the foreseeable future, not to offer the course. "It just isn't worth it," he said. "Professors who teach race issues encounter such a culture of hostility, among some students, that some of these questions are simply not teachable any more, at least not in an honest, critical way."[15]

In both cases, well-situated white professors discovered the risks involved in teaching culturally diverse, race-related subjects. Their logical conclusion, similar to the advice I received about course evaluations, was "to not do them." The idea that it is not worth it—meaning, "They don't pay me enough to put up with this abuse"—is a luxury that not many faculty of color can afford. In academia today, women of color are still the last hired, first fired, and must prove themselves several times over. Walking away from what we are hired to teach, which is usually connected to our color, is not an option. Besides, for me as an American literature specialist, there *is* no "safe" course. Traditional, supposedly neutral courses in the modern American novel and the American short story necessarily include ethnic writers for the simple reason that African Americans, Chicanos, and other ethnic minorities have, indeed, written novels and short stories. Alongside European American authors, there is no justification for excluding ethnic writers of color. Thus, American literature *is* multicultural literature even if this is still not accurately identified in course catalogs. Because I teach American literature and because North American society has always been multicultural, my courses are necessarily multicultural.

While white faculty cited here seem to worry about appropriate compensation for teaching "risky" courses, I am more concerned about how to do my job without being punished for doing it. In today's politically charged classrooms, the teacher's subject position is necessarily her starting point. Knowing, from years of experience, that both my race and gender made me vulnerable in front of the classroom, I once had the bright idea of team-teaching a course on American Indian literature with my visibly white husband. My diabolical scheme was to have a white man share, or perhaps help neutralize, the hostility usually directed at me. Thus, I accepted an invitation to guest teach the course at an Ivy League university. At the second class meeting an Asian American student pulled Jerry aside and told him that the students wanted him to speak, not me—even though we had informed the class at the outset that I was the primary on the team (Jerry's doctorate is in British literature). Flabbergasted, my husband invited the student to drop by our office after class. She refused to come and subsequently dropped the course.

We consider this one of the most successful courses either one of us has taught. As for the course evaluations, they were generally favorable. One point stood out, however. Even though most students rated us as a team, a few went out of their way to rate us separately. Of these, across the board Jerry's ratings were higher than mine.

For faculty women of color, professorial authority cannot be taken for granted. "English professors don't look like you" continues to be the prevalent student response to my physical presence. From this initial reaction follows a significant and at times prolonged struggle. A student may go through an entire course without coming to terms with his or her sense of what psychologists call "cognitive dissonance." There is no polite way to say it: this is racist. An insidious aspect of racism is that the racist blames the victim for not fulfilling his or her expectations. From my years of experience as an educator I find that the script tends to play out along the following lines:

— Professors are white men. You are not a white man. Therefore, you are not a professor.

— English professors are white. You are Asian American. Therefore, you cannot be an English professor.

— Asian Americans are quiet, humble, and submissive. You have strong convictions and you are not humble. Therefore, you are a failed Asian American.

This line of thinking explains why the student cited above wanted my white husband to teach what was essentially my course in American Indian literature. In her mind, the white man has the authority to teach this nonwhite literature, while the Asian American woman does not. This is a manifestation of what two women of color theorists would have called "internalized racism."[16]

Given the complexities of such interaction, ethnic students and ethnic faculty need space to work out racial issues among themselves. Under the scrutiny of white-folks-in-charge, however, this is virtually impossible. When the ethnic professor holds the ethnic student to some standard of intellectual rigor, she is likely to be cast as the villain. Her white colleagues may view her as engaging in a squabble with another "minority." Once, when an ethnic woman colleague and I asked why a graduate student was assigned my colleague's graduate course in postcolonial literature to teach, our white feminist colleagues said, "Why would you begrudge another woman of color a line on her vitae?" This viewpoint reinforces the perception that there is no distinction between women of color professors and students. A valid issue of protocol is typecast as jealousy among ethnic women.

As a visibly Asian woman in America, I know that race will continue to be a part of my life. As an ethnic literature professor, I will continue to address racial issues in my courses. Openly acknowledging that race is a problem in the classroom provides a starting point. This brings me back to the stranger who told me that I was a lousy teacher. What I said to him was, "*You* don't tell me who I am. I've had to listen to people like you all my life and I'm not about to put up with you." From a brochure, I later realized that the man had been a former president of the professional organization hosting the convention. His smug deportment suggested that he was used to dishing out such insults and getting away with it. My dramatic response obviously caught him by surprise. After a half-hearted attempt to laugh off the confrontation, the man got up to leave. I held out my hand to shake his. "Nice meeting you," I said calmly, "and see you for the next round."

Practicing the art of open confrontation has transformative potential. Deconstructing racial stereotyping requires both parties at the table. The stranger was not prepared to engage me as an equal, so he ran. In the college classroom, open discussion and active engagement among class participants is an integral part of the learning process. If issues of race prevent such give and take, the instructor must find ways to get the class past this reticence. Good teaching requires risk-taking. A good teacher encourages students to take that extra step, to venture beyond their normal levels of comfort and areas of knowledge. Collective brainstorming—one of the more effective classroom activities—does not occur when students are invested in politically correct behavior to hide their thoughts and feelings. To push, prod, and goad students beyond such a defensive posture requires a hands-on, interactive teaching strategy. In a racially charged climate such as the ethnic literature classroom, an occasional blowup is inevitable—and even healthy. Standardized evaluations applied to these courses prevent such active teaching.

Once considered progressive, anonymous course evaluations sanction racist attitudes among students, place women of color faculty in special jeopardy, and undercut the efforts of multiculturalism in higher education. Knowing that the evaluation system is flawed should be a call to action. Publicizing the problem is a first step. As committed educators, we should collectively pressure our institutions to devise a better way of assessing teaching. Being forced to compromise our standards and pedagogical goals to avoid low student evaluations is simply not an option.

NOTES

This essay was first published in *Amerasia Journal* volume 27, issue 2, summer 2001 (UCLA Asian American Studies Center).

1 Thomas Trzyna and Martin Abbott, "Grieving in the Ethnic Literature Classroom," *College Literature* 18:3 (October 1991), 1–2.

2 United States, National Commission on Excellence in Education, *A Nation at Risk: The Imperative for Educational Reform* (Washington, D.C.: GPO, 1983), 5.

3 Peter Sacks, "In Response," *Change: The Magazine of Higher Learning* 29:5 (Sept./Oct. 1997), 29. See also Peter Sacks, *Generation X Goes to College* (Chicago: Open Court, 1996).

4 "New Research Casts Doubt on Value of Student Evaluations of Professors," *Chronicle of Higher Education* (16 Jan. 1998): A12+.

5 Dinesh D'Souza, *Illiberal Education: The Politics of Race and Sex on Campus* (New York: The Free Press, 1991), 228–229.

6 Sacks, *Generation X*, 29.

7 Benjamin Bowser, Gale S. Auletta, and Terry Jones, Preface, *Confronting Diversity Issues on Campus*, ed. Bowser et al. (Newbury Park, Calif.: SAGE, 1993), xii.

8 Bowser et al., *Confronting Diversity*, xiii.

9 Gerald Graff, *Beyond the Culture Wars: How Teaching the Conflicts Can Revitalize American Education* (New York: W. W. Norton, 1992).

10 Johnnella E. Butler, "Toward a Pedagogy of Everywoman's Studies," in *Gendered Subjects: The Dynamics of Feminist Teaching*, ed. Margo Culley and Catherine Portuges (Boston: Routledge, 1985), 236.

11 Butler, "Toward a Pedagogy," 236.

12 Johnnella E. Butler, "Transforming the Curriculum: Teaching About Women of Color," in *Transforming the Curriculum: Ethnic Studies and Women's Studies*, ed. Johnnella E. Butler and John C. Walter (New York: SUNY Press, 1991), 83.

13 David Schoem et al., eds., *Multicultural Teaching in the University* (Westport, Conn.: Praeger, 1993), 293–311.

14 Ann E. Larimore, "On Engaging Students in a Multicultural Course on a Global Scale: Risks, Costs, and Rewards," in Schoem et al., 218.

15 D'Souza, *Illiberal Education*, 197.

16 Virginia R. Harris and Trinity A. Ordoña, "Developing Unity among Women of Color: Crossing the Barriers of Internalized Racism and Cross-Racial Hostility," in *Making Face, Making Soul/Haciendo Caras: Creative and Critical Perspectives by Feminists of Color*, ed. Gloria Anzaldúa (San Francisco: Aunt Lute, 1990), 309.

KARYN D. MCKINNEY

WHITENESS ON A WHITE CANVAS:

TEACHING RACE IN A PREDOMINANTLY WHITE UNIVERSITY

PHOTO: AMIR MARVASTI

Being white is, in my personal point of view, like being free.
It is like when you were a child and watched birds flying
around—swooshing down and then soaring above the
clouds—and you wish that for even a second you could
touch the sky. Well the bird probably never even thinks
about his freedom in flight, he just flies.

—Tim, a student in a race and ethnicity course[1]

Teaching race and ethnicity courses has been one of the most rewarding and challenging experiences in my academic career. In the university, I confront three groups when I teach the sociology of race and ethnicity. My most frequent interactions are with white students, who are the majority in my classes. A different type of encounter usually goes on with students of color. My interactions with the university administration and my colleagues regarding the pedagogy of race are sometimes overt, but more often they exist as unseen players in each semester's drama. Teaching race and ethnicity also causes me to be more aware of my own identity as a white, female, Southern, middle-class assistant professor of sociology.

KARYN D. MCKINNEY is an assistant professor of sociology at Pennsylvania State University, Altoona. Her research focuses on race, ethnicity, and gender. Among her scholarship is a coauthored article in the *Indiana Law Review* and a forthcoming book (coauthored with Joe Feagin) titled *The Costs of Racism* (Rowman and Littlefield, 2002).

McKinney examines student responses to her course assignment, a "racial/ethnic autobiography." She demonstrates the fine balance instructors must maintain between countering misconceptions—such as "the fiction of whiteness as a liability"—and "making the classroom as safe a place as possible to discuss issues of race."

RACIAL ENGAGEMENT IN A
PREDOMINANTLY WHITE UNIVERSITY

I begin my introductory level race and ethnicity course each semester by defining concepts and discussing theories of race and ethnicity. I do not take anything for granted at the beginning of the semester. For example, I spend part of a class period asking students why, at the beginning of a new millennium, are we still talking about race? In doing so, I try to involve them in defining the course as valuable. We move on to discussions of the social construction of race, considering issues of power, race, and racism as they relate to specific ethnic groups. At the end of the semester, I engage students in a discussion of white racialization and white privilege.[2]

For many young people in the United States, college is the first place they encounter people of different racial groups.[3] It may also be the first time they seriously question the beliefs that their parents have taught them. Thus, a course like mine is often a lightning rod for various modifications students are making to their identities.

My interactions with students of color are a concern in the predominantly white university in which I teach. This university is also located in a rural community with very little diversity. Students of color speak of their discomfort in both the campus setting as well as the community at large. I strive to be a supportive ally, so that these students may see my class as "safe." I fear these students face a unique type of pressure in my race and ethnicity courses. Despite my best intentions to avoid tokenism, students of color often become coteachers of white students in our group conversations. Even if this participation is voluntary, I am aware of the burden it places on these students.

As an untenured faculty member in my university, I have considered that the way I teach about race could affect my evaluation. Students enter my class with many preconceptions. For example, last semester a student told me that in high school, sociology was "where we sat around and talked about our opinions." I often face resentment from such students, who feel they've been duped—sociology is supposed to be "easy," and my class is too difficult. Further, because students perceive much of the course material to be "opinions," they often believe I am trying to force my opinions on them. Additionally, because some white students feel I am unfair to white people at large, I worry that they may evaluate my fairness to students poorly.

For many students, the course is not what they expect it to be. One white male student apparently desired a "tour" of other people's ethnicity, complaining: "I thought this course was going to just be about people's foods, traditions, and stuff."[4] I answered that I teach the course from more of a conflict perspective.

Unless they have taught a similar course, few of my colleagues understand the intensity of student reactions to the class. Possibly even fewer in the administration understand how difficult it is to teach the course without angering some students. Each time I begin a semester, I consider new ways to approach the class so that students do not close their minds. I struggle with how much to compromise to ease the discomfort they will surely experience, and strive to create a balance between walking on eggshells and confronting students' fears.

REVEALING WHITENESS ON A WHITE CANVAS

When I was a child, I longed to be a visual artist like my sister and father. Unfortunately, I never developed that type of talent. I did, however, enjoy paint books made up of outlines on white paper. The outlined figures were not colored in. All I had to do was to take a wet brush and "paint" the white page in order to reveal the colors of the figures.

I find the task of teaching about race in a predominantly white university to be similar, but more difficult. Most white students come to college with only the faintest outlined knowledge of who they are, racially. They know that they are "not black," "not Latino," and not of any recent immigrant group. However, they have no real substance with which to fill in their racial identity or to decipher where they fit into this country's racial hierarchy. It is a singular challenge to reveal the contours of whiteness on the white canvas of a predominantly white university.

As part of the course, students write a racial/ethnic autobiography, in which they describe how they learned about their own and others' race and ethnicity. They discuss their perspectives about racial identity and race relations, linking their personal experiences with concepts they have learned in class. After hearing the assignment, many white students approach me with incredulity, complaining that they simply do not know how to begin a discussion of race and their racial identity. This confusion has been more near panic in the rural area where I now teach than in urban settings where I previously taught. However, the discomfort white students express when required to speak of race is common across all social classes and regions.

In the autobiographies, there are often thinly veiled criticisms of me and of the course. I remind myself that while it seems their reactions are directed at me, often students are using me as a sounding board, working out ways to absorb disturbing new information. Each semester, the autobiographies serve both as a source of information for me as a researcher, and as a gauge of how students are receiving the course. Most students who disapprove register discomfort with the course in their autobiographies, rather than in person. They often explain that they like the course, but there are some things about it they disagree with. These statements perhaps reflect the fact that many students believe sociology is a subjective discipline. In race and ethnicity courses, this notion is particularly an obstacle. If the course content is supposed to be only theories and opinions, students' previously held notions about race are to them as valid as anything they read in their textbooks or hear from me. I have spent hours outside class listening to white students recounting reasons that race relations are not a concern, or that the only concern today is how whites are being victimized. No matter their stance, these students explain their arguments to me patiently, as if I have never heard them before. Sometimes their audacity is almost endearing. Other times, it is frustrating.

White students' responses to my course can be described in various ways. Most often, they deny the very existence of racism. They are equally opposed to the notion that all white people to some degree benefit from it. Ironically, many perceive that there is still disadvantage according to race, but cannot acknowledge that there is also racial advantage. Some even believe that it is whites who are disadvantaged by race today, rather than people of color. A few students carry on a running debate with me all semester, while others simply sit, silently disgruntled. Still others manifest a sense of shame for being white. Some of these students remain locked in guilt, and seek unattainable redemption through class discussions. Finally, some question their racial and ethnic identity, and even begin to see entrenched racism in society.

Researchers have found that young whites consider themselves color-blind, and see whiteness as a liability.[5] White students fail to recognize racism as not only individual-level bigotry but also institutional discrimination.[6] Other researchers have suggested the need to explore the role of whiteness in pedagogy.[7] To better understand the particular challenges faced by faculty who teach about race and ethnicity in predominantly white universities, and to devise ways to address resistance and denial, it is important to explore white students' reactions to course material. The following analysis draws on my ongoing research into young whites' conceptions of racial identity and racism.

DENIAL OF RACISM

Frequently, white students protect themselves from discomfort by arguing that racism is no longer a problem, or at least not *their* problem. For example, consider my student Seth's statements:

> I identify myself with my race. I don't think that in America, at least for white people, ethnicity is a major role. Especially because I am not of a pure ethnic background. I relate to being Scottish but I don't play the bagpipes or wear a kilt. . . . I know I am white but I don't see that as being very important unless other people make [it] that way. For example, I am so tired of hearing how the "white man" has screwed everyone [over] everywhere. I personally am not responsible for any discrimination or hatred towards anyone and I am tired of being referred to in those terms. . . . I think that my race gets blamed for the problems of other races in this country much more so than necessary. I understand what has happened to other races by mine, but these things happened many years ago and I am tired of being blamed for the mistakes of my ancestors. Also, I think that minorities (including females) blame white males for their problems in the workplace, etc. Again, I know these things happen but to put the blame on all white males like they are some sort of disease is wrong. These extremist groups of people are the biggest hypocrites in the world. They want equality but mean to attain it through inequality.

Students frequently express such ideas and few believe racism is a major concern today. Another student, Julia, turns an example of white dominance on her predominantly white campus into the fault of students of color. She believes in a meritocratic campus situation where people of color are free to choose to participate in campus activities. When Julia sees that they are not participating, she perceives them as troublemakers: "[T]hey choose to segregate themselves. . . . It truly sickens me that people sit and complain, but yet they are not doing anything to change it. . . . It truly frustrates [me] that people cry wolf with discrimination, when the truth is they do it to themselves."

Similarly, Will believes most claims of racism are false:

> I think more minorities bitch and complain more than they do anything else about their problems. Most people are not out to get someone because

of their race. I know this for a fact because the people that I hang out with view people of different races as the same as one another. I know that there are people out there who like to make life difficult for others. . . . But everyone is not out to get minorities. There is a problem, but blaming people who are not racist is totally wrong. They like to say, "it's because of people like you that I am the way I am." This really pisses me off mainly because I would not do anything to discriminate against anyone. If someone has it harder, they need to put forth a little more effort to reach their goals. I am sure I would have to do the same if I lived . . . somewhere like China or Japan. The point is that these minorities who constantly force into their minds that everyone is exploiting them are digging the hole they are in deeper and deeper. If other minorities can do it, then others should be able to as well.

Carefully omitting group names, Will suggests that in our meritocracy, hard work should overcome any obstacle—some "model" groups have succeeded in the United States, so all of them should be able to.

Finally, Iris articulates ahistorical denial by saying that "There are a few blacks in the class that feel that they can't get a job or will ever be able to move up in the world due to the fact that they are black. They bring up the fact that they were slaves, etc. They weren't slaves and slavery hasn't been around for many, many years. Yeah, maybe their great great grandparents were slaves, but that was a long time ago."

LIABILITIES OF WHITENESS

Because they have difficulty seeing existing racism, some white students assert that the real racial problem today is that whites are victimized, particularly by affirmative action. Julia tells a story that is common in the autobiographies:

I remember when I was applying to colleges, I wondered why on every application it asked your race and religion. . . . I went and asked my guidance counselor and she told me that schools have to fill quotas. I thought that was the most ridiculous thing I have ever heard. I never knew that schools based these important decisions on how many slots there are to fill. Affirmative action began to take on a whole different meaning. I thought it was insane to let an unqualified person into a school because they are required to. I know that I worked very hard, and I thought that all that work would pay off with an acceptance letter. I was wrong. I know a girl named Erica that attends [another university]. She is Chinese and relatively smart. I know that my SATs and grades were a lot higher than hers, but I was rejected to [that school] and she was not. I felt like I had been the loser in this rat race. I think that deep down she knows that she was the product of the quota system, but she enjoys the advantage. I began to have the feeling that being a white female, I was at a severe disadvantage. I did not seem to be getting any breaks.

Many young white students believe that being white put them at a disadvantage in university admissions. They fail to realize that universities do not admit students only as a "reward" to them. They also admit students based on what the student will contribute to the university.

Some white students not only believe they have already been the victims of "reverse racism," but forecast that they may be victimized in seeking employment. For example, Jerry argues:

I am only a sophomore in college, but my eyes have already been opened to the way the world works. When graduating high school and going through the scholarship process, I thought for the first time that it would not be too bad to be black. Had I been black I would be a National Merit Scholar and had I been black I would not be taking a small loan to be here. Several of my very close friends who I had dreamed of attending college with since we were young were not accepted to the [state university]. Mostly because of their own lack of effort in high school, but being white and from a decent family did not greatly increase their chances. I am sure that when I do graduate college and attempt to trade bonds, on Wall Street, I will probably for the second time in my life wish that I were black.

Not only does Jerry believe he has been treated unfairly as a white person, he goes further to state that he has actually wished to be black. This statement can only be made by a person who both denies continuing racism against African Americans, and also sees whiteness as a liability.

Another liability of whiteness revealed in the autobiographies is a sense of empty ethnicity. For many white students, my course reveals that they know little about their own ethnic backgrounds. This may lead them to envy students of color, or it can motivate them to try to research their heritage. In some cases the course makes them more aware of being white. After students realize they know little about their ethnicity, they are typically left with only a racial identification. For example, Ned writes:

"What am I?" This is a question I have never been asked before. It is probably a good thing because the only way I would have known to answer that question before would have been "white." And now I have been asked what is white and I do not know. I cannot begin to describe to you what it means to be white. The only way I can think of describing my whiteness is to say that I am not Black or Indian or whatever else. I cannot give you a definition of white. Now I ask myself: Who can I be if I don't know what I'm being?

For these students, whiteness lacks substantive content that is easily accessible as cultural resources. Today, young whites who reject white supremacist discourse and know little of their ethnic heritage are left with a "mirrored" whiteness: whiteness defined in terms of what it is not. On a predominantly white campus, with few "others," whiteness may therefore remain invisible.

Then there are the students who feel a lack of "culture" and believe that being white is "boring." This is what Lori says about her vague sense of being "European":

> My family is European. My grandfather's ancestors were Irish. That just means he got toasted for St. Patrick's Day and developed an affinity for green. My grandmother on my real father's side (he died before I was born) once told me that I was related to Charlemagne. That might have meant something except that at that point I had no idea who he was. Is my world influenced internally because of ethnicity? Nope. I don't celebrate anything that isn't inherently "American" or have customs that I have to explain. . . . I have no idea when my ancestors came over on the boat or whether they owned slaves or what. But I have slowly begun to see privileges that I have because I am part of a dominant culture. . . . In a country whose latest fad is rediscovering their roots, I am grasping at straws. There are people who could not shed their ethnicity no matter how hard they might try. I have nothing to take on in this category. I have no new facet to add to my identity. . . . I never had any "specialty dishes" to bring on cultural awareness day. I feel neutral, plain about my ethnicity. It is only recently that I have realized that others may not see my race that way. I took it for granted that I fit into the apple pie, girl next door, American backdrop. My last name is "Smith." It's like "being everybody else." Or not.

During the course of the semester, students often analyze their names, appearance, personality, and family traditions, searching for any indication of their ethnic heritage. Lori offers her last name as evidence of her being "plain." Similar to Lori, Stephanie writes: "When I think of my life, I am almost disappointed that I do not have more culture in my heritage. Being born in the United States to white parents also born here is almost boring to me."

One might say that this cultural envy is the pinnacle of white privilege: not only do whites receive social and economic privileges, but some have the audacity to overlook them and to resent their status as part of the dominant group. While it is because of their dominant position that these white young people are able to construct whiteness as a liability more than a privilege, their doing so marks a shift from the attitudes of white people in the generations immediately preceding them. Rarely would a person in those generations have spoken of being "disappointed" to have been born white in the United States. The social construction of whiteness has transformed in this generation so that whiteness no longer seems to be as rewarding as it once did.

EPIPHANIES OF WHITENESS

As a result of taking the course, some students have what could be called epiphanies of whiteness. Jennifer comes to an understanding of white privilege through hearing stories of African American students:

> The more class progressed the more I learned about myself. I realized that compared to the other races and cultures in the class, I knew nothing about my own race and ethnicity. I considered myself white and couldn't describe it to someone or put a value on it. I never thought about it because I never had to. I was never discriminated against because of it, and if I received privileges because of it, I was so accustomed to it that I didn't even notice. I began to realize through the stories told by the African American students, that I never had to worry about being accused of shoplifting, or fear police, or even be forbidden to live in a particular neighborhood. My race wasn't a factor in my life, but I began to realize the impact that my race had on others' lives.

Two other students also came to define whiteness through an understanding of white privilege. Beth explains: "Whiteness, to me, is not having to think about being white. I have nothing to prove to society, nobody will look at me and pass a judgement on my entire race on the basis of my individual actions, and I can make myself invisible in a majority of situations." Sawyer sees white privilege both in society at large and in the university:

> Society is much less likely to doubt a white person's word than a black person's, especially if their words are conflicting. . . . Also, we are viewed as being generally less lazy, more intelligent, and more competent. I believe that in general, it would be easier for a white person to find a high-

paying job than an equally qualified black person would. I find that in college, that black students tend to have to prove themselves and their eligibility to be there more than white students do.

Finally, two students who began the course resistant to information about racism changed some of their views over time. Ned ended his paper this way:

> Throughout this class a lot of my ideas, opinions, feeling, and intentions have changed. . . . I was never taught to feel that way [racist], especially not by my parents, but I also have never learned not to feel that way. One of the main reasons that this class has made changes in me is because I am being educated. . . . I now know that as a white male I receive privileges that others have never had. I also understand that those privileges are what cause me not to see the hardship, unfairness, and inequality of others. . . . I feel that education will be the only way to overcome the trouble. . . . I really want [my son] to grow up with much more of an open mind than I did. If for no other reason but the fact that he is a white male and will soon be the minority.

Rianne also came to college with strong negative feelings and family influences about people of other ethnic groups. She writes:

> The diversity at the university level was phenomenal. . . .You can probably guess the remarks made by my family: "How funny it would be if you got a black roommate." Honestly, at the time I was petrified of this. . . . In retrospect, I realize this was only because I knew nothing about the "other" races. . . . one thing was different compared to high school, I was actually exposed to the "other" races. . . . I would try to instigate conversations with other minority groups, but would inevitably fail. Could this mean my father had been right? At the time I concluded just this. However, now I realize that I was practicing the benefits of being white. I was talking to other groups as if they were like me. In other words, I did not understand why they could not be like me. . . . The most recent learning experience I have had is being in your class. . . . The most important information that I think I have learned from this class is the notion of the benefits associated with being white. . . . This class has given me the base knowledge about other races and ethnic groups to better understand what is going on around me, rather than scapegoat the "other" groups. . . . In our world today, not understanding people's differences gives us an automatic disadvantage.

Partially due to her class experiences, Rianne is able to insightfully analyze the most micro-level workings of white privilege.

SEEING RACISM

Some students write that because of the course, they have begun to see racism in society when perhaps they did not believe it existed before. Sawyer writes:

> Education about racism has allowed me to see racism more clearly. Although being white only gives me an outside view upon black people, I still get to see instances of racism. I see white people hesitant to sit next to black men on the bus. Sometimes people will purposely go into a store to get out of the way of an oncoming group of blacks when they will not for a group of whites. I even see store workers come to assist me when both of us know that a black customer was there first. Knowing about such racist acts allows me to tell the worker that the other person was there first and not me.

Another young man, Ben, describes in detail an experience he had when he returned home for Christmas:

> I was all about sharing my experiences with the remainder of my family. . . . Everything was fine until I asked my grandmother about my cousin Jill who married an African American. Her expression immediately turned sour and she said, "I don't want to have anything to do with Jill." Much to my surprise, I retorted, "Well Grandma, you could be a great-grandmother." She said with more conviction, "I don't want anything to do with Jill and any bastard nigger children she may have spawned!" My mouth gasped to the table. . . . It wasn't as if I hadn't heard that word before, but it sounded so evil coming from the mouth of my own flesh and blood. To know that your own grandmother harbored such potent racism and possibly even instilled her views on my father was too much for me to handle. It ruined my Christmas. . . . Come this Christmas she is planning on visiting my family. . . . I hope she can control herself, for I don't think I can say the same for myself. After what my Cultural Diversity class has done for me, I cannot tolerate overt and/or subliminal racism.

Upon returning home, students may find that their views regarding race no longer match those of their families. Another student, Rhonda, discusses how she has ended friendships with other whites that she realizes are racist:

> Before taking this class I would have said that anyone who told me I had privileges because I was white was crazy. Now I think that it is a true statement. I have gained a much deeper understanding of racial issues through this class. . . . Knowledge is power. One of the sorriest statements about my race is that the majority of white people just don't get it. They don't

understand the pain and frustration that people of color go through every day of their lives. If you try to explain this as a fact of some people's lives, most white people, in my experience, look at you like you've lost it. I think that in the future I expect most white people to remain apathetic to racial issues, because for them the status quo is working just fine. For me the most important thing I can do is to educate the people around me.

Being in the class has helped to convince Rhonda that racism is a "fact of some people's lives," and she feels a sense of responsibility to try to educate other whites.

A WHITE WOMAN FROM THE SOUTH

Teaching about race allows me to know students in a way I do not when teaching other courses. I believe that the opposite is also true—students come to know me in a different way, whether or not this is my intent. This past semester, a white male student told me and then wrote in his autobiography that he does not think he can learn about race from a "white woman from the South." I wrote back to him a treatise in which, while trying to remain impersonal, I encouraged him to reconsider his views of a notable North–South difference in race relations today. I added that any difference may be more attributable to differences between whites who have grown up in rural versus urban areas. Still, the challenge he posed to my qualifications based solely on my identity reminded me that I am not racially or regionally unmarked in the classroom, and that my identity impacts how my message is received.

At the end of the semester when I teach this class, I usually receive e-mails from students thanking me for the course. Some students are unequivocally positive. Usually, these are the white students who made up the choir for me, the reluctant preacher. Others, perhaps the more candid, thank me for helping them think about things differently, but also voice disagreements with some of the course content, one last time. I find myself wondering if writing to thank me was a pretense to remind me that I had not convinced them of the necessity of considering race and racism.

Teaching about race and racism creates a situation in which all the normal considerations of pedagogy are magnified. It is not enough simply to be accessible; I feel I must be willing to spend hours discussing class issues with students. It is not sufficient to be open-minded; I am required to listen calmly as students recite views that in other settings would anger me. Finally, it is often not enough to be fair. I must also find ways to praise and encourage even those students who refuse to learn.

When speaking with students, for whom class discussions of racism are perhaps the first they have had away from their family dinner tables, we instructors must carefully define our terms. It is sometimes because of a confusion between individual and institutional racism that white students believe they personally are being called racist in race and ethnicity courses. Because they confound the terms "race" and "ethnicity," white students draw false parallels that cast whiteness as an apparent liability.[8]

In order to challenge structural racism, whites must relearn what it means to be white. Perhaps the best venue for this re-education is the college classroom. Antiracist instructors should place U.S. and global race relations in a historical context so that the fiction of whiteness as a liability is disrupted. We must be certain not only to point out the seriousness of the problem of racism, but also suggest how whites may become antiracist allies to people of color. It is crucial that young whites do not leave a course on racism believing either that there is nothing they can do—or that simply by taking the course, they have done all they should do to dismantle racism.

Finally, instructors who teach about race must recognize what students cite as one of the enduring obstacles to becoming active in antiracism: fears of social awkwardness or racial tension. One student, Kim, discussed this fear:

> The first few times our class met, all I could do was sit there and think how stupid everyone was and wonder why they didn't realize that everything they were saying about racism and discrimination was just a facade. As the class continued to meet . . . I began to think that maybe I was the one with the wrong idea about [it] all. I used to have such a strong opinion about it all, but now I am more confused. I now think that in a way it is unfair for me to even speak my opinion to anyone else because I couldn't possibly know what it is like to be someone of a different race. It is because I am white that I do not see racism as a problem in our country.

Other students express discomfort in offering their views in class for fear that they will be seen as racist. Although some may use this as an excuse, we as teachers have a responsibility to try not to alienate the white students who are part of our classrooms. Yet we have a conflicting duty to combat the denial of white privilege that is so evident in the words of young whites. It is important that instructors make the classroom as safe a place as possible to discuss issues of race. However, we who teach about race should not try to remove all racial tension from classroom discussions, because written and verbal expression of these concerns can be enlightening for young whites, and beneficial for people of color. As the autobiographies show, white students respond to courses on race and ethnicity in many different ways. We must try to understand and address these reactions without imposing a monolithic view on students that stifles the learning that only begins in our classrooms.

NOTES

1 Quotations from student papers on four campuses are reprinted by permission of those students. Names and other identifying characteristics have been changed to protect student privacy. I am indebted to the students who gave their written permission allowing me to use their words.

2 Michael Omi, "Racialization in the Post–Civil Rights Era," in *Mapping Multiculturalism*, ed. Avery Gordon and Christopher Newfield (Minneapolis: University of Minnesota Press, 1996), 178–186; Peggy McIntosh, "White Privilege and Male Privilege: A Personal Account of Coming to See Correspondences Through Work in Women's Studies," in *Race, Class and Gender: An Anthology*, ed. Margaret L. Andersen and Patricia H. Collins (Belmont, Calif.: Wadsworth Publishing Company, 1998), 94–105.

3 Mary C. Waters, "Optional Ethnicities: For Whites Only?" in *Race, Class, and Gender*, 403–412.

4 bell hooks, *Black Looks: Race and Representation* (Boston: South End Press, 1992).

5 Charles Gallagher, "White Racial Formation: Into the Twenty-First Century," in *Critical White Studies: Looking Behind the Mirror*, ed. Richard Delgado and Jean Stefancic (Philadelphia: Temple University Press, 1997), 6–11.

6 Joyce King, "Dysconscious Racism: Ideology, Identity, and Miseducation." in *Critical White Studies*, 128–132.

7 Henry Giroux, "Racial Politics and the Pedagogy of Whiteness," in *Whiteness: A Critical Reader*, ed. Mike Hill (New York: New York University Press, 1998), 294–316.

8 Robert Blauner, "Talking Past Each Other: Black and White Languages of Race," in *Race and Ethnic Conflict*, ed. Fred L. Pincus and Howard J. Ehrlich (Boulder, Colo.: Westview Press, 1994), 27–34.

RAJINI SRIKANTH

GIFT WRAPPED OR PAPER BAGGED?:

PACKAGING RACE FOR THE CLASSROOM

This essay is a recounting. It's a report of the sudden fierceness with which the issue of race seized my pedagogy, of my captivity to its power, of my gradual release from its hold, and of my now current "comfortable" accommodation with its urgency. In the fall of 1999, a majority of students in my graduate seminar the "Teaching of Literature" staged a minor revolt. They were fed up with politics, they declared, frustrated by what they saw as my preoccupation with questions of race in literature. About midway through the semester, they delivered a passionate outburst of their objections. Before the class met again the following week, I wrote them a twelve-page letter as a response. That letter was the first time that I had seriously articulated, both to myself and to others, the intersection of aesthetics and politics in my teaching, with specific reference to the politics of race. The students felt that I had thrust race upon them; their reaction made me interrogate the effectiveness of my approach and made me examine the strengths and limitations of my pedagogy.

After much reflection, I came to the conclusion that I would have to rethink my method of confronting students with questions of race and craft

RAJINI SRIKANTH is an assistant professor of English at the University of Massachusetts, Boston. Her coedited works include *Contours of the Heart* (creative writing and photography by South Asian Americans and Canadians); *A Part, Yet Apart* (multidisciplinary essays on South Asian Americans); *Bold Words: A Century of Asian American Writing;* and *White Women in Racialized Spaces.*

Srikanth writes that when she attempted to approach her graduate seminar from a racial standpoint, students reacted with "resistance, frustration, and anger." She argues that by approaching race obliquely and being more accommodating of her students, she has reclaimed authority and control of the classroom.

and employ a more subtle approach. At the same time, I wondered whether I was capitulating to the unwillingness of the white students (of the fourteen students in the seminar, all but one were white) to acknowledge and deal with the pernicious hold of race in our lives. After having taught the seminar a year later with a less race-immersive approach, I feel comfortable in saying that my willingness to "soften" my style has given me greater power and authority and made me a more formidable advocate of confronting issues of race in the classroom. Yet employing this altered tactic is by no means an irrevocable decision; I fully expect the seminar to metamorphose with every offering, my pedagogy seeking the changing nooks and crannies in each new batch of students, searching for the spaces in which to settle and take hold in the frontline of classroom dynamics.

ALL DESCRIPTION IS POLITICAL

I teach at an urban commuter campus. The graduate student body is largely white, although the undergraduate student body reflects the racial and ethnic diversity of Boston, and, in addition, a healthy mix of immigrant and U.S.–born students. The majority of students who take the teaching of literature seminar are contemplating careers in education—teaching either at the high school or community college level (a smaller number wish to continue with doctoral study and a career in higher academe). Therefore, what they study in my seminar is not entirely for their consumption alone. I continuously enjoin them to consider the cultural and demographic makeup of the classrooms in which they might or hope to find themselves and to reflect thoughtfully on *how* they, as teachers, will construct knowledge for their students. I make very clear to the students that this is not a "how-to" course. While we do discuss strategies for opening discussion on specific texts or alleviating discomfort with teaching poetry, the mode of the course is perhaps best described as "critical interrogation." Seminar participants are asked to dwell on the role of literature in the sociocultural fabric of the United States. They are asked to probe their fundamental assumptions about important social forces and to determine the impact of these assumptions on their pedagogy. Toward these ends, they read such scholars as Terry Eagleton, for his stance that the term "literature" itself comes loaded with unexamined value judgments; Edward Said, for the ways in which the nonwestern Other is constructed as the uncivilized and irrational foil to the West's conception of itself as civilized and rational; Stanley Fish, for his position that we interpret texts on the basis of a set of assumptions shared by a community of interpreters and that these assumptions are contextual; bell hooks, for her passionate call to make the classroom the site of transgression and revolutionary thinking; Gerald Graff, for his opinion that not all students of literature come to the subject through a love of language, that in fact for many students the motivation to study literature lies in the controversies surrounding literary texts and that in teaching these controversies one shows the relevance of literature to life; and Raymond Williams, for his analysis of the deep relationship between class and the hegemony of certain types of sociocultural values.[1] In all of these interrogations of how we come to know what we know—that is, in the analysis of the institutional structures that shape knowledge—I urge students to consider the role of race.

I've been asked by some of my colleagues whether this self-probing within the context of an "obvious" politicization of literature ultimately equips students with the tools they will need to stand up in front of a classroom and lead a discussion on, say, John Updike's short story "A & P" or Emily Dickinson's poem "Because I could not stop for death—." I take my colleagues' question seriously. After all, one cannot deny that a course on the teaching of literature ought to help students understand how language is used and why it is used in certain ways and, further, enable students to find the means to shape such understanding in *their* prospective students. For instance, what image is evoked by "windhover," the word that Gerard Manley Hopkins coins to describe the flight of the falcon, or how does one discuss with students the sexually laden language in the closing lines of Richard Wright's short story "The Man Who Was Almost a Man"? Of course, we talk about such literary matters in the teaching of literature seminar. But this is not all we do; nor is it what we do primarily. The methodological inquiry takes place against the backdrop of philosophical or pedagogical inquiry, and quite frequently the backdrop becomes the foreground.

Like Salman Rushdie, I believe that "redescribing a world is the necessary first step toward changing it."[2] And like Jean-Paul Sartre I hold that literature is an art form that necessitates foregrounding rather than silencing its politics: "The serious error of pure stylists is to think that the word is a gentle breeze which plays lightly over the surface of things, grazing them without altering them . . . To speak is to act; anything which one names is already no longer quite the same; it has lost its innocence."[3]

That race plays a central role in my teaching is less a factor of my being a woman of color and more a function of my desire to spotlight one of the deepest fissures in U.S. society.[4] Elsewhere in the world other imperatives organize societies: religion in the Middle East, ethnicity in the Balkans, civil liberties in totalitarian regimes, for example. My consciousness of race as a significant social force in the United States came to me only in my late twenties; in India, my identity was constructed along parameters of class, degree of westernization, regional affiliation, and, to a lesser extent, religion. Now, after twenty-five years in the United States, it is clear that race has become predominant and deeply imbued within my identity.

Before coming to the University of Massachusetts in Boston, where I have taught since September 1998, I worked for a year at an elite prep school. There I taught a new course in multiethnic American literature. All fourteen seniors who signed up for the course identified themselves as students of color or as multiracial. During the previous year, they had lobbied vociferously for such a course. The readings included Native American, African American, Asian American, and Latino/a texts. The year-long course was one of the most tumultuous and stimulating that I have ever taught. From the outset, the students set the direction of the course, and, because their agenda accorded with mine, I did not have to justify to myself the validity of an approach that took as given the intersection between aesthetics and politics, in this case the politics of race. The students had spent several years being trained in formalist methods, largely through the examination of Eurocentric literature, and were therefore skilled practitioners of close reading—the practice of looking at a text as a self-contained literary object and of paying particular attention to how language and other artistic elements are used within the text. Thus, their desire to view literature through the lens of their politicized perspectives as students of color in an overwhelmingly privileged white environment was intertwined with a sophisticated understanding of literary craft. They belied the view that a political reading of literature comes at the expense of an appreciation of literary technique. The students were passionate and articulate, bold and brutally honest. An African American male student admitted that he had never thought of Asian Americans as sexual beings and that Shawn Wong's "Eye Contact" was a revelation to him.[5] Multiracial students fiercely objected to statements by their peers that lumped all whites as racist. An African girl from Botswana confessed her puzzlement at the anger and bitterness she detected in most African American literature; while acknowledging similar hostile feelings on her part about the British, whose colonization of Botswana ended in 1966, she also spoke of the intricate and myriad ways in which the English language and culture pervaded her being. Her classmates were thus able to understand differences between the legacies of slavery and colonization.

The discussions were eruptive and heady. At the end of every class period, I felt depleted but enormously gratified. Those students gave me a glimpse of the truly transformative power of literature. It was this vision and hope that I carried with me to U Mass Boston. After all, I reasoned, if literature has such transformative potential, what better audience to demonstrate that potential to than a group of prospective teachers of literature? And thus it was that I carried the banner of race into my graduate teaching of literature seminar.

THE TEACHING OF LITERATURE:
RACE HEAVY VERSUS RACE "LITE"

The two offerings of the graduate seminar were a year apart. With the exception of one woman of color, the students in the first seminar were white, and they were on average in their mid-twenties. The primary texts we worked with in this seminar included Joseph Conrad's *Heart of Darkness*, William Faulkner's "The Bear," Shakespeare's *The Tempest*, Mary Shelley's *Frankenstein*, Frank Chin's *Donald Duk*, and Nella Larsen's *Passing*. *Heart of Darkness* describes the late nineteenth-century journey of a British seaman down the River Congo into Belgium controlled territory, and Conrad has been savagely attacked by Nigerian novelist Chinua Achebe for his racist depiction of Africa as a dark land of unimaginable savagery. "The Bear" is at one level a hunting and male coming-of-age story, but at another level it is a fierce indictment of slavery. *The Tempest* focuses on Prospero, the Duke of Milan, and his young daughter Miranda, stranded on an island in the Bahamas due to the treachery of the Duke's brother. *Frankenstein*, published in 1818, explores the limits of man's learning and arrogance and studies such complex subjects as the creator's responsibility for his creation, the human need for companionship, and the criteria of monstrosity. *Donald Duk* describes the growing pride in a Chinese American teenager of what it means to be descended from men who built the transcontinental railroad. *Passing* is a glimpse into the 1920s phenomenon of some high-society African Americans passing for white. Also part of the curriculum were short stories and poems from a range of authors and periods. Secondary material was largely of the left-leaning camp, and primarily centered on race. I erred in confining my secondary readings to this narrow ideological framework, as became apparent to me later.

As the course progressed, students began to reveal in subtle ways their discomfort with the material. Their resistance peaked after reading Ronald Takaki's analysis of *The Tempest*. Takaki contextualizes the play historically and advances the thesis (buttressed by sixty-four footnotes from primary sources) that the play is an allegory for the English colonization of the New World. Although I had never suggested to the students that this was the only way in which to view *The Tempest*, many of them assumed that my reason for assigning the Takaki reading was precisely that I saw it as a definitive interpretation of the play. In fact, I included Takaki because I was reasonably certain that the students would not have encountered a postcolonialist reading of the play and would therefore find it intriguing.[6]

Takaki, however, became my undoing. The thrust of my graduate students' objection to him was that he was a historian by training, and therefore what could he know about literature? Although not every student saw his essay as irrelevant, a critical mass of them did. It provided the stimulus for an avalanche of criticism. One student, an immigrant from Poland, felt that discrepancies of power and discrimination exist the world over, that in other societies these practices fall along lines of religion or ethnicity or national origin. So why make such a to-do about race? No society is free from its defective practices, he declared, so let's get on with the business of literature and literary appreciation and not become embroiled in controversies of power.

A second student, an immigrant from Ireland, found the issue of colonization resonated with his own experiences. However, this same student wondered whether all the talk about race was healthy. He believed that students in a South Boston classroom (predominantly white in its demographics) might turn against a teacher who brought up race too frequently. Several other students shared this view. They felt that in certain classrooms in the Boston area raising the issue of race would only compound the stickiness of race relations and heighten tensions within the classroom. In environments with few students of color, such a focus on race could result in white students directing their ire against the students of color, they said. This view echoes conservative scholars Thomas Sowell and Dinesh D'Souza, who conclude that "racial conflict occurred at those schools with strong liberal pro-diversity and pro-affirmative action policies."[7]

The one person of color in the class felt that the focus on race came at the expense of a focus on other injustices—particularly, sexism. She was an Asian American (Indian American, to be precise) from California and said that she had always been part of a multiethnic and multiracial environment. She didn't see what all the fuss was about. She thought that the class had paid insufficient attention to gender relations; this was the area, not race relations, in which she had suffered the most oppression.

That the majority of students in the first seminar were challenging me was obvious. For a brief period, I wondered whether my being a woman of color had anything to do with the boldness of their confrontation. But dwelling on that possibility was not going to lead me anywhere. Instead, I was interested in incorporating their outburst into the structure of the course and making it illuminate one of the class's primary objectives; that the process of self-interrogation is something in which both students *and* the teacher must engage. My letter to my students was my first step toward making a change in my practice. Writing the letter enabled me to uncover some of my deepest motivations and discover which pedagogical imperatives I was unwilling to compromise. It was a manifesto of sorts; in providing me the opportunity to articulate a portrait of myself as a teacher, it also freed me to contemplate the ways in which I would be prepared to modify that portrait. Here are some excerpts:

> I focus on race not because it is my pet peeve or my only interest in literature, but because I believe that it provides the most challenging platform on which to initiate discussion of the volatile dynamics embedded in situations in which we will invariably find ourselves embroiled at regular or intermittent points in our teaching career. In learning to negotiate the minefield of race, I reasoned, one could pick up the skills necessary to negotiate through any minefield—for example, gender, class, sexuality, and religion. . . .
>
> One of the most interesting poets . . . is Adrienne Rich, who made a journey from writing poetry that was highly acclaimed for its stylistic fidelity and conformity to the tradition of the old masters to writing poetry that is unabashedly political. W. H. Auden praised the poems in her award-winning first collection for being "neatly and modestly dressed." The poems, he noted approvingly, "speak quietly but do not mumble, respect their elders but are not cowed by them, and do not tell fibs."[8] David Zuger speaks of Rich's transformation from this decorous writer to a "poet of prophetic intensity and visionary anger bitterly unable to feel at home in a world 'that gives no room / to what we dreamt of being.'" . . . If, like Rich, we see literature as the "bomb that rips the family home apart," as that

which creates turbulence, then it is likely that we will teach literature in the same way.[9]

Lest the letter be seen as a defensive move, let me quickly put that thought to rest. An important element of my pedagogy involves leading potential teachers to recognize that they must be willing to question their own assumptions and perhaps even to modify them. The injunction becomes tricky, admittedly, if students see themselves as having more power than the teacher and somehow get the impression that challenging the teacher is their right, and that the administrative power structure will support them in their efforts to undermine the teacher's approach. And if that teacher happens to be a woman in a male-dominated classroom, or a person of color in a white-dominated classroom, then the teacher may often feel under tremendous pressure to accommodate her students' demands. Thus, while I advocate the mode of negotiation and accommodation, I do so fully cognizant of the complex ways in which these approaches must be practiced. The teacher's willingness to negotiate must never be seen as a gesture of capitulation; rather, it must be seen to proceed from a position of strength and security, almost as though the teacher were saying to her students, "Okay, I acknowledge that you take issue with my approach. Because we entered this classroom committed to ensuring that learning takes place within *all* of us, I am willing to change. Are you?" The last question is the critical one, and the students should see clearly that the teacher's readiness to respond to the students' resistance must be accompanied by their corresponding readiness to engage with the teacher's perspective.[10]

Having made clear my pedagogical orientation in my letter, I was now able to engage the task of addressing the students' specific objections. I made four significant changes between the two offerings of the course. First, I included secondary material that presents views on literature and teaching that are distinctly different from those I hold. I had naively believed, in my first attempt, that students would take me at my word when I announced that I welcomed opposing points of view in the classroom—that I in fact appreciated controversy as a constructive mode of education. I had hoped that they would be provoked by the poststructuralist secondary readings—critiquing traditional and orthodox cultural institutions, practices, and ideas, and interrogating systems of thought that preserve the status quo and resist change—and would debate the ideas presented in them. Instead, the students told me that they saw the readings as an attempt on my part to indoctrinate them into a certain way of thinking. They felt themselves constrained, believing that if they disagreed with the views presented in the readings they would invite my displeasure and see it reflected in their grades. Recalling their early discomfort in verbalizing their intellectual disagreements, I realized how unreasonable I had been in expecting them to trust my enthusiasm for constructive argument. Thus, on the second attempt at teaching the course, I gave *evidence* of my fondness for dissent by including writings by literary scholars who valued approaches that were formalist—that is, focused on craft—and who privileged aesthetics over politics. Conservative thinkers they read include Harold Bloom, T. S. Eliot, and Matthew Arnold.; in a similar vein, but not exactly conservative, they also read Helen Vendler and Susan Sontag, who questions whether interpretation is an appropriate response to literature. That I was right to make the change became clear to me when students plunged into spirited debate, juxtaposing ideologically opposed readings against one another. No longer did they feel the necessity to read *me*; instead, they turned their attention to the secondary material.

The second significant change is that I heighten rather than diminish the time I spend in explaining the politics inherent in the act of teaching literary texts. I underscore the deeply political nature of my teaching, but I do so in the context of letting students know that this is a *choice* I make, not an approach that I have had thrust upon me; I remind them that they too will have to make choices. In this revised version of the course, the first two course sessions are characterized by a running commentary on the political underpinning of every decision I have taken in putting together the syllabus and discussing with them the material for this course. I demonstrate, perhaps excessively, the self-examination I bring to teaching, in the hope that they will be convinced of the usefulness of doing the same for the courses that they will teach.

In both courses—first and second versions—I began by engaging students in a discussion of how to teach the poem "Facing It" by Yusef Komunyakaa. The poem's speaker records the complex emotions that overwhelm him as he stands before the Vietnam Veterans' Memorial. The poem is rich in form and content and permits a discussion that encompasses both these aspects of literary analysis. However, what I find most appealing about it is that it enables me to demonstrate economically several types of pedagogical decisions I make. The poem deals with race in a rather indirect and perhaps even contradictory fashion. One can teach the poem quite effectively without highlighting the issue of race, but one can also teach the poem to engage it. It begins with the lines "My black face fades, / hiding inside the black granite." Some students see "black face" as not necessarily referring to an African American speaker but as the color the speaker's face takes on when reflected by the highly polished black granite surface of the memorial. A not unlikely reading. But this line, when viewed against other lines toward the end of the poem—"A white vet's image floats / closer to me, then his pale eyes / look through mine. I'm a window"—suggests that the speaker is African American, because he is drawing attention to the skin color of a veteran who is not. Then there is the question of the lines "his pale eyes / look through mine." Do they mean that the white vet doesn't "see" the black vet and looks right through him as though they have nothing in common, or do the lines mean that the white vet and black vet have a great deal in common and the white vet sees *with* the eyes of the black vet, that the black vet is the white vet's window into the war? Komunyakaa's poem, in its unobtrusive treatment of race, places the onus on the teacher of whether or not to dwell on the issue. Even as I bring up race, I tell them that this is a poem that doesn't require a race-infused reading for a rich interpretive experience. I tell them that how they choose to teach the poem is their choice.

When I taught "Facing It" in the first offering of the seminar, I coupled it with a screening of the documentary *Maya Lin: A Strong Clear Vision*, a film about the young architect who designed the Vietnam Veterans' Memorial. I prefaced the screening by talking about the controversy surrounding the design, fueled in part by Ms. Lin's being considered by some veterans as an inappropriate person to memorialize the Vietnam War dead, in light of her Asian American ancestry. There were other elements to the controversy, but I wanted students to view the film in the context of how a nation chooses to remember its dead and whom it is willing to invest with the right to honor its heroes. When I screened the film in the second version of the seminar I still presented this perspective, but I also asked students to attend to Maya Lin as an artist, to the vision and imagination that enabled her to conceive of the wall as a form for the expression of grief and as a place for the beginning of healing. The question of race is thus coupled with the question of artistic representation.

I have gone one step further in deflecting the targeted focus on race. My third change is to demonstrate the construction of a literary "unit" on the Vietnam War with a cluster of texts and varying thematic emphases. In addition to the Komunyakaa poem and the documentary, students now discuss three other texts: Tim O' Brien's frequently anthologized short story "The Things They Carried," which provides an eloquent and moving portrait of the hopes and despairs of a group of young American men sent to fight the war; Vietnamese American playwright thúy lê's solo performance piece *Red Fiery Summer*, an angry and impassioned outburst against the ravaging of Vietnam and the disruption of lives there; and Anne Sexton's poem "I'm Dreaming the My Lai Soldier," a graphic and nightmarish vision of a soldier involved in the My Lai massacre in Vietnam and an unequivocal indictment of men as initiators of war. I explain that my pedagogical approach is to give play to differing voices and perspectives on the Vietnam War. The result is that students are more willing to engage the subject of race than when I had focused on race exclusively.

SEXISM TO THE RESCUE?

The fourth change I made to the original version of the course was to insert Charlotte Perkins Gilman's narrative "The Yellow Wallpaper" between the discussions on how to teach Conrad's *Heart of Darkness* and Shakespeare's *The Tempest*. Whereas my illumination of the issue of race in Conrad and Shakespeare was seen as excessive and too political the first time, the shift to a discussion of patriarchy, paternalism, and the constraints of turn-of-the-nineteenth-century womanhood engendered by "The Yellow Wallpaper" provides the perfect space in which to raise questions about power. Not surprisingly, Gilman's story is a highly successful text with white women students and serves also to politicize the less politically inclined students—male and female—in the seminar. This newly stimulated political sensibility then further encourages students to engage the issues of race and power in *The Tempest*.

AM I ECLIPSING RACE?

In juxtaposing sexism with racism, I recognize that I run the risk of marginalizing the impact of racism. Law professors and feminist race theorists Trina Grillo and Stephanie Wildman believe that the "sex/race analogy perpetuates patterns of racial domination." They list the detrimental effects of linking sexism with racism:

> (1) The taking back of center stage from people of color, even in discussions of racism, so that white issues remain or become central in the dialogue; (2) the fostering of essentialism, so that women and people of color are implicitly viewed as belonging to mutually exclusive categories,

rendering women of color invisible; and (3) the appropriation of pain or the denial of its existence that results when whites who have compared other oppressions to race discrimination believe they understand the experience of racism.[11]

Despite the validity of Grillo and Wildman's observations, I believe that there are contexts in which making the analogy between sexism and racism can serve a useful purpose. In the case of my classroom, making sexism the central issue for one class period awakened those students who never before had an opportunity to see the ways in which difficult issues can be repressed to realize how easy it would be to teach "The Yellow Wallpaper" as a gothic horror text rather than as a cry for female liberation. That knowledge led them to consider the ways in which similar silences can be enforced and are frequently enforced around race and led them to see their own complicity in that silence.

Students who continue to want to render race invisible and silent bear out the truth of Dana Takagi's observation that the current sociopolitical climate in the United States signals a "retreat from race."[12] Frustrated as I am with their resistance, I nevertheless believe that confrontation is not the answer. Rather, I am interested in exploring with them possible new ways to talk about race. The choice is not between aesthetics and politics or between talking about race and ignoring race; rather, the objective ought to be the continuous effort to encompass both possibilities. In the final analysis, what I hope students take away from the teaching of literature seminar is that while it is by no means my intention to mandate that they make the issue of race visible in their classrooms, I do urge them to consider the ramifications of their pedagogical decisions given the realities of the communities in which we live and work.

NOTES

1 Students read excerpts from Terry Eagleton's *The Ideology of the Aesthetic* (1990); bell hooks' *Teaching to Transgress: Education as the Practice of Freedom* (1994); Edward Said's *Orientalism* (1978) and *Culture and Imperialism* (1993); Stanley Fish's *Is There a Text in this Class?* (1980), particularly "How to Recognize a Poem When You See One"; William Cain's *Teaching the Conflicts: Gerald Graff, Curricular Reform, and the Culture Wars* (1994); and Raymond Williams' *Marxism and Literature* (1977).

2 Salman Rushdie, *Imaginary Homelands: Essays and Criticism 1981–1991* (London: Penguin, 1991), 14.

3 Jean-Paul Sartre, *"What Is Literature?" and Other Essays* (Cambridge, Mass.: Harvard University Press, 1988), 36–37.

4 The literature on the impact of race in U.S. sociocultural and political life is too numerous to list in its entirety. However, two large volumes, both edited by Richard Delgado and Jean Stefancic, provide an excellent survey: *Critical Race Theory: The Cutting Edge* (Philadelphia: Temple University Press, 1995) and *Critical White Studies: Looking*

Behind the Mirror (Philadelphia: Temple University Press, 1997). See also Michael Omi and Howard Winant, *Racial Formation in the United States* (New York: Methuen, 1986) and George Lipsitz, *The Possessive Investment in Whiteness: How White People Profit from Identity Politics* (Philadelphia: Temple University Press, 1998).

5 "Eye Contact," in Jessica Hagedorn, ed., *Charlie Chan Is Dead: An Anthology of Contemporary Asian American Fiction* (New York: Penguin, 1993), 500–527.

6 Ronald Takaki, *A Different Mirror: A History of Multicultural America* (Boston: Little, Brown & Company, 1993), 24–50.

7 Dana Y. Takagi, *The Retreat From Race: Asian-American Admissions and Racial Politics* (New Brunswick, N.J.: Rutgers University Press, 1998), 167.

8 Adrienne Rich, *A Change of World* (New Haven: Yale University Press, 1951). Foreword by W. H. Auden.

9 *Contemporary Authors: New Revision Series*, Volume 20, 394. See also Adrienne Rich, *Your Native Land, Your Life: Poems* (New York: Norton, 1986), 16.

10 See Indira Karamcheti, "Caliban in the Classroom," in *Teaching What You're Not: Identity Politics in Higher Education*, ed. Katherine J. Mayberry (New York: New York University Press, 1996), 215–227.

11 Trina Grillo and Stephanie M. Wildman, "Obscuring the Importance of Race: The Implications of Making Comparisons between Racism and Sexism (or Other Isms)," in *Critical Race Theories*, 621. See also Samina Najmi and Rajini Srikanth, eds., *White Women in Racialized Spaces: Imaginative Transformation and Ethical Action in Literature* (forthcoming from the State University of New York Press, 2002), especially the introduction.

12 Takagi, *The Retreat From Race*, x.

THE QUESTION OF COMFORT:

THE IMPACT OF RACE ON/IN THE COLLEGE CLASSROOM

"The problem of the color line," identified by W.E.B. Du Bois as the key issue facing the twentieth century, still remains paramount in the twenty-first—especially in the state of Alabama and particularly in the city of Birmingham, with its pretensions of being culturally diverse. A million people comprise its metropolitan area.[1] But the city proper, with its intrinsic racial problems, merely mirrors in microcosmic form the broader based county and state problems, which, combined, impact and shape the attitudes of faculty, staff, and students at the University of Alabama at Birmingham (UAB)—whether or not members of this urban university, the city's largest employer, are conscious of their effects.

During the ten years that I have taught at UAB, I have been in numerous situations where, when race has entered a conversation, white people have become extremely uncomfortable. Diversity, which in this southern setting means black empowerment, is met with resistance. For example, a proposal for upgrading a minor to a major in African American studies led to campus-wide dissension and student marches. The introduction of a cultural studies

---

VIRGINIA WHATLEY SMITH is an associate professor of English at University of Alabama at Birmingham, specializing in African American literature. Her work has appeared in *African American Review, Mississippi Quarterly,* and *Approaches to Teaching Native Son.* Her collection of essays, *Richard Wright's Travel Writings,* is published by University Press of Mississippi.

Smith analyzes the effects of systemic racism, both societal and institutional, on her teaching and working relationship with students and colleagues. She explores the question of why white English majors have not been taking her African American literature courses. This essay provides a close-up view of a black professor's ongoing struggles in the trenches of academe.

concentration to diversify the traditional Anglocentric canon in the English department precipitated heated debates. One such confrontation took place recently when I asked three key administrators in our department, another faculty member in African American literature, and a student advisor for the School of Arts and Humanities to attend a meeting. The paramount issue was the way that the English department, by retaining its Anglocentric curriculum while consistently devaluing African American literature, had in effect created a system of de facto segregation. Needless to say, the four white participants were shocked by the assertions I laid out in a two-page memorandum which concluded that the department was in violation of the 1964 Civil Rights Act and the ongoing 1983 court decree of Knight v. Alabama, mandating desegregation of Alabama's institutions of higher education. During the discussion two of my white colleagues asked, "Why does everything always have to do with race?" and "Do white students feel comfortable in African American literature courses?" Both questions reflect systemic policies in politics and education that produce racism in Alabama's culture and, in effect, foster conditions of racism in the college classroom.

THE CAUSE: RACISM AT THE TOP

With its history of slavery and nineteenth-century Jim Crow policies in public facilities, Alabama, like other Deep South states, adopted and stringently enforced racially biased ideas in all aspects of society, including educational institutions. The infamous image of former governor George Wallace defying federal troops in the 1960s to prevent Autherine Lucy from entering the University of Alabama at Tuscaloosa (UAT) illustrates how the top-ranking system of power, the governorship, controls knowledge at educational institutions. UAB, a predominantly white institution, falls below UAT in the systems of power operating between and among the state's institutions of higher education (although it has its own prestige as a medical school). At UAB, a similar chain of knowledge-access operates in descending order (president, provost, dean, department chair, faculty, students). A subordinate group's intellectual capacity to function is always controlled by the power above it.

Consequently, the subordinate ranks of English department chair and faculty reproduce the institution's systems of power, including racial policies. When a white colleague asked why everything always had to do with race and I replied, "Because you make it into race when you ignore my voice," our combative exchange reflects how, according to the philosopher Albert Memmi, such white consciousness remains transhistorical in its attempts to erase or ignore "blackness" and all of its problems.[2] I resisted quoting Du Bois's "double consciousness," or Ellison's "inner and outer eyes," or Wright's "blindness and sightedness" at this moment; it seemed futile.[3] My white colleague, who sincerely attempts to foster healthy race relations like the majority of my colleagues, still invariably exercised the privilege of looking at the world through white tunnel vision. I, as a bicultural African American, on the other hand, was compelled to read the world double-consciously in black and white. My area of expertise, African American literature, exemplifies this black–white dichotomy in terms of how its endorsement depends upon whether it measures up to the accepted model—the white canon—and what value the department places on Africanist subject matter. From 1991 to the present, I have developed several courses in African American and African literature. Over the years, course catalogs, departmental brochures, and fliers looked progressively more impressive; in reality, there was a conspicuous absence of students. The question still lingered: Why are white English majors not taking these courses?

The absence of white English majors (both undergraduate and graduate) in my African American literature courses has been puzzling me for years. Time after time I have asked faculty in the hallways, on an individual basis, and in department meetings, "Why don't I see English majors?" Up until this year, I couched my words carefully. I never cited the race of the absent English majors about whom I was questioning. The reason is that I never advertised my courses in African American literature as being designed to attract a specific racial group, whether in my capacity as an English professor or in my service position as UAB's first director of African American Studies from 1994 to 1999. While I noticed that my African American literature courses drew the attention of a few white non-English majors from other disciplines across campus, I observed that only in rare instances would I see an English major. The few I did see were black in ninety-five percent of the cases and in pursuit of educational degrees. As I broadened my course offerings, I would encounter new or repeat black students in my classes. In responding to my inquiry a colleague or the department chair would reply that they would "have to look into that" or "I don't know." The issue was not important to my white colleagues; my concerns as an African American teaching African American literature were politely dismissed.

Gradually, the racial pairings of white English majors with white faculty became clearer to me because of a ritual, year-end event. Each spring, we have a faculty meeting to nominate undergraduate- and graduate-level English majors for scholastic awards. I have rarely been able to make a contribution about the merit of any of the nominees because I have no contact with the white student candidates (only on one occasion did a black undergraduate student make the list). As far as graduate level, I have never served as a thesis director for a white graduate student. Ten years ago, there was one black female student in the MA program who never finished her degree but for whom I briefly served as advisor. About that time and the only instance, I did serve on a thesis committee for a white female student. Since that time period, I have not served on a thesis committee in any capacity. At the spring meeting, therefore, I merely sit and listen as white faculty members exchange enthusiastic and knowledgeable commentary about these students.

How has this racial divide, reminiscent of bygone Jim Crow practices in education, managed to survive in the UAB English department—causing great discomfort for faculty despite my efforts to bring the matter to their attention? One development contributed to the problem but also revealed others to me. When the state of Alabama mandated that all four-year colleges and universities develop a core of courses matching two-year colleges, so that students could transfer to four-year institutions with impunity, this affected me directly. My courses were not required for English majors and had no specific function in the curriculum other than to satisfy electives. Thus, enrollment in my 300-level survey courses dropped as students opted for the newly identified, traditional 200-level core courses. Other 300-level courses in the department were similarly affected. However, African American literature was what I was hired to teach, and my survey courses were all at the 300 level. I finally realized that the only consistent enrollments in my classes were students from the African American studies program, nondegree students, and undeclared majors. Mind you, this revelation did not happen overnight; it took years to deconstruct the complex layers of academic requirements. But, as a former Equal Employment Opportunity Specialist in the U.S. Department of Housing and Urban Development, I was trained to track patterns of racial discrimination and could see that my courses—and I as an African American teaching them—were being shunned. In seeking redress in the English department for this "race problem," I incurred a backlash from my white colleagues: I was labeled a racist, a whiner, a complainer, and even a "bad cop." In my ten years at UAB, I have observed that black faculty are labeled "good" if they are silent or accommodationist and "bad" if they are outspoken or considered uncooperative. While my white colleagues do not go around thinking about "black this" or "white that," many, through their actions and words, exhibit some inherent notion that African American literature is not "American literature" and, thus, not important.

THE EFFECT: RACISM AT THE BOTTOM (IN THE CLASSROOM)

Racial comfort is not a phrase one would use to describe the state of Alabama. If the state, city, and county schools do not require students to study African American culture; the university does not require diversity training for faculty, staff, and students; and the department does not require its majors to take courses in African American literature, then systemic racism will persist, and the conflicts between blacks and whites will continue unabated. One case exemplifying this transhistorical problem is the ten-year "race war" between incumbent and ex-mayor Richard Arrington, who is black, and white incumbent city councilman Jimmy Blake that was and still is played out daily in the media. The reopened trial of Ku Klux Klansmen for the bombing of Sixteenth Street Baptist Church, which killed four black girls, is another. Black and white native-born students who enter UAB are generally immune to racial conflicts because it is the norm in their lives. However, transfer or foreign-born students are more likely to see this racial divide. Several years ago I had a young white male student enrolled in my American Studies course titled "Race and Justice in America." After four classes, he informed me that he was returning to Louisiana because he could not cope with the daily racist remarks he heard white students making about blacks. He said racial problems were worse in Birmingham than in New Orleans. I myself make an effort to leave the state every two months to ensure that I, too, never become blind to injustice.

The state and Birmingham have proven over time that to change racial attitudes in favor of intellectual growth requires great struggle. Some forty years after the major civil rights conflicts in this city, racial division on campus still exists. It took four years to design and get approval for a major in African American studies. The university-wide committee on the major that I chaired had to leap extraordinary hurdles to gain faculty approval while the same faculty, without hesitation, approved traditional degree proposals in a year's time. This protracted struggle signifies the inequality of the validation process and stands as a gauge of how black culture is devalued in the state of Alabama and, at the institutional level, within UAB. It also indexes why I have had a ten-year struggle to get the department of English, still out of sync with the rest of the nation, to require its undergraduate majors in English to take a course in African American literature—thereby validating the subject, its black faculty, and 22.2 percent of UAB's students.[4] The absence of such validation not only exacerbates the "absent" English majors' cultural ignorance in classes but also impacts the "present" black and white student body by enabling racial conflicts.

As a result, essentialist notions of the biological inferiority of the African American subject are inextricably interwoven in the minds of some white faculty, staff, and, by default, students affiliated with UAB and the department. There is an assumption that the courses in African American literature are for blacks only. During the meeting to discuss defacto segregation, I asked the members present if white students were ever advised to take courses in African American literature or if they were even advised not to take them. This was during the early part of the meeting when tempers were bristling and hostility was acute. Those present tried to suggest that student advising fell solely on the shoulders of the school advisory representative. I said I found it difficult to believe that three key officials running the English department never had contact with students in any advisory capacity. One person retorted defensively, "But do white students feel comfortable in your courses on African American literature?" Here was the stock repartee I have heard more than once; the well-being of white students seemed to be of paramount concern. I countered by asking why white professors weren't concerned if black students were comfortable in their literature classes—or if they cared.

If white professors are only concerned with the comfort zones of white students, what racial messages do they convey in the classroom that affect student values, perceptions, and actions? I have had three white students on separate occasions express to me their unawareness that slaves like Frederick Douglass resisted captivity. All have told the same anecdote about attending a history class where a white instructor teaches that slaves were in fact content with their conditions. This miseducation of the student is unconscionable. Descendants of slaves are today made to feel stigmatized. In-state students arrive in my literature classes aware of Booker T. Washington, his accommodationist policy for blacks to appease whites, and Tuskegee Institute's location one hour from Birmingham. Interestingly, I have had just as many black students as white react with shock when they learned about the real horror of slavery after reading *Our Nig* or *A Gathering of Old Men*, or watching the film

Sankofa. Equally pernicious in K–12 and college-level classes is the white instructor in American literature (or British or world literature, for that matter) who omits inclusion of black authors on a syllabus. Two years ago I had two black males in their thirties who were products of the public schools in Selma and Birmingham acknowledge that they had never heard of or been taught about W.E.B. Du Bois. Both were mesmerized by Du Bois's emancipatory message in *The Souls of Black Folk.* And certainly the English department is not without blame when, for instance, a white instructor dilutes a black text's message of racial discrimination by focusing only on gender and class, thereby whitening the text. The bottom-level group (the impacted student or graduate teaching assistant) then becomes the next purveyor of misinformation in the classroom. Both message recipients have been taught to be racially ignorant and racially insensitive, since the English department has signaled that the African American literature courses are not worthy. On several occasions, graduate teaching assistants who have never taken an African American literature course have asked me for help in interpreting a text or have borrowed books from me on Africanist culture. These are the next generation of racially insensitive English teachers that UAB is training.

RACISM IN THE CLASSROOM: THE REALITIES OF THE MULTICULTURAL CLASSROOM

My approach to teaching is to address issues of race and ethnicity directly. As an African American professor teaching in the Deep South, my presence in the classroom invariably creates discomfort for some white students. One American literature class I teach has a high enrollment of thirty-five students, since this course meets the humanities core requirement for many disciplines. Some white students disappear after the first day (probably because they have never dealt with a black professor). Others look at my multicultural syllabus and decide that they do not like it. I use *The Heath Anthology of American Literature*, a culturally diverse textbook that includes formerly excluded white women writers and writers of color. Even though I offer a legitimate rationale for using this anthology, some students dislike the readings and drop the course.

Black students in these same classes are frequently uncomfortable as well. Besides being totally outnumbered, ongoing Jim Crow practices in the South teach them to be passive. Their reticence around whites changes little on a college campus with 10,420 undergraduates comprising the total 16,081 student population, and only 76 black faculty among the 1,688 employed. All are located at an institution in a predominantly black city that is the largest urban area of the state. And even though UAB has the highest percentage of black students on a predominantly white campus in the southern region (22.2 percent), they experience classes where they find themselves few in number and rarely see a black professor. Of the thirty-five students usually enrolled in the American literature course, perhaps seven or eight are black. To establish comfort, oftentimes three or four will cluster in the front row near me. If they sit in other seats, two generally sit together and, in a few instances, one black student will sit apart from the rest. Because Alabama has a history of brutal slavery and ongoing civil rights struggles, most black students band together in classrooms for comfort. This clustering follows the protective tactics formerly used by slaves and freed blacks known as "safe haven" spaces. Regardless of economic class, black students almost always form racial clusters in classrooms where white students dominate. In my African American literature classes where black students are the majority, white students tend to disappear after a few sessions. The white students who stay tend to be more loquacious than the black students—possibly because they have always had the privilege of unbridled speech.

In anticipating racial tensions in the classroom, I include a stock code-of-conduct statement on the syllabus for every composition and literature course that says: "This course may challenge one's notions about what constitutes American culture. Students are requested to respect the opinions of others while in the classroom." Because I use nontraditional, multicultural texts to redefine American culture, my students are often exposed to a variety of customs foreign to their own. This applies to my African American literature courses as well. Naturally, students raise mild objections about some texts. I have stopped teaching texts dealing with race that are too dense for 200- and 300-level undergraduates, such as William Faulkner's *Absalom! Absalom!* and Toni Morrison's *Beloved.* Otherwise, their objections during group discussions usually pertain to moral issues in texts such as Ernest Hemingway's "Hills Like White Elephants," in which a single white woman succumbs to pressure from her male partner and chooses an abortion, and August Wilson's *Fences,* in which a married black woman yields to the pressure of her husband to adopt the child of his deceased lover. I remind students that cultural mores arise out of time-based practices and that customs must be read in such contexts against today's principles. They are still misled by their assumptions. For example, students in my African American literature class have misread the sexuality of the former slave Olaudah Equiano, assuming that he was homosexual because he learned the barber's trade. They also missed the issue of his white-collar privilege of not being made a field slave.

Students exhibit the strongest reactions when race and ethnicity are the focus of discussion. I do not dilute the premises of the texts in order to provide students with a false sense of comfort; instead, I address the theme of race and ethnicity directly to promote intellectual development which, in my eyes, is the mission of teaching. Frequently, as we commence to explore slavery and the resistant voices of people of color and white women to white male dominance, some of my students will express their discomfort through note-passing, body language, or whispering. The "N" word still causes racial tensions when used by a white author or white person. In my "Writers of the Great Depression" course, we read *Jews Without Money, The Girl, God's Little Acre*, and *The Grapes of Wrath*—novels by white authors who periodically portray blacks as indolent, immoral, or unintelligent. But "nigger" is still a trigger word to blacks, like waving a red flag to a bull. In my team-taught class "Race and Justice in America" two years ago, a very intelligent white female student used the word in a sensitive, tasteful manner during discussion. Nevertheless, a black female student immediately reacted by sending her a note with the word "bitch" scrawled on it. I generally discuss the "N" word briefly in all my classes, but this incident was more volatile and required more explanation about the word's contradictory use by blacks. I pointed out James Weldon Johnson's definition of the term to mean "fellow" in *The Autobiography of an Ex-Coloured Man*, and how Langston Hughes condemns use of the word by anyone in *The Big Sea*.[5]

Body language in the classroom can also reflect discomfort with race. I noticed a white male student in one American literature course who spoke quite intelligently in class but often appeared flushed. I learned of his racial rage near midterm when he burst into my office with his white male tablemate complaining about the D grades on their papers and implying that it was because they sat on the left side of the room. They never used the word "race," but it was their subtext since it appeared that only whites, by then, sat on that side of the room. Whispering is another expression of discomfort. Most students do it. At times, white students become bolder and bolder in their whispering until I have to invite both parties to share their information with the whole class. Black students, on the other hand, tend to remain silent or impassive in the tradition of their parents or the public school teachers who yearly attend the English department's high school articulation conference and remain mute. What white students whisper among themselves can be racist. A black student reported to me that two white females behind her were whispering to each other that Ann Petry's novel *The Street* was "ghetto literature." This label was ironic since we had also read Meridel LeSueur's *The Girl*, a novel about the corruptive influence of an urban criminal subculture on a white female.

In extreme instances, students have become aggressive in the classroom because of interracial hostilities. White students often go to the dean to register complaints. On two occasions, black militant students who were members of the campus chapter of the Malcolm X Grassroots Organization have acted out their political agendas in my classroom. Several years ago I was teaching black women writers and using Patricia Hill Collins's groundbreaking book *Black Feminist Thought*, a study that presented the first in-depth theory on black female consciousness and empowerment. When we got to the chapter arguing that white males, white females, and black males could also ideologically become feminists, the black militant students could not accept this new proposition.[6] It countered 1970s essentialist arguments still prevalent in the 1990s that biology (race) and gender (female) were the qualifying criteria. I learned that the black male ringleader, supported by two black female allies, had been pointing fingers and shaking fists at some white female students in the classroom and then verbally threatening them during breaks on the balcony. I had to act quickly: first by verbally warning them to desist, next handing written letters to them, and finally referring them to the university judiciary officer for counseling. This was a blatant case of interracial bigotry. Most often, however, black students turn to forms of intraracial destruction as described in August Wilson's play *Ma Rainey's Black Bottom*.

Such an incident occurred in our race and justice in America class following the "N" word incident. I team-teach this course with a white historian who is mild-mannered and perceived as a "good cop" since, most often, I have to resolve racial incidents involving black students who dominate the class. In this case, a black female student and president of a black organization on campus loudly assaulted her organization's black male vice president and student classmate twice in one class meeting while at break or when my colleague was lecturing. I had to break up both confrontations and, after class, ask the campus police to patrol the hallways for the final two class meetings. Another black student informed me that the loud black female student suffered from low self-esteem because of her dark skin coloring, and the Malcolm X organization had taught her self-love which she, like others, interpreted as showing aggression. Her case is an example of how Alabama's systemic racism has psychologically scarred blacks to believe they are racially inferior. My white colleague informed me that the young woman enrolled in her class the following term and was a model of decorum. Having left the black safe haven of my class, the young woman altered her behavior in the next class, which was predominantly white.

A second example comes from my developmental reading class one term. Typically ninety-eight percent black, these conditionally admitted students resisted typecasting as remedial readers. Yet like the several white students in the class, they tested out at fourth-to-eighth grade reading levels although they did well in math and science. The class was a struggle all term because I frequently had to counsel one black female student who was loud and insulting toward me when she received poor grades. My white colleagues encounter student resistance, but rarely to this degree is their experience racially grounded.

The first graded paper or midterm examination often acts as the catalyst for exposing brewing racial hostilities. Many departments on campus still do not have black professors because whites argue that they cannot find any who are "qualified" to fill positions; I have also been in meetings where I have heard white professors state that "they don't belong here"—meaning black students. If figures of authority have such biased views, how can the bottom-level student not be affected? In such a climate I must resort to syllabi that run seven to ten pages long, in contrast to my white colleagues' much shorter versions. I must cite all required and supplementary textbooks, examination requirements, report expectations, grading scales, and assessment processes in precise detail. This includes grading.

The papers that I return to students are bloody with red marks. I do not have the luxury simply to write "sp" for a spelling error, "awk" for an awkward phrase, "dict" for a word choice, and then write a brief commentary as do my counterparts; I have to overjustify. I have had white male students complain to the dean about me being racially biased. One student in the race and justice in America course claimed that I had assigned him a C grade for his literature paper because I was prejudiced. I later learned that my colleague assigned the student a C on his history paper and the student never complained. At the other extreme, I have experienced intraracial bias on two separate occasions because black students expected lax attendance policies and easy grades from me while they skipped my classes. Both students were education majors from other institutions who dually enrolled in courses at their main campuses. Each proceeded to harass me with scenes of crying after the male student received an F grade, and numerous telephones calls from the female petitioning to attend class once a week. With both I had to be firm in enforcing the attendance policy that applied to other members of the class.

Course evaluations also enable both black and white students to express their racist postures. Because I teach literature that students often resist, I know that I will never receive an Ingalls Award for excellence in teaching. Generally, black students in my classes are not vindictive (even the problem ones), because they are so grateful to have been exposed to their own culture in a course. One exception, however, was the developmental reading course. Teaching this course was a painful experience for me. I followed the syllabus designed by the reading committee and voluntarily assigned extra credit and initiated extra counseling sessions. At the end of the term, I left the classroom during student evaluations according to policy. From down the hallway, however, I could hear the black female ringleader loudly coaching her classmates. Of the twenty-two forms turned in, fifty percent were in the below average and poor categories. These were the worst student evaluations in my entire career. I will never teach the course again.

Teaching American literature from a multicultural perspective has its pitfalls as well. Students in general do not always appreciate my good intentions. Where the evaluation form asks what was good or bad about the course or instructor, they take "good" and "bad" literally, often based on how comfortable they felt in the course. For years I have gotten comments from white students in my American literature course such as, "I didn't know this was a course in African American literature." Since African American literature is my area of expertise, I believe that I have just as much right as any of my white colleagues to refer periodically to this expertise to make valid points. Some white students resent reading or hearing about more than one nonwhite author, even though I explain that a course on American literature is necessarily multicultural and multiethnic. The most negative evaluation I have ever received was a typed sheet attached to the standard evaluation form. In other words, student X had been waiting to exercise his or her power with the pen.

RACISM IN THE CLASSROOM:
THE POSSIBILITY OF CHANGE

The conversation on race and comfort that arose in the combative department meeting to remedy the problem of a balkanized, Anglo-centered curriculum reflects racial issues larger than those of my department, the school of Arts and Humanities, the University, the city of Birmingham, or the state of Alabama. I do not expect that requiring a few hundred white English majors to take courses in African American literature will immediately rectify a transhistorical state and national color-line problem. I have cited cases involving campus-wide student racism in the classroom, but do not exempt those absent white English majors from being any less racially biased than those who have appeared in my classes. More than likely they bear similar traits, since all are victims or practitioners of systemic racism. Our mission as a university and department is to ensure the intellectual and cultural growth of all students, and this requires validation of the African American subject. Encouragingly, our meeting ended on a positive note: we presented a proposal to the English faculty to require all English majors to take one course in African American literature. Of the twenty-three voting members, only three voted against this. The new course requirement will be implemented next term, even though it will take two years for the course catalog to be updated. With the department taking strong actions to correct its undergraduate requirements by developing a curriculum of inclusion, and perhaps later by developing similar requirements for English majors in our masters degree program, we take a step towards truth. In addition, with the migration of Chicanos to the Deep South at an impressive rate, I predict that the department will be developing and implementing a cultural studies concentration for the English major soon. In light of such evolving demographics, I foresee that a new multicultural challenge not only awaits my institution, but other state institutions as well.

NOTES

1 W.E.B. Du Bois, *The Souls of Black Folk* (New York: Penguin, 1989), 13.
2 Albert Memmi, *Racism*, trans. Steve Martinot (Minneapolis: University of Minnesota Press, 2000), 100–21. In his chapter "Definition," Memmi discusses many characteristics of racism such as biological differences, valuation of differences, refusal to see others, etc., and reactions of the accusers or victims with hostility, fear, or aggression. On whiteness studies, see Richard Dyer, *White* (New York: Routledge, 1997), 3; Michellet Fine, et al., *Off White: Readings on Race, Power and Society* (New York: Routledge, 1997), vii; and Thomas K. Nakayama and Judith N. Martin, eds., *Whiteness: The Communication of Social Identity* (New York: Sage, 1999), vii.

3 Du Bois, *Souls*, 3; Ralph Ellison, *Invisible Man* (New York: Vintage, 1980), 3–4; Richard Wright, *Native Son* (New York: Perennial, 1966), 103–105.

4 University of Alabama at Birmingham, "Student Enrollment," Institutional Studies and Services, Fall 1999, http://www.main.uab.edu>, October 23, 2000. All statistics pertinent to UAB cited herein refer to this source.

5 James Weldon Johnson, *The Autobiography of an Ex-Coloured Man* (New York: Penguin, 1990), 67; Langston Hughes, *The Big Sea* (New York: Hill and Wang, 1940), 268–269.

6 Patricia Hill Collins, *Black Feminist Thought* (New York: Routledge, 1991), 33–37.

ROBERTA J. HILL

FAR MORE THAN FRYBREAD:

THE TENDER ISSUE OF RACE IN TEACHING LITERATURE

PHOTO: TIMOTHY FRANCISCO

Race, a charged word in our national history, is, if anything, becoming even more of a "dirty" word in the new millennium than it was when I began to teach. The discussion of race causes intellectual and emotional difficulties, leading students to reveal their own traumatic experiences with race. This happens as well in areas of academic expertise. I teach a number of courses in American Indian literature. One way to engage students in the literature is to study it by explaining material culture. Like frybread, a flour dough fried and eaten in homes and sold at powwows, other cultural innovations show that Indians adapted, using creativity, our "Injunuity," to generate cultural cohesion. Studying only that, however, misses other important aspects in many texts. From the moment I first entered the classroom as a professor over twenty years ago, I have necessarily included discussions of race with the discussion of literature. In studying race, classes are tense. I do not claim to be an expert on the subject, and recognize that as a nation, we need scholars who are experts with race as well as in their areas of academic expertise. In my class, we discuss racism not just as a personal dilemma, but also as a manifestation of the European system of exploitation and colonization in the Americas and the Caribbean. Through the lens of American Indian literatures, we gain insight

ROBERTA J. HILL, an Oneida from Wisconsin, is a poet, fiction writer, and scholar. A professor of English and American Indian Studies at the University of Wisconsin, Hill's books include *Star Quilt* and *Philadelphia Flowers*. A biography of her grandmother, Dr. Lillie Rosa Minoka Hill, the second American Indian woman physician, will be published by the University of Nebraska.

In her essay, Hill explores the connection between material culture and literature, explaining her pedagogic strategy. She argues that student responses in American Indian literature classes demonstrate a predictable five-step process in relation to race, moving from "incredulity" to "skill with oppositional and syncretic epistemologies."

into racism as a global phenomenon which altered the social orders of indigenous peoples in Africa, Australia, New Zealand, and Asia as well. Racism, the students learn, is both an ideology and an oppressive practice, codified in institutions, laws, and norms.[1] The discussion gets personal whenever the concept of race leaves the formerly cosseted pen of abstraction and pads like an ocelot with a piercing screech into the midst of twenty students.

I want to share my experiences with an imaginary class, a composite created from the many I have taught. Freshmen through seniors enroll in American Indian Literature: Social Issues in American Indian Literature; the course fulfills an ethnic studies requirement. The University of Wisconsin system requires a course in ethnic studies to prepare students in the discourse of race, class, gender, and ethnicity before they go forth into a rapidly globalizing world. Many students wait until the final semester of their senior year to fill the requirement. Some are not inclined to believe the subject matter important. I save space for freshmen and sophomores because with a wider age-range of students, it is possible to have more challenging discussion.

Students in my class travel a journey, stopping at various sites (that is, texts). While I developed the course in terms of content, theme, conventions, and ideas to explore, I did not consider that in our discussions of race we were moving together through a five-step process: incredulity, emotional tension and release, recognizing social facts, awareness of interiors (motive, attitude, value), and skill with oppositional and syncretic epistemologies. This is not a lock-step process: some students remain incredulous the entire semester. These steps surface at different junctures in the ripening of our encounters with each other.

Before we meet the class on the first day, I want to share one key experience in my teaching. In my early years of college teaching, I understood that my being an Oneida woman challenged my students. I was an adjunct, teaching a composition class that required students to do research. I had chosen research into Chicano culture. The class discussed Rudolfo Anaya's *Bless Me, Ultima*. Stephen, a young student who participated frequently in class discussions, was chagrined about reading a novel about "Mexican Americans." He did not see the point in studying about *curanderas* and a Mexican American boy's coming of age in New Mexico. The students were white, most of them freshmen and sophomores from the Midwest. I told them the projected population statistics: Before the end of this coming century, the country's population would change "color" from a white majority to a brown majority. The Hispanic population had one of the highest birth rates. Stephen leaped up from his chair, inflamed by passion and purpose.

"We can't let that happen," he cried. "We were here first!" He looked at me, expecting my agreement, wanting the class to agree it would be horrible for white students to become a minority in "their country." The class was silent. A teaching moment! I wondered how to approach his rally for white privilege and power. Then Sara in the back of the room asked him, "Do you know whom you're talking to?" The silence deepened. Her awareness significantly jolted our perceptions. The tension was thick. It was a wonderful gift, an illustration of situational irony. I had to laugh and they laughed, too. "Indians" were here first. We had been socialized to accept as natural the "discovery" of America. I told them Stephen's question had to be taken seriously, because others in the country believed in the meta-narrative of European conquest and settlement, but the story we were discussing was more complex than the myth of conquest. We needed to explore what it meant. I asked why he felt such legitimacy and passion in his claim to possession. We unpacked the rallying call to analyze its origins, its truth, the fear beneath it, how characters in Anaya's novel might experience his comment, and what public policies have supported and continue to support the system of racial hierarchies.

At the time this happened, I represented a ratio of less than 0.2 percent of the faculty in U.S. colleges and universities. In their important work *Faculty of Color in Academe*, Caroline Sotello Viernes Turner and Samuel L. Myers, Jr. analyze both the patterns and nature of minority underrepresentation and the overrepresentation of white males. Currently, whites represent 88.9 percent, blacks represent 5.7 percent, American Indians 0.2 percent, Asians 3.4 percent, and Hispanics 1.8 percent of the faculty in U.S. colleges and universities. Their work has helped me understand the complexity of such experiences.[2] It was analysis unavailable to me at the time.

As we head back to the imaginary class, I try to keep in mind that the tensions and complexity of that early experience are a continuing undercurrent in many discussions of racism. The teaching moment happens more subtly now than in the period of the civil rights movement. I am also more aware than I was then of my particular place within academe. As we head to class, I hope we did not get the oven or the lab; in the first room, the lack of windows and poor ventilation closes down discussion after the first half-hour's worth of air is gone, and in the second, the rigidity of long lab tables bolted to the floor prevents students from discussion. In earlier years, I would be assigned an abysmal room and stick it out to the end of the semester, but no more. The room must fit my teaching style: movable desks, windows that open, and a clock. At the first meeting, I am pleased the class has an unusual number of Indian students: seven out of twenty, a rare experience. Usually I have one or none. There's a good balance in student ranks, freshmen through seniors. One foreign student, Anna, and several students taking a certificate in American Indian studies will bring more depth of knowledge to our cross-cultural interpretations. Classes evolve a sensibility that is greater than the input of students and teacher. This class will keep me awake at night off and on for the next sixteen weeks.

Because there are so few American Indian women professors, I was their first, possibly their last, and wore no buckskin. With my curly hair, I never looked like most expected. In my early years of teaching, one girl wrote on the evaluations that she had wanted to be taught by "a real Indian." I accepted the persona of an "unreal Indian." In the course I expected them to read, write, think, role play, dance, sing, and test one another's assumptions. They struggled over issues of race, that big four-letter word they flung and sometimes cut themselves or each other with. Race, a razor cutting through the class. I found myself worrying about the books, methods, course objectives, and the psychopathologies of at least two students. Although some days I dreaded the unresolvable tensions that erupted, I understood that we were dredging a deep channel. It was supposed to affect us. Sometimes, no matter what I tried, the energy was not right. I do evaluate the class each semester and change what I can. However, such tensions are not always due to anything I taught or the way I hoped the students would learn it. I believe these tensions come from the complexity of racism as represented in the literature, the effects of historical traumas, and the challenge the literature presents in making ourselves conscious of the impact racism has in our lives, in the lives of others, and in our recognition of the institutional racism that we still encounter. To interrogate racism—whether overt, covert, unintentional, institutional, or internalized—is not something that can be done in one course.[3] Although course texts varied, this semester we were reading *Fools Crow, Love Medicine, Mean Spirit, Almanac of the Dead,* and *The Lone Ranger and Tonto Fistfight in Heaven.*[4]

With the introductory essays "The Sacred Hoop" by Paula Gunn Allen and "Oppression" by Marilyn Frye, and a discussion of racist ideology of the 1850s, students learn how the language of manifest destiny works to distort, mystify, and oppress.[5] Some students do not want to believe that the historical documents are accurate. The five-hundred-year-old reality of warfare, slavery, starvation, and disease can be hard to wrap our minds around. Whether they read a literary or historical essay or the first novel, *Fools Crow*, for example, the class divides into two camps, the majority skeptical of new knowledge. Katy, a junior, asks, "Why didn't I learn about any of this in high school?" Bill, an American Indian freshman, speaks up and shares how in his high school, only a few paragraphs in his history book mentioned Indians. Students from other marginalized communities bring their voices to bear on the discussion. Their opinions enrich and broaden our interpretations. Without American Indian students and students from a diversity of American marginalized communities, the white students do not understand as clearly how racism affects all of us. Some students will continue to think the course does not bear on their lives in any way. Some never leave the hermeneutics of doubt. They believe throughout the semester that this literature is on some fringe of knowledge they will never meet again. Most squirm, thinking about how a racist ideology promotes a status quo whereby those who dominate the society's economy, polity, and other key institutions legitimately, it appears, keep the social wealth. We discuss ethnic stratification and tie it into definitions of class and privilege. My intention is to get them to understand that race is not a biological factor but a social construction designed to establish who has social power and who fits within a particular caste. On this continent, the colonization of the Americas and the debates over whether Native Americans were human beings grew into the formation of racism. *Fools Crow* offers awareness and understanding of the worldview of an Indian nation, the Pikuni, and the relentless nature of American settlement. It portrays the racism of the frontier. With these stories, the submerged history of indigenous nations comes out of the ravine.

Students begin to see that control of the language is power. They also see that reading the literature, they will want to be sensitive to the social facts of each character's situation. Frye's article helps students consider that the usual response—that the oppressed ought to help themselves out of their oppression—might not work if those who are oppressed are blind to "the bars on the cage"—the beliefs, policies, and social practices which keep them from obtaining social power. The article and the unfolding of the process in a novel helps students understand that blaming the victim keeps the system intact.

By the time we are into the second novel, the class shifts into three camps: adamant white seniors in their final semester, fulfilling the ethnic studies requirement; some of the Indian students, including seniors, who draw support from a recognition of their common points of reference; and some

Indian and white students from all ranks who wanted their literature free of any emotional strife or queasy self-realizations. They read, write, and think about the novels—raw, ribald, tough, and gritty, beautiful in their pathos and the way they elicit rage, fear, and sadness as well as hope, joy, and compassion. I believe emotions contain knowledge and that the emotional tenor in the class aids in the construction of a point of view and opinion. At the second site, the cave of emotional tension and release, these novels bring into consciousness rage and disappointment, shame and rejection of shame, and the need for pride and self-esteem that oppressed people experience. A novel like *Almanac of the Dead* brings into consciousness internalized racism and the experiences of oppression.

At this point, the course can keep me awake at night, thinking of ways to mediate discussion. It comes to the point of who gets to speak and what they get to say. One Indian student, Miranda, is very angry and challenges students to consider the depth of rage she feels for the oppression of Indian people. Other Indian students echo her emotional truth. Some students do not want Miranda to speak about it. Anna, the foreign student, cannot grasp why she is so angry. The emotional impact of the fiction can affect the class in the most distressing way, because an intellectual analysis can offer some clarity, but there is no easy answer to the complexity of human emotion. We need to see and listen to each other.

I ask them to take what they are learning and check it out in their world. Does racism still exist? Are these fictions pure fantasy or are there truths here? Sometimes the class requires an examination of the dynamics of discussion. When students work together in groups, I propose to them that who speaks and who stays silent may be a duplication of our socialization in a racist culture. I want them to listen to everyone and for every student to speak. In a situation where the tension becomes difficult and we must address it, I might ask them, "If Miranda cannot speak up about her experience, including her emotions in response to what she reads about in American Indian literature, where else can she do this?" We want Miranda to share her ideas and feelings. Miranda must also listen. Clare tells us she comes from a ghetto in Baltimore. She understands oppression. Sherman Alexie's work reminds her of her home. If Miranda wants others aware of her interpretation of how racism affects characters, then Clare wants Miranda to understand other students have emotional conflicts. Other students know about class and gender oppression. At some point, a student like Joseph who has been writing exquisite papers but not speaking up begins to share his interpretations. He will put another spin on the discussion when he says, "I feel like Lipsha. I don't know who I am. I feel like a no-brain white and half-worst kind of Indian. I'm a mishmash of cultures, but I don't belong to any of them. My dad is Cherokee and lives in Oklahoma, but my mom is Irish and Italian. They're divorced so she expects me to be a normal Catholic American. I wish I could go to powwows and be accepted." Dealing with both the emotional and intellectual conflicts enables us to broaden our interpretations, to tease out the dynamics of the characters' situations and how events affect them, and how the choices a character makes leads sometimes to unforeseen consequences.

The students relate to the novels' imaginary worlds and begin to understand the complexity of five hundred years of a dynamic encounter coded into the literature. Some are frightened by characters like Silko's Awa Gee, a genius bent on destruction of the electric grid. They struggle with prophecies in that novel: "How will the end come about?" "Is the power of dreams more potent than weapons?" "Will we all dream the same dream when the electricity fails?" "What did you think about Tilly Shay, the colonic irrigation therapist, and her theory about the link between chronic constipation and the violence in Anglo-Saxon males?"

Sometime after mid-term, when we've stopped at the next two sites, most students know they must be cognizant of the social facts of the characters. They gain skill with making inferences, determining motives, values, and beliefs, and understand "things may not be what they appear to be on the outside." They are struck by the recognition that the war on drugs is also a war on citizens. They are challenged by Silko's world where alcohol and drugs are intended to keep the people weak, to keep the oppressed from demanding justice. They are shocked to discover how the prison system works to destroy the power of black and other marginalized peoples' votes. They recognize that people face limitations and that these limitations as well as opportunities affect an individual's beliefs, values, and motives. We recognize and discuss how some have more opportunities than others. We begin to see that privilege and limitations are not just individual and natural "givens," but are also part of a world, a social system. We recognize how racism, class, and gender discrimination affects lives. Useful in these discussions is James Banks' discussion of the stages of ethnicity, a typology that theorizes ethnicity as a process. This typology proposes a model of diversity within ethnic communities. Some people are held captive by their own internalized racism, others have self-acceptance and a positive attitude toward their "race," and others can function well within several cultures.[6]

Before the last four weeks, some students who used "either/or" categories begin to play with and tease out the multifarious interrelationships in the characters, gleaning how history, representations, public policies, and social power affect them. Some who took the course for an ethnic studies requirement—who wanted the content tucked into neat themes, placed in some grid and forgotten—are awakening to the idea of synthesis. Many have a better understanding of the amorphous complexity of racism. The literature reveals how pervasive and perverse racial hierarchies are and how some people, represented by characters in the fiction, struggle with shame and oppression day after day. Some may still want to believe that race does not really matter. Yet American Indian literature attracts and challenges them to reflect on their own identities and what choices are open or closed to them in a country constantly shifting under the discourse of race and equality.

In this imaginary class, it should be clear that the racial heritage of the students in the classroom and the environment created affect both the discussions and the course objectives. The race of the instructor (a tender issue in academe) affects the ways in which students interact, the course evaluations, and peer-to-peer reactions among colleagues. In some classes I feel I have not handled these tensions well. I never feel totally prepared, but I have learned that the dissembling anxiety is what keeps me thinking, writing, and reading. I live within a racist system and don't expect a quick transformation, although I do believe "a change is gonna come." Some faculty retreat from challenging students because the possibility of reprisals exists and can be time-consuming. In only one instance did I go to the department chair and ask for a discussion with a student. He was in the class the first day, raising his hand at every opportunity and threatening me. I wanted the chair and the student to discuss with me his intention in taking the class; if it was not to learn, then why was he there? He never came to the meeting and dropped the course.

Course evaluations base their assumptions on a level playing field for all faculty; however, teaching ethnic requirements poses a risk, because many of the students are not in the course because they love the material. Teaching ethnic studies courses semester after semester can make a scholar long for a class in which all of the students are there because they are interested in the literature. It makes me understand the nature of my own discipline and my own place, race, and marginality. Many universities are committed to broadening students' understanding about issues of race, class, gender, and ethnicity. In a fractal universe, the tension in the class reflects the tension in the society. Public universities have both the power and responsibility to teach about justice and moral vision. If they do not commit themselves to this effort, then the unjust society which may be created returns to all of us. I do not want the brown kindergartner, already placed in a special education class, to have no other choice than to be a member of an underclass. As I have told students, I teach and learn from them not only in that semester, but for our common future as well.

Some of the good work being written on racism makes teaching the works of American Indian authors very exciting. Rather than focus on critical studies within the field of American Indian literature, I find several texts on racism particularly helpful in placing the work in context. George Lipsitz's *The Possessive Investment in Whiteness* and collections of essays like *Race and Ideology* help me bear in mind that racism as an institution continues to oppress us.[7] Sharing these studies with students, engaging them in the issues, has convinced me that the study of race deepens their awareness of the frybread—the material expression of culture, and the pattern of relations and resistance that support those expressions. A long road, a long revolution is ahead. I offer what I can and hope that the next generation is more aware.

NOTES

1 James Banks, *Teaching Strategies for Ethnic Studies* (Boston: Allyn and Bacon, 1991), 74–76.

2 Caroline Sotello Viernes Turner and Samuel L. Myers, Jr., *Faculty of Color in Academe: Bittersweet Success* (Boston: Allyn and Bacon, 2000), 71–81 discusses the statistics.

3 For an essay on the types and difficulties of dealing with racism, see Gloria Yamato, "Something About the Subject Makes It Hard to Name," in *Race, Class, and Gender: An Anthology*, ed. Margaret L Andersen and Patricia Hill Collins (Belmont, Calif.: Wadsworth Publishing Company, 1992), 65–70.

4 Louise Erdrich, *Love Medicine* (Harper Perennial, 1984, 1993); James Welch, *Fools Crow* (New York: Penguin, 1986); Leslie Marmon Silko, *Almanac of the Dead* (New York: Simon & Schuster, 1991); Sherman Alexie, *The Lone Ranger and Tonto Fistfight in Heaven* (New York: Harper Perennial, 1994); Linda Hogan, *Mean Spirit* (New York: Ballantine, 1990).

5 Paula Gunn Allen, "The Sacred Hoop," in *The Sacred Hoop* (Boston: Beacon Press, 1986), 54–75; Marilyn Frye, "Oppression," in *The Politics of Reality* (Trumansburg, N.Y.: The Crossing Press, 1983) 1–16.

6 See Banks, *Teaching Strategies*, 65–69.

7 George Lipsitz, *The Possessive Investment in Whiteness: How White People Profit from Identity Politics* (Philadelphia: Temple University Press, 1998); Arthur K. Spears, ed., *Race and Ideology: Language, Symbolism, and Popular Culture* (Detroit: Wayne State University Press, 1999).

MENACED BY RESISTANCE:

THE BLACK TEACHER IN THE MAINLY WHITE SCHOOL/CLASSROOM

Black people are the magical faces at the bottom of society's well. Even the poorest whites, those who must live their lives only a few levels above, gain their self-esteem by gazing down on us. Surely, they must know that their deliverance depends on letting down their ropes. Only by working together is escape possible. Over time, many reach out, but most simply watch, mesmerized into maintaining their unspoken commitment to keeping us where we are, at whatever cost to them or to us.

—Derrick Bell, *Faces at the Bottom of the Well*

When the African walked into the court of Western letters, she or he was judged in advance by a fixed racist subtext, or pretext, which the African was forced to confront, confirm, or reject. Given that these fictions of racial essence were sanctioned by "science," the Africans had little hope indeed of speaking themselves free of European fantasies of their "Otherness."

—Henry Louis Gates Jr., "Talkin' That Talk"

If Gates' proposition above is a reasonable one—and I believe it is—then relatively few people of African descent ever have any hope of "speaking them-

---

GÎTAHI GÎTÎTÎ teaches African, African American, Caribbean, Latin American, and comparative literatures at the University of Rhode Island. His work has been published in *The Johns Hopkins Guide to Literary Theory and Criticism, Companion to African Literatures, Current Writing, Paintbrush,* and *Left Curve.* He is also a translator and poet.

In this essay, Gîtîtî asserts that while whites are rewarded for any work related to "diversity," people of color are not; his essay includes several memorable illustrations from his own career. Inspired by James Baldwin, he makes the case that institutions that are not working to eradicate racism "perpetrate great violence against students of all backgrounds," with their administrators functioning as prison guards of student and faculty minds rather than true educators.

selves free" of American "white" fantasies of their "Otherness." In the context of academia, this would apply as much to prospective students and faculty members as it would to public speakers and visiting scholars. The exertion involved, conscious or otherwise, particularly in confronting and rejecting the racist subtext or pretext, is tremendous and exhausting to the body and the spirit. The waste of energy, talent, and human possibility is simply enormous.

The devastating cost of eradicating racism has been noted by many, including Joe R. Feagin and Hernán Vera in their 1995 book *White Racism:* "From the perspective of U.S. society as a whole, the human time and energy expended in planning, staging, and implementing racist actions is extremely wasteful, and this waste is catastrophic for both black victims and white perpetrators."[1] Elsewhere, Feagin and Vera remark on "not only the very heavy material and psychological costs for African Americans but also the serious material, psychological, and moral costs for white Americans"; they lament that, in all areas of American life, "the abandonment of efficiency because of a racist mythology is thus highly wasteful in concrete material terms. In addition, all who invest in such inefficient corporations lose materially from racism."[2] It is necessary here to include colleges and universities as corporations which traditionally have invested monies, and received millions in gifts and grants, from anything between apartheid-era South Africa and racist transnational companies. Equally, it is necessary to state without flinching that those colleges and universities which condone white supremacist practices, however veiled those may be, perpetrate great violence against students of all backgrounds, and implicate their administrators, like prison guards, in the continuous imprisonment of minds —the very antithesis of education that liberates the mind. But colleges and universities are far from acting alone.

In his incisive "A Talk to Teachers" address, originally titled "The Negro Child—His Self-Image," delivered in October, 1963, James Baldwin reminded his audience that they must understand that "in the attempt to correct so many generations of bad faith and cruelty, when it is operating not only in the classroom but in society, you will meet the most fantastic, the most brutal, and the most determined resistance . . ." Baldwin remarked that American society at that historical juncture was "desperately menaced, not by Khrushchev, but from within."[3]

In the ensuing essay I want to extend Baldwin's insightful observation on the purpose of education and the obligation of "any citizen of this country who figures himself as responsible—and particularly those of you who deal with the minds of young people . . ." by taking a look at the state of education in the university classroom almost forty years after Baldwin's talk to teachers. It is important, at the very least, to gauge whether any substantial changes have occurred in the areas that matter most: the American mind, the curriculum, pedagogy and its practitioners, educational administration, and the power that corporate and political interests wield over the form and content of education. My personal experience in teaching at various U.S. colleges and universities will be augmented with readings from contemporary radical-thinking writers and cultural activists in the areas of literature, pedagogy, cultural studies, and multiculturalism.

Baldwin warns that those committed to fostering enduring changes must be prepared to "go for broke." In today's social, cultural, and political climate, how does the "Negro child" that Baldwin spoke about now become adult—"go for broke" in the socializing and formative terrain of the American university today? Essential to this discussion are questions pertaining to the constraints, pressures, and hostilities faced by would-be agents of change, albeit in apparently minimal ways. What, for example, do white students *see* when I, a black instructor, walk into the classroom on that first day of the semester? When I open my mouth and a "foreign accent" comes out? Does my blackness (or my speech) do anything to their comfort level, perhaps causing some to seek their comfort in another course or with a different instructor? While some students may not doubt my competence to teach a particular course prefixed with African American, African, Caribbean, and so on, is it possible that they do not understand why I am teaching them something called American literature, poetry, short story, film?

It is not enough to ask this kind of question of students alone. One must consider also what and how students learn in other courses taught by one's colleagues. Do students bring with them facts, attitudes, prejudices, and mental habits that complicate (often unnecessarily) the classroom dynamic? What influence do parents, family members, and peers exert on the students I teach or hope to teach? What of the much-vaunted institutional culture that each university or college claims to develop, maintain, and promote? Much of contemporary academic discourse is laced with such buzzwords as "diversity" and "cultural competence," and a good number of university administrators and teaching faculty, mostly white, have been gathering awards and monies for their work in promoting diversity, multiculturalism, and so on. Finally, there is talking about race, writing about it, doing research in matters of race, publishing papers and books on race, conducting local and countrywide workshops and seminars on race, and nabbing research grants for race questions. All told, it is evident that when white people do it, it is worthy and meritorious work, deserving of timely reward; if black or other nonwhite people try to do it, they are just whining, or perhaps incapable of, or unwilling to do, other kinds of scholarly stuff.

What remains in question are the precise components of such diversity, especially as these apply to recruitment and retention practices for students and faculty of color, as well as to curricular content and the relative stability of those disciplinary areas in which students of color should see reflections of themselves—in the subject matter and in the faculty who teach them.

In the aforementioned essay, Baldwin asserts that the purpose of education, "finally, is to create in a person the ability to look at the world for himself, to make his own decisions, to say to himself this is black or this is white, to decide for himself whether there is a God in heaven or not. To ask questions of the universe, and then learn to live with those questions, is the way he achieves his own identity."[4] Baldwin posits that "what is upsetting the country [in the 1960s] is a sense of its own identity," arguing that if one were able to change the curriculum in all the schools so that African Americans learned more about themselves and their contributions to American culture, "[one] would be liberating not only Negroes, [one] would be liberating white people who know nothing about their own history. And the reason is that if you are compelled to lie about one aspect of anybody's history, you must lie about it all."[5] If, as Baldwin asserts, one attains a fuller consciousness of one's identity only through an incessant questioning of one's complex sociocultural universe, if one must learn to live with not only those questions but also with the sometimes unsettling nuances of the answers they yield, then it appears that contemporary American education, with its overly nationalistic emphasis on a Eurocentric cultural heritage, fails to encourage students (and their instructors) to explore more deeply and widely what it means to be American. The attempted omissions and erasures of every American's other "self" predispose one to think of oneself in either–or terms, the facile notion of the melting pot notwithstanding. The certainty with which we carve our identities as culturally or genetically unalloyed, the absolute truths that we teach our children and students, particularly with regard to what "we" are not—and others certainly are—may well be the insidious lies that Baldwin sees as historically inscribed in the culture of American education and socialization.

The sad truth of Baldwin's observation manifests itself, for instance, in the plight of the white female student who complains bitterly to us in class that her son, born of a black father, has been "put down [in some official document; the phrasing is hers] as 'black.'" Why, she demands of us, can't the child be listed as white, the color of its mother's skin? One sees here a troubled replay of the "one drop" rigmarole: in the past, one drop of "black" blood used to be the sole measure of one's blackness. Today, does one drop of "white" blood make the child in question white, or black? Does it matter, should it matter, what color the child is? Should color ever be the basis of familial love and achievement? The student's question is not a challenge to the entrenched system of racialized identities; in the asking of the question the student reveals her investment in the latter. The lies that Baldwin writes about have worked too well. Clearly, the impact of the lies of American history can only be injurious to interracial couples, families, and other human associations.

Part of the series of myths that pass for contemporary American identity is the myth of the death or disappearance of race as a central and controlling issue in American daily life. The white undergraduate and graduate students I teach routinely repeat the mantra of how far we have come, how much economic and social progress African Americans have achieved since the 1960s, or how education will soon have converted all racially prejudiced Americans into models of civic righteousness. Needless to say, this is deeply confused behavior. In her essay "Representations of Whiteness in the Black Imagination," bell hooks examines the classroom dynamic in her own teaching experience, and notes how white students respond with "disbelief, shock, and rage" when black students provide observations, stereotypes, and so on of white people that are offered as "data" gleaned from close scrutiny and study. According to hooks, "Their amazement that black people watch white people with a critical 'ethnographic' gaze, is itself an expression of racism. Often their rage erupts because they believe that all ways of looking that highlight difference subvert the liberal belief in a universal subjectivity (we are all just people) that they think will make racism disappear."[6] In addressing this aspect of white student behavior in the context of mixed-population classes, hooks notes that white students "have a deep emotional investment in the myth of 'sameness,' even as their actions reflect the primacy of whiteness as a sign informing who they are and how they think."[7]

My own classroom experience provides related examples of this closet racism on the part of white students, and consequently of the intractable, if sometimes dormant, character of racism. The year is 1993. I am teaching a course titled Introduction to African American Culture. A preliminary question is: How do we define "African American," given the complexity of origins, geographical distribution, intermixture, and so on? Before the racially diverse class could even make a tentative attempt to answer the question, a white student vehemently objects that "this business of some people [attaching prefixes such as 'African' to their identity category] is the cause of division and conflict in America." Why, this student wants to know, can't people be *just* Americans?

A vigorous exchange follows this outburst. Are there not Americans who identify themselves as Irish, Italian, Polish, Anglo, and so on? he is asked. Do such categories not observe holidays and rituals, and symbolically enact some of their ethnic being? Many such questions later, the student is compelled to answer in the affirmative. He later "shares" with his classmates that his family are recent immigrants from Eastern Europe, that some of them have had racial slurs thrown at them by white Americans.

Or take the case of my 1997 graduate course the Novel Across the World, which required students to recognize especially the motif of resistance to domination, whether it be internal or otherwise. Inevitably, imperialism, European or American, is encountered again and again. So are the motifs of revolution and "necessary violence" as counterhegemonic strategies. The students' own resistance to the idea of other nations, peoples, and "races" mobilizing against their own colonization—and often meeting violence with violence—was most determined. Are there no alternatives to revolutionary violence, almost all of them demanded? Doesn't the use of violence simply guarantee an endless cycle of violence? When I asked the students whether they would push this argument for the American or the French revolution, I received incoherent or sophistry-laden answers. Might the race or geographical origin of the self-liberators be a factor in the students' denunciation of armed resistance, I asked. Silence or indications of hurt feelings were what I got. When students, scholars in the making at the very least, refuse to entertain or engage ideas or propositions even in an intellectual fashion—because race (or one's investment in race) is a nasty subject best left to die a natural death—what does that say about their capacity to "ask questions of the universe, and then learn to live with those questions"? Baldwin has told us that "the obligation of anyone who thinks of himself as responsible is to examine society and try to change it and to fight it—at no matter what the risk. This is the only hope society has. This is the only way societies change."[8] For me as a teacher, the question that this begs is: What price does intellectual complacency and avoidance of the unpleasant exact on a nation, especially when institutions of higher learning become the hotbeds of reactionarism and the now-familiar dumbing down of the American mind?

I have often thought that the status of the black teacher in an all-white school as being akin to that of the black police officer in an all-white neighborhood. The black teacher may, hopefully, count on his or her colleagues to vouch for his or her character or qualification for the job. Similarly, the black police officer may hope for the same validation by his or her fellow officers. But in neither situation is such validation in any way guaranteed, or without its limitations and caprices. In any case, the white teachers and the white police officers have constituencies behind them—white students and parents and white citizens, respectively, that the black teacher and the black police officer decidedly do not.

The black teacher in a predominantly white school, even when part of a minority group, fares only slightly better, if at all, just as a black police officer in a predominantly white force fares only slightly better than his or her lone counterpart in an all-white force. And if black American citizens, most of whose histories are as old as the Republic, if not older, encounter this questioning of credentials and belonging, what do you think black people of different geographical origins and histories encounter? For the black persons involved, are there realistic career prospects in such scenarios?

At issue is the idea of ownership—ownership of power and the institutions that power creates to maintain and protect itself. Institutionalized power creates insiders and outsiders; it draws boundaries and marks of identification. By these marks it manages to include or exclude, to certify or to disqualify. So it is that the socialization of children entails an imprinting of what "we" own by right, who or what we do not touch. So it is that children and students learn what kind of teachers they "should be" provided with, and which ones they should not be; what kind of education—and what form of instruction—they should or should not be exposed to.

So it was that, as a graduate student at the University of Minnesota, when I first stepped into a classroom to teach Spanish to a beginning class, the students refused to believe that I was their instructor. This went on for three days in a row. When I persisted in being present, they finally gave up, but not before a good number of them had dropped the class or shifted to another section. Since then, such student behavior no longer surprises me. Indeed, I have known students to drop the class at precisely that moment when they set foot in the room and see the "guy who's going to be teaching us." For some reason, when I give students their syllabi, I never prefix my name with any of those titles beloved of academia. In most cases, students take that as a sign that I have only minimal academic achievement, and are quick to let me know by their behavior and attitude.

Happily, not all students, and not all families, are as invested in race and social status as others. Many students share with their classmates stories involving parents who ask with dismay why in the world their son or daughter is wasting time on something called "African this" or "Black that," whether it be literature, art, history, or whatever. Many parents and family members express shock or disbelief that a black instructor is teaching their child. Conversely, many wonder just how it is possible for a black instructor from the other side of the world to be teaching American poetry, or drama, or novel. But students who do their own thinking know that the cultivation of the mind, and of the person, has nothing to do with the color of the source.

There seems still to be scant attention paid to the price that the scholar of African descent pays daily in the course of performing his or her teaching duties. Both anecdotal and research evidence attests to the prevalence of discriminatory tenure review procedures, heavy formal and informal teaching loads, excessive committee assignments, burdensome student advisement, and mentoring demands. But the psychological burden associated with the black scholar's typical "one minority per pot" status gets little press. It is bad enough that my own colleagues typecast me as the one who teaches "black" courses, going so far as to characterize me—to incoming graduate students, to boot—as the "specialist" in "Afro-Caribbean studies," whatever that means. It is terrible that a former department head, playing messenger for the dean's office, once pointedly warned me to "go easy on standards," as many students, initially expecting an easy ride in the classes I was teaching, were dropping classes—thus costing the university, or department, valuable tuition money. I was, clearly, being warned that my chances of promotion and tenure would be in jeopardy unless I "acted right." It is deplorable that my students, weaned mainly on a Eurocentric intellectual diet, feel the need to seek validation of what I teach from their white professors. The worst is, of course, the combination of intellectual and social isolation I experience in the institutional setting and in the outside community. Wrestling with student antipathy and institutional ostracism generates often unbearable levels of stress, to say the least. The psychological stress is made worse by the lack of any usable or friendly resources outside of the shrink's office. Having continually to invent individual stress management strategies imposes not just psychological harm; it has a negative effect on sustained productivity and a sense of being anchored, and consequently it has its own economic costs on the individual and family unit.

I am tempted at this point to write a little about how enormously difficult it is to deal with bereavement in such a setting, but I think the point has been made. The routine trivialization of my grief, personal suffering or loss, including injuries from accidents, is hard to deal with. What does one say about a university community where the human problems of black people are not even noticed?

I spoke earlier of typecasting based on race. While my academic credentials in a general sense determine what range of courses or material I am considered fit to teach, are there nevertheless certain expectations of how I should teach them—expectations colored by departmental ideology, the internalized "fittedness" of black people to teach black courses (and vice versa). A perverse twist of this typecasting revealed itself recently during the course of a job search in the English department. Black candidates were repeatedly questioned about their ability to cater to the needs of white students. One curiously self-indulgent question put to white candidates was whether they believed that a white person can be just as effective and competent to teach courses in African American literature and culture, and to interact professionally and effectively with students of color.

My presence at those interviews and presentations reminded me of my own initial interview, during which I was practically asked whether I could pledge to be a role model for students of color. Now, if I am expected to be a role model for black students (or other students of color), does this mean that I am unqualified to play role model for any other kind of student? Does it mean that my white colleagues may in no way be bothered with requests to play the same role for nonwhite students? The question, then, becomes: Are there levels of socially acceptable prejudice that have resulted in a collective myopia to how "race" informs our actions? Is this prejudice bred into the next generation by the present one? In other words, is it just possible that I teach, with enormous tear and wear to myself, students whose "race" infection is congenital, through the school system and outside of it?

One of the saddest reflections of the contemporary status quo in academia is the continued use of the descriptive "American" as a metonym for "white" or

"Caucasian." Whenever "American" is attached to history, literature, art, philosophy, cinema, and so forth, it effectively excludes African American, Native American, Asian American, Latin American, and other integral components of America. Even worse, these latter categories are typically reduced to "ethnic" or "area" studies with the status of elective or "cultural" requirement. The marginalization of these curricular areas (or their total elimination in many institutions) impoverishes not only the education that universities claim to make universal; it deprives students of all cultural backgrounds the opportunity to broaden and deepen their knowledge of themselves and the world they inhabit. There can be little intellectual benefit to be derived from a purposely thinned-down curriculum, both for students and their instructors. Nor can the practice be conducive to social justice, whose ambit encompasses the right of students to receive an education that accurately represents the world they live in, as well as their aspirations and dreams. When schools and instructors signal to their students that there are qualitatively "better" instructors or "more culturally suitable" content areas—based on race or culture—then the schools and instructors have abdicated their moral responsibility to ensure parity of status for courses of instruction. Even worse, they have signalled their complicity in curtailing the career progress of nonwhite scholars, as well as the intellectual and social development of students.

It is not necessary here to rehearse the reasons for and the history behind the de facto positioning of the majority of African-descended peoples at the bottom of the American ladder (or at the bottom of the well, to quote Derrick Bell). Suffice it to say that the inadequacy of redistributive measures that would radically improve economic, social, and political conditions for African Americans lies in the widespread and persistent lack of political will among whites that is, in its turn, based on their investment in what accrues to them by virtue of their race. As Derrick Bell has observed in *Faces at the Bottom of the Well*,

> Throughout history, politicians have used blacks as scapegoats for failed economic or political policies. Before the Civil War, rich slave owners persuaded the white working class to stand with them against the danger of slave revolts—even though the existence of slavery condemned white workers to a life of economic privation. After the Civil War, poor whites fought social reforms and settled for segregation rather than see formerly enslaved blacks get ahead . . . The "them against us" racial ploy—always a potent force in economic bad times—is working again: today whites, as disadvantaged by high-status entrance requirements as blacks, fight to end

affirmative action policies that, by eliminating class-based entrance requirements and requiring widespread advertising of jobs, have likely helped far more whites than blacks.[9]

I contend that the permanence, or persistence, of race in America offers a major reason for the widespread but mistaken white notion that people of color in particular, and women in general, have the jobs or opportunities they have solely by virtue of affirmative action. In the opinion of the majority of whites, blacks are not hired on the basis of merit but rather in accordance with affirmative action objectives.

The adverse effects of this belief on the victim are serious and deeply troubling. In this context, according to Marcia E. Sutherland, "professors of color are preemptively construed as lacking the requisite qualifications, credentials and experience. This is only one of many outcomes which flow from the attribution of Whites that Black academicians are solely affirmative action appointees."[10] Sutherland argues that "ascribing token status to Blacks informs Whites' tendency to offer Blacks low salaries and nontenurable positions," and, further, that "the temporality implied by these appointments fosters a climate in which the Black scholar remains peripheral and inconsequential to the White institution."[11] As far as faculty of African descent are concerned, it is no secret that predominantly white institutions practice the dictum "Keep this nigger running." Hired disproportionately at the lowest ranks, socially isolated and intellectually segregated from other professional colleagues, deprived of information on the informal processes to upward academic success, black faculty frequently just up and leave, and in their wake a myth takes root about their well-known inability to tough it out.

In the context in which this discussion is situated, the classroom environment is structured mainly by race. Upon entering college, significant numbers of white students admit to being exposed to students or faculty of color for the first time. The racial demographics of students, faculty, and administrators have already been made predictable by so-called tradition. What may not be so predictable is how the black instructor must negotiate the tensions that necessarily arise in the course of classroom discussion. If white students are reticent to contribute to discussions that involve American history or race, or American involvement in world affairs, what does the instructor do to get them involved? If the same students, mistakenly or otherwise, believe themselves to be the victims of generalized "anti-white" sentiment, is the instructor obliged to be their consoler and defender? Since the white students will let the instructor know what they think in their student evaluations, how does the instructor negotiate this minefield? Should he or she have to worry so much about these subjective and often retaliatory evaluations?

That is not all. Through a combination of factors students, both white and black, consistently are led to believe that the courses assigned to black instructors are—or should be—"easy" courses. The relative value attached to such courses, many of which are placed in a culture cluster or some such lower-rated academic category, is frequently an indication of the institution's priorities. Be that as it may, black instructors are not "supposed" to be rigorous in their scholarship, teaching, and insistence on performance standards. When, alas, they act out of character and pose a threat to student's grades, they are deemed to have gone too far. As Sutherland reports, "Untenured faculty receive tacit messages to strive for a 'proper fit' with the White institution. In the customary conservative White academic culture this is best attained by the avoidance of challenges to White supremacy. One must avoid the image of being a 'trouble maker.'"[12] Inhospitable working environments motivate people to relocate to what appear, at least in the short term, to be more amenable environments. However, the cost of being on the move so much is the instability it engenders, internalized by the person affected, and used as a stigma by those who judge the "constant mover."

Partly in recognition of the commonplace that language is everything, academia has revised some of its language. Certainly political correctness is bandied about every day. The drones insist that PC is an attempt to muzzle freedom of expression. All that aside, it is safe to conjecture that not too many white faculty members are to be found who address their black students as "Negroes" or "niggers." How, then, is it possible that students at all levels continue to churn out in their speech and writing—without qualification or any sense of irony or insult—such terms as "tribesmen" (in referring to Africans, for instance), "primitive societies," "Bushmen," and "inferior cultures"? Could race have died but forgotten to take its vocabulary along with it?

When white faculty members and administrators tell me that I am very articulate, or that I speak English exceptionally well, what I hear behind their voices are students complaining or cursing because I corrected their English. The unspoken thought is that language acquisition is race-based. That is, a black person like me has no business being truly intelligent, or having strong command of not just English, but several other languages as well. When a black person can do all these things, ways must be found to bring him or her down a notch. Hence the recourse to "you can't understand them because of their accents," or "so-and-so is such a tough grader, you better not take that class." Incidentally, faculty members who abet students in this kind of behavior do themselves no service. If indeed I am a tough grader, a demanding teacher, what does that say about my accusers or their abettors?

Numerous recommendations have been made for combating or eradicating racism. The most challenging (or challenged) include the kind that Derrick Bell suggests in the opening excerpt, that "only by working together is escape possible." Real change begins, many now argue, when whites begin to recognize that the destruction of racism is in their own interests. Feagin and Vera suggest that "Meaningful solutions to racism involve making the waste caused by this racism painfully evident for all Americans . . . In our view a strong defense of antiracist education and public policies such as reparations must show white Americans that contemporary racism is a waste of energy for *everyone*."[13] One hopes that white people are listening. Their humanity, and that of their coming generations, is at stake.

NOTES

1 Joe R. Feagin and Hernán Vera, *White Racism: The Basics* (New York: Routledge, 1995), 167.
2 Feagin and Vera, *White Racism*, 168–169.
3 James Baldwin, "A Talk to Teachers," in *Multi-Cultural Literacy: Opening the American Mind*, ed. Rick Simonson and Scott Walker (St. Paul, Minn.: Graywolf Press, 1988), 3–12.
4 Baldwin, "A Talk to Teachers," 4.
5 Baldwin, "A Talk to Teachers," 8.
6 bell hooks, *Black Looks: Race and Representation* (Boston: South End Press, 1992), 167.
7 hooks, *Black Looks*, 167.
8 Baldwin, "A Talk to Teachers," 4.
9 Derrick Bell, *Faces at the Bottom of the Well: The Permanence of Racism* (New York: Harper Collins, 1992), 8.
10 Marcia E. Sutherland, "Black Faculty in White Academia: The Fit Is an Uneasy One," *Western Journal of Black Studies* 14.1 (1990), 19.
11 Sutherland, "Black Faculty," 19.
12 Sutherland, "Black Faculty," 20.
13 Feagin and Vera, *White Racism*, 191, emphasis in original.

PHOTO: TIM TRUMBLE, ARIZONA STATE UNIVERSITY PHOTOGRAPHER

KAREN J. LEONG

STRATEGIES FOR SURVIVING RACE IN THE CLASSROOM

When I prepared to begin my first semester as an assistant professor in a women's studies program, my friends, committee members, and colleagues all warned me to adjust my expectations and that I would be teaching students very different from me. They were correct. Significantly, this difference not only included our social and educational backgrounds or aspirations but also extended to my being a Chinese American woman at the front of the classroom. The factors that visibly identified me challenged my students' perceptions of how a professor should appear and act. The dual and contradictory position I embodied as native informant and authority figure was difficult for all of us in the classroom to negotiate. In this essay I discuss how I learned to make sense of race in the classroom.

My first and primary teaching assignment was to teach the women's studies core course that focuses on the experiences of women of color in the United States. This gender, race, and class course has almost always been taught by a woman of color, and, according to my colleagues, has always been a challenging course to teach because it inspires student resistance and hostility. Students are asked to question their own positions within the hierarchies of

---

KAREN J. LEONG is an assistant professor in the women's studies program at Arizona State University. Her teaching and scholarship examine the intersections of gender, race and ethnicity, class, and sexuality in U.S. history, particularly as manifested through women's experiences, social institutions and policy, and American popular culture.

Leong tells how she deals with the student resistance and hostility she encounters as a beginning professor. She describes times when her "perceived dual authority"—as a woman of color as well as a professor—creates unexpected classroom tension, and times when students' minds begin to open.

gender, race, and class that structure our society. This is not always comfortable, and students understandably respond with resistance. As someone who simultaneously represents the very subject of what the students are learning, however, I soon realized that this resistance took on a particularly personal dimension.

My background in feminist and critical race theory encouraged me to try to demystify the classroom experience. Nonetheless, I was not prepared to deal with the ensuing power dynamics in the classroom. My first semester as a professor in the classroom was a revelation of student resistance and hostility. The tensions of the classroom manifested themselves in my course evaluations. I have found that many students do take the time to provide thoughtful feedback and critiques, and I rely on these comments to shape revisions to my courses. But several of my evaluations revealed deeper discontent. Numerous students complained that in a class that was supposed to be about women of color, I only talked about Asian American women (interestingly, this was the class for which I had omitted most of the readings about Asian American women). Several complained that this course focused "too much on race," and they were tired of hearing about oppression. Others expressed their weariness of hearing so many "complaints" about society from so many "victims."

I have since learned that my experience of race in the classroom was similar to those of other women faculty of color. The dynamics of race in the classroom reflect broader dynamics of power relating to gender, race, and class in academia and society at large. Administrators, scholars, and pedagogical theorists alike exhibit a reluctance to acknowledge and address the particular experiences of faculty who are women, and who are not white. Whether we like it or not, the politics of identity shape our interactions with our students and the very dynamic of learning within the classroom.

I shared with someone, whose opinion I greatly admired and respected, my frustration and surprise that my attempts to demystify the learning experience were unsuccessful. I explained that I had been inspired by several books about teaching to challenge traditional models of pedagogy with my students. She, in turn, expressed amazement at my surprise, and pointed out that these authors were either older white males with whom students associate academic authority, or a celebrity scholar of color. "When he appears to be vulnerable, the students already respect him and so respect him more because he is clearly choosing to bridge the distance they perceive between their role and his. But you—" and here she laughed. "You don't have to try to be any more vulnerable—you already are!" And she was right. I had overlooked my own difference, which in itself made a great difference. And at this point it was too late. My classes were already enmeshed in the ambiguities of my position and the contradictions of power and authority in the classroom—and truthfully, it would have been a great learning experience for all of us if it weren't so awful.

The director of my program at the time sought to support me by acknowledging that race was part of the student reaction. She provided me with a report on the status of Asian Pacific American women in higher education, in which Shirley Hune summarizes, "APA female faculty find they are evaluated differently and lack a sense of community with their colleagues. Their expertise and authority is [*sic*] often contested in the classroom and in their departments."[1] Another study, one that examines the variables of gender and race in college course evaluations, concluded that nonwhite women faculty tend to be ranked lower in these evaluations than any other group. In general, women received lower evaluations than men, and faculty of color received lower evaluations than white faculty. Analysis of how gender and ethnicity affected student evaluations of faculty showed that male students were more likely to rank male faculty higher than female faculty. Furthermore, "women [students] were found to give the highest ratings to minority male faculty and the lowest ratings to minority female faculty, with the ratings of Anglo female and male faculty falling somewhere in between."[2] The study thus suggests that race and gender intersect to negatively shape students' perceptions of minority female faculty. Given the disproportionate number of women faculty of color hired to teach courses about race and difference in women's studies courses—which anecdotally are some of the most difficult courses to teach—women of color faculty are at a disadvantage before class even begins. Although the study highlighted the how race and gender skew students' course and faculty evalutions, addressing specific factors that shape these outcomes obviously was beyond its scope. The color and gender lines extend far beyond the students and the classroom to American society at large. Race in the classroom is not so much about students and classes as it is about social structures that are replicated uncritically in academia, inside and outside of the classroom. Indeed, I increasingly noticed how the very dynamic that shaped my courses and interactions with students continually manifested itself as deeply embedded in all levels of higher education.

Throughout my first few semesters, I attended numerous teaching workshops desperately seeking tools to construct an alternate mode of teaching in the classroom. Most of these workshops recreated the very dynamics that we sought to deconstruct in our teaching. Gender and race worked together to determine who would speak and who would be silenced, who would be asked to speak for different groups, and whose experiences would be legitimized. During one workshop about incorporating theater exercises in the classroom, the faculty participated in creating living sculptures, positioning other workshop participants to create pictures of oppression or homophobia. A pattern began to emerge where the faculty of color present were chosen to represent people of color, the woman with the short and spiky haircut was asked to portray the lesbian, and so on. Even though all of the participants had discussed at length how students of color are often are called upon in class to "translate" their apparent differences, we nonetheless uncritically performed that same scenario over and over again, substituting bodies for voices throughout the workshop.

In order to create productive learning spaces, we in academic positions of authority must engage in self-questioning and frank dialogue about difference if we expect our students to do so. I have found that many administrators and faculty members are still very uncomfortable even acknowledging the realities of difference that shape our institutions from the top down. How can we expect our students to feel any more comfortable than we do? The desire on the part of some to slip issues about race and difference into our curriculum without our students noticing defeats the whole purpose. Differences are *not* comfortable. No matter how much we try to make it comfortable for our students, or ourselves, at some point we must face the reality that structures of difference in our society place some of us in positions of power and advantage over others. Implicit messages from colleagues that we should not challenge our students in this way, because learning is less likely to occur in a hostile environment, are embedded with white privilege. Our very presence as faculty of color may be perceived as a challenge in and of itself. Regardless of what we say or how nicely we say it, our presence will threaten some students. This is not to suggest that we abandon civility or professionalism, but that we recognize and expect that our bodies will be read personally within the classroom context, changing the very dynamic of the learning environment. By consciously incorporating this dynamic into the educational process itself, I believe that it is possible to empower our students and ourselves to learn to confront and negotiate the multiple permutations of race that shape our classroom as well as our society.

This realization resulted from my own process of learning how to negotiate race in the classroom. I am fortunate to work at a university large enough that other faculty of color were present and willing to encourage me by sharing the scars of their own battles in the classroom. One senior faculty member, a major scholar in her field and well-known for her teaching, sought me out to ask how my first year was progressing. She encouraged me to take charge the first day in class, to state from the outset my credentials and establish my authority; more importantly, she shared her own tales about a classroom of male students literally standing up in class to challenge her knowledge and authority. An African American faculty member will never know how much of a difference she made to me when she spoke during a roundtable discussion following a graduate student's performance about gender and race. Sharing eloquently her own experience of segregation as a child, and the continued racism she experiences as a woman of color faculty member on campus, she observed, "One learns to protect oneself—to wear armor." She paused. "Every day before I enter the classroom, I pull on that armor." This acknowledgment that as women of color we must protect ourselves, that when we are out there in front of the class we are no less vulnerable than when we as students sat in the class, moved me to tears of recognition.

I do not know why I expected being a professor would be any different than being an undergraduate or graduate student. As perpetual outsiders within academia, those of us who represent the underrepresented have long learned mechanisms of survival. My mistake was in thinking that my being a faculty member automatically conferred some sort of privilege upon my person in the academy. Even though our training provides us with some authority in the classroom and elevates our social status to some extent, our very presence as faculty continues to be contested. We must remind ourselves again and again that we do not enter academia as students and faculty with our acceptance a given, nor with our armor fully assembled. We learn over time—specific to the circumstances in which we find ourselves—when and how to protect ourselves and, just as importantly, when we can put down the armor and with whom. I have found that many colleagues are not comfortable relating their own stories from the front. Perhaps these memories are still too painful, or perhaps they fear that to give voice to the struggle means giving ground for which they have fought. I can empathize. At the same time, I know that others sharing their experiences helped me to not internalize my own sense of inadequacy as a teacher, and allowed me to acknowledge the pain and anger of particular interactions with students and colleagues. Now, in specific contexts in my classroom or in my interactions with colleagues, I reserve the choice to be vulnerable—but I will not do so as indiscriminately as I did before.

Rather than erase race or any other differences from the classroom, this microcosm of society, we need to acknowledge these differences and the tensions that result.[3] One of my colleagues suggested that I discuss openly in class the ways in which race was shaping the classroom dynamics. She suggested that this could be a way to ask my students to critique their own assumptions about gender, race, age, and authority. At the time, I did not have the confidence to pull this off. I now recognize, however, that this is as important a strategy as openly critiquing the mechanisms by which we professors gain authority in the classroom. In my classes I now discuss my own privilege of education, a middle-class background, and social status; I do this to show how even as a woman of color I may be located in privileged positions relative to my students and to other women of color. In turn—and depending on the students in the class—I may borrow from my insightful and courageous colleague who asked her colleagues in a teaching workshop, "What is it like to wake up white?" When I ask my students this question that they are often surprised, upset, and annoyed—some seem literally stunned with guilt. If I push them a bit more and am lucky, at least one of my students will protest, "That's not fair! How can one person represent all white people?" And then I will exclaim, "That is precisely the point! Is this fair to anyone?" Thus we begin our discussion of white privilege, how whiteness has been normalized in American society and culture, and how, as Gloria Yamato explains, guilt is not the point—active intervention in the processes of privilege is.[4]

I now realize that teaching is a performance on multiple levels; we constantly juggle different roles in order to evoke different responses from our students. As women and nonwhite faculty, moreover, we are performing gender and race in new ways for many of our students—we may be the first female, non-white professors they have had in college. The key is to convey this to our students; they must understand that we are performing our pedagogy in order to facilitate learning, and that we are not necessarily representing our own selves in the front of the classroom. Indeed, performing identities may be the most productive way for women faculty of color to negotiate the multiple expectations of the students in the classroom.[5]

I also try to enter the classroom with an awareness of how history has shaped my own life as well as the lives of my students. Many of my students have grown up in neighborhoods marked by homogeneity in socioeconomic status and racial composition, many have been taught a national mythology that silences the voices of a wide range of men and women, and many have never been challenged to examine the structures that simultaneously advantage and disadvantage them. Awareness of these realities calls for a patience rooted in humility and empathy: to become conscious of one's own privilege is a painful experience, and it is a process that my students and I will inevitably share over the course of the semester.[6] At times, my students will teach me from their own experiences, from their expressions of enthusiasm or frustration, and even from their silences, precisely what I am trying to convey to them—and when those moments converge, they can be transformative for all of us.

I seek to develop a learning environment conducive to these moments, a sense of sharing a common journey that requires combining our individual resources and abilities. Every semester I am made acutely aware of my shortcomings and limitations in this process. Recognizing my own frustrations as I learn to teach reminds me that hope is an essential element of education. Learning about the divisions in our society and in our classrooms is indeed painful. Students need to know, and be reminded throughout, that the process of learning is worth it—that what they are learning matters. In practical terms, I infuse my curriculum with moments in history when individuals have transcended immediate limitations to create what bell hooks describes as "beloved community."[7]

My role in creating beloved community in my classroom fundamentally requires a constant awareness of my own position as a person in authority. This entails knowing that, as a nonwhite professor, students of color may scrutinize my words and actions more closely. Sometimes I am so solicitous of the white students' feelings, and afraid of appearing to blame whites for all of America's social ills, that I do not correct racist statements that are painful to other students—particularly students of color. I thus privilege the feelings of the white students at the expense of the nonwhite students. During one lecture, I passed over one student's comment about rap—I thought it was too obvious, and I hoped that one of my students in this very talkative class would address it. But no one said a word. After class ended, two African American students communicated to me that they had found the comment full of offensive stereotypes about blacks. I agreed, and explained that I had hoped that students in the class would speak up. One of the students, a male, explained, "I know that people probably expected me to respond. But I don't want to always have to be the one to speak up for African American males." I knew what he was talking about. I may consciously choose to identify myself as a woman of color and acknowledge that my critique of structures of inequity comes from that strategically essentialist position. Yet it is quite a different matter when others continually expect or assume that my words or actions, because I am a Chinese American female, represent those of all Asian American females. In this case, I realized that the students were looking to me to wield my professorial authority in response to a comment made by an older white male student. Was part of this because he was older and white? Was there no immediate response to his dismissive comments because we who found the comment questionable thought it was so obvious that surely someone else would say something? As the professor, and perhaps more so as a professor of color, students may look to me to speak out about these issues. I am still learning when to speak and when to challenge my students to speak through my silences.

Negotiating my position of power in the classroom also means being aware of when my identity as a Chinese American and visibly identifiable woman of color will converge with my position of authority in the classroom. During class discussions about race, I may overcompensate out of concern for how my students of color view me. At other times, it is just difficult to know when to say something and when not to. During one class, Abby, a white female student who had been working hard to participate in class even though what we were learning was clearly challenging to her, responded to another student's comment. As she paused mid-comment, I jumped in to define her terminology, sharply stating, "You mean *white* women, right?" The student faltered, looked uncertain, and said "Yes, that's what I meant—white women." Quickly concluding her statement, she fell silent. And having interjected my point, I felt the entire class recoil at my tone of voice, which had come out sharply, perhaps even accusatory, in tone. At that moment I realized that my perceived dual authority in this classroom discussion about race—as a woman of color in addition to being a professor—had lent my words and tone an extra weight that I had not intended. I hesitated. If I acknowledged that I overstepped my authority, would I end up undermining my authority in the classroom? If I did not, what kind of lesson would my students take away from class discussion? I took the easier way out, stopping Abby after class and asking her to come to my office where I apologized to her for interrupting her and for my tone of voice. Surprised and relieved, she expressed her fear of saying the "wrong" thing in class. I assured her that I could see that, and that I appreciated her efforts in participating. I added that I too was afraid of making mistakes.

Finally, I remind myself what a privilege it is to stand in front of the classroom, and to challenge students to think in new ways and to grapple with new ways of seeing and knowing. I think of Kerry, a young woman in my class who sat in the front row in the seat farthest to the right. A copious note-taker, Kerry rarely spoke up in class. Right before the midterm, as we reviewed concepts from the class during my office hours, I learned that she and her husband lived with her parents, and she initially had thought I was "white-bashing" during the first two weeks of class. But she added, "I'm beginning to realize what you were doing." I heard this with some relief. Even so, she and her classmates visibly struggled with the course materials. She nodded when other students commented that Peggy McIntosh's list of forty-six examples of privileges whites enjoy in American society was overreaching the point.[8] After the midterm, Kerry stopped by my office just to chat about my expectations for the her final research paper. Then, abruptly, she changed the subject. "You know how you're telling us that the American Dream is a myth?" I nodded. We had been talking about the myth of meritocracy in class, and how it shaped social policy and people's attitudes. Kerry hesitated. "Well, I went home and told my mother what you said, you know, about the American Dream . . . being a myth." She looked at me with a puzzled expression. "And do you know what she said? She said of course it's a myth." As her eyes filled with tears, Kerry explained, "All my life she's told me that I only needed to work hard, all my life she's told me to believe in the American Dream. And now . . . and now she's telling me it's all been a myth." Kerry looked at me with surprise and sadness in her eyes, her voice almost a whisper. "Can you believe that?"

Over the semester, Kerry stopped by to tell me that she had not realized that she, her husband, and her parents together were bringing in a household income just barely over the poverty line. During class she began to speak up more often, asking me to clarify a question or statement, or to write a term on the board. Toward the end of the semester we read Ward Churchill's piece on the racist practices involved in the use of Native Americans as school mascots, and I showed clips from the documentary *In Whose Honor?* about Charlene Teters' attempts to end the use of Chief Illiniwek at the University of Illinois at Urbana-Champaign.[9] A heated discussion ensued about whether the mascot should be removed or not. Some students adamantly argued that to remove the mascot was simply caving into political correctness. A couple of the students of color, most of whom sat together in class, stated passionately that those sentiments were racist. Other students of color acknowledged that removing the mascot would be expensive for the school and for the local business community—encouraging more students to speak up and question whose rights and whose history should be considered when the university administration made decisions about the mascot. Several students began looking at me nervously, trying to figure out where I stood on this issue, and concerned that I was focusing so much on the economic issues brought up by the administrators in the documentary. At this point, Kerry, who had been listening intently, raised her hand. Making my way through the outstretched hands of students impatiently wanting to speak, I finally called upon her. Kerry stated, "When slavery ended, there was an economic cost, but we ended slavery because it was the right thing to do. Even if it costs money, the university should change the mascot because it is the right thing to do." The class fell momentarily still and we looked at her as she looked at me. Some students nodded in agreement while others frowned, deep in thought. I turned to the class. Did anyone have anything to add to what Kerry had said? Hands rose again, but not as quickly, as students responded to Kerry's comment.

My final strategy for surviving race in the classroom: enjoy moments like these and treasure them. This is why we're here.

NOTES

1 Shirley Hune, "Executive Summary: Asian American Women in Higher Education: Claiming Visibility and Voice," Association of American Colleges and Universities Program on the Status and Education of Women, *Women of Color in the Academy Series* (Washington, D.C.: Association of American Colleges and Universities, 1998), No. 3, 3.

2 Bianca L. Bernstein and others, "Contributions of Faculty, Student, and Course Characteristics to Student Evaluations. Report on Student Evaluations of Female and Male Faculty at Arizona State University." Faculty Women's Association, Arizona State University, Tempe, Arizona (May 1995), 27–28.

3 Audre Lorde, "Age, Race, Class, and Sex: Redefining Difference," *Sister Outsider* (New York: Crossing Press, 1984), 114–123.

4 Gloria Yamato, "Something about the Subject Makes It Hard to Name," in *Making Face, Making Soul/Haciendo Caras: Creative and Critical Perspectives by Feminists of Color*, ed. Gloria Anzaldúa (San Francisco: Aunt Lute Books, 1990), 20–24, 21.

5 A study analyzing student expectations of faculty based on gender only suggests this as well: "Perhaps female professors are more adept at displaying wide range of teaching behaviors, which allow them to match their teaching style to the particular demands of students in certain classes. In this case the woman is viewed as somewhat of a performer, using her wide repertoire of interaction skills as needed." Anne Statham, Laurel Richardson, and Judith A. Cook, *Gender and University Teaching: A Negotiated Difference*, SUNY Series in Gender and Society (New York: SUNY State University of New York Press, 1991), 107.

6 Cornel West, *Beyond Multiculturalism and Eurocentrism, Volume I: Prophetic Thought in Postmodern Times* (Monroe, Maine: Common Courage Press, 1993), 3–7.

7 bell hooks, "Beloved Community: A World without Racism," *Killing Rage: Ending Racism* (New York: Henry Holt & Company, 1995), 263–272.

8 Peggy Mcintosh, "White Privilege and Male Privilege: A personal account of coming to see correspondences through work in women's studies," in *Race, Class, and Gender: An Anthology*, 1st edition, ed. Margaret Andersen and Patricia Hill Collins (Belmont, Calif.: Wadsworth Publishing Company, 1995), 76–86.

9 Ward Churchill, "Crimes Against Humanity," in *Race, Class, and Gender: An Anthology*, 3rd edition, ed. Margaret Andersen and Patricia Hill Collins (Belmont, Calif.: Wadsworth Publishing Company, 1998), 413–420; and *In Whose Honor?* (Champaign, Ill.: Jay Rosenstein, 1996).

BRENDA BOUDREAU
TAMI EGGLESTON

TRAPS, PITFALLS, AND OBSTACLES:

CHALLENGES TO CONFRONTING RACISM IN ACADEMIA

Bring up the topic of racism on many college campuses, particularly pre-dominantly white campuses, and you will often hear responses such as, "Why can't we all just get along?" or "I don't see color—I see people," or "If everyone would stop focusing so much on race, everything would be fine," or "We don't have a problem on *this* campus." These responses are examples of what Joan Olsson would call "traps"—patterns of guilt, defensiveness, and denial—that allow white people to delude themselves into thinking that racism does not exist or to find ways to avoid confronting the damaging effects of racism. These traps can be even harder to see on a college campus, an arena we expect to be committed to social justice. A true commitment to social justice begins with an open dialogue about race and racism. White educators need

BRENDA BOUDREAU teaches at McKendree College in Lebanon, Illinois. Boudreau is an assistant professor of English and the director of the gender studies minor. Most of her research and teaching focuses on race, class, and gender in contemporary American literature.

TAMI EGGLESTON, who received her Ph.D. in social psychology from Iowa State University, is an assistant professor of psychology at McKendree College. She works with faculty development efforts to combat bigotry and racism.

In their essay, Boudreau and Eggleston look at some traps white faculty fall into, even with good intentions. With rigorous self-criticism, they relate their encounters with massive faculty resistance to a "community and diversity" shared theme for a freshman seminar. Although their account is a cautionary tale, it also serves as a call to informed activism.

to recognize that when we don't engage in a dialogue about racism, we are necessarily helping to perpetuate it. Discussing race in the classroom can be difficult, uncomfortable, and sometimes even frightening or threatening. It can also, however, be incredibly productive and rewarding. Recognizing the traps we fall into as white educators, even with the best intentions, is the key to making sure that this dialogue continues.

Our personal efforts to better understand how to discuss race in the classroom began when we attended a Building an Inclusive Community Workshop sponsored by the National Conference on Community and Justice, a one-day workshop focusing on personal and institutional racism. As professors of English and psychology, we both already incorporated some focus on race, class and gender in our couses, but this workshop made us realize that we could (and more importantly, should) be doing even more to confront racism. After that workshop we continued to involve ourselves in antiracism training programs, and we participated in a weeklong Dismantling Racism Institute, also sponsored by the National Conference on Community and Justice. This kind of training can be expensive, and it is often difficult to get funding, particularly at smaller institutions. McKendree College is a small, predominantly white, private liberal arts college in Southern Illinois, twenty-six miles east of St. Louis. We were able to attend the Dismantling Racism Institute only when we elicited the support of the director of multicultural affairs and negotiated sharing the costs with this office. During the week at this training, we discovered that while dealing with racial issues in an academic way is important, to really confront racism we first had to confront our own white privilege and internalized racism. This was a realization that allowed us to identify a much broader sphere of influence for ourselves as white educators.

We left committed to finding ways to more effectively confront racism on campus. One opportunity to do this presented itself when the director of the Freshman Seminar (FRS) Program at McKendree College decided to incorporate "community and diversity" as a theme for the freshman seminar class, a one-credit hour course for incoming students. The course is designed to acclimate students to college life, both socially and academically. It is taught by instructors from virtually every discipline on campus, working with a junior- or senior-level student peer mentor. As instructors in this program, we took responsibility to restructure the course to deal seriously with this theme. We devised what we thought was a cohesive, innovative, and thematic series of activities and exercises to be used by all fifteen course instructors, adapted from a variety of antiracism training manuals. We developed worksheets, discussion questions, and assignments, along with specific instructions for integrating these into the modules.

Initially the other instructors seemed, if not enthusiastic, at least receptive to the theme and the pedagogical rationale for the activities in the manual. As the semester progressed, however, we met with resistance, which manifested itself in a variety of ways including excuses, refusals to participate, questioning the value of the theme, and even blatant hostility. When our colleagues started to respond so negatively, we were taken aback. As one white female professor said, "We don't want to make freshmen *uncomfortable*, do we?" And from another colleague, "Well, I don't really get how I can talk about this stuff—I'm white."

This sense that white people are somehow not "raced"—that white people are the norm against which all other races are compared—is often the place social justice educators have to start with white students, so these comments from colleagues were surprising. We had to remind ourselves, however, that while most educators might be more sensitive to racial issues, most of our colleagues had never had to think about their own racial identities because they are white. Most of the faculty at McKendree College are individuals who have been teaching for more than ten years, and who have been trained as educators in a very different time. Perhaps even more significantly, professors in other disciplines outside the humanities and social sciences do not necessarily deal with such topics in the classroom at all. When individuals receive Ph.D.'s in any given discipline, they frequently do not go through any training to be teachers at all, other than to perhaps do some teaching as graduate teaching assistants. And, if they did receive teacher training, it most likely did not include anything about diversity issues.

After this initial meeting, when we realized the limitations of our colleagues' backgrounds, we decided to offer a training workshop for faculty and peer mentors to go over the pedagogy supporting several of our worksheets. The turnout for the workshop was disappointingly low. Even more significantly, the response was resistant. One colleague raised her hand and said, "I don't see how I can possibly deal with this diversity stuff and still really cover the history of McKendree and money management." Another colleague, seeing our obvious frustration, tried to answer this question for us: "Well, you can do diversity in the last ten minutes of the class." We were dumbfounded and basically told our colleagues that we shouldn't be dealing with these kinds of issues in the classroom at all if we were not going to take them seriously. I think we realized at that moment that we were not just trying to defend our pedagogical rationale but were indeed dealing with individuals who did not see racism as their personal responsibility.

One of the initial problems we encountered when discussing diversity issues with colleagues illustrates a clear case of cognitive dissonance. The resistance our colleagues felt began with very simple comments such as, "Why do we need to talk about race? I don't even have any black students in my class." This initial resistance turned into full-blown noncompliance when faculty began to admit to us that they either "didn't have time for these diversity activities because there is too much study skills information to cover, " or that they had just "decided not to do that diversity discussion thing." Sometimes we would argue with these colleagues and try to push our beliefs about the importance of these activities; other times we would just give up. On the one hand, we believed strongly in the theme and wanted people to deal with these tough issues. On the other hand, we wanted the group to get along.

We also saw a different version of this dissonance in the ways that the other faculty members explained their outright refusal to participate in the diversity segments. They recognized the importance of the theme but could not overcome their personal discomfort. They fell into typical responses: individuals either change their attitude ("Why do we need to discuss diversity anyway?"), change their behavior (start including diversity in the classroom), or explain away their behavior ("I don't have training to discuss diversity," or "I don't have time to discuss diversity"). In other words, educators don't like experiencing dissonance so they develop a variety of ways to cope with these feelings. Many professors want a classroom that is harmonious and cohesive, while at the same time one that challenges students. When discussing racism, some of the desirable harmonious classroom dynamic will inevitably be altered. Students often get upset or angry, and they tend to withdraw if pushed too far. This constant push and pull is why so many faculty members may find it easier to simply ignore the tough topics of racism, sexism, heterosexism, and classism.

Of course the ways white people choose to avoid race are complex. This is particularly interesting when dealing with educators, who we assume will be liberal and open-minded, and indeed want to educate students in terms of social justice. These are presumably people who understand the importance of social justice but who do not want to directly confront it in their own classrooms. Even educators who are personally dedicated to teaching social justice will fall into traps that allow for denial and defensiveness. We have recognized in the course of working on this specific freshman seminar project that it is only by identifying these traps that we can overcome them.

The traps that white educators fall into can be highly visible or they can be subtle, which makes them even harder to challenge. For us, one of the most insidious traps occurs when faculty and students refuse to see a problem, essentially falling into the rose-colored glasses trap: "We don't have a racism problem here at *this* school." Within the first two weeks of the semester, we decided to proceed with the first step in the diversity sequence—to show the first hour of the John Singleton film *Higher Learning* and then lead a discussion about it after the viewing. One of us agreed to be there each night, recruiting a few other faculty who we believed had the same commitment to dealing with racism. The turnout of students was excellent, and the discussion that followed the film was interesting and provocative. Students were very willing to discuss racial issues from this safe distance: "This happens at other, bigger schools."

When we tried to lead students into asking whether these same problems existed at McKendree, they were sincere when they responded "no." This included the few students of color who were present. Ironically, the response that racism was not a problem at our school further reinforced this belief among some of the FRS faculty. Even though these students had only been on campus for a few weeks, seasoned faculty were perfectly willing to take these observations as truth.

Sometimes in meetings our colleagues would turn to us and ask, "Well, give me an example. What kinds of specific problems are students of color having?" Of course, we had lots of examples, but what we have realized is that when we get too focused on trying to articulate specific problems, we lose sight of the bigger picture that racism is a broader social and institutional problem. Part of the personal journey we made doing antiracism training was to realize that white people have a vested interest in combating racism for white people. White people need to see, as Beverly Tatum notes, that "the role of the ally is not to help victims of racism, but to speak up against systems of oppression and to challenge other Whites to do the same."[1] This was a difficult thing to try to convey to our colleagues, however.

When we did try in faculty meetings to call our colleagues' attention to some specific problems students of color face, defensiveness quickly set in— an example of the shifting responsibility trap. These colleagues felt like they were being attacked and responded with such things as, "I'm not a racist—I'm trying," or "I tried but the students didn't want to talk about it." This particular trap manifested itself on a variety of levels. In the middle of the semester, it became obvious that many of the faculty were not doing any of the diversity assignments, and in fact were belittling some of the assignments we had designed in front of other students. When we questioned them on this, they responded defensively: "Don't blame me. I tried and my students were very uncomfortable," or "I ran out of time, and I felt like my students needed to spend more time on study skills."

Another trap many of our colleagues fall into is believing that once students are in an academic setting, the playing field is made equal. This trap occurs when individuals insist that we live in a meritocracy—where if you work hard enough, you will get what you deserve. For example, when we tried to say that many students of color were having trouble assimilating into the residence halls, one colleague argued, "They just need to be more assertive and outgoing and try harder to fit in." Blaming the victim is particularly problematic in an academic institution because rather than thinking critically about what the institution can do to eradicate social injustice, it reverts the focus back to the students. We say that the students are all at ground zero when they are admitted to college; but then, many of our minority students are placed into remedial English, a course that does not allow them to simultaneously enroll in the freshman seminar. Ironically, the students who most need an orientation to college life are excluded from the program. When these very students fail to succeed academically, to get involved in campus activities, or to develop good study habits, rather than question institutional policies, we completely blame the students for their failures.

Most of the FRS faculty supported the community and diversity theme, but they did not want to remove their own rose-colored glasses—a denial that often leads to what we call the lip service trap in academia. At McKendree, as is the case on many campuses, our mission statement includes a commitment to diversity: we have a director of multicultural affairs (who also coordinates the black student organization), we offer an ethnic studies minor, and we require all students to take a cultural diversity class. On the surface, it would seem like we have a commitment to diversity as a campus community. In reality, however, we rarely discuss the serious underlying issues that provoke racist behavior.

On paper, programs such as the FRS focus on community and diversity makes it look like the college is making a concerted effort to address diversity. In fact, however, most of the FRS faculty were simply skimming the surface. When we insisted that there needed to be more deliberate and consistent discussions about racism throughout the semester, one faculty member suggested moving the diversity theme to a one-week module. What faculty failed to see is that to really explore the complexities of racism, time to process and reflect is key. Throughout the semester, the activities we had developed started to get less emphasis in the classroom and in our faculty meetings, and in fact, alternative assignments not related to the theme were made available.

When things got too difficult, we were ready to throw in the towel and blame the lack of success on our colleagues. As problems and difficulties continued to arise we wanted to ignore them, saying things like, "These are just bugs; they will work themselves out. " This denial gave way to anger, which of course was counterproductive. At times during the meetings, one of us might attack other faculty members. For example, when one faculty member said that he did not have "training" to deal with diversity issues, one of us retorted, "Any educated college professor should be able to discuss these issues. We have already done all of the preparation for you; you just need to hand out the worksheets!" These angry outbursts were followed by our own retreat—we started to ignore or avoid some of the faculty members who had been most resistant. We realize in retrospect that we were probably perceived as sanctimonious and controlling.

After concluding that divisiveness and hostility were not the answer, we attempted bargaining, encouraging our colleagues to attend diversity workshops, and making more concerted efforts not to lash out when we felt frustrated by certain responses. We also dropped some of our initial ideas and activities to try to show that we were willing to change and modify our ideas, even though we felt that we were compromising the integrity of the theme. We were angry and resentful, realizing that many of the activities were not even being attempted and that the diversity theme was being abandoned. It seemed like more work to try to convince people of the importance of dealing with racism than it was worth. Our next response was a feeling of hopelessness and a resigned acceptance that we couldn't effect change given the resistance of the campus climate; we even considered dropping out of the program the following year.[2] We had unintentionally fallen into a trap ourselves by deciding to walk away, forgetting that it was our own white privilege that allowed us to selectively deal with racism.

We have not quit the program as we had originally threatened. After talking to students and reading the course evaluations, we realized that even though a substantial dialogue about racism did not occur in most of the sections, students' awareness and attitudes did get challenged—at least in some small way. We have realized that compromise does not negate our commitment to teaching for diversity and social justice. We asked that there be more training the next time FRS was taught and a more focused curriculum.

The following semester we saw our colleagues fall into another trap, which is to assume that a person of color can better train white educators to deal with diversity issues. Many white people believe that only people of color can teach them about racism. Significantly, our first training session of the semester was led by a recently hired African American psychology professor. We wish we could say we saw a marked difference in the response from some of our more resistant colleagues, but many of the same patterns emerged. To amplify this point, this semester, even though the theme is still being touted as community and diversity, the diversity worksheets have been relegated to the appendix of the freshman seminar student workbooks.

In processing everything that took place, we still do not have definitive answers. Maybe the freshman seminar has too many goals to seriously address such a complex topic. Perhaps there were too many instructors, most of whom have had little or no training in dealing with sensitive issues. Perhaps our enthusiasm for course content in which we had invested so much time made it difficult for us to anticipate obstacles. And perhaps our investment made it difficult not to take failures as personal affronts. Ultimately, we have decided that it is not in the best interest of our goals to constantly criticize our colleagues; rather, we should help them recognize the traps that we all can fall into on a predominantly white campus.

Despite the problems, we are still committed to finding where we can best exercise our sphere of influence. This past spring, for example, we team taught a new introductory class in race, class, and gender with a third faculty member, and we were far happier with the results. This was largely due to the fact that we had total control of the course design, and we had three hours per week rather than one to grapple with these issues. Furthermore, students taking the class knew exactly what the course focus would be and were willing at the outset to engage with the material. This is not to say that there were not difficult and intense moments in the class, but overall students' learning experiences were good ones, and we hope to make the course a permanent one.

We have realized that exercising this sphere of influence can be difficult when traditional pedagogies may have to be altered to allow for the effective teaching of social justice. Many faculty do not see the place for emotion in traditional teaching methods. Essentially we have two conflicting pedagogies: the traditional model of intellectual, distanced, factual dissemination of information, and an emotional, personal, student-centered model of learning. This dichotomy became radically clear to us during the race, class, and gender course when an assignment asking students to write a reflective essay about their own feelings about race was deemed not academically rigorous enough by the third instructor. As bell hooks notes in *Teaching to Transgress*, "Ideally, education should be a place where the need for diverse teaching methods and styles would be valued, encouraged, seen as essential to learning."[3] Transgressive teaching, however, is not the type typically valued in the traditional assessments. The choice to work against the grain has consequences, both in terms of potential negative student evaluations and negative colleague perceptions that question the academic seriousness of a class. These are choices often made by nontenured faculty, the most vulnerable members of an institution.

Writing this essay has been a cathartic experience that has allowed us to process our experiences. We go into this next semester a little more realistic, better able to anticipate the traps and obstacles that often occur when discussions of race enter the classroom. We also begin the semester understanding the importance of allies, realizing that we can have a big impact on both faculty and students at different points in their thinking, and recognizing that small steps can be productive. We still hope to see faculty and students on this campus make big steps toward continuing the journey on the road to social justice. As Joan Olsson says, "Every experience takes us deeper into new territory and the complexities of racism, expanding our vision of the possibilities of a future without racism. Each turn brings us face to face with another set of potential traps and reversals. Like traveling unmarked roads, staying on the right track demands constant attention and intention."[4] We intend to continue to work together as allies to deal with the inevitable dissonance, attend to the traps, and stay committed to being change agents within the classroom.

We cannot eradicate racism, but as white educators we have an important sphere of influence to help white students and colleagues recognize that racism affects us all, not just people of color. Part of this sphere of influence is our ability to facilitate dialogue about racism both within and outside the classroom. We believe Beverly Tatum's directive that "we cannot continue to be silent. We must begin to speak, knowing that words alone are insufficient. But

I have seen that meaningful dialogue can lead to effective action. Change is possible. I remain hopeful."[5] We do too.

NOTES

1 Beverly Tatum, *"Why Are All the Black Kids Sitting Together in the Cafeteria?" and Other Conversations About Race* (New York: Basic Books, 1997), 108.

2 When dealing with our faculty members during the semester, we engaged in some rather typical psychological responses. Elisabeth Kübler-Ross, in *Death: The Final Stage of Growth* (New York: Simon and Schuster, 1975), explains five stages of the dying process that are common to most people: denial, anger, bargaining, depression, and acceptance. Our responses to the difficulties with our faculty members could be easily identified by these five stages.

3 bell hooks, *Teaching to Transgress: Education as the Practice of Freedom* (New York: Routledge, 1994), 203.

4 Joan Olsson, "Trap-Spotting for White Anti-Racists," *National Conference for Community and Justice DRI Training Manual* (2000).

5 Tatum, *Why Are All the Black Kids Sitting Together*, 206.

PART 3

TRANSFORMATIVE PRACTICES

In *The Courage to Teach,* the highly acclaimed activist educator Parker Palmer recommends that instead of struggling as isolated individuals against an intransigent organization, would-be agents for change look beyond their institutions. He points out how the civil rights and women's movements developed a "movement mentality" that eventually benefited from institutional resistance:

> In both of these movements, advocates of change used organizational resistance as a trampoline to spring themselves free of organizations. They found sources of countervailing power outside of those structures, then consolidated that power in ways that eventually gave them leverage on the structures themselves.[1]

From the various national and international movements that he studied, Palmer identifies roughly four stages of development: (1) locating a new center outside the institution, (2) developing a support network with other kindred spirits around a shared vision, (3) "going public" with issues, and (4) developing a system of alternative rewards while pressing for institutional change.[2]

However unpremeditated, it can be said that the contributors to *Race in the College Classroom* have embarked on such a collective enterprise. The essays here identify a shared commitment to the open discussion of race. To address race and racism is also to engage in the eradication of a major—if not *the* major—system of oppression in the United States. This volume verifies that at both the interpersonal and institutional levels, racism is far from over. As discussed earlier, the level of discomfort exhibited by students when the R-word is used confirms that, as a society, we have a problem. We are not, nor have we ever been, a "color-blind" society. Relegating race to a taboo subject only forces racism underground, and this disease will not disappear of its own accord. As responsible educators many of us believe that we need to do our part in combatting racism. From our perspective, interrogating and challenging white-skinned privilege is the very essence of education.

Contributors here describe transformative models of antiracist pedagogy. In recounting their teaching practices, they variously offer a pedagogical paradigm that reflects the partnership of conflict and love. It is important to remember that we teach because we care. Teaching well without avoiding the issue of race is challenging work. At times, addressing race in the classroom borders on the grotesque—something from which all those present would like to avert their eyes. The very humanness behind such an impulse should keep us in the struggle, however. In an interview, the writer Tomás Rivera once made a similar point. He had seen some grotesque things in Chicano theater, he said. But he accepted these things because "they're so damn human." As he further explains, "At one time there was one individual who thought he was saying something beautiful. The fact that he thought about it that hard, to me makes it beautiful."[3] The ethical, caring stance behind such a worldview reflects the position of many contributors to this volume. With such a pedagogy of acceptance and love, higher education cannot help but be transformed.

NOTES

1 Parker J. Palmer, *The Courage to Teach: Exploring the Inner Landscape of a Teacher's Life* (San Francisco: Jossey-Bass Publishers, 1998), 165.

2 Palmer, *The Courage to Teach*, 166.

3 Juan Bruce-Novoa, *Chicano Authors: Inquiry by Interview* (Austin: University of Texas Press, 1980), 160.

José L. Torres-Padilla

CONFRONTING THE "SCREAMING BABOON":

Notes on Race, Literature, and Pedagogy

PHOTO: LEE VERA

Before it can adopt a positive voice, freedom requires an effort at disalienation.

—Frantz Fanon, *Black Skin, White Masks*

There is still much national solace in continuing dreams of democratic egalitarianism available by hiding class conflict, rage, and impotence in figurations of race.... Freedom ... can be relished more deeply in a cheek-by-jowl existence with the bound and unfree, the economically oppressed, the marginalized, the silenced.

—Toni Morrison, *Playing in the Dark*

At one point in *Beloved,* one of the characters, Stamp Paid, ruminates over the state of affairs of African Americans in Reconstruction America and the role of racism in their lives. In his mind, the distance between blacks and whites appears impossible to narrow, because the latter believe that "under every black skin was a jungle."[1] Stamp Paid understands, in his own way, that this "jungle" and other related images such as the "screaming baboon" are the imaginary constructions of a white racist ideology developed by a fearful, loathing white population: "The screaming baboon lived under their own white skin."[2] It is an entrenched ideology not easily transcended or eliminated. Stamp Paid's

José L. Torres-Padilla, previously chair of English at the University of Puerto Rico, Cayey, is an associate professor of English at SUNY Plattsburgh. A published writer of poems and stories, he focuses his teaching and research on U.S. ethnic literatures. His latest project is a critical anthology of early U.S. Hispanic short fiction.

Torres-Padilla expresses reservations about a recent course that students rated favorably. In his words, "the discussions were often muted or clothed in clichéd, guarded, humanist-speak." His essay focuses on his plans to challenge students more and to confront them more directly with the "race demons" he himself faces.

realization, tragically sobering for his times, unfortunately remains relevant today. More than a century after slaves were proclaimed free, the racist ideas and beliefs that sustained and justified slavocracy still prevail; they fester in practically every aspect of American culture and society, and threaten to further divide the nation and subvert its democratic principles. When we consider the growing population of people of color in the United States, it is not inconceivable that if the nation does not confront its institutional racism, and race relations steadily worsen, the country could fall victim to prolonged interracial violence and future race-related uprisings.

Most Americans resist this scenario because they truly believe racism is something archaic, and that racial relations are much better today. Their perceptions of racism are generally aligned with the grisly stories that occasionally make it to television: the brutal killing of James Byrd, Jr. in Jasper, Texas; the beating of Rodney King; and, more recently, the Diallo and Louima cases. These are the acute racist manifestations, too ugly for the media to disregard, but perverse enough to present as isolated cases. But every day there are other racist attacks on people of color in America. Some get reported to the FBI and recorded within the growing number of hate crimes; far too many go undocumented, but the damage to an individual's self-dignity and worth is immeasurable and irrevocable. These are the discriminatory practices and prejudiced behavior that make life harder for people of color in this country. Psychologists John Dovidio and Samuel Gaertner write that within a society that is experiencing a deterioration of racial relations, the prevailing form of racism in America is not the more blatant type usually attributed to white supremacists but rather a "more subtle, often unintentional, form of bias" they call "aversive racism."[3] Aversive racists generally hold "strong egalitarian values" and believe that they are nonprejudiced, but they also possess unrecognized negative racial feelings and beliefs stemming from "discomfort, uneasiness, disgust, and sometimes fear."[4] In other words, they have a "screaming baboon" on their backs.

If Americans were honest with themselves they would agree that racism still thrives in the country, and they would confront it. Denial and evasion are not going to cure this deep-rooted social disease. Awareness of the problem is crucial; we all need to return to the basics of raising consciousness about racism. We must all become agents for change, because the alternatives are destructive and thus unacceptable. As a professor of literature and language, I have come to the conclusion that even a seemingly innocuous (some would say irrelevant) field such as literary studies can play a part in changing minds about racism and transforming passive individuals into agents determined to change the racial status quo. As a teacher that is what I try to do in the classroom. Such a project requires an intelligent, resourceful pedagogy suitable for the environment in which you are teaching; it is equally important to accept the risks involved in the undertaking. Especially crucial is how you, as a teacher, view and position yourself in that classroom. For me, questions of race have not been easy to comprehend and engage. As a Puerto Rican, I have inherited complex and retrogressive cultural perceptions and ideas of race. I have struggled to rid myself of that cultural baggage even as I coax students to cross borders. Moreover, as I have recently discovered, teaching race through literature takes on different meanings and dimensions depending on where you teach.

I taught English at the University of Puerto Rico for nearly twenty years. There, I included themes on race in every course I taught. Race in Puerto Rico is a problematic, even vexing topic. For most Puerto Ricans, race is ever-present in the formation of our identity even as some try to deny it. Indeed, this diversionary tactic concerning race actually informs our identity. The standard, cultural construct disseminated by most Puerto Ricans is that we are a mulatto nation, a people with strains of African, Spaniard, and Taino (the indigenous people of the island). We proclaim ourselves the rainbow people, but signs of racism abound everywhere—the scarcity of black faces on local television, the growing factions of *rockeros* and *cocolos*, the discrimination of usually darker Dominicans on the island, the annual selection of a Miss Puerto Rico who is invariably very European-looking with light eyes, the increasing synthesis of poverty, race, and criminalization, and the ghettoization of darker Puerto Ricans in caserios (public housing). These are among some of the more salient manifestations of racism in Puerto Rico.[5]

The failure of Puerto Ricans to embrace the cultural discourse on race at a very practical and personal level makes it that much more difficult to discuss racial issues in the classroom. Students often accept that racism exists, and even accept the familiar line that we are racially mixed, but they do not see the many insidious ways in which it operates socially or ideologically, or, more importantly, in their lives. That Negroid part, *la taja*, which all Puerto Ricans are supposed to have, becomes submerged; darker skin becomes *trigueño*—the Spanish word referring to the color of wheat.[6] In Puerto Rico, no matter how dark you may be, "Negro" is something that someone else is. I have lived this type of racism intimately. Throughout my life I have constantly fought with my mother to recognize the blackness of her late father, my grandfather. To this day, she still insists that *abuelo* had "Indian blood." Moreover, the culture takes on the attitude that since everyone is mixed there is no problem of racism in the island. Racism, some claim, is an import from the more virulently racist United States. As Miriam Jiménez Román has argued, this attitude leads to the unfortunate "double silencing" of black Puerto Ricans, and the neglect of Africanism in our culture as a whole.[7] To make young Puerto Ricans aware of these issues and to motivate them to celebrate our shared Africanism is a difficult task. Yet I sympathize with how hard it is to assimilate such views when you are presented with the black and white paradigm of racism that exists in the United States. I remember as an undergraduate forced to decide between sitting at the black table with the "bloods" or with white friends. If a black person demanded that I declare myself black, I would certainly have a problem. At the same time, I have never identified myself as white. I continue to be angry over having to make that type of decision given my cultural background, especially since that type of pressure stems from America's obsessive Manichean view of race. Puerto Rican racism is definitely homegrown, but undoubtedly the United States' hegemonic influence over Puerto Rico impedes the island's development of a genuinely Antillean and Caribbean hybrid sense of race and culture.

In the fall of 2000, I started a position at Plattsburgh State University, a campus of the State University of New York (SUNY) system. I am now living, to quote Martí, in "the belly of the beast." I enter a classroom with the same dedication, even as I bear the cross of cultural racial ambiguity. Truthfully, I do not feel endangered in this part of New York. I'm not ingenuous enough to think that racism does not exist in the North Country. In fact, I know that it does because my black colleague has encountered it. I have not, but I am also aware that as a light-skinned Puerto Rican—whom people have mistaken for an assortment of other ethnicities—racism does not tend to touch me in the very same way it does others. But, unlike my mother, I embrace my grandfather's blackness and therefore the blackness in me. I come to the conclusion that my true freedom depends on rejecting the idea that I am somehow entitled to an "easier way of life" because I have a lower level of melanin. My resistance reveals the essential problem. Our society is fundamentally racist and racialized, and it must change.

The college newspaper asked students about diversity on campus, and one of the respondents replied that it was needed because "we're just a bunch of rednecks around here." In many ways that self-deprecating response is revealing. The college community, for the most part, desires diversity and the institution has promoted initiatives along those lines. New York is not Mississippi, but Plattsburgh State is not New York University. PSU has an African American president, but he has had some difficulties that some partly attribute to racism (while others vehemently deny those charges). Students of color make up less than 10 percent of the total population, and underrepresented faculty range around the same percentage. Discussing racism and race here would not be any easier than in Puerto Rico, although for very different reasons. Now, I am not one Puerto Rican talking to a group of younger Puerto Ricans. I am a Latino talking to a predominantly white class about a subject they have been taught to evade like the plague.

One of the courses assigned to me is called "Visions of America." Visions is a course that contemplates, according to the course syllabus, the myths, dreams, and nightmares of American culture. I see the course as a way to explore issues related to American identity, nationhood, and culture—and a serious investigation of such issues would perforce include race. I agree with Robert J. C. Young that any culture's construction of the "other" invariably involves racism. Culture and racism, he writes, "are inextricably clustered together, feeding off and generating each other. Race has always been culturally constructed. Culture has always been racially constructed."[8]

In the United States, with its history of slavery, it is not hard to accept Young's assessment. Toni Morrison has written on the African presence in American culture, and particularly how the othering process Young describes operates in the nation's literature. Morrison argues that various concerns and ideals, especially of "freedom," were "made possible by, shaped by, activated by a complex awareness and employment of a constituted Africanism. It was this Africanism, deployed as rawness and savagery, that provided the staging ground and arena for the elaboration of the quintessential American identity."[9]

Morrison has written eloquently and movingly on this and other matters related to race and the African American experience in the United States. After being assigned the course, I knew that I would include a unit on race, so I turned to her novel *Beloved*. Choosing a proper text for such a unit requires serious consideration. There are several alternatives, but considering the objectives of the course, *Beloved* seemed to me the best choice. The novel raises the issue of slavery and its impact on the nation's thinking on race. It is also a beautifully written work that is not didactic. Complex and multilayered, *Beloved* still gazes directly at the brutality of slavery and its aftermath, especially at how it affects the individual. I knew that the novel's seductive narrative voice, a hallmark of

Morrison's style, would attract my students, would lead them to territory they are accustomed to avoiding. Once there, they would have to face the racist ideology and the issues that I raised in the class discussion.

An excellent literary text should be the center of such a unit—for an English class, anyway—but it is certainly not enough. Most students, especially at PSU, come with historical gaps or a limited, unsophisticated knowledge of slavery and its history. Ancillary materials are therefore important to round out the text and give them a better understanding of the period and the workings of slavery as an institution. To complement their reading of *Beloved* I showed them the first part of the documentary *Africans in America*, so that they could understand the origins of slavery and see for themselves the horrors of the Middle Passage. Visuals can be very powerful, so I use them whenever I can. Besides the video, I had them view *Amistad* outside of class, and in class I passed around a book titled *Lest We Forget*, which includes interactive materials such as a facsimile of a check paying for a slave. The students were particularly moved by a picture of a slave who had scars on his back from being whipped. I showed them this picture for them to better visualize that image of the "chokecherry tree" on Sethe's back. The students were also assigned a reading of a slave narrative and to write a response paper on it. To question whatever contentions existed that blatant racism is "a thing of the past," I had the students log on to the Yahoo boards on race relations. Some students were genuinely startled, some visibly upset, to encounter that level of open racism on the Internet.

I had taught this course my first semester at PSU and was frustrated at the silence during the classroom discussion. After almost one year at this institution, I'm beginning to think that these students are very quiet for several reasons. Most are first-generation college students, from the working or lower middle class, whose high school preparation is not always the best. Some have honestly stated to me that they do not want to say something stupid in class, or that some other student sounds so much more intelligent that they feel intimidated. At any rate, even though most topics will not bring forth a gush of enthusiastic chatter, the discussion seemed that much more eerily silent when we approached the "R" word. In fact, some students confided that when it came to race they were afraid to say anything that would offend a person of color. Perhaps these are sensitive words, but they still represent a disconcerting form of evasion. Race relations in the United States will not improve if people continue finding ways to avoid talking about race and racism.

Assigned the course in the second semester, I decided to confront the evasion issue head-on. First, I assigned readings from Gloria Anzaldúa's anthology *Making Face, Making Soul.* I had them read an excerpt from her introduction in which she discusses the problems she faced in teaching the issue of race in a course on women of color. Anzaldúa discussed the evasion tactics people use to avoid confronting their own racism. At one point, she writes, "the people who practice Racism—everyone who is white in the U.S.—are victims of their own white ideology and are empoverished by it."[10] Although I agree with the last part of that sentence, I find it difficult to believe that only white people practice racism. I have met some bigoted Latinos and blacks in my day. Unfortunately, some students, bothered by this, pounced on that part of her assertion without critically considering the latter, which tells me that everyone seems to function at a high level of anxiety and defensiveness when discussing this topic. This is something that teachers should be aware of, but especially those of color. We need to analyze that defensiveness without resorting to generalizations. When we discussed Anzaldúa's introduction in class, I told the students that I found her comment unfortunate. In the journal that I kept during the three weeks of this unit, I wrote that her comment seemed "standoffish," that "people of color cannot enter this dialogue looking for people to blame. . . . The blame game," I wrote, "is a lame game." Later, as I read for the writing of this essay and deepened my understanding of racist ideology, I realized that perhaps Anzaldúa was working from a different definition of racism. In her very instructive book *"Why Are All the Black Kids Sitting Together in the Cafeteria?"* Beverly Daniel Tatum argues that racism is not only a behavior of prejudice, but a system that in the United States "clearly operates to the advantage of Whites and to the disadvantage of people of color."[11] If Anzaldúa's perspective is indeed coming from this position, then any white person who does not take an assertive antiracist stand is racist because they benefit from the status quo. I don't completely agree with the logic of this assertion, although I agree that racism systematically and primarily privileges whites. However, in any structured racialized society some people of color will also find ways to benefit. Certainly, this new information casts a different dimension on talks about racism and in the future I will introduce it into the class discussion. Tatum's definition of racism should spark some response.

From Anzaldúa's anthology I also included Pat Parker's poem "For the white person who wants to know how to be my friend," and Gloria Yamato's

220 ■ *Transformative Practices*

essay "Something About the Subject Matter Makes It Hard to Name." Both of these pieces are highly provocative, and I chose them purposefully for that reason. The reaction these materials spurred was limited—honest but mainly defensive. One student mentioned that racial division exists in her town. A few talked about racist relatives. One bizarre comment from a student pondered why, if slave owners saw slaves as less than humans, they wouldn't also consider eating them. (This seemed, to me, after trying to understand it, an over-logical question based on the scene in *Beloved* where Slave Catcher considers the value of a slave as compared to a rabbit.) I understood the question as a sort of defiance, of trying to perhaps undermine, in a very odd way, Slave Catcher's thinking. I responded that the rhetorical insistence on dehumanizing slaves was a strategy to rationalize and justify slavery that nonetheless was consistently contradicted by other actions, such as slave owners taking on concubines. To the comment made by a student that the slave owners could have treated the slaves better, another student responded that slavery was slavery no matter what type of treatment slaves received. This brought up the Garners in the novel, and one white student plainly stated that if he had been a slave and given more benevolent treatment, he would still find a way to kill his master or escape.

These rare moments held up possibilities, some hope, but I decided early on to assign a journal on the novel and the unit. A journal, I believed, would present the students with a method for breaking their silence; it would provide a safe haven for their personal thoughts on race and racism. A journal also allowed for more discursive space for every student, a written document of these ideas available to me for careful critical analysis. From the journals I realized that most students engaged the issues discussed in class with directness and honesty. I gave the students a series of questions to guide their journal writing, and one of them was, "Are you a racist?" Several admitted that they had some racist ideas. A white female wrote, "sadly, yes, except I camouflage them as harmless stereotypes . . . But is any stereotype really harmless?" One Asian international student wrote that she was racist against "Chinese people."[12] Another admitted that he was a racist, but added, "I'm not saying that I'm going to rush right out and buy a pillowcase, then cut two eyeholes in it and run around burning crosses." A black Latina wrote, "We are slaves of racism." But many more resisted the idea that they were, in any way, racist. Some declared that they came from very liberal homes where racial slurs were never uttered, and the use of them would be reprimanded. One white female actually wrote how upset she was at what she understood to be my comment that "everyone is racist." "I have to say that I disagree with that statement, " she writes, " I am not a racist. I have never acted like one, and I never will . . . I took great offense to this comment." Although some take this attitude, they still acknowledge that they are not immune from racism. Apparently, this younger generation sees a difference between how they perceive race as opposed to their parents and grandparents. Several wrote about racist relatives. One white female wrote about her grandmother who talked about black people "as if they were beneath her." This student, like many others who mentioned racist relatives, tended to soften their relatives' racism by situating it in a more racist past. In an interesting entry, another white female calls her stepfather "a racist man." She continues that "he doesn't try to be, but he works in a prison and most of the population in the prison is black people." She attributes her stepfather's behavior to being surrounded by black prisoners. But the stepfather's seemingly unintentional racism ("he doesn't try to be") appears more blatant when she describes his making comments such as "damn raccoons, they are stinking up the whole place," as he stands behind black people in a line at a Disney theme park. This student wants to be antiracist, and she tells her stepfather that she does not appreciate his comments with a sarcastic remark about "making him stand there no matter what." She is not confronting her stepfather directly about his racism, but deflecting it. Tatum writes that antiracist whites such as this student, who are going through what she calls the "disintegration level," need strategies to deal with these situations and they also need support to get through this level towards a healthier white identity—that is, one not dependent on racist othering.[13]

If white students, consciously aware of society's racism, do not find support then they can easily slip back into their more passive way of viewing racism—or they can become angry and frustrated with their feelings of guilt and shame. One white female writes: "I am beginning to feel as if all the racist troubles in the United States are being blamed on me." Another declares that she is "sick about talking about race," and in a separate entry rails against affirmative action even as she admits that the journal writing forced her to "look at my own views and if I really understand if they're racist or not." A white male writes of his friendship with an African American and declares that "after seeing first-hand the racism that he has experienced," he tries "to be more considerate towards other races." A few sentences later, however, this same writer states that affirmative action is "a pointless and ignorant concept," and that "people are hired for jobs on the basis of their race and not on their skill or qualifications."

Another student, writing against reparations for African Americans, states: "the absolute truth is that African Americans would not be in the United States today if there is no slavery." Later this same young white man writes, "I am a better person for being involved in this unit." Clearly, there is confusion among these students, and I believe that this unit exposed them to information and ideas that confronted their established perceptions, leading them to the discomfort that most people experience at this level. That discomfort comes from looking at the racist past of the country and how it brutalized human beings. There is very little connection, in the minds of these students, however, of that past and its racist ideological foundations and the reasoning behind their opposition to some issues (affirmative action, reparations, and so on).

There are positive moments in these journals. Students write about friendships made with African Americans and the learning experienced through those bonds. There are remarkable admissions, like the young white woman who says she is attracted to black men but is afraid to act on it because of racist attitudes. There were some gratifying comments that demonstrated an acquired awareness of the problem and sensitivity to people who suffer racism. One white female wrote, "I am really glad that we got the opportunity to do these journals. It made me think a lot about how other people might feel who are in a different position than me." Another white female said, "I learned a lot about slavery and racism and it got me thinking of where I stand on certain issues myself." Yet another writes: "The completion of this book has left me with an awareness and intimacy with the treatment of people in slavery." One white female states eloquently that "the ghost Beloved haunts and in many ways corrupts the house 124; it is in comparison to this that I can say racism haunts and corrupts the United States of America." Another young woman writes simply, "Sooner or later, I have to learn to eliminate racism from my life."

That these students reached a level of consciousness about racism, and brought that newly acquired knowledge to a more personal level, makes me feel good about my efforts. It is sad to think, however, that all of them expressed a deep resignation to the continuation of racist thinking and practice in our society. One of the guideline questions was "Do you think racism will be eliminated in your lifetime?"—and not one thought it could be done. Sadder still were the remarks of one Asian female. After describing an incident in elementary school where a young boy taunted her daily, calling her "chink" and saying that she was "stupid" because she couldn't speak English that well, she goes on to say that "the bottom line is people have their own beliefs and ideas and no matter how many discussions there are about racism it's not going to make a huge difference." She adds: "I don't mean to sound so negative but everyone is racist, racism has existed for so long that I don't see its departure in my lifetime." The most uplifting comments were those few that not only demonstrated awareness but also showed a desire to do something about the problem. One student writes that ignoring racism will not make it go away and stresses the importance of "starting early in elementary school, trying to teach children young in hopes that these ideas will carry with them and the next generation will look differently upon race and color." One white female writes that we have to listen to one another, and be respectful of each other's thoughts. "After we listen," she adds, "we must act, and attempt to make a change." The unit's "new gained knowledge," writes a white male, "will allow me to educate others and expand the concepts that filled my mind."

In my first journal entry, I wrote of the trepidation with which I started the first day of the unit. In Puerto Rico I was speaking to a class full of my people. They may not have liked talking about it, but I never felt that they could turn on me. There was no cognitive dissonance at play. At PSU, I found myself in front of mainly white faces. These students would evaluate me after all of this was done; my fate at this institution was partly in their hands, and I would be challenging them on an issue that made them very, very uncomfortable. Receiving this challenge from a person of color would not be the same as receiving it from someone white. There are other dynamics operating. For instance, would this situation compromise my commitment? You mention race and there is a silence. It is not a silence full of expectation and excited energy, but a deadening silence, both tense and threatening. The journals made my efforts meaningful, but I cannot say for sure if they dispel my fears. A professor of color can never be certain of the reaction he or she will receive on evaluations. The studies on aversive racism conducted by Dovidio and Gaertner contained a very troubling finding: "discrimination against the black applicant was most apparent . . . when the applicants were highly qualified."[14] The reason for this? Through post-experimental evaluations, the two psychologists found that

> the ratings revealed that participants described even high-ability black partners as significantly less intelligent than themselves. Blacks may be regarded as intelligent, but not as intelligent as whites. It therefore appears that although whites may accept that a black person is intelligent on an absolute dimension, white participants are reluctant to believe that a black person is higher or equal in intelligence compared to themselves.[15]

Who can say if these students have completely liberated themselves from this seemingly pervasive form of racism? Have I thrown fuel into the fire by making them squirm for three weeks of the semester, making them confront a topic they simply do not want to approach? Who knows? The evaluations may have answers. However, I cannot allow this type of fear to shake my resolve or undermine my principles. This is certainly one of the pitfalls of bringing race into the classroom, especially for a person of color. Once you leave the comfort zone of safe and neutral discourse and enter dangerous discursive ground, you must face all the demons that inhabit it. If I go by the journals, then I have accomplished something significant with some of these students. Equally important, I have also learned from this experience. A good teacher should improve from past mistakes. In the future I will have to work from a better definition of racism. Tatum's definition forces the white student to look even deeper at his or her role in racist society; it presents more clearly the hegemonic quality of racism in the United States expressed in Arthur Spears' claim that "America cannot be America without racism."[16] From this position, it is more possible to connect racism to other issues such as affirmative action, something that many could not do. Finally, I must incorporate a sense of agency into this pedagogy. I cannot have students walk away with misguided awareness. It is important that these students, particularly the white ones, know that people consistently fight against racism and make a difference in the lives of others. They need to learn about white heroes like Morris Dees. They must learn that our contributions need not be heroic in proportion. Tatum tells us that we all have a "sphere of influence . . . some domain in which we exercise some level of power and control. The task of each of us, White and of color, is to identify what our own sphere of influence is (however large or small) and to consider how it might be used to interrupt the cycle of racism."[17]

As teachers, we must use our sphere of influence to alert these students to theirs, so that we can break the insidious cycle of racism. As I write these words, Cincinnati, the setting for *Beloved*, is paralyzed by hate and racial tension. The police in that city have killed five black men in the last eight months. The city's African American citizens are upset and some have taken to the streets in violent protest. Such violence may erupt again in other cities across the country. The first step toward a permanent peace is for America to finally confront its deep-rooted racism. Literature teachers can assist in reaching this goal by developing pedagogy that includes race and racism as topics and utilizes literary texts, among other materials, to foment consciousness and agency.

NOTES

1 Toni Morrison, *Beloved* (New York: Plume/Penguin, 1987), 198.

2 Morrison, *Beloved*, 199.

3 John F. Dovidio and Samuel L. Gaertner, "On the Nature of Contemporary Prejudice: The Causes, Consequences, and Challenges of Aversive Racism," in *Confronting Racism: The Problem and the Response*, ed. Jennifer L. Eberhardt and Susan T. Fiske (Thousand Oaks, Calif. and London: Sage Publications, 1998).

4 Dovidio and Gaertner, "On the Nature," 5.

5 On *rockeros* and *cocolos*, see Roberto P. Rodríguez-Morazzani, "Beyond the Rainbow: Mapping the Discourse on Puerto Ricans and 'Race,'" special issue of *Centro, the Journal of the Center of Puerto Rican Studies*, Focus/En Foco: Race and Identity 8.1&2 (1996): 150–169. In the same issue see Kelvin Santiago-Valles, "Policing the Crisis in the Whitest of all the Antilles," 42–57, on poverty, race, and criminalization.

6 In Puerto Rico there are two popular sayings that articulate ideas on race. One of them, *el que no tenga dinga, tiene mandinga*, refers to two African tribes and means that if you are not from one, you are from the other. In other words, every Puerto Rican has African ancestry. The other saying, *¿y tu abuela donde está?* ("and your grandmother, where is she?"), exposes the hypocrisy of some Puerto Ricans who deny their blackness.

7 Miriam Jiménez Román, "Un hombre (Negro) del pueblo: Jose Celso Barbosa and the Puerto Rican 'Race' Toward Whiteness," *Centro* 8.1&2 (1996): 8–29.

8 Robert J. C. Young, *Colonial Desire: Hybridity in Theory, Culture and Race* (London and New York: Routledge, 1995), 54.

9 Toni Morrison, *Playing in the Dark: Whiteness and the Literary Imagination* (Cambridge, Mass.: Harvard University Press, 1992), 44.

10 Gloria Anzaldúa, ed., *Making Face, Making Soul/Haciendo Caras: Creative and Critical Perspectives by Feminists of Color* (San Francisco: Aunt Lute, 1990), xix.

11 Beverly Tatum, *"Why Are All the Black Kids Sitting Together in the Cafeteria?" and Other Conversations About Race* (New York: Basic Books, 1997), 7.

12 I am intentionally being vague throughout this essay when it comes to identifying a student's ethnicity to protect the student's privacy.

13 Tatum, "Why Are All the Black Kids Sitting," 98–101.

14 Dovidio and Gaertner, "On the Nature," 18.

15 Dovidio and Gaertner, "On the Nature," 20.

16 Arthur K. Spears, *Race and Ideology: Language, Symbolism, and Popular Culture* (Detroit: Wayne State University Press, 1999), 11.

17 Tatum, "Why Are All the Black Kids Sitting," 105.

CENTERING THE MARGINS:

A CHICANA IN THE ENGLISH CLASSROOM

Growing up in Laredo, Texas, on the U.S.–Mexican border, I was not aware of difference, except perhaps the difference that comes with inequality of class— I did have that awareness. I knew children who wore store-bought clothes; families who didn't have to work in the fields; other families who migrated north, *al norte*, to work every year, following crops, leaving in spring and returning in the fall. In other words, I knew families different from mine. I didn't know we were poor, nor did I question why others had more or fewer material goods. I do not remember our poverty as deprivation. In my barrio we were all poor. Since we were all *mejicanos* (my parents' preferred term of self-identity) I did not perceive racial difference in my community, a world insulated and totally *mejicano*, save for the few interactions with the non-*mejicanos*, who invariably held positions of authority: my father's boss, *el jefe*, at the smelter; store owners; the bankers for whom my mother had worked as a nanny before marriage; the priest at San Luis Rey Church, Father Jones. These same non-*mejicanos* peopled the stories in our textbooks, the television programs, and the movies. Some of our teachers offered the reality of a world that was drastically different from the one we knew. That world has changed, yet the world I grew up in still

NORMA E. CANTÚ is a professor of English at the University of Texas in San Antonio. She is the editor of a book series, *Rio Grande/Rio Bravo: Borderland Cultures and Traditions,* from Texas A&M University Press. Her book *Canícula: Snapshots of a Girlhood en la Frontera* won the Premio Aztlán award in 1996.

Drawing from her Chicana cultural background, Cantú uses personal anecdotes to analyze her experience as both student and teacher in the U.S. educational system. Race and class continue to be major factors for her as an English professor, she concludes, but they do not deter her from her love of teaching.

exists along the border and in many school districts; poor children still contend with the ugly realities of racism. Many students still don't see folks like themselves in the literature, in the media, as teachers. I am a survivor of that world, and I am not alone.

To better understand my survival, I often resort to a recounting of my early schooling. My maternal grandmother, Bueli, taught me to read and write in Spanish before I ever went to school. At age five I attended Señora Piña's *escuelita* where I learned even more: songs, rhymes, all the wonderful linguistic tricks of wordplay, *trabalenguas* and *adivinanzas*, the riddles and tongue twisters that I would not learn in English until much later. Such joy in language shaped my life. I can truly say I am a professor of literature, a writer, and a lover of words because of that early experience with language. Already I had two things going for me: a bilingual education and a love of learning instilled at Bueli's knee. Perhaps that is why, when I had to choose a major for my teaching degree, I chose English. I wanted to share my joy and also to help students gain the power that I felt such knowledge had given me.

I am often asked how I came to be a professor of English. I too ask myself how it was that I survived when all the messages in school and in my community told me I would not. How could a Spanish-speaking child of a working-class family ever dream of a college education, of being a writer? Most of my friends were majoring in education; a few dared venture into fields like psychology or sociology. In the sixties, not many of us majored in business or thought of pre-law or pre-med. Only a few whose class status made it possible went into law or medicine. In fact, my double major in English and political science was designed to give me the option of going into either law or teaching. I begin with such musings because I believe it was racism that kept many others from succeeding in the educational system whose game rules I learned early on. I don't have the statistics to prove it, but I bet it is the junior high English classroom that is the proving ground. If you succeed there (and in math class), chances are you will graduate from high school.

Over the years I have become more and more aware of the role race, ethnicity, and class play in the English classroom, and I cannot ignore its influence on how I am perceived as a Chicana professor of English. I have faced many challenges as a university teacher who believes that teaching responsibly requires an honest and searching examination of race. I also believe that class is integral to any discussion of the education of marginalized groups. Yet with an optimist's view of the new millennium, I believe that we can learn to transcend our differences as members of the human race.

It is not surprising that I present here an autobiographical view of a Chicana in the English classroom, for in my work I often insert the autobiographical as a referent; it seems only natural to make the personal political. I take bell hooks's "passion of experience" as license and, in my theoretical projects, I often include insights gleaned from experience.[1] In approaching the negotiations required of faculty of color in predominantly white institutions and the changes forthcoming in higher education as demographic changes force those groups traditionally at the margins to move toward the center, I once again rely on my own experience to anchor my observations. Only a radical reform of the educational system will overthrow the status quo of center and margins—so that every child, every student performs to his or her utmost ability and so that everyone becomes, to borrow Abraham Maslow's concept, a self-actualized citizen of the world.[2] Eternally optimistic, I see that it is possible, but I also see the improbability of it happening in the near future. For it would take each and every one of us—not just those in the academy or the educational system—but all of us in the country to believe that it is possible and to take the steps necessary to make the educational experience one of inclusion and not exclusion, one of joy and not anger or resentment, one of accomplishment and not frustration and defeat.

As I reflect on my own experiences, I realize that my racial and ethnic identity has also afforded me a unique vantage point in my life as a student and teacher. As I explore the pedagogical implications of my own racial and ethnic identity in English departments that have been exclusively white, I realize how it is that my political and social positions have sustained and allowed me to discern the apparent contradictions inherent in my academic work. I cannot divorce the issue of class from any discussion of race and ethnicity in the classroom, for it is evident to me that the prejudices that impact student–teacher and student–student relationships are there even though the middle class myth obfuscates the divisions.

I was a graduate student when I first heard the word "shibboleth" applied to what happens to many students aspiring to a higher education—indeed even those aspiring to nothing more than a high school diploma. In graduate school, I came across someone who used the Biblical story of the Gileads in the Book of Judges to illustrate how pronunciation identified who was an outsider and therefore an enemy. The professor further applied the story to the traditional

English classroom where often teachers use knowledge of standard English as a shibboleth. At the time, however, I didn't understand that for the gatekeepers in the English classroom it is also a matter of class and race. I view Terry Eagleton's discussion of how English came to be a subject to be studied in school as a discussion of how that shibboleth was instituted and why.[3]

THE STUDENT/THE TEACHER

Teaching in South Texas at universities with a majority of Chicano and Chicana students affords me the opportunity to engage in a different kind of cross-cultural teaching; I am often a bridge between the faculty and the students. The ethnic makeup at faculty meetings, where I am often the only person of color, contrasts sharply with the makeup of my classes where a mix exists that more truly reflects the community where I teach: largely Chicano, a few whites, the occasional Puerto Rican, African American, or Asian American student. I am convinced that if the faculty more closely resembled the classroom mix, my job would be easier. While teaching the literature of the groups the students come from, I have to dismantle the learned othering acquired in the traditional English classroom—that is, the classrooms led by some of my colleagues whose own experience in teaching the literatures of people of color in the United States focuses on erasing the ethnic and racial difference of the students in the class. Often such classes are so sanitized that ethnic and racial contexts (not to mention the gender issues) have no place in discussions. For example, a professor teaching the literature of the nineteenth century, in an effort to be inclusive, asks me what would be a good text by a Latino or Latina writer to include in her class. I offer a few titles, and she goes off happy and adds one of my suggested titles to her reading list. But in teaching the work *The Squatter and the Don*, she does not mention the historical context of the novel or of the obvious class and race themes that Amparo Ruíz de Burton presents. I am really touching on two issues here: the content of the course and the pedagogical approaches to teaching "nontraditional" literature. If the professor teaching nineteenth century American literature had used the historical reality of the novel, if she had noted the class issues between the characters and in the plot, if she had guided the discussion toward an open analysis of the gender and ethnic cultural clashes, then the students—not just the Chicanos and Chicanas but all students—would have engaged the novel in a different, perhaps more meaningful, fashion. So, in terms of content, it is not enough to add a title by a Chicana or Chicano writer. The world of the text and the world where the students live include race, class, and gender issues.

The second issue, the pedagogical implications of teaching at a university with a majority of Latino students, is related to the fact that most of the faculty are white. Faculty of color and white faculty may not always acknowledge that they are teaching about race, but the very position they take in discussions, their text selections, and their interactions with students are all shaded by their own racial subject position within the academic world. I did not realize how much race has impacted my teaching. My academic career spans from a teaching assistantship in the early 1970s in Kingsville, Texas, through a doctorate in Nebraska, to my present professorship in San Antonio, Texas.

Armed with my baccalaureate degree in English and political science, I began teaching a freshman English class at Texas A&I University in Kingsville in the fall of 1973. The chair of the department had awarded me the coveted teaching assistantship after a brief interview and mostly as a favor to Alan Briggs, his colleague, and my mentor at Texas A&I in Laredo. Although I was a little older than the traditional graduate, because I had had to wait until the university branch opened in Laredo so that I could finish my baccalaureate degree, I was no less naïve than many of my peers in terms of the reality of our marginal status in academia. I once heard a statistic that shocked me: eighty percent of the Mexican American children who had entered first grade when I had did not finish high school. I was not ready to understand the reasons for this or to question the fact that I had somehow, miraculously it seemed, made it—not just out of high school, but out of college, too. My students at Texas A&I were similarly positioned. Sons and daughters from working-class communities in South Texas, their aspirations led them to Kingsville to pursue college degrees in education and business. They were the survivors, for the dropout rates were just as high then as they had been for my generation. But, there was hope. The war on poverty and other federal programs, including the GI Bill that several Chicano Vietnam vets were using to complete their college education, made my classrooms diverse. Many of these returning GIs and poorly prepared students from the high schools in South Texas would not finish.

I felt that I was part of the problem as I struggled to teach the standard English that the university demanded; English was the shibboleth that kept many of my students from completing a degree. One particular student, Joe, had received his GED in the service and was in my freshman English to begin his college career.[4] Vastly unprepared and possibly suffering a learning disability, he consistently received D's and F's on his essays. He was tenacious, though, and would not drop the class. Joe ended up with a failing grade. Then there was Oralia, who had graduated in the top 10 percent of her high school class but whose writing showed poor preparation. She too failed that first college English class, as have thousands over the years. In some institutions, the class weeds out those who are meant to continue from those who "have no business in college." I felt like a failure that first year. The students who already had the skills did well and passed the course. But those with weak skills did not, and I had not taught them enough to enable them to make English work for them. The department chair saw my despair and offered consolation with maxims he repeated like mantras: "You can't reach all of them," and "The only way to learn to write is to keep writing." As chair, he and the other senior faculty had designed the syllabus for the freshman English class I was teaching. Students were required to write ten persuasive and argumentation essays even when they had little to build on. The fact that I too had suffered at the hands of a Chicano English professor my first year at the community college made me empathize with my students, but, as a lowly teaching assistant barely starting on a master's degree, I had few skills and merely did what had been done unto me.

As a first-year student in Professor García's class, I, too, had felt out of place. I first felt the difference of economic and social status that I would later acknowledge. When the first papers were returned three other students and I had received A's. The professor asked which high schools we came from; I was the only one to come from the public high school. My classmates were from the private Catholic schools. I couldn't understand why I never made another A in all my subsequent papers. The Anglo students, and those who came from the private schools, generally received A's and B's. I remember crying when I received a C on the cause-and-effect paper. If it was class and ethnicity that singled me out for my professors, however, I fit right in with my peers: the majority were *mejicanos* like me. The racist teachers did much harm. In Laredo, we believed ourselves immune to the racist world outside of our community. It was many years later that I recognized the subtle and even blatant racist comments and actions for what they were. The racists whose good intentions kept many of us from taking the college prep courses in high school, the racists whose notions of helping us included punishment for speaking Spanish or speaking with an accent—they were our teachers, who thought we would end up married with a dozen kids, who believed that we did not value education, who were convinced that we just didn't have what it took to make it in college.

Language, the English language specifically, became both my passion and my greatest concern. While I loved my English classes and kept writing poetry and short stories, the speech class was another matter. The speech professor became one of my tormentors. In his efforts to eradicate the heavy Spanish accent of our speech, he taunted and teased and made fun of our mispronounced "sheet" and "keys." One day I ran out of his class crying; I swore I would not return. Of course, I did, since I was on scholarship and could not drop the course. Terrified of the professor, I never complained; I swallowed my pride and accepted the low grade. (In her book *Borderlands/La Frontera*, Gloria Anzaldúa speaks of having to take similar speech classes around the same time only a few hundred miles down river from Laredo.)[5] I still remember how insecure I felt. As I washed dishes at home or did some other household task I memorized the ten vocabulary words and got perfect scores on the weekly quizzes; I strained to hear the difference between *these* and *this*, *chip* and *cheap*, and *chip* and *ship*. Only years later, after Dr. Briggs patiently worked with me one-on-one, did I learn to pronounce the troublesome pairs. I don't recall having access to tutors and we didn't have any real advising.

What made me stick with it? Perhaps because I am *terca*—stubborn—but perhaps it was my love of language and literature, or my dream of becoming a teacher, that made me persevere despite the humiliation, in spite of the difficulty finding rides or money for the bus. I recall how my family and I sacrificed during that one year of community college classes that the Rotary Club scholarship afforded me. As the oldest of eleven children, with my brother off to Vietnam, I could not stay beyond that first year—so I quit and began working. I returned to night school a couple of years later. Because of the geographical isolation of the border, there was no university within 150 miles of Laredo. Faced with the reality of my family's financial need and the impossibility of my ever going out of town to a university, I had to forgo my dream of becoming a teacher. Some of my friends who managed to secure scholarships or whose parents were able to survive without their income did leave. There were even a few lucky ones whose families were better off, and these individuals went on to college right after high school. None was from my neighborhood or circle of friends, though. Class defined our limits and geography exacerbated the restraints on our educational attainment. We simply did not have access to a university unless we moved away from our families and, for those like me who had to work to help support the family, moving was not an option. It took seven long years but, when a branch of Texas A&I University opened in Laredo, I enrolled and received a bachelor's degree in 1973. My experience only underscores the fact that it is not only one factor but many that impact our education as Chicanas and Chicanos. For me, it was certainly the racist teachers and the internalized racism, but it was also the geographic discrimination by the centers of power and the burden of having to contribute to the family's income that affected how and when I could proceed with my educational goals.

Yes, my racial and ethnic identity as well as my class affected how I was treated as a student; when I became a teaching assistant, it seemed I had not learned much. Although I treated students more humanely, I was using the same teaching methods my teachers had used. At Texas A&I, I worked with Upward Bound students in the summer and prepared them for the college English classroom by also working on their pronunciation and writing skills. I don't think I fully functioned as a role model for my students. They probably saw me as inspiring and someone who had made it; they probably also regarded me with some pity—for it seemed to them that I didn't party or have any fun the way they did. They may have perceived that I had lost some of our common heritage. I feared that I was losing my culture, forgetting who I was. I decided to read more books in Spanish and even to audit Spanish classes in linguistics although they were not required for my masters in English. I wanted to empower my students with the English skills, but I also wanted them to remain whole—to remain true to their culture and their reality as *mejicanos*. Academia is an alien enough world and, without the diversity of age and without family around, I felt as if I had landed on another planet. To my Chicano and Chicana students I became a link to home. I recall one particularly homesick group of undergraduates from Laredo who came over one evening; we had baloney sandwiches and Kool-Aid for supper.

GRADUATE SCHOOL

As racist as Kingsville, Texas, was, it did not prepare me for life as a doctoral student in the Midwest, where the majority of my students were white. Only in ethnic literature and writing workshops did I encounter students of color. I again became the mentor for Latino and Latina students—students from Venezuela, Puerto Rico, and the Dominican Republic. Of course, the Chicanos and Chicanas from Nebraska flocked to my classes. Not all students welcomed me. In my second semester as a teaching assistant, one student walked out the first day of class and dropped the course. The reason? He didn't have anything to learn from a Mexican. I don't know how I found out—perhaps he wrote it on the drop form—but it stunned me.

In Nebraska, I learned much about teaching and about the issues that confront students in educational institutions designed for the white majority. For me as a Chicana, the interracial issues came to the forefront in a few instances. In one case I faced a charge of discrimination by a disgruntled African American student who expected "at least a B" because he had turned in all assignments although he had been absent for more than half the class meetings. It didn't matter to him that he had no grades above a C and that he had repeatedly ignored requests to meet with me to go over his papers. Had it not been for the fact that I worked with many other African American students for whom I was an advocate and with whom I felt I was successful, I don't know if I would have questioned my own position of power as a teacher in the classroom. I saw myself as having a common bond with the students of color but, after this incident, I began to see classrooms as sites where power is played out, and my own position of power as the teacher vis-a-vis the students. I began reading Paolo Freire and working through pedagogical issues in the classroom.

In the multicultural classrooms I taught I began to see both the commonality and uniqueness of our experience as people of color in the United States. My students included those whose eastern European language background from several generations ago still surfaced in their sentence construction. There were African American and Native American students as well as several students on work release from the penitentiary, whose grades were always better than the others in the class. As I discovered that my pedagogical passion was leading me to change my teaching, I found teaching to be an exhilarating experience. I was successfully engaging students in the literature and with their own lives. Issues of class, race, and ethnicity as well as gender took center stage in our discussions. A Korean American student in one of my children's literature classes cried in my office one day after a class discussion on the scarcity of materials by and about Asian American and other ethnic children in the literature. She had never acknowledged her heritage or spoken up in class about the invisibility she had felt, but never addressed, reading the stories about white children. I could identify with her. I became the unofficial advisor for not only the Chicano and Chicana students but also the other students of color, for there was such a dearth of faculty of color at the institution and the few who were there were overwhelmed with the demands on their time.

BACK TO TEXAS

In 1980, after a year's hiatus doing research on a Fulbright in Spain, I went from the mostly white educational environment of Nebraska, with few but rich multicultural islands of learning, to an almost exclusively Mexican American student body (at what was then Laredo State University and later became Texas A&M International University [TAMIU]). Given that I was from the community, you would think that all would go smoothly. I was met with both awe and hostility. On more than one occasion, I felt like the African American physician in the emergency room whose black patient requests a white doctor. I had become an outsider. My students resisted my use of the term *Chicano*, even after I explained why I used it and even though it was used in the literature they were studying. The dean spoke to me about student complaints, and I had to reassess why the students were reacting in such negative ways. Only a few students who came from elsewhere—California, or perhaps Chicago—understood. The internalized racism that I too had been subjected to was still there; the schools were still teaching that "Spanish is for the birds," as my eight-year-old nephew informed me one day in 1981. My students had succeeded and survived the educational system because they believed what they had been taught. Now I was asking them to reassess their position, to look at their ethnicity and celebrate their history and origins, to be themselves in the classroom as they were in the bilingual/bicultural community where they lived. While open to discussing discrimination or racism, they were reluctant to see how race affected them directly. Students in my linguistics class found it easier to discuss the bilingualism of communities along the U.S.–Canadian border than our own.

Even as the students questioned my credentials, however, many were my allies and worked hard on a women's conference, joining me as tutors for the local literacy effort and teaching classes in the community. Because many of them were the first in their families to go to college, as I had been, they knew what I knew: that knowledge was power, and learning to read and write in English was power in this country. Many of my students had been migrant workers, and many were working to help support families. Class issues they could understand; racism was not as clear to them. Yet the fact that I had picked cotton as a child seemed to give me some sort of legitimacy. When I taught Shakespeare or Faulkner, or any "difficult" writer, they found solace knowing that I could read these works and discuss them informally during breaks or out of the classroom in Spanish with those for whom Spanish was the preferred language.

My classroom was, and remains, a safe space for discussions about language, about literature, about life. For me, teaching is how I become actualized as a human being.

Teaching and working in an academic setting is when I feel most alive. The educational environment is where I feel I have had the most impact. Almost twenty years after I arrived back home, I noticed a marked change. No longer do the university students in Laredo shy away from issues like homosexuality, linguistic pluralism, Chicano politics, or the violation of immigrant rights. During my final year at TAIMU, I taught Chicano literature, a course on multiethnic literatures of the United States., and a graduate seminar on the U.S.–Mexico borderlands. Such courses did not exist when I was a student nor when I returned as an assistant professor. The local university has changed radically, and I would like to believe that in my various roles as faculty and adminis- trator, I have had some part in making the changes happen. The university has had a tremendous impact on the community's educational system and on indi- vidual lives (like my own, and that of my siblings). The teaching staff of the local school districts has changed from approximately twenty percent Mexican American when I was in school, to eighty percent in 2000. But it has not been easy. It took a lawsuit filed by the Mexican American Legal Defense and Edu- cation Fund to secure funding that was sorely needed to expand the educa- tional opportunities in South Texas. In 2001, the Texas legislature voted against a package of financial support for the region. The severe needs for health care and basic services, such as running water, impact education. The rapid growth (Laredo is the second fastest growing city in the United States) has exacer- bated many of the problems that poverty and government policies like the National Free Trade Agreement have wrought.

COMING HOME

Coming from such a community along the border has afforded me a unique vantage point as a student and teacher. As I explore the pedagogical implica- tions of my own race and ethnic identity in English departments that have been exclusively white, I realize how it is that my political and social positions have sustained and allowed me to discern the apparent contradictions inherent in my work in the academy. I no longer feel like an alien in the department of Eng- lish, although some of my colleagues may still question my credentials and want to be mollified that I do indeed know the Western literary canon. My colleagues in Renaissance or medieval literature are not expected to know twentieth-century U.S. writers, but I am expected to know the traditional canon. This suggests that, somehow, my work is not as valuable.

The study of English as a subject in the university curriculum matters for Chicanos and Chicanas in many ways. For those of us on the geographical margins of the United States and cultural and linguistic margins of the so-called mainstream, it is especially important to learn the language of power and to read the literature that has shaped this country. It is often in the English classroom, I tell my students who will be English teachers, that the future is shaped. High school and elementary school teachers will have to confront teaching situations that until fairly recently were unique to the border area—students with limited English skills who either are recent immigrants and therefore have high levels of Spanish literacy, or who are life-long residents of the area and dominant Spanish speakers, but with limited literacy skills. The latter is now a common experience for teachers in North Carolina, Idaho, Nebraska, Virginia, and many states whose 2000 census figures indicate a surprising and unprecedented increase in the Latino, mostly *mejicano*, population.

Because I cross the traditional discipline boundaries within English—I work in folklore and ethnography—my colleagues in English remain suspicious of my abilities or believe that my ethnicity has allowed me certain privileges. At a recent conference, a white female colleague and I were discussing the possibility of her moving to another university when she blurted out, "You have it made being Chicana." I pondered her observation. What she meant was that I had more job mobility than she. Although I have had others make similar observations that belie true feelings (such as the fellow graduate student in Nebraska who told me that the only reason I received a Fulbright was that I was a minority), I had hoped that as a full professor with extensive publications, I was beyond feeling offended by such comments. In fact, I had naïvely assumed that such perceptions were no longer prevalent. My position is that even if affirmative action got me into a doctoral program, I know that it was because of the lack of affirmative action, bilingual education, support for schools, attention to the curriculum, and teacher training that many Chicanos and Chicanas did not become writers, or teachers, or doctors, or scientists. The loss in human potential, in "cultural capital," has been tremendous even if it's unquantifiable.

Researchers who have studied diversity in classrooms may want to focus on the position of faculty of color at predominantly white institutions versus those with a majority of students of color. I don't regret majoring in English and pursuing a graduate degree. I love to teach and I love to teach literature and languages. I know that, being Chicana and of working-class origins, I am marked as an outsider in the field both by my white colleagues and by my students. Nevertheless, I am an optimist and believe that, just as Chicanos and Chicanas are in many instances no longer the minority but the majority, the same will happen in the English classroom as more marginalized students move toward the center through mastery of the English language. Perhaps then the English composition class will not be what stands in the way of a high school diploma, nor will it be a subject that so many college students fear. Perhaps English will become the one subject that students love, for it will give them the tools to master not just the language but also their own destinies. Perhaps.

NOTES

1 bell hooks, *Teaching to Transgress* (New York: Routledge, 1994), 192–193.

2 Abraham H. Maslow, *The Farthest Reaches of Human Nature* (New York: Viking, 1971), 91–92.

3 Terry Eagleton, *Literary Theory: An Introduction* (Minneapolis: University of Minnesota Press, 1971), 17–53. See his discussion on how and why English became part of the instructional content in technical schools in England in "The Rise of English."

4 All faculty and students' names have been changed to protect their privacy.

5 Gloria Anzaldúa, *Borderlands/La Frontera* (San Francisco: Aunt Lute Books,1987), 54.

DANIEL P. LISTON
SIRAT AL SALIM

RACE, DISCOMFORT, AND LOVE IN A UNIVERSITY CLASSROOM

INTRODUCTION

We write both as teacher and student. We write in hopes that we may describe some of the thoughts, feelings, and experiences we've encountered when we have confronted issues of race and white supremacy in the classroom. In this process we have both learned about the worlds we inhabit, the worlds of others, and ourselves. We write so that others might take our experiences and articulate their own. We present two voices and versions. There were many more. But our personal strengths and weaknesses, our shared insights and blindness, have combined to emphasize two important elements. When examining race in the university classroom we need two types of pedagogy: we need a pedagogy of discomfort and a pedagogy of attentive love. A pedagogy of discomfort engages students and teachers in an examination of their assumptions, beliefs, and locations in a racist society. When we practice a pedagogy of discomfort, pain and anguish surface. A pedagogy of attentive love recognizes this pain and attempts to connect students with the classroom

DANIEL P. LISTON is a professor in the School of Education at the University of Colorado at Boulder. His areas of interest include radical educational theory, curriculum theory, and teacher education. A widely published scholar, he has a forthcoming book from Routledge titled *Love and Despair in Teaching* (2002).

SIRAT AL SALIM is an African American educator, organizer, and activist. While pursuing his Ph.D. in education at the University of Colorado at Boulder, he directs an outreach project, CU in the House, and serves as educational coordinator and curriculum specialist for the Veterans of Hope Project based in Denver, Colorado.

Liston and Salim, a white professor and a black graduate student/activist, each reflects on the racial conflicts both experienced in two of Liston's graduate courses. Struggling across the color line is difficult, they concede, but applying a pedagogy of truth-telling, testimonial reading, and attentive love offers hope.

material. Attentive love focuses on seeing students and ourselves (as teachers) more clearly. Both approaches are needed. It is not an easy story to tell but we think the telling is important.

THE SETTING AND BACKGROUND (DANIEL)

I teach prospective and practicing teachers and doctoral students about the intellectual foundations and ideological contexts of public schooling in a white research-oriented institution. I work hard to create a classroom environment that is both supportive and challenging, a place where students can read and react honestly without fear of dismissal and with an expectation of support and understanding. I thought I knew something about the intricacies of exploring race and culture in these and other classes. I've written articles and books on the topic. I've taught in the field for seventeen years working with undergraduate and graduate, professional and liberal arts, young and old—predominantly white, middle-class—students. But this last academic year I have come to believe that my explorations of race, class, and culture may not have been as shared as I had thought. This last year there were times I went home disheartened, frustrated, and angry about the conflicts the students and I were experiencing. This last year I learned a lot and I'm sure I have much more to learn.

In the past I've shied away from overt expressions of conflict and confrontation in the classroom. This year I couldn't, and have slowly learned not to want to smooth things over. This year Sirat Al Salim, a doctoral student at the University of Colorado at Boulder and middle school teacher in Denver, practiced a pedagogy of discomfort in my classroom. His pedagogy of discomfort is a form of truth-telling, and it is a practice that has stirred a strong sense of conflict and ambivalence in my own and my students' hearts, minds, and souls. At times Sirat Al's truth-telling feels like accusation, pointing fingers at other students for wrongs he perceives. At other times I thank the educational gods that he pushes to extend the limits of our discussions. Some days I think Sirat Al is much too quick to judge others harshly. And during those same moments I know that were I in his place I might very well make the same judgments. I hope it won't be the last year I encounter these emotions and beliefs. Sometimes at the college level we forget that teaching can be an emotionally challenging endeavor. At the university we seem to imagine that we can cut through the butter of emotions and get right to the rational, hard core. That's an illusion. At the university we can't expect to address over two centuries of white violence directed at blacks and not experience conflict, painful emotions, and heartache.

In the past I tried to create a classroom that was caring and not acrimonious—one that was intellectually challenging but not personally discomforting. I now believe that I strove for an unrealistic and not very helpful ideal. I still strive to create a caring and supportive ethos, but I now also want to support and make safe the expression and reception of anger and frustration. I have come to believe that if white faculty and white students are going to examine issues of race and racism in the classroom then conflict, struggle, and discomfort must be present. We need to learn how to express emotions and ideas, especially painful ones. I'm still learning. But I've come to believe that we need to experience and explore what the feminist scholar Megan Boler calls a pedagogy of discomfort.[1] According to Boler, "Learning to live with ambiguity, discomfort, and uncertainty is a worthy educational ideal."[2] This is difficult territory, but if we are going to deal with race in a white university setting then we need to make some new paths. However, as we experience and explore this pedagogy of discomfort, we also need to offer a pedagogy of attentive love. Without elements of attentive love, a pedagogy of discomfort can result in a kind of conflict and confrontation that easily turns ugly, mean-spirited, and harmful. If we disregard attentive love we neither heal nor nurture each other; without a pedagogy of discomfort, we may not confront the issues we need to address. We may come to believe that we are all innocent and not culpable in white supremacy.

In the fall of 2000 Sirat Al enrolled in "Curriculum Theories," a graduate-level course. That was our first course together. There were eighteen students, fifteen of whom had taught in the public school and were coming back for a master's degree. Sixteen students were white, two were black, and fourteen were women. It was the most silent class I've ever taught. Two male students tended to dominate discussions. One of these students, Sirat Al, tended to be quite critical. He intimated that my ordering of one week's readings was racist and that my overall selection of readings represented a white rather than a diverse curriculum. He found my characterization of white students' reluctance to address racial issues to be much too protective of those students, and he criticized other students for their inability to address race and racism. Many of the white students were uncomfortable with the dynamics and eventually chose to be silent. I talked with the white male student about his tendency to dominate discussions. He said that he understood and altered his pattern. I was reluctant to talk to Sirat Al as I feared that my own frustration, anger, and ambivalence would surface, and I didn't trust myself. I was frustrated that I had helped create a classroom setting in which students felt vulnerable and intimidated. I was angry with myself for not finding a better way to deal with the situation and angry with Sirat Al for his blanket criticism of "white folk." I was conflicted and ambivalent about what to do.

During one class session when Sirat Al criticized his classmates for their inability to adequately address the issue of race in education, many other class members finally voiced their disagreements with him. At the end of class that evening many students left upset, frustrated, and angry. Sirat Al was also dismayed and troubled. He had developed relationships with some of the other students. I figured it was time for Sirat Al and me to talk about the class dynamics. In order to initiate and carry out my role in that conversation I knew I had to inhabit a different space. I had to occupy a space that registered but did not become inflamed by my own reactions. I needed a space that saw and heard Sirat Al clearly and affirmed his basic goodness, while also taking into account his classmates' concerns. My own reactions were a major impediment. I had to be able to speak clearly and tell my own truth about the classroom situation. I doubted that I would speak truthfully and feared that my emotions would erupt. I had to more fully develop what others and I have come to call attentive love.

Teaching with attentive love entails the following: the presumption that good exists within each student; the attempt to discern and see our students more clearly and justly; and the understanding that in order to see more clearly we need to reduce the noise of our selves. When we accomplish this, students and teacher learn more about the world and about themselves. It is a concept and practice others have touched on. Simone Weil developed the notion of attentive love in writings and reflections composed during the 1930s and 1940s; Iris Murdoch extended it in her book *The Sovereignty of Good;* Sara Ruddick elaborates elements of it in *Maternal Thinking;* and Lisa Delpit underscores it in her published work.[3] Attentive love in teaching is frequently a struggle and a sacrifice. It asks us to see beyond our egoistic and culture-bound selves in order to see our students more clearly and connect them and ourselves with the lessons at hand. Attentive love doesn't guarantee success, and I certainly didn't perform any magical transformations. It did enable me to persist during some difficult times by allowing me to see myself, Sirat Al, and our class a bit more clearly. It allowed a kind of grace to settle in between. It allowed me to walk into our next course (on radical educational theories) together, with a commitment to listen to Sirat Al's truth-telling and experience more fully a pedagogy of discomfort. Usually it is the official teacher who initiates this pedagogy; here it was one of the students.

A PEDAGOGY OF DISCOMFORT
IN THE WHITE CLASSROOM (SIRAT AL)

At the beginning of a graduate course on radical educational theories, Dan Liston asked students to share their names, their academic and professional interests, and their activities over the preceding winter break. We shared recent events, introduced ourselves, and became familiar with each other's interests. We were encouraged to engage in the political act of naming and positioning our selves, of claiming identity, purpose, and vision. I remember thinking how appropriate and necessary the introductory activity was given the course topic. I wondered whether the activity foreshadowed a curriculum and pedagogy that would center all of our lived experiences, identities, and purposes or would be yet another example of a white curriculum. Would this learning experience be meaningful, culturally inclusive, nonalienating, and grounded? Despite my enthusiasm for the promising beginning, I could not assuage my concern over the limitations and constraints imposed on learning at an isolated, overwhelmingly white research university. Many faculty and students of color have described the university atmosphere as toxic, and I agree. The constraints and limitations are real and have forced some to leave. Just the previous year, the School of Education experienced an exodus of the first and only African American faculty and approximately thirty percent of the African American graduate student population.

"Story" was the preferred form of sharing our experiences over the break, and I was intrigued by how each experience positioned us with respect to class, race, and gender. While each story was descriptive and valuable, many seemed to revolve around relaxation such as vacations and skiing trips, or the joys and frustrations of visiting family members and friends over the Christmas holidays. I shared my experience of communing with elders in Cleveland, Ohio, but I did not mention that Cleveland was once known as the City of Hope and "the Crossroads." It served as a fueling station for many enslaved Africans searching for freedom en route to Buxton, Canada.[4] One hundred and forty years after emancipation, I had traveled to Cleveland. In many ways I was retracing my ancestors' footsteps in search of—and hoping to replenish—my faith.

The only other student of color in the class, who is also African American, shared a story about an experience at a local Radio Shack store. As she waited at the counter for service, a white male sales clerk (unconsciously or consciously) ignored her and waited on an elderly white male customer who had just walked up to the counter. She confronted the clerk and later the manager, who became angry and hostile regarding their practice of racial profiling and discrimination. They seemed unable to comprehend the insult or the extent that their actions perpetuated racism. She shared with the class her disgust and anger at continually being asked to do the work of eradicating white supremacy—a task that largely involves educating white people. She also expressed her disappointment in the two white men as their humanity was stunted, in part by their failure to understand that white supremacy was *their* work to do.

Several classmates responded with questions: "Where is the store located?" or "What did you do then?" One classmate subtly questioned the analysis and interpretation of the offense, though most students simply sighed or nonverbally expressed passive empathy. Then the class went on with business as usual.

This testimony and accompanying class response demonstrate the dynamic nature in which race, class, and gender are intertwined to produce and reproduce oppression in our society. The students' empathetic response allows us to explore two key concepts in Megan Boler's elaboration of a pedagogy of discomfort: passive empathy and testimonial reading.[5] While my analysis does not do justice to the full scope of Boler's theory, I wish to use the notion of testimonial reading to expose and name some of the constraints of learning within predominantly white institutions.

The racial profiling and discriminatory practices of the two employees at Radio Shack reveal the extent to which class, race, and gender are dynamically interconnected and layered to produce domination. Though we do not know the particular motivations and intentions behind the white men's actions that dismissed the African American woman, they share a commonality with many—perhaps most—of my white classmates: a failure to fully comprehend that white supremacy represents work white people must do. To be sure, many distinctions exist between the two hostile white men and my empathic classmates, but neither hostility nor passive empathy produces meaningful shifts in existing power relations—and neither eradicates racism. As Boler suggests, "passive empathy absolves [us] through the denial of power relations."[6] It rarely results in sustained "reflection or action, either about the production of meaning, or about one's complicit responsibility within historical and social conditions."[7]

The point is not to dismiss empathy or my classmates' capacity to express it. Empathy is a potentially important act of identification with the other. Even more so, it recognizes that suffering is real and caused by internal and external factors (i.e., "I'm not you but I understand what you're going through"). While empathy is often a byproduct of fear (the fear that one will be subjected to the other's suffering) and can inspire action in an immediate, real-life context, empathy rarely eradicates the other's suffering or produces justice.[8] Would the empathy the class expressed result in some students' taking action against Radio Shack? Would students stop shopping there? Would they organize a boycott? Would any student question or reconsider their worldviews? Would they explore the extent to which passive empathy perpetuates white supremacy and gendered domination?

Like Boler, I am concerned with who and what benefit from the production of empathy. What is gained when students and professors occupy fantasy spaces through empathy that decontextualizes the moral problem? Moreover, as Boler points out, "what is gained and/or lost by advocating as a cure for social injustice an empathetic identification that is more about [self than other] . . . If no change can be measured as a result of the production of empathy, what has been gained other than a *good brotherly feeling?*"[9] Hollywood continues to produce soporific tales in movies like *The Green Mile* or *Driving Miss Daisy.* Here we were doing the same damn thing.

What is really needed, as Boler argues, is a "testimonial reading" that involves empathy but also results in responsible action on the part of the listener.[10] For Boler, "testimonial reading inspires an empathetic response that motivates action: a historicized ethics . . . that radically shifts our self-reflective understanding of power relations" and critically examines our complicit role in oppressive social forces.[11] Within the context of testimonial reading and beyond passive empathy, the questions include: What responsibilities did the white students have to my black sister's story? What actions were required that would move them beyond their mechanized lives? Instead of a consumerist focus on identification with "this black woman's experience of discrimination," were the white classmates required to rethink their own assumptions? Were they obligated to identify and eradicate their own complicit roles in the social forces that produce the racism and sexism?

After reading Boler's *Feeling Power* later in the semester, my friend shared her Radio Shack story again in an effort to make the above points. I directly asked my white classmates and Dan what they thought their responsibilities were in such a situation and what actions were required of them. I was astonished by the class's initial silence and their inability to respond adequately to the question. I was reminded of a comment Dan made to a class the previous semester in an effort to help students get beyond the inhibitions and difficulties of talking about race and racism. To paraphrase him, "Talking about racism for some white people is like calling a black person a nigger." While Dan's intent may have been to provoke discussion, silence was also this class's response.

I believe that Dan's comment and the students' silence represent a crisis of truth, where many white people are frequently unable to move beyond feelings of shame, guilt, fear, and indifference over the historical reality of race and racism in the United States. This seriously undermines their ability to talk meaningfully about race or to explore their complicit roles in white supremacy. As Boler suggests, "To raise the specter of racism does not mean for the white person that 'guilt' is the permanent or only option."[12] Through experiencing and exploring testimonial readings and a pedagogy of discomfort,

> it is possible to explore the emotional dimensions and investments . . . and the histories in which these are rooted. We can explore how our identities are precariously constructed in relation to one another, so that to suggest change may feel like a threat to our survival. At a minimum, one might offer a responsible accountability for how these emotional investments shape one's actions, and evaluate how one's actions affect others.[13]

Dan, who I believe has exhibited a refreshing willingness to expand the world he inhabits, has suggested in conversations that I am too presumptive in my observations about the motivations and silence of classmates and him. I see his point and admit it is sometimes a daily battle to quiet and negotiate my own feelings of outrage and impatience: outrage at the insidious reality of white supremacy and impatience with the slow process of testimonial readings, pedagogy of discomfort, and attentive love.

However, if we are to engage a pedagogy of discomfort, it seems necessary to explore my classmates' silence which, in part, represents a failure to move beyond passive empathy and empathetic identification. Moreover, when the range of our emotions about issues of race oscillates between hostility, fear, guilt, shame, and passive empathy, the range of potential actions are severely restricted. I believe my classmates' inability to articulate any necessary actions when asked to reconsider the testimony is reflective of the limitations of passive empathy as an educational practice. What internal and external obstacles prevented my colleagues from rethinking their assumptions about race and critically examining their complicit role in white supremacy? Beyond this minimal task, what prohibited the students from articulating or engaging in other possible actions such as letter-writing campaigns, phone calls, boycotts, or other meaningful efforts of redress?

Testimonial reading requires both action and accountability. My classmates' passive empathy, silence, and inability to take action fail to engage the deeper implications of racism in our society or classroom. Moreover, passive empathy and inaction risk confirming the permanency of white supremacy. It represents a failure to comprehend that white supremacy is the work white people must do—it is their project.

This situation and others like it begin to expose the limitations and constraints that students of color, particularly African Americans, experience in overwhelmingly white educational institutions and classrooms. How do students of color have meaningful relationships with white classmates when the relationship is inauthentic (built upon empathetic identification) and perpetuates our objectification and consumption as other? How meaningful is a learning experience shaped by empathy borne of fear, guilt, and self-interest? Passive empathy permits a fantasy-like identification with the other. While this kind of empathy may feel good, particularly for many of my white colleagues, it continues to alienate and objectify students of color. As an educational practice, passive empathy—coupled with the larger, often repressive dynamics of race, class, and gender on college campuses—produces a toxic campus atmosphere. This is especially detrimental to students of color.

In part, my classmates' empathy, like the actions of the two racist and sexist representatives of Radio Shack, symbolizes a failure to accept their complicit roles in the reproduction of white supremacy. Their empathetic identification with the African American female student did not require them to shift their understanding of power relations. My white classmates did not seemingly reconsider what it means to be black and a woman in our society. Maybe if we had read Patricia Hill Collins's *Black Feminist Thought*, some reconsideration would have occurred.[14] Nor did they seemingly critique the extent to which their daily actions or inactions perpetuate the social forces that seek to subordinate and oppress. Collins's chapter "Toward a Politics of Empowerment" would have encouraged such a critique.[15]

Under these conditions, serious constraints are imposed on students of color, and their abilities to have meaningful learning experiences are compromised. What do we gain from educational practices that decontextualize knowledge, that divorce knowledge from responsibility and action, that alienate and objectify us, that omit or negate our cultural ways of knowing and make them foreign, that deny possibility itself and function as a destructive force? In the face of such contradictions and fraud, how do students of color seriously engage white classmates and professors in a collective educational project?

As students of color struggle to make meaning in white classrooms, they are often asked or expected to do the majority of the work—to shoulder the responsibility when it comes to grappling with issues of race and racism. In this class, like other graduate courses, when I engage a pedagogy of discomfort and testimonial reading to expose complicity in the perpetuation of white supremacy, I am problematized and characterized as "adversarial." The discomfort and conflict are real and evident, but the capacity and presence of attentive love are not. I don't mean to imply that African Americans and other people of color should not and need not have a role in eradicating white supremacy—particularly since I do not believe that most white people can do this work without some initial leadership from people of color, especially African Americans. However, I do mean to suggest that as people of color, we need to decontaminate our psyche by divorcing ourselves from white supremacy. Our story transcends racism and oppression. Until white people begin doing the majority of the work of eradicating white supremacy, racism is likely to remain a permanent feature in our classrooms and society.

Nevertheless, we must continue to engage testimonial readings and a pedagogy of discomfort; this is an ultimate act of love out of which we can emerge as fully realized human beings. As law professor Derrick Bell reminds us, "This engagement and commitment is what black people have had to do since slavery: making something out of nothing. Carving out humanity for oneself with absolutely nothing to help—save imagination, will, and unbelievable strength and courage. Beating the odds while firmly believing in, knowing as only [we] could know," that the odds are stacked against us, but we must have the "unalterable conviction that something must be done, that action must be taken."[16]

A PEDAGOGY OF ATTENTIVE LOVE (DANIEL)

I find it difficult to support students who are harshly critical of others. This was one of the difficulties I was having with my perception of Sirat Al. At times he seemed to assume he could discern the motivations behind white students' contributions and silences. "White folk" became a monolithic category, and that categorization polarized our classroom. But that was neither my only perception nor my singular understanding of Sirat Al. In our interactions inside and outside of the classroom, in his interactions with his peers, and in observing him work with his students, I have found Sirat Al to be a man who examines and criticizes not only the practices of others but his own as well. He encourages his students and is respectful in his interaction with colleagues. While at times he may seem to me to be more externally than internally critical, he continually enters a white institution with the expectation that somehow his and the more general African American experience will not be diminished but valued. He participates with the belief and hope that the history and legacy of his people will be honored; and that I, as a white other, will strive to understand my legacy and role in it. In this respect, he gives me and his white classmates the benefit of the doubt. We have taken the time to talk on a number of occasions. When we've sat and talked I've had to bring this understanding with me. I've needed to acknowledge the good within him and I've had to be open to hearing the ways in which he felt I had diminished him and was inadequate before the task. Over time, I have come to see Sirat Al as an educational and community activist motivated by a love of his—and all—people. It took me quite some time to see this. In order to see his love I had to get beyond my reactions to his anger.

All of us seek to understand, to reach out beyond ourselves for that which is good. It is a desire that may not always be consciously present and certainly conflicts with other desires and needs. But it is a yearning that defines, in part, what it means to be human. We long to reach beyond ourselves, to see and participate in something larger than ourselves. I also believe that our students come with the expectation that they will be treated decently. As Simone Weil has commented: "At the bottom of the heart of every human being [is the expectation] that good not evil will be done to him. It is this above all that is sacred in every human being."[17] Our students are sacred in that they search for good in this world and yearn for a good beyond themselves. When I approach students with this understanding I hope to honor them: honor their good within, and honor their search.

Iris Murdoch claims that we attend to others throughout the moments of our days and reminds us that this can be a difficult task:

> Our attachments tend to be selfish and strong, and the transformation of our loves from selfishness to unselfishness is sometimes hard even to conceive of. . . . The love which brings the right answer is an exercise of justice and realism and really looking. The difficulty is to keep the attention fixed upon the real situation and to prevent it from returning surreptitiously to the self with consolations of self-pity, resentment, fantasy, and despair. . . . It is a task to come to see the world as it is.[18]

When we are engaged in teaching, our egos and cultures can get in the way. Our own conceptions, anxieties, discomforts, apprehensions, satisfactions, and dreams both obstruct and illuminate.

With Sirat Al, I found myself wondering if I could ever get out of my white skin and understand more thoroughly my white frameworks. I thought I had already examined my assumptions and beliefs, but there were times when our pedagogy of discomfort felt very discomforting. In many ways I have become the "white Boulder professor" I wasn't ten years ago. And there were times when I thought that Sirat Al needed to be more self-reflective. However, over time I have come to see the double bind my curricula and courses have created for him, the need to examine the context that constructs and construes him as "problem," and the "whiteness" of my curricula. In many ways I have relied on Sirat Al's presence and voice to raise the difficult questions, to initiate a pedagogy of discomfort. When he does the work and raises the discomfort level, he can be perceived by others and me as creating problems and, at times, as being a problem. While I wished he would find other less adversarial ways to raise these issues, Sirat Al frequently was the one who initiated the critical tasks and when he did so others (including me) found his message discomforting. Being black and critical in a white institution put Sirat Al in a double bind: in raising the problems, he became a problem. Being a white professor in a white institution that envelops and restricts students of color, I need to find ways to disrupt equating problem poser with "pain-in-the-ass," to make problematic a context that constructs the critical voice as the problem voice. I can do some of this conceptually and theoretically, but I am still working on doing it pedagogically. Sirat Al also pointed out ways in which course readings fit white and not black understandings. He pointed to the color and hues of the issues. This reflected the cultural gap I thought I had overcome, but found that I continually needed to bridge.

I think it's a struggle to tend to students. The struggle is not that attentive love requires attending to each and every student in every class session. Rather, it is a task to suspend our own expectations, bracket our own agendas, and set aside our own concerns so as to see the matter at hand from our students' points of view. How do we as white teachers put our beliefs on hold to attend to the other before us? How do we reduce the noise of our egos? We talk with others; we attempt to see the good in the situation or student; and we refocus our attention on an object that is a source of contemplation and energy. During this last year I have engaged in all three. I have endeavored to see the good, talked with colleagues, and refocused my own energies. Murdoch writes that "What is needed is a reorientation which will provide an energy of a different kind from a different source. . . . Deliberately falling out of love is not a jump of the will, it is the acquiring of new objects of attention and thus of new energies as a result of refocusing. . . . There is nothing odd or mystical about this, nor about the fact that our ability to act well 'when the time comes' depends partly, perhaps largely, upon the quality of our habitual objects of attention."[19] Conversing with others, tapping each individual's goodness, and reorienting our gaze allows us a degree of detachment from the noise of our selves. None is, for sure, a guaranteed method. However, all seem to provide a measure of the redirection and self-detachment needed for attentive love.

CONCLUSION

We continue to talk about and engage both attentive love and a pedagogy of discomfort. It is a complicated undertaking, compounded by the world and ourselves. We don't always agree, but we have found ways to understand and respect each others' angers and fears and to voice our disagreements. We share many of the same hopes and dreams. It is a long journey that we are beginning and must continue to take.

NOTES

1 Megan Boler, *Feeling Power: Emotions and Education* (New York: Routledge, 1999).

2 Boler, *Feeling Power*, 197–198.

3 Sara Ruddick, *Maternal Thinking* (Boston: Beacon Press, 1989); Iris Murdoch, *The Sovereignty of Good* (New York: Schocken Books, 1971); Lisa Delpit, *Other People's Children* (New York: New Press, 1996); George Panichas, ed., *The Simone Weil Reader* (Wakefield, R.I.: Moyer Bell, 1977).

4 Jacqueline Tobin and Raymond Dobard, *Hidden in Plain View* (New York: Doubleday, 1999).

5 Boler, *Feeling Power*, 197–198.

6 Boler, *Feeling Power*, 164.

7 Boler, *Feeling Power*, 164.

8 Boler, *Feeling Power*, 159.

9 Boler, *Feeling Power*, 164; emphasis in original.

10 Boler, *Feeling Power*, 158.

11 Boler, *Feeling Power*, 158–159.

12 Boler, *Feeling Power*, 197; emphasis in original.

13 Boler, *Feeling Power*, 197–198

14 Patricia Hill Collins, *Black Feminist Thought* (New York: Routledge, 2000).

15 Collins, *Black Feminist Thought*, 273–290.

16 Derrick Bell, *Faces at the Bottom of the Well: The Permanence of Racism* (New York: Basic Books, 1992), 198–199.

17 Panichas, *Simone Weil*, 79.

18 Murdoch, *Sovereignty*, 91.

19 Murdoch, *Sovereignty*, 55–56.

MOONWALKING TECHNOSHAMANS AND THE SHIFTING MARGIN:

DECENTERING THE COLONIAL CLASSROOM

I teach Native American Literature—works written by Native (Uramerican) authors about Native people and issues—a subject that did not exist when I was a college student. Often, however, my classes consist of extended attempts to disrupt the ethnostalgia of Euramerican students for a lost origin called "Indian" because, for the most part, my students in the university classroom— even in Native American studies, but especially in an English department—are seldom indigenous. The one or two or sometimes three or four Native students in my literature classes find themselves nearly always in an odd position: they suspect that they have a certain authority within the text, yet they must struggle for a way to acknowledge such authority within the classroom where to claim that authority is to claim possession of the stereotype of "Indian" brought to the classroom context by their white classmates. Outnumbered and outflanked, the Native student must, as Philip Deloria argues in his book *Playing Indian*, step into the constructed role of Indian to be heard by their fellow non-Native students.[1] Most Native students refuse the gambit and hold to a silent margin. But not always.

LOUIS OWENS is a professor of English and Native American Studies at University of California, Davis. He is the author of numerous essays, critical studies, works of fiction, and personal narratives. His publications include *Other Destinies; Mixedblood Messages; I Hear the Train; The Sharpest Sight; Wolfsong; Bone Game; Nightland;* and *Dark River*.

Owens draws on his two decades of experience teaching Native American literature. He analyzes one unusual class in which European American students did not form the privileged center of the classroom. In the essay's climax, Owens describes a Native student fashion show that contains lessons for educators and all Americans as well.

The "catachrestic gesture," we are told, is the gesture of "the postcolonial artist or critic who interrogates, turns round, (mis)appropriates the terms or symbols of Western discourse."[2] What happens, however, when catachresis becomes the tool of the "minority" student, when the margin achieves a critical mass and appropriates the center in the classroom, when the formerly marginalized student mimics not the dominant center but that center's marginalizing gestures and seizes the authoritative high ground of privileged discourse? Homi Bhabha's celebrated destabilizing "ironic compromise" slips away with the vanishing center as, in the particular case I have in mind, the formerly dominant center of the white (Euramerican) classroom finds its nostalgia for lost origins repudiated by the Indian (Uramerican) margin that transcribes the stereotype into another discourse.[3]

In the spring of 1991, I offered a course called "The Native American Novel" to students at the University of California at Santa Cruz—the first such course in the history of the campus. Perhaps because of the novelty of the class, and undoubtedly influenced by the recent popularity of that insidious film *Dances with Wolves*, more than three hundred students applied for admission to the class of forty-two.[4] I had joined the UCSC faculty in the fall of that academic year, and, because I served as faculty advisor for Native American students, I had gotten to know the small group of Native students on the campus fairly well. At least they had gotten to know me well enough to sign up for my class in unusual numbers—perhaps mostly out of curiosity.

Those of us who have taught university courses in what we call Native American literature are accustomed to finding one or two Native students in such a class, always surrounded and engulfed by a classroom sea, or pond, of non-Natives. In my Santa Cruz Native American novel course, a dozen of the forty-two students were Native Americans, an astonishingly high number. Those of us accustomed to teaching Native students in any classes are used to seeing them sit silently in the back of the class, listening but seldom speaking. Such silence, we know, results from complex pressures. In some cases Native students come from traditional homes where young people are taught to respect their elders and listen, not asking questions. In some cases, confronting intense culture shock, they are simply private and shy in public—especially if they've grown up in a reservation community where English may not be the first language at home. Always, they are aware that theirs is not the privileged place or voice in a classroom where the texts are someone else's, and the dominant voice—the only voice allowed—is a weapon that has been used against

Native people for half a millennium. If they've come from a reservation school, they are often acutely conscious that the education they received was not the same as their fellow students'. Consciously or unconsciously, they react to these shaping forces. America needs to remember that when Indian students sit in a U.S. classroom, they sit in a colonized classroom surrounded by heirs of the invaders, and consciously or unconsciously they know this.

The Native student is never at the privileged center of the class or text and must select words from another's language to explore literature from and about that other. With whom, for example, does the Navajo or Lakota or Choctaw student identify in *Tom Sawyer, Moby-Dick, The Catcher in the Rye, The Waste Land,* or the poems of Sylvia Plath? While great literature obviously speaks to the human heart across all boundaries, Twain's "Injun Joe" and Melville's Queequeg nonetheless provide distorting and limiting mirrors for the Native student. Holden Caulfield offers a fun-house reflection at best for the student from a remote corner of the 25,000 square mile Navajo reservation or the ravaged rural worlds of many reservation communities. If stories are supposed to give us back reflections of our selves, as Vladimir Nabokov's mad editor Kinbote understands so well in the novel *Pale Fire,* where does one find the Lakota reality of Pine Ridge, South Dakota, or the Blackfeet Reservation world of Montana reflected back from the literature taught in American classrooms? I was used to Native American students who sat in the back and seldom spoke. In grade school and high school, as a Choctaw-Cherokee-Irish-Cajun sharecropper's kid transplanted from the Yazoo country of Mississippi to the strange world of California, I had done the same.

In my Santa Cruz class, however, the familiar dynamics shifted suddenly and radically. Rather than disappearing into the depths of the room, the Indian students sat at the front of the class. More astonishingly, they spoke, gaining confidence and enthusiasm from the first day so quickly that by the second class meeting they were dominating discussion. They were an eclectic, pantribal group from places and peoples as disparate as Tlingit communities in Alaska, the San Carlos Apache reservation in Arizona, the Pine Ridge Lakota reservation in South Dakota, the Yurok and Hoopa rancherias in northern California, and the Navajo Nation of the Southwest. Some had grown up securely in the center of their tribal cultures, and others were urban Indians, the children of displacement and federal relocation programs. Some were the products of the most brutal impoverishment in America, and some came from upper-middle-class California families. Together they brought to my class a very mixed but extraordinarily broad knowledge of what it meant to be Indian in contemporary America. Almost from the beginning, they were eager to volunteer knowledge, information, and opinions, talking about the reservations or urban Native communities and families from which they came, about their experiences in schools like the experiences of the books' protagonists, about being mixedbloods in a world where authenticity was commodified, about being silenced like the characters in so many Native novels, about poverty and anger but also about grandmothers who told stories and basketball teams that swept down the court like war parties. They explained aspects of Native life ranging from the angst of cultural displacement to exotic elements such as frybread and fancy-dancing to their classmates and laughed at the inside Indian jokes about apples and snagging that their classmates didn't get. Most of all, they mocked and ridiculed the stereotypes and clichés that make up the world's idea of something called "Indian." The first two rows of the class, the Native rows, became almost from the first moment a carnivalesque space of released energy and excitement, but behind those first rows things were different.

The University of California at Santa Cruz is a rather special place. The Santa Cruz campus sits on an exposed shoulder of the coastal mountains looking down upon the stunning blue bowl of Monterey Bay. Between the campus and bay is a small, expensive town that was for several thousand years an Ohlone Indian site before the Ohlone people were enslaved in a Spanish mission and nearly exterminated. The settlement became an Italian fishing village and then a seaside resort, and finally an affluent, New Age college town. Set within a redwood forest that climbs for miles up the Santa Cruz range, the campus is surrealistically lovely.

Tucked into shadowed redwood groves above the campus, within the close tree circles called fairy rings, students have for years created secret shrines and altars, places where they gather at night to light candles, make small offerings, and generally pay mysterious homage to the nature that saturates their world in a religion made of fragments they are shoring against spiritual ruin at the end of one millennium and beginning of another. Bits and pieces of what the students—in a confused and intensely naïve fashion—conceive of as Native American spirituality are appropriated and puzzled into the fabric of this poignant new religion in random and wistful ways, fragments taken from books and movies and the overarching American metanarrative that has taught them about Indians.

Santa Cruz students were the numerical minority in the classroom, but none was alone. Tlingit, Yurok, Lakota, Apache, Navajo, Hoopa, Blackfeet, Delaware, Cherokee—they were all acutely conscious of being Native American together. They were also an unusually mature and very bright group, including several sharp critical readers and fine writers. They were interested in the subject and had a personal stake in it. Perhaps for the first time in a college classroom, they realized that they had authority, that the privileged voice was for the first time theirs. Every detail of the novels I had assigned touched someone among the Native students directly and powerfully.

The reaction of the non-Indian students in the class was fascinating. They were not used to being silenced. They were bright and talented and had come from very good secondary schools, and they had always been in the privileged position in the American classroom. The texts in those classes had spoken their language, had dealt with the details of their shared world. The non-Native students had come to my class eager to read this new kind of fiction—had come, as Trinh Minh-ha has written of her own audiences, "to listen to that voice of difference likely to bring us *what we can't have* and to divert us from the monotony of sameness."[5] Though there were naturally very different degrees of awareness and sensibility among the students, they had for the most part come, as Trinh adds, in search of "a difference or otherness that will not go so far as to question the foundation of their beings and makings."[6] They had come in search of what, in my book *Mixedblood Messages*, I have termed "literary tourism." This is precisely what so many ethnic classes indeed offer, perhaps particularly those classes taught by representatives of minority discourse who desire to fit Trinh's definition of the "Third World representative the modern sophisticated public ideally seeks . . . the *unspoiled* African, Asian, or Native American, who remains more preoccupied with her/his image of the *real* native—the *truly different*—than with the issues of hegemony, racism, feminism, and social change (which s/he lightly touches on in conformance to the reigning fashion of liberal discourse)."[7] In short, many of the white students in the class had come bearing an enormous burden of preconceived, authoritative knowledge. They had grown up knowing about Indians because European America invented the Indian to replace the indigenous person. The Indian lives inside the Euramerican, never outside in the real world. The students for the most part didn't know or know about indigenous Native Americans, however, and when, in the second class meeting, a non-Native student spoke up to point out that in one of the novels a Native man's legal rights had been violated and thus question the novel's verisimilitude, several of the Native students laughed outright. While Native Americans can also fall prey to the Euramerican construction of Indianness and unconsciously play the role of Indian for white America, these students came from reservation communities and had seen Indians' legal rights violated again and again all their lives. Their fellow student's naiveté struck them as hilarious. Humiliated by the sudden laughter, the young woman abruptly fled from the classroom in tears, and at once one of the more self-confident and mature of the Indian students, a Yurok woman who read and wrote brilliantly, got up and followed her from the room—not to apologize, as I later learned, but to tell the fleeing student that she needed to grow up and face realities instead of running off like a baby.

By the third meeting of the class, despite my efforts to subtly mediate what was shaping up as a political and cultural crisis, the non-Native students were coming one after another to sit in my office, often in tears. Their stories were the same each time: never in their lives had they been afraid to speak up in a class; never had they felt silenced, afraid that what they said would not be "right" or that they didn't simply misunderstand the material but lacked the necessary knowledge to understand at all. The Blackfeet world of James Welch's *Winter in the Blood*, the Pueblo world of Leslie Marmon Silko's *Ceremony* or N. Scott Momaday's *House Made of Dawn*, the trickster chaos of Gerald Vizenor's Anishinaabe fictions—these were foreign and dangerous to them, particularly when the body of knowledge that had prepared them for life seemed oddly to lack legitimacy. More critically, there were "others" in the class who had privileged insight into the texts and whose cultural authority trumped their own. To the white students' utter surprise, they had encountered not a safely colorful "other" world, but an articulated otherness that questioned, in Trinh's words, "the foundation of their beings and makings."[8] For the first time in their lives they felt marginalized, disenfranchised, deprivileged. Indians had seized the colonized classroom, taken over the fort. Faced with something like what Henry Louis Gates, Jr. has termed the "multiplication of the margins" and the "coming to voice" of the "other," they were experiencing what postcolonial critics have called a "deterritorialization" of the knowledge that defined their cultural and social selves.[9] For the first time in their lives they undoubtedly suspected that theirs was abruptly a subjugated knowledge.[10] The tables had been turned and the experience was painful.

At the beginning of the fourth class meeting I brought the issue up for discussion, describing the fears students had acknowledged in my office and inviting analysis of the classroom torsion that might bring about such fears. I pointed out to the white students that this was the kind of experience those on the margins of American society experienced every day in not just every classroom but every social situation, every medium of exchange outside of their own close communities. In every classroom from preschool to Ph.D., the Native American student faces a canonical liturgy of legitimization that excludes her or him. The Choctaw or Chickasaw student was expected to read about Tom Sawyer without wincing at Injun Joe—the tortured breed plotting in his dark cave—or to comprehend the intricacies of Indo-European mythology and culture and history in *The Waste Land* or *The Sound and the Fury* without ever encountering Old Man and Old Woman of Blackfeet origin stories, or the dancing bones of the Choctaw primal flood, or Coyote inventing life and death. The Indian student was always on the outside looking in, never at the center of the text. When the same student went to the theater, he or she saw Kevin Costner in the role of a white god, extracting Indian culture and spirituality and identity as if it were a fossil fuel to be taken back East at film's end.

For the first and very likely the only time in their lives, I suggested to the students, they had a rare opportunity to experience the Other's experience—to know what it was like to find their voices silenced, their authority erased, to read the text from the margins rather than the center. This Native American novels course was a serendipitous experiment that had fallen into their collective laps, a perhaps frightening but sadly temporary tour through the world of otherness—like one of those adventure vacations where the dangers seem palpable but the ticket home is safely secured.

The effects of this discussion were extraordinary. A few students vanished from the class before the next meeting, but only a few. The self-confidence that had initially marked the white students—including she of the flight and tears—returned in a gingerly fashion as they cautiously formulated questions and responses from within a newly strange context of cultural displacement. Authority unquestionably remained with the Native students, but the class opened up and blossomed—becoming the finest teaching experience I have had in my career.

The social selves that these students, Uramerican or Euramerican, had brought into the classroom suffered a sea change that quarter in Santa Cruz. Language was the medium, and—putting aside some of the complexity of the issue—the question of whether the subaltern can speak was answered as a subaltern literature allowed voices to be heard that had been accustomed to being silenced. The power dynamics of the classroom might have been the work of Trickster. Not only were the Euramerican students forced to confront assumptions and issues of language and power most of them had never before considered and to make their voices heard from a newly revealed margin, but, just as significantly, the Native American students found themselves forced to articulate what they had never before put into words and to resist the comfortable roles of "authentic" others offered seductively by both text and context.

It wasn't a utopian paradise, certainly. Feelings were hurt and subtle grudges formed but, even better than utopia, it was a frontier space, which I have defined elsewhere as "always unstable, multidirectional, hybridized, characterized by heteroglossia, and indeterminate"—a carnivalesque space standing in sharp contrast to a static territory such as the infamous Indian Territory, which is designed to contain and control wild *indigenes*.[11] The Native American students had been accustomed to sitting in classrooms defined as territories, where the boundaries were clearly drawn to paradoxically both contain and exclude them.

Ten years after that UCSC course, two Native students from the class—one now an Indian rights lawyer and the other a candidate for chairmanship of her tribe—still express anger and a touch of humorous contempt when we talk about the young woman who couldn't believe a reservation Indian's rights could be so violated by U.S. justice. Anyone who grew up at Pine Ridge, as the Lakota lawyer did, could only laugh at such comfortable innocence. And perhaps the young woman herself still winces at the memory. In the end, however, although that class was an astonishingly rich experience for me as a teacher and writer, the thing that stands out most clearly was a paper written by a young woman who had grown up in a middle-class family in northern California. Not Native American herself, she recalled an Indian boy from the Pomo Tribe who had been in her high school English class. The boy always sat near the back of the class, she said, and never spoke—not once during an entire term. One day, however, as they were passing assignments in, she noticed that the boy's printing was so small that she couldn't read it. She turned around to ask him if he always wrote in such a minute hand. For the first time in her memory the boy not only spoke but laughed out loud. Yes, he said, explaining that his math teacher had to use a magnifying glass to grade his work.

This student had never given much thought to the Pomo boy's strange behavior before, but after a quarter spent reading Indian novels and being part of discussions of those novels led by Native American students, she saw things differently. She had seen in novels how Native people had experienced not merely literal genocide but five hundred years of linguistic and cultural erasure: seeing their religions abolished, their cultures and languages destroyed in a federal system that embraced a philosophy of "kill the Indian and save the man," as the founder of a prominent Indian school declared. She had seen the ways in which this erasure continues today in America as Native Americans see themselves represented only in ethnostalgic caricatures—as if real "Indians" had ceased to exist more than a century earlier. More important, she had felt what it was like to be almost silenced, to be forced to the margins. She suggested eloquently that the boy's mute presence in the classroom and the minute, almost indecipherable handwriting demonstrated the trauma of cultural erasure and silence. But she had also read in these Indian novels about subversion, about writing back, about Trickster's ubiquitous presence in the Indian world—and she argued persuasively that out of his near silence the boy had forged a subversive weapon. It was a small gesture perhaps, a brief moment of very serious play, but with his gesture the boy had forced the dominant culture to engage his near silence on his own terms—to look at his words through a magnifying lens, the very act itself a brilliant illumination of everything crucial in the moment. It was as if the boy had, through a subtle trick of language play and power, turned magnifying glass into mirror for Euramerica. It was a painful story, the student acknowledged in her essay, and the Pomo boy's near silence was unquestionable testimony to an unbearable reality—but it was also a trickster story of subversive survival, the resilience that has kept Native American people and cultures alive through half a millennium of what can only be described as genocide.

In the late spring of that same year, the Native American Students Association at UC Santa Cruz decided to put on a fashion show for the campus community. The impetus behind the show came from a student who had been a fashion design major at the Institute of American Indian Arts in Santa Fe, New Mexico. Enthusiastic and intense in most of her endeavors, the young woman from a pueblo near Santa Fe was convinced that such a show would be good for Santa Cruz's non-Native student body and fun for all involved. She made phone calls and recruited funds and arranged for friends from IAIA to arrive on campus for the show, advertising it heavily around the community.

The night of the show, one of the dining commons on campus was filled beyond capacity with several hundred students anxious to see beads and bone chokers, deerskin and feathers and all the lovely accoutrements so familiar from *Dances with Wolves* and *Pocahontas*. They wanted a safe tour of Indian Country, and when a young Cherokee woman from the Art Institute came onto the stage wearing long braids and a demure, Pocahontas-like doeskin dress and offered an opening prayer in Cherokee, the white students in the room seemed mesmerized. What they were seeing was familiar and comfortable, for this was the kind of Indian "other" the American metanarrative had taught them about. The audience had no idea that they were being set up in a brilliant trickster move. When the curtains parted and a Choctaw-Hopi dancer crashed onto the stage to the sound of violent heavy-metal music, thrusting a dangerous looking spear and wearing a hubcap helmet, a breastplate made out of radio transistors, an inverted deer pelvis face mask with a metal-canister mouth, stomping wildly in heavy boots, the whole crowd shrank back with a collective gasp. As the dancer, who called himself a "technoshaman," jumped and spun and danced down the catwalk and then back through the curtain, the crowd fell silent. Nor did the audience have a chance to recover, as a line of svelte young Native women from the Institute of American Indian Arts began to walk onto the stage wearing dazzling and outlandishly daring deerskin and feather-and-bead apparel as wild as anything Paris or Milan could have imagined, from a magnificent white beaded doeskin evening gown cut outrageously high on the sides and scandalously low in front and back, to daring mini-dresses of leather and feathers. One after another the models paraded out and back, shocking the Santa Cruz campus in a way it undoubtedly had never been shocked. While the white audience sat in complete and palpable silence, the Klamath Indian student beside me whooped and shouted, "This is what I call tradition!"—and some of the other Native students fell all over themselves laughing.

The fashion show ended with the Choctaw-Hopi dancer moonwalking in a beautifully beaded deerskin version of Michael Jackson's drum-major outfit, white gloves included. When the moondancing technoshaman disappeared through the curtains and the Cherokee fashion designer announced the end, there was a scattering of timid applause that vanished quickly into the over-whelming quiet of the room. Then the three hundred students filed out in almost total silence. I heard no one comment or protest or even whisper. Nor in my subsequent three years on the campus did I ever hear a reference to the Indian fashion show, except from the Native American students who to this day still laugh about the best joke ever played at politically correct Santa Cruz—the campus where students might not understand why a Washington Redskins baseball cap was offensive but recoiled at a risqué evening gown, where Native

Americans were supposed to be spiritual and close to the earth but not claim authority or voice. The campus's reaction was to erase the subversive show from the narrative, but within the counternarrative—the Indians'—it is told and retold to this day.

The best education must arise out of the most earnest kind of play, and the classroom must never be a safe territory. Trickster lives in every utterance, ready to subvert and pervert, to question, to violate, to challenge, to change, and, when one finds oneself defined by the dominant Other—colonized in canon or classroom—one immediately searches for the tools of mimicry and subversion, even if those tools must be forged from silence imposed or tradition commodified. As teachers we must strive to bring that that subversive energy and consciousness into the classroom so that our students negotiate frontiers rather than static territories, and so that privilege is put into question and centers do not hold.

NOTES

1 Philip Deloria, *Playing Indian* (New Haven: Yale University Press, 1998).
2 Bart Moore-Gilbert, *Postcolonial Theory: Contexts, Practices, Politics* (London & New York: Verso, 1997), 136.
3 Homi Bhabha, *The Location of Culture* (London and New York: Routledge, 1994), 124.
4 For more on this film, see "Apocalypse at the Two-Socks Hop: Dancing with the Vanishing American" in Louis Owens, *Mixedblood Messages: Literature, Film, Family, Place* (Norman: University of Oklahoma Press, 1998), 113–131.
5 Trinh T. Minh-ha, *Woman, Native, Other: Writing Postcoloniality and Feminism* (Bloomington and Indianapolis: Indiana University Press, 1989), 88.
6 Minh-ha, *Woman, Native, Other*, 88.
7 Minh-ha, *Woman, Native, Other*, 88.
8 Minh-ha, *Woman, Native, Other*, 88.
9 Henry Louis Gates, Jr., "African American Criticism," in *Redrawing the Boundaries: The Transformation of English and American Literary Studies*, ed. Stephen Greenblatt and Giles Gunn (New York: MLA, 1992), 315.
10 Leela Gandhi, *Postcolonial Theory: A Critical Introduction* (New York: Columbia University Press, 1998), 43.
11 The quote is from Owens, *Mixedblood Messages*, 26.

THE COLORBLIND CYBERCLASS:

MYTH AND FACT

FROM AFFIRMATIVE ACTION
TO THE COLORBLIND CYBERCLASS

For those of us who came of age in the 1960s, it is impossible to forget the intensity of that era. School desegregation, civil rights legislation, the Birmingham church bombing, Martin Luther King, Jr.'s assassination, and subsequent civil unrest literally changed the complexion of that decade, and of all the decades to follow. America's complacency about race was challenged, more than it had been since the Civil War. The affirmative action policies put into place were just footnotes to the many amazing race-related events that altered our lives.

Affirmative action was supposed to be a short-term, stop-gap remedy that would make itself obsolete after it reversed the rabid racial inequities in the United States. Yet affirmative action did not solve the disparities in the American educational system, and the "race issue" did not disappear in America.

SHARON PACKER, M.D., is a psychiatrist in private practice in New York. She is an adjunct faculty member at New School University, where she teaches online courses in media, psychology, and cultural studies. Packer has published articles dealing with psychiatry, religion, and culture, and is currently researching racial revelation in the colorblind cyberclass.

This essay traces the roots of racial utopian dreams for cyberclasses and contrasts those dreams with the reality Packer has observed in teaching eight different psychology courses online. Packer notes a division between students who volunteer racial information in cyberclass discussions and those who do not. Her essay suggests that the difference between the two groups, which affects student participation and involvement, must be incorporated into the current paradigm for cyberclasses.

Some critics claimed that affirmative action created different problems for several other ethnic groups, without necessarily helping those whom it was intended to help the most. The pros and cons of affirmative action remain complex, and are still being debated today in the courts as much as in the classroom.

This essay is concerned with another landmark invention—one that arrived about a quarter-century later, after cyberspace and the Internet information age came into being. Just as affirmative action was breathing its last breath, new technology paved the way for online college classes. These classes could be delivered to an invisible, ether-based audience, and so could be "colorblind" in the truest sense of the word—or so it seemed. This new and innovative "colorblind cyberclass" could conceivably cure pre-existing race-based economic and educational incquities.

The concept of the colorblind cyberclass rode on the shoulders of an unbridled cybertopian belief system. Faith was placed in a cyberspace-based, semiutopian society. Early enthusiasts foresaw the end of national boundaries and personal property, thanks to this seamless and shared cyberspace that existed everywhere and nowhere. In cyberspace all "cybernauts" could coexist peacefully—exchanging information, cooperating with international and inter university research projects, and establishing unprecedented personal ties, all because they could bypass time zones, put aside passports, avoid both real baggage and personal baggage. Freed of the constraints of the material body, people would embrace and accept one another for whom they really were, rather than for what they represented through their physical form.

Equally importantly, the colorblind cyberclass could rationalize and legitimize a product that promised remarkable profits for educational entrepreneurs. By focusing on the potential social benefits of cyberclass, these developing online educational enterprises could enlist popular support for their efforts to colonize cyberspace, and to stake their claims in the natural resources of this new frontier. The colorblind cyberclass was a wonderful selling point for a product that already existed.

Eradicating racial differences was not, however, the stimulus for creating the cyberclass. The colorblindness was accidental rather than intentional. Because of the technical limitations of the early Internet, early cyberclasses could not be anything other than colorblind; there was no way to add an image or a photo or a sound clip to the text. The colorblind cyberclass thus reflected the realities of the Internet at the time it was developed.

The first cyberclasses in the early 1990's were completely text-bound, and based on the DOS operating system. They didn't have sound or image, and couldn't even connect to other parts of the Internet. The class was a series of virtual blackboards, composited from written material provided by professor and students. Even when cyberclasses moved to the more user-friendly Windows system, they often crashed from overload. As a result, most early users learned to make do with a bare-bones system that would stay up and running. They avoided the havoc that could result from adding space-gobbling image files to cranky old computers.

Deprived of the ability to engineer cyberspace to meet social specifications, academicians did the next best thing: hypothesized. We prognosticated about the potentials and the pitfalls of conducting college classes online, just as social scientists and financial analysts speculated about all other aspects of cyberspace.[1] These early predictions were based on hope and hype, and reflected our own feelings more than proven fact. Since most academicians sincerely believed in the importance of equal educational opportunities for all, many devised facile explanations about the ways that cyberspace could facilitate these foreseeable goals.

It was said that everyone would really have equal opportunities to a college education, once students and professors "dematerialized" and "disembodied" in cyberspace in true sci-fi fashion. Once we were freed of the physical reality of race—and other potentially damning aspects of the physical personae such as gender, age, appearance, or disability—we would be free to be ourselves, and to be accepted for ourselves. Because racial discrimination had wrought so much destruction in the past, it was automatically assumed that shedding racial identity would be to everyone's advantage.

Few people considered the fact that psychological identities develop around one's physical persona, and that this persona includes race, among other things. Few people considered the fact that complex intellectual, artistic, political, and philosophical positions accrue around race, and that dismissing its existence could simultaneously dismiss the importance of these positions. Even fewer people expected that "erasing" race could put students of color at a disadvantage: adopting an "invisible" identity in cyberspace enforced the unspoken expectations that the standard or default race of unseen cyberstudents is white.

Admittedly, not everyone was enthusiastic about the college cyberclass. There were nay-sayers who predicted that online college classes would actually impede equal access to higher education, because computers were still out of reach to disadvantaged socioeconomic groups. They worried that the Internet would widen the racial divide by enhancing educational opportunities for students who could afford personal computers, who attended expensive private schools with high-tech equipment, or who lived in affluent public school districts with subsidized classroom or library computers. Cyberclasses would only continue to privilege the already advantaged without doing anything to change the station of those who needed the innovation most.

It wasn't long before the emphasis on economics, as opposed to social engineering, grew. Cybercollege was a relatively late arrival in the Internet arena, and by the time it did appear much of the debate about cyberspace had turned from morals to money. Speculation about the Internet's ability to deliver college classes online grew among the business community once efforts to expand markets for this brave new technology were underway. Many of the university professors who opposed the proposed cyberclasses were also motivated by individual economic interests, and by their fears of losing their hard-won lecturing livelihood. Prodded by anxiety over their already tenuous job security, traditional professors tended to downplay the advantages of cyberclasses. They published oppositional articles in publications such as *The Chronicle of Higher Education* and *Lingua Franca*.

The most outspoken opinions appeared at the peak of the "high-tech bubble," when Internet stocks rose to unprecedented peaks and fortunes were made (and often later lost). As virtually everyone took note of the "new economy" brought on by rising technology stocks, people suddenly forgot their dewy-eyed plans to deliver free online information. They focused on the profit potential of cyberclasses instead.[2] This economic enthusiasm obscured the fact that financial interests were not—and never were—the sole predictors of personal attitudes toward technology. When studies revealed that even affluent African Americans were less likely to own and use a computer than their white economic counterparts, most people were surprised.

A new expression was coined to describe this unequal access to and unequal enthusiasm about the Internet: The phenomenon came to be known as the "digital divide." Now that this syndrome had a name, it was time to investigate the reasons behind it and to see what could be done or what should be done about this new manifestation of race-based inequality. It was in this climate that my research study of racial revelation in the colorblind cyberclass began. As a psychiatrist who had taught over a dozen college classes online through a pioneering program at the New School for Social Research, I was particularly interested in the cultural and psychological influences of Internet use, and had already collected years of data. I had reason to believe that the myth of the colorblind cyberclass did not measure up to fact.

COMPARING CYBERCLASSES
TO CORRESPONDENCE COURSES

When cyberclasses began in earnest in the mid-1990s, the uninitiated assumed that computer-based classes would be a high-tech equivalent of traditional correspondence courses. Because human beings imagine uncharted territory in familiar terms, people conjured up images of dreadfully dull lectures delivered by a puppet-like professor who spoke to students through the television. It was assumed that quizzes would be mailed out and term papers completed through the mail, and that no one, not even the professor, could identify anything about anyone in class—except, perhaps, their signatures on their term papers and canceled checks.

Yet the cybercampus has next to nothing in common with the static "TV College." It shares even less with the laboriously hand-delivered lectures of correspondence schools. What ultimately separates the cyberclass from these other modes of off-site class delivery is its interactivity. This interactivity is even more impressive than its ability to enhance lectures by linking to an infinite number of Internet sites and by accessing libraries online, worldwide.

What's more, an asynchronous cyberclass allows students and teachers to post lectures and responses on their own time, rather than during "real time." These postings appear on a virtual blackboard, that is accessible twenty-four hours a day, read by each participant independently at a time and place that is convenient. There is no concern about people talking out of turn, because everyone can post at will. No one needs to worry that two people speaking simultaneously will drown out each other's voice, because printouts of written text display both people's opinions without depending upon sound. This asynchronous interactivity permits unlimited opportunities for student–student and student–teacher interchange, whereas an onsite class is limited by real-life concerns about acoustics and decorum.

Student participation in a cyberclass is essential to the success of the course, since students and teachers create a virtual classroom out of a vacuum as they write their lectures and their responses, sitting in separate spaces and logging on from their own computers without seeing another soul. They can use hypertext to make their postings appear bigger, or bolder, or in italics, and they can add emoticons to substitute for unseen facial expressions. They can add weblinks to their responses. But they cannot appear in the flesh, at least not yet. More recent versions of online classes permit the posting of personal photographs, and aspire to enliven classes though the use of personal video-cams that produce indistinct images, like those in convenience store surveillance systems. But, by and large, the virtual environment of the cyberclass is completely distinct from all existing models of communication, and defies comparison to current systems.

It should be noted that each cyberclass is more or less unique, and reflects the predilections of the professor and the attitude of the class. Some universities standardize cyberclasses, while other universities allow more latitude in design and implementation. Some classes encourage more interactivity than others, and some professors exercise their own creative capabilities. Some instructors orchestrate more (or less) interactivity than others. Different subject matters lend themselves to different types of presentations online, just as they do onsite.[3]

Because the cyberclass transcends real space and real time, it can include students from far-flung places. More and more, cyberclasses include international students, although these international students must live in relatively developed nations with reliable Internet connections. When international students identify the place they log on from, everyone is automatically aware of a diversity of "place." It is assumed that students realize that some places are more likely to be populated by specific "races." Students have the option of posting an ethnic, racial, religious, national, linguistic, or any other kind of description of themselves in their introductions, although in practice next to no one identifies him or herself by race without first alluding to place.

Although physical persona ceases to exist in cyberspace, each student's name appears above his or her posting. Because many surnames as well as given names have ethnic identifiers, and because most names are gender-specific, a great many people inadvertently broadcast their ethnic, racial, national, or gender identities without directly specifying them. At the same time, people of mixed ethnic ancestry run the risk of being counted as members of groups that they do not identify with.

Some people may be comfortable with this totally disembodied existence, but most people prefer to retain some semblance of earthly reality and strive to attain a sense of presence in this strange place we call cyberspace. They do this by describing themselves in word, if not in image. Furthermore, in order to overcome the anonymity and sterility of a potentially alienating and dehumanizing environment, most cyberclasses start with personal introductions that are more extensive than ordinarily occur in onsite classes. These introductions make for more cordial relationships among students, facilitate discussions, and often lead to long-lasting friendships outside of class. More immediately, students' introductions appear to predict their participation during the course, and often correlate with their interest in joining the class. It is up to the instructor to set the tone for these introductions, and it is entirely conceivable that an instructor who states an identity in terms of race would elicit similar descriptions by students.

EXPECTATIONS AND EXPERIENCES OF CYBERCLASS

The consensus was that race would cease to exist once cyberclass arrived. Such expectations were established in part by the early armchair theorists, and were embellished by sensationalistic reports about people who switched gender identities online and who misrepresented themselves in any number of other ways.[4] Some of these expectations were seeded by films that were fashionable around 1950, such as Elia Kazan's *Pinky* (1949), *Imitation of Life* (1959 remake), or *I Passed for White* (1960), which depicted light-skinned black women who "pass" when the opportunity arises. Yet hands-on experience proved that these preconditioned expectations were unfounded.

Students with ethnic first or last names invariably referred to their origins in class, emails, or term papers. Although students in my own cyberclasses did not initially allude to their race (or their physical appearance, for that matter), this changed somewhat when the technology permitted the posting of photos. At that time, some students of color posted personal photographs in their introductions. (One never knows how many students of color did not post photos of themselves, nor does one know if the posted photos were authentic.) Students who identified themselves by national or linguistic group—and who disclosed their identities through place rather than race—did not post photos or refer to their race, but spoke freely about the specialness of their own communities. This pattern repeated itself, in class after class after class, and even in faculty forums.

It was impossible not to react to this pattern. Perhaps these photo postings were political ploys intended to elicit response, and preplanned by special interest or lobbying groups. Or, these selective disclosures could be part of someone's social science study and a clever way to collect data about online reactions to race. But, presuming that these postings were genuine (and, indeed, they turned out to be), this seemed to be a way to express discomfort about erasing race entirely and with being forced to adopt an invisible online identity. Upon questioning, students stated that people presume that someone is white unless they specifically state otherwise. Such students said that they needed to communicate that they were not what they were presumed to be.

The only other people besides people of color who posted their photographs were actors, singers, models, and performers, who depend upon physical appearance to ply their trade, and who adopt a "persona" when they go on stage, and middle-aged, married men who hinted that they were on the move, and who had reason to emphasize their physicality. What was most curious was that students of color who had been silent before posting their photos suddenly became more interactive in class. There seemed to be something liberating about reuniting with one's physical form and with revealing who one really is, even if such revelation exposed someone as being different from the presumed norm.

Conversely, those students with ethnic names or those students who identified their heritage by place or religion (rather than race), tended to be interactive from the start. They made references to their cultural and ethnic backgrounds, and seemed to be especially energetic when asked to elicit information from parents and grandparents and community members for field projects and other class assignments. There seemed to be a clear-cut correlation between racial revelation (and any other kind of revelation of group identity) and comfort in participating in an otherwise invisible cyberclass.

After witnessing the way that some students were struck silent after shedding such physical identifiers, and then hearing them regain their voices, after posting their photos, it became more and more conceivable to me that race functions as more than just the external persona or mask worn by actors. In classical Greek theater, actors donned these masks before performing on stage. The audience identified the actors through these personae, and the actors themselves abandoned their own internal identities (or their "animae," to use Jungian terms) as they performed for the public through the aid of these personae.[5]

It was curious that actors and persons of color were the two groups who posted their photos in a place where everyone could readily remain invisible. Actors willingly accept and specifically seek out the imposition of an alternate and ascribed identity, whereas persons of color and other minorities have historically had not a choice about adapting to an identity that is ascribed by outsiders (and often by hostile outsiders, at that).[6]

There was a possibility that persons of color were just playing a role, like actors, or like the black-faced minstrels that Spike Lee parodied in his film *Bamboozled* (2000). But the patterns of behavior seen in the cyberclass implied that assigned and self-perceived racial identity are far more closely connected in many people, and that many people of color do not experience the dissonance between one's external racial persona and one's internal anima—which people of noncolor may presume. Perhaps the cyberspace atmosphere, which deprives people of the opportunity to project their racial or ethnic persona automatically could be suffocating the anima inside and forcing people to swim to the surface, to gasp for air, by posting their personal photos.

In these early cyberclasses it was unclear if racial revelation was important to everyone, or if there was something unique about the individuals who chose to reveal their race online before they felt free to "speak" in cyberclass. It was equally unclear as to whether these effects were nothing more than reactions to my own unstated issues with race and related matters. Before proceeding further, it was incumbent upon me to investigate my own attitudes, to see how they impacted upon class.

JEWS AND GENES

As is true for anyone, my own life experiences molded my approach toward racial revelation and concealment. As a Jew, and as a psychiatrist, I was well aware that people often have complex, sometimes hidden identities that affect the most minute aspects of daily functioning—and that would certainly be expected to come to the fore in cyberclass.

In spite of this awareness I was unprepared for my own reactions, and for that sudden moment of self-consciousness in a disembodied state in cyberspace. I knew that not everyone acclimates to cyberclass at the same speed, and I also knew that virtually every instructor and every student struggles to find an own online voice, before one can think-type almost automatically, so that conversations flow effortlessly.

It just so happened that this first cyberclass happened to be about the psychology of religion, and invoked the issue of race automatically. Much to my surprise, not one of the students in this first class was Jewish, even though the university was based in heavily Jewish New York City. Many were from the South, and often from rural regions where past Klan activities contributed to their reputations for being unwelcoming to Jews. (Two students eventually disclosed their Jewish roots; one had intermarried and converted to Christianity, while another had an estranged Jewish grandparent.)

Yet there I was in cyberclass, a Jew who had inherited a nonethnic surname, who could theoretically pass as a Gentile in such an environment were I not so uncomfortable with such inauthenticity, and were my personal identity and intellectual pursuits not so intertwined with my Jewish roots. This inauthenticity became an issue, because I was a member of a minority religion in a class about religion, and I, as the instructor, was present to assume a position of authority. To compound matters further, much of my base of information about the psychology of religion derived from research studies conducted about Judaism. I also had a much more extensive Jewish education than many Jews my age.

I had two choices: I could allow students to assume that I was someone I was not, and therefore forfeit the opportunity to share my religion-specific research (which was the reason I was running this class in the first place). Or I could reveal my religion and acknowledge my minority status, and seize the opportunity to showcase my solid—but circumscribed—base of information. To be fair, my choice was already made for me, because my resume was on display and students were well-aware of my research interests—and of my ethnic-specific education—before signing up for the class. Still, I was surprised by my own trepidations at facing a class of "others," and I was even more surprised by the relief I felt after addressing this issue directly and encouraging students to share their own experiences and areas of expertise.

This issue alone would have sufficed to make me wonder about ways that people of varied races react in cyberclasses where everyone is invisible, but where many people claim to "see" their classmates as they read their words. But there was an even stronger reason why I could not forget the concept of race and the racial implications of "Jewishness." Being Jewish today means practicing the religion, being born to Jewish parents, or participating in various ethnic rites. But these associations are a relatively recent switch from much more searing racial implications that peaked some sixty years ago.

Having been born shortly after the end of the Second World War, shortly after the Holocaust was committed, I was acutely aware of the concept of race and of the "Jewish race" in particular. Jews were exterminated by Hitler not because of their religion but because of their "race"—specifically, because they were deemed to be an undesirable and polluting race, one that could be compared to vermin and exterminated just as swiftly. Racial constructs were a reality, an unavoidable reality, that meant the difference between life and death. It was irrelevant whether or not this concept of race held up to scientific scrutiny; the damage from the Nazis' spurious race science was already done, and could not be undone even after the war. True, this concern with race was not the same as the racial concerns of contemporary America, but it was a cause for concern for *me* nonetheless. The expression "a member of the Jewish race" was still heard in the 1950s. The epithet gradually disappeared, after prodding by Jewish groups and after the civil rights era imprinted the concepts of "black" and "white" race on the collective American consciousness.

In spite of this alleged racial heritage of Jews, which continues to be debated in scientific circles to this day, it was difficult to identify a Jew with certainty were one to rely upon appearance alone.[7] Consequently, Hitler required Jews to wear a yellow star on their lapels. That way, even "mischlinge" or "mixed-race" people who had intermarried with Jews or who did not possess the caricatured facial features of "stereotypical" Jews could also be counted. They, too, could be confined to ghettos and conscripted to concentration camps. By inventing the yellow star, the Nazis dispensed with imaginary medieval stereotypes of Jews, which portrayed them as having horns and hidden tails, resembling the Devil and thus embodying evil incarnate.[8]

Frantz Fanon, the Carribean-born psychiatrist who went on to become the most influential voice in pan-Africanism, wrote about the implications of this yellow star (and about the implications of the veil donned by Algerian female freedom fighters as well). In his books *Black Skin, White Masks* and *The Wretched of the Earth*, Fanon made a point of distinguishing this externally identified "reversible race" of the Jews from the "irreversible race" of most African peoples. Fanon also emphasized the significance of speech and language, in identifying Creoles of mixed race who were common in his native Martinique.[9] One wonders what Fanon would have said had he lived to see the creation of cyberspace, where people type the same way that they talk and where nuances of ethnic, racial, class, and social identity manifest themselves even in the utter absence of the physical persona or audible speech.

It was revealing to see how much my concerns about racial revelation in the colorblind cyberclass were informed by Fanon's theories of racial determinism.[10] It also made me wonder if my own long-standing discomfort with racial classifications that congealed in the United States in the late 1960s was impacting on my cyberclass. It was no new revelation to me that I did not identify with any of the racial categories imposed around 1970, even though I theoretically fit into the rubric of "white." But I identified myself as a Jew, and, like many American ethnics, resented being pigeonholed as either black or white just so I could be counted neatly in a census or in affirmative action statistics. Because I, as the instructor, could set an example for the students to follow, when I chose *not* to describe myself in terms of a race, I could be the one who was inadvertently closing off opportunities to students for revelation.

PROJECTING FROM THE PERSONAL

This introspection about the distinction between assigned identity and accepted identity made me more and more concerned about the reactions of minority students, who could conceivably feel as uncomfortable in a place that did not directly address race as I did in a place that did not address religious or ethnic origin. Fortunately, I was able to conduct detailed interviews of student and professor volunteers. Much to my surprise, I found that most people did not even think about race in cyberspace, and that many people who offered an opinion often conducted themselves in a way that contradicted their stated opinions.

Anthropology students, students who lived in racially torn cities, and German exchange students were all acutely aware of race, as were American students of color, while most others had no such concerns. Asian Americans were often outspoken on this subject and stated repeatedly that they were "overlooked" and lumped with whites. People who were intermarried, or who were children of intermarriages, or who held nonmajority sexual preferences, were also interested in these issues. Not surprisingly, professors who taught courses on European languages, literature, or history stated that such issues were irrelevant, whereas American literature instructors who stressed inclusiveness offered many useful anecdotes. Visual artists, who dealt with imagery, voiced intense interest.

Although this project has not reached its end, it is already apparent that the racial concerns of the 1990s are not the same as the concerns of the sixties. The issues that vexed the twentieth century are different from the issues of the twenty-first century. That conclusion should not be surprising, considering that everything evolves over time, including concerns about race and identity. The most recent census report in 2000 confirmed just how much racial identity has changed since the institution of affirmative action. Twice as many people consider themselves to be of mixed race as in 1970, and fewer and fewer young people feel themselves constrained by race.

Perhaps our real discomfort in addressing race in the cyberclass stems from the fact that our suppositions about race have not kept pace with changing demographics, social practices, and options, and with changes in the world in general. Our vision is bound to be blurred if we try to view a new phenomenon such as a cyberclass through the lens of the 1960s and 1970s. Perhaps we are simply feeling the pain of trying to force this procrustean fit. Perhaps the distinction between black and white and yellow and red will become as outmoded as the distinctions made between Jewish and Gentile some sixty years earlier. The introduction of something totally new, such as the cyberclass, is possibly what is needed to signal the end of the old era, and to remind us that it is time to redefine identities that were constructed to meet the needs of three decades past. As essential as this reconstruction is, it has yet to be completed. Some would say that it has not even been sincerely attempted. Either way, it is doubtful that it will be accomplished if universities continue to maintain unwavering faith in the myth of the colorblind cyberclass, without questioning if this medium meets its own goals—or society's greater goals.

NOTES

1 Sherry Turkle, *Life on the Screen* (New York: Touchstone Press, 1995), 210–232.
2 Merritt Roe Smith and Leo Marx, *Does Technology Drive History?* (Cambridge, Mass.: The MIT Press, 1994), 1–37.
3 Susan Ko and Steve Rossen, *Teaching Online: A Practical Guide* (Boston: Houghton Mifflin, 2001), 218–234.
4 Turkle, *Life on the Screen*, 255–269.
5 Carl Gustav Jung, the controversial psychoanalyst who incorporated wisdom from Greek myth and theater into his psychoanalytical theories, emphasized the distinction between a person's public "persona" and that person's private, hidden sense of self, the "anima."
6 Jean-Paul Sartre, *Antisemite and Jew* (New York: Schocken, 1965), 111–141.
7 Hillel Halkin, "Wandering Jews and their Genes," *Commentary* 10, no. 2 (September 2000), 54–61, takes up the issue of racial background.
8 John Efron, *Defenders of the Race: Jewish Doctors and Race Science in Fin-de-Siecle Europe* (Baltimore: Johns Hopkins University Press, 1994), 13–57.
9 Frantz Fanon, *Black Skin, White Masks* (New York: Grove Press, 1967), 157–163, 173, 180–182.
10 Fanon's theories fueled the African American identity movements of the 1960s.

GARY L. LEMONS

SKINWALKING AND COLOR LINECROSSING:

TEACHING WRITING AGAINST RACISM

PHOTO: ARTHUR COHEN

We learned early that our devotion to learning,
to a life of the mind, was a counter-hegemonic act,
a fundamental way to resist every strategy of white
racist colonization.

> —bell hooks, *Teaching to Transgress*

ENVISIONING A NONRACIST SOCIETY:
ERASING (E-RACING) THE COLOR LINE

Visionary, progressive teachers committed to struggle against racism must impart to our students hope that coalition movement for building racial equality and social justice is possible. Such a coalition requires that white people divest themselves of the power of institutionalized whiteness, and that nonwhite people transgress the color line to forge multiracial alliance with antiracist whites. Students must come to know that the struggle against white supremacy will never be waged successfully by nonwhite people alone; colorism remains a central issue in communities of color as a prime feature of racist colonization. The increasing multiracialization and multiethnic recomposition of communities of color suggests that African Americans, Latino(a)s, Asian Americans, indigenous Americans, and other U.S. nonwhite people can no longer construct a litmus test of color to determine who is authentic and who is not. People of color loving people of color must know that our political allies

GARY L. LEMONS is a professor and the chair of race, ethnicity, and post-colonial studies at Eugene Lang College at New School University. He teaches courses on feminist antiracism, black feminist theory and cultural criticism, and critical pedagogy. He has held two NEH fellowships for college teachers and a Rockefeller post-doctoral fellowship. He is the founding director of the Memoirs of Race Project.

This essay describes how Lemons uses autobiographical writing about race to help empower his students in the service of racial healing. He sees the practice of "auto(race)critography" as a significant oppositional strategy to the ideology of white supremacy and its practice in everyday life.

may not always look like us. At the same time, white people can no longer claim to be purely white.

Visionary people of color and progressive, antiracist whites must be committed to taking risks across the color line. We must move to contest a politics of white supremacy that reinforces the myth that our social, political, and spiritual destinies are separate—for the clear reality is that our futures are inextricably tied. Political alliance to end racism will come about when the nation comes to grips with its miscegenated past rooted in the history of slavery. In understanding the "whiteness of blackness" and the "blackness of whiteness," we begin the hard process of erasing (e-racing) the color line. To find the racial Other in oneself will surely lead to an identity crisis, particularly for those whose skin color has afforded them centuries of undeserved privilege. But precisely this risk must be taken if the nation is to heal itself of the holocaust of American slavery.

People of color need visionary, antiracist white people at the front line of the struggle against white supremacy, fighting for their own humanity. I believe it is a vision of progressive, antiracist whites fighting at the front line with like-minded people of color in the struggle for racial equality that will initiate a revolutionary coalition movement predicated upon a love of justice and a love of human rights. If we can believe that men can be feminists, standing against sexism and the power of patriarchy; that heterosexuals can be outspoken advocates for equal rights for gays and lesbians; and that folks with economic privilege and institutional resources can employ them to eradicate poverty, then we must believe that whites and people of color can cross the color line to affect a radical coalition for a nonracist society.

As an African American college teacher whose pedagogy is grounded in antiracist practice rooted in feminism, I am committed to the classroom as a place where student and teacher work together to resist the power of white supremacy. This is the singular goal of every course I teach. The classroom can be a critical location of resistance to advance the struggle against racial injustice—most strategically waged at the intersections of sexism, classism, and homophobia. In this essay, I show the evolution of a teaching strategy aimed to combat racism and white supremacy. I call it *a pedagogy of racial healing.*

I teach writing against racism through an antiracist–feminist pedagogy situated in the study of memoirs of race. Although I use a rather esoteric term to describe this methodology—auto(race)critography—it is easy to explain. "Auto" stands for autobiography, the narrative form that acts as theoretical and pedagogical anchor for the method. "Race" marks the method's focus of investigation, and "critography" signifies the "critical study of." In short, this method offers a study of race through autobiography in order to teach feminist antiracism. My goal is to teach the race memoir as an act of racial transgression.

TEACHING THE PERSONAL AS POLITICAL

Three years ago, I began teaching a first-year writing course called "Writing from Margin to Center: bell hooks and the Political Essay." Having worked with hooks as one of my dissertation directors at New York University some years ago, I acknowledge the major influence her feminist work on autobiography and race has had in my life as a feminist thinker, scholar, and teacher. Hooks strikingly shows how one's personal roots can function as a wellspring for incisive critiques of self and society. From her relationships with family, students, and other persons linked intimately to her, she merges the confessional with well-wrought feminist and cultural critique to take on the politics of race, culture, identity, gender, class, and sexuality. Her use of autobiography as a strategic writing technique linked to critical analysis works to demonstrate to students the power of personal narrative that is politically engaged in the struggle against racism. In her writing the personal is *always* political. For hooks, autobiographical writing constitutes a political act: survival against cultural domination.

My class examines the style of writing that has become the trademark of hooks's voice—the autobiographical essay. Focusing on hooks's ability to weave intensely personal strands of her life into a complex fabric of black feminist critique, the books we use are *Talking Back: Thinking Feminist, Thinking Black* and *Remembered Rapture: the Writer at Work.*

Teaching feminist antiracism in a majority white institution. I believe it is crucially important for students—and particularly white students—in my classes to know the transforming power that African American autobiographical writing can have not only in the lives of nonwhites, but also in the lives of whites. All students need to understand that writing against racism and white supremacy can initiate a process of critical race thinking that is healing to the mind, body, and spirit. Because people in the United States live under a regime of white supremacist ideology, we all suffer from the disease of racism. Whites—some who are consumed by racial hatred; others who claim well-meaning, liberal notions of racial "tolerance"; and even those who oppose ideas of racial superiority—suffer from racism's dehumanizing effects. Because of racism, many people ofcolor suffer terribly from ill health mentally, spiritually, and physically—as manifested in patterns of self-hatred, self-mutilation, self-annihilation, and violence against one another. Autobiographical writing against racism pushes students toward an intense process of racial self-reflection. This is the point of Writing from Margin to Center.

At the beginning of the semester, students confront one of the most provocative writing assignments in the course. I ask them to recollect in writing the earliest memory of being racialized. Drawing on this narrative in various ways during the term, they move to engage hooks's autocritographical method through a series of writing workshops. I base each workshop on a subject taken from one or more of the style analysis papers, which explore some of the subjects hooks addresses. In the process of each two-week reading and writing cycle, students write their own auto(race)critography on the topic that has emerged from the workshop. Their writings acts as an analytical reservoir to help students think critically about the social implications of the narratives.

For example, a workshop might examine the issue of race and its relation to education. Thinking about the subject from hooks's feminist standpoint, each student produces a personal narrative forged in critical resistance to the interrelated ways racialization in U.S. education perpetuates gender, class, and sexual oppression. At the end of the first week of a writing workshop, students will have produced two to three style analysis papers and a memoir of race based on them. During the second week of the workshop, each student reads her or his memoir in class. Collaboratively, with assistance from a writing fellow assigned to the course and writing groups of three students each, students read and systematically critique each others' work outside of and in class. As the final writing assignment, students select one of their three to four autobiographies written during the term to develop into a longer version. This version requires that the student draw upon other secondary sources to broaden the range of analysis. The class prepares students to study and to write the race memoir in the second half of my course sequence, "The Whiteness of Blackness, the Blackness of Whiteness: The Novel of Passing," which is also a first-year writing course.

Getting students to talk about racial secrets in class is never easy. Challenging white and nonwhite students to share their dehumanizing effects of racialization depends on the willingness of students to disclose intensely painful personal experiences as well as the critical maturity of students to interpret these experiences against the systemic and institutionalized practice of racism. Another key feature of my pedagogy is the race journal, which works as a mediating writing space for students to speak candidly about race; of course, they share in class only those experiences they feel comfortable revealing. The journal functions as a safe place for students to write out their experiences without worrying about critical feedback.

TEACHING THE NOVEL OF RACIAL PASSING

The prologue of Ralph Ellison's *Invisible Man* marked a profound turning point in how I taught race and writing. As a black male who was educated in majority white institutions for over thirty years, I had not fully understood the power of African American literature as a tool against racism. I learned the signifying relationship between blackness and whiteness from the novel's title character. The signifying trope of racial invisibility in a culture of white supremacy, the phrase "invisible man" represents a body of contradictory and intersecting racial signs. He is black, but at the same time he is invisible. He moves, speaks, and lives as a racial oxymoron—a slippage, a gap, a rupture on the faultline of color. The invisibility of his blackness is simultaneously a disadvantage and an advantage. It renders him faceless, nonexistent to whites; on the other hand, it allows him to "pass" over the color line.

A seen-but-not-seen racial identity becomes a provocative location to theorize racial passing and its potential as launch site for writing against racism. Several important questions arise in this consideration. Could whiteness exist without blackness, when it depends so much upon the Other for racial superiority? If blacks could pass for white, who would be black—the signifier of racial "inferiority"? Who could really, without a shadow of doubt, claim to be white? From Ellison's paradigmatic novel on the "blackness of blackness," these questions would chiefly inform my conceptual thinking for the Whiteness of Blackness, the Blackness of Whiteness course. This course explores racial contradictions found in biracial identity to expose the myth of white superiority, while calling out stereotypical falsehoods associated with blackness. The course does not suggest that race mixing is the solution to racism. Rather, by focusing on the problematic of black/white and white/black racial dynamics in the formation of biracial identity in the novel of passing, it determines to get under the skin of racism, to the bone of the ideas that give it form. In the service of antiracist teaching, the novel of passing—a genre in African American literature that can be traced back to the slave narrative but is most realized in the Harlem renaissance—becomes a powerful tool for critical race consciousness. I maintain that in the novel of passing it is always and already the biracial body, capable of passing as white, which contests the color line and thus undermines notions of racial purity associated with whiteness. In an earlier essay, I maintain that "Teaching the 'novel of passing' is a transgressive act against white supremacy, essentialist ideas of racial purity and the fallacy of racial categorizing. Advocating student responsibility to antiracist thinking, I position an analysis of the (mis)treatment of mixed-race persons in the 'biracial' novel as a crucial strategy for both white students and students of color to begin divesting themselves of white supremacist ideology."[1]

In the Whiteness of Blackness class, we read and write about novels such as Harriet Wilson's *Our Nig* (1859), which, as a "fictional autobiography," introduces students to the first African American novel published in the United States. About Wilson's significance as a black woman writer, Henry Louis Gates, Jr., has said, "Her legacy is an attestation of the will to power as the will to write. The transformation of the black-as-object into the black-as-subject: this is what Mrs. Harriet E. Wilson manifests for the first time in the writings of Afro-American women."[2] The notion of the black-as-object into the black-as-subject in Wilson's novel and others is liberatory, but it is the very idea of the "black" object/subject that I ask students to question, particularly with regard to the biracial subject/object character we encounter in each text. Should we consider the biracial individual "black"? By whose definition of blackness? If a biracial character in a novel of passing can indeed cross the color line without detection, who has the right to refuse her? What does the one-drop rule have to do with any of this? These, and many more, complex questions come up during the semester as we push against the boundaries of skin color, which are interrelated with gender, class, sexuality, the institution of slavery, and laws of racial segregation.

In analyzing each novel, students deconstruct the politics of the color line represented in the social construction of biraciality as the invisible signifier of racial transgression. Always attempting to get at the ideological apparatus that configures the mixed-race body, we look everywhere for insightful clues. In William Wells Brown's *Clotel or the President's Daughter* (1863), we examine the political relationship between its author and the protagonist he creates. The remaining novels all feature an interracial main character confronting the harsh realities of the color line. They include *Autobiography of an Ex-Colored Man* (1912) by James Weldon Johnson; *Quicksand* (1928) and *Passing* (1929) by Nella Larsen; *Plum Bun* (1929) by Jessie Fauset; and *Black No More* (1931) by George Schuyler.

SKINWALKING: LIVING IN THE SKIN OF AN(OTHER)

... we all "skinwalk"—change shapes, identities, from time to time, during the course of a day, during the course of our lives.
... line-drawers have the authority to describe the world for everyone in it. They are exercising enormous power, power they have grabbed or earned or received or simply found. But they have it, this power to locate the line, to decide who stands where in relationship to the line, and to divide community resources based on that decision.

—Judy Scales-Trent, *Notes of a White Black Woman*

Similar to the conceptual framework that organizes the whiteness of blackness as a writing and literature course on the novel of passing, the second part of the course sequence, "Skinwalking," shifts our focus onto the examination of biraciality as represented in contemporary memoirs of race.

Reading Judy Scales-Trent's autobiography *Notes of a White Black Woman* was the first time I had come across the term "skinwalk." Scales-Trent notes in her use of the term that it is a translation of a Navajo belief that "there exist certain powerful creatures who, although they appear to be mere human, can change shape whenever they wish by taking on animal form. . . . They are called 'skinwalkers.'"[3] I have appropriated this term as a provocative idea to engage the notion of students' emotionally committing to understanding the life experiences of individuals living on the color line as if the experiences were their own. To move toward an empathetic imagining of the biracial life of another, students read contemporary autobiographies of people who have a lived knowledge of mixed racial identity. I challenge students continually to evoke personal memories of having been marginalized, discriminated against, ostracized, hated for being different—for being an Other. Through empathetic imagination, students come to know intimately the biracialized lives of the writers we read.

I use Jane Lazarre's *Beyond the Whiteness of Whiteness* as a rhetorical model for teaching the memoir of race. Lazarre weaves together personal narrative and social critique in a style that is intellectually rigorous but reader-accessible. Moreover, the very self-conscious and self-critical way she multiply positions herself as a white mother of black sons at the intersection of gender, Jewish culture, and educational practice makes her life story instructive in teaching racial healing. Lazarre accomplishes exactly what I want my students to do in the autobiographical race narratives they produce: to be always critically aware of the integral relation between the social context of race and the personal experience of it. The students too must continually demystify the interplay of identity politics in the stories they tell. In the prologue of her memoir, Lazarre brings much clarity to her attempt to link autobiographical narratives of race to an incisive social critique of white supremacy:

> In all my work . . . especially in this book, I have tried, in a way to use memoir to transcend itself; not only to recall and describe experience but to understand its significance beyond the self. Indeed, the unnatural split between individual and historical consciousness, where the one seems to emerge and prevail wholly independent of the other, is part of a distorted vision resulting from privilege, part of an ideology of individualism fraught with false stories which are dangerous to personal as well as to political life. The link between an individual life story and the collective story which gives context to that life is a defining formal and thematic aspect of African American autobiography.[4]

As a white woman writer and educator acknowledging the power of African American autobiography that is so much about the fundamental importance of the personal to the political, Lazarre's memoir shows the influence of this tradition in both form and content. White students and nonwhite students writing against racism need to know the lived experience and practice of antiracist white people, because still too few white people identify as antiracist and most whites still believe antiracist education is the sole responsibility of nonwhites. There is an integral relationship between the tradition of African American autobiography and the contemporary memoir of mixed-race subjectivity that continually subverts the power of whiteness as a sign of racial invisibility (that is, no race) and blackness as the preeminent marker of racial hypervisibility. I maintain that it is blackness that gives whiteness color; without color, whiteness would continue to exist as invisible, an empty sign of race. Thus, a pivotal task in teaching the memoir of race is to make whiteness visible so that white students come to acknowledge and go on to become accountable for the privileges that come with being white.

In her essay "White Privilege: Unpacking the Invisible Knapsack," Peggy McIntosh speaks about the necessity of whites becoming critically race conscious:

> I think whites are carefully taught not to recognize white privilege . . . I have come to see white privilege as an invisible package of unearned assets, which I can count on cashing in each day, but about which I was

meant to remain oblivious. White privilege is like an invisible weightless knapsack of special provisions, maps, passports, codebooks, visas, clothes, tools and blank checks.[5]

For nonwhite students, acknowledging and becoming accountable for internalized racism rooted in white supremacist colonization also means coming to know the liberatory power of critical race consciousness. When the critique of racism is situated in a pedagogical content authorized by nonwhite, biracial, and progressive white voices, nonwhite students in particular feel empowered to speak and write freely about the effects of racism in their daily lives.

Several years ago, I founded the Memoirs of Race Project to promote the practice of critical race consciousness and antiracism beyond the classroom. Six students in the project presented their work in an historic conference called Poets on Location, convened by Jacqui Alexander to honor the twenty-fifth anniversary publication of *This Bridge Called My Back*. Project members continue to present in high schools and universities. Sharing their memoirs in these varied locations, my students become practitioners of racial healing. Their work is inspiring. Impassioned and deeply moving, it critically transgresses the color line. It articulates a new, liberatory line of antiracist communication that defies simplistic notions of race and the myths and stereotypes that inform its inherently flawed representation. Students promoting racial healing outside the classroom is the final step in a layered process where antiracist theory leads to transformative social practice. Students publicly reading the memoir of race challenge their listeners to step imaginatively inside the skin of another. My hope is that those who hear their work will embrace the concept of "skinwalking"—challenging the racist ideology of the color line rooted in the history of white supremacy.

NOTES

1 Gary Lemons, "Teaching the (Bi)Racial Space that Has No Name: Reflections of a Black Male Feminist Teacher," in *Everyday Acts Against Racism: Raising Children in a Multiracial World*, ed. Maureen T. Reddy (Seattle: Seal Press, 1996), 162–163.

2 Henry Louis Gates, Jr., "Introduction" to Harriet Wilson, *Our Nig; or, Sketches from the Life of a Free Black* (New York: Vintage Books, 1983), iv.

3 Judith Scales-Trent, *Notes of a White Black Woman* (University Park: Pennsylvania State University Press, 1995), 127.

4 Jane Lazarre, *Beyond the Whiteness of Whiteness: Memoir of a White Mother of Black Sons* (Durham, N.C.: Duke University Press, 1995), xviii.

5 Peggy McIntosh, "White Privilege: Unpacking the Invisible Knapsack," in *Race, Class, and Gender in the United States*, ed. Paula S. Rothenberg (New York: St. Martins Press, 1988), 165.

A. YEMISI JIMOH
CHARLENE JOHNSON

RACING INTO THE ACADEMY:
PEDAGOGY AND BLACK FACULTY

In the 1970s, following the political upheavals of the 1960s, many major universities responded to calls for diversity in students and faculty on their campuses by hiring people of color, most often—depending on demographics—African Americans.[1] Frequently these faculty members served the dual purpose of providing newly arriving students of color an advisor with whom the students could feel something of a connection, and of teaching courses that expanded the standard selections in most university course catalogues. Clearly, this increased interest in diversity on university campuses was fueled by identity politics, with all of its pitfalls as well as its benefits. Nearly thirty years later and in a political climate that is

A. YEMISI JIMOH is an associate professor of English at University of Arkansas. She teaches and researches multiethnic literatures of the United States while specializing in twentieth-century African American literature. Her scholarly study *Spiritual, Blues, and Jazz People in African American Fiction: Living in Paradox* is forthcoming from University of Tennessee Press.

CHARLENE JOHNSON is an associate professor of education at University of Arkansas and teaches foundation courses that focus on the psychology of teaching and learning. Her research focuses on the implications of culture for early adolescent development. She coedited the book *Practicing What We Preach: Preparing Middle Level Educators,* published by Falmer Press.

Jimoh and Johnson offer substantive analyses of personal experiences with disrespectful and hostile students. In clearly laying out the issues, sequence of events, and outcome, they provide insight into racial dynamics between students and black faculty in the university classroom. They conclude with concrete suggestions for both individual and institutional change.

approaching—though not quite—the antithesis of the openness of previous years, many of these same universities continue to wrestle with issues centered on the diversity of faculty, students, and course offerings.

Today, these issues not only allow us to raise the question of who gains access to the university but also allow us to interrogate, in complex ways, the conjuncture of power, privilege, and implicit political and cultural messages which sanction the image of the intellectual as well as the ideas that are welcomed within the academy. Among many of the faculty that have diversified universities in the United States in recent decades there are now pressing concerns about the impact our presence has made on the academy. How, for instance, do university students' perceptions, even if erroneous, of an African American professor's background, ideology, and competence affect students' receptivity to the material she presents and the students' confidence in her evaluation of their work? As we endeavor to conceptualize a new pedagogy that recognizes and values multiple perspectives, we must acknowledge honestly that questions of race as well as gender have the ability to complicate classroom dynamics. This means that we must be willing to admit that many African American faculty encounter educational and professional consequences resulting from some students' feelings of dissonance and disequilibrium when they are required to situate black faculty comfortably within their conceptions of power, intellect, and knowledge.

Insights from critical race theory and cultural studies allow us to think through this classroom problem and to move toward a new pedagogy that displaces the privilege that this culture locates in "whiteness, elitism, [and] maleness."[2] Cultures sustain themselves by replicating crucial social discourses. People who are located within any given culture unconsciously internalize innumerable tacit or silent beliefs along with the explicit concepts and ideas by which their culture operates. In the United States today, tacit racial discourses are prevalent. This means that unacknowledged—though perhaps conscious as well as unconscious—racialized and gendered beliefs and perceptions are part of this nation's cultural inheritance. These deeply rooted and often naturalized suppositions about race and gender coexist with a more recent social context that purports to enact sanctions against explicit racialism as well as sexism. Racialized behavior in particular has now gone underground within the dominant culture.[3] Yet even underground or unconscious, the presence of racialism is still palpable in the lived reality of those against whom it is directed; this reality has critical implications for those educators whose university classrooms are sites where students might expect to find their intellectual comfort zones challenged and whose black and female presence potentially may double a student's conflicted response.

What we are suggesting here is that for universities with limited diversity, an African American professor, in particular a female professor, frequently runs the risk of creating cognitive disruptions in students who may perceive us as "matter out of place," or matter which defies purportedly fixed racialized and gendered categories.[4] As we conceptualize it, a new pedagogy will seek to ameliorate if not rid the academy of the damaging effects of student as well as institutional attitudes that result from viewing the black faculty as anomalous to the university environment. Both of us taught courses at a mid-Southern public research university. Universities are certainly microcosms of society, and, as the following two anecdotal case studies suggest, our pedagogy must be able to account for the presence of racial and gender complications in the classroom.

TEACHING STUDENTS TO THINK ABOUT TEXTS AND IDEAS (A. YEMISI JIMOH)

Halfway through a semester of my African American literature survey, I assigned Booker T. Washington's "The Atlanta Exposition Address" for students to read and discuss in class. In the weeks before our in-class discussion of Washington's essay, I had introduced the students to literature by several nineteenth-century black writers and provided them with (in my estimation) a challenging and provocative historical context within which they could operate. This context included a discussion of the Revolutionary War success of the United States, which was just 112 years in the past, and the proliferation within the culture of democratic ideals based in freedom. I also encouraged students to consider how, during Booker T. Washington's era, the dominant culture abandoned the ideals that we find in the Declaration of Independence—especially when the citizenship rights of black people were under consideration—and how the antebellum Constitution of the United States of America was complicit in the subordination of black people.[5] As had been my practice when teaching Washington's address, I also required the students to read "Of Mr Booker T. Washington and Others," W.E.B. Du Bois's response to Washington's ideas on the social and political positioning of black people in the United States.

I juxtapose these two essays primarily as a way to expose students to the often intricate (though divergent) bases on which both Washington's and Du

Bois's ideas are located, as well as to demonstrate to students that African American intellectual ideas, even on racial issues, are not and have not been monolithic. The Washington and Du Bois exchange is a clear example of this alterity among black intellectual thinkers, even on important social and political issues.

Following a lively in-class discussion in which students, both black and white, responded positively to the issues in Washington's as well as Du Bois's essay, one student approached me after class with further questions about Du Bois's resistance to Washington's ideas. I explained to this student that Washington's plan implicitly positioned all black people outside of intellectual education and moved black people outside the political (e.g. voting) realm as well, as Washington—in the midst of encroaching modernity—publicly encouraged an agrarian-based industrial education for black people and discouraged voting rights. Washington, I explained further, was creating a scenario that comforted white southerners by suggesting to them that the social order, if not the total economic order of the antebellum South, would remain in place. While I was making my point, another student who had been listening intently to this discussion not only intervened but also interrupted to, I conjecture, set things straight. This second student, Ryan, entered the conversation by saying directly to the first student, Josh, that what I was saying was "wrong."[6] Ryan went on to say that I was not placing Washington within historical context. I briefly pointed out that Du Bois was not alone in his critique of Washington, that Reconstruction's failures were clearly evident by the time that Washington made his speech in 1895 and that his willing acceptance of segregation was not the form of freedom and citizenship that should be foisted on all black people. Ryan, addressing his comments to Josh, insisted that I was wrong and that I did not know the history of the era.

I ended the conversation at this point, as I perceived that Ryan, perhaps without consciously recognizing this, was unwilling to engage in a discussion of Washington on the terms that I had established and within the historical context that I was presenting to Josh and that I had presented in class for the last nine weeks. Ryan seemed to view me, and perhaps my course, as "matter out of place," something that was improperly positioned in the university setting in which he found them. Ryan also did not see Du Bois and Washington, I later came to understand, as two intelligent men who disagreed on an issue and whose ideas deserved analysis. He saw them as part of the "black problem" that troubled white people—the *true* citizens of the United States whose position he wanted me to validate, even though I was focused on the impact that Washington's and Du Bois's ideas might have on black people.

Ryan was not the only student who had an alternative reading of Washington and Du Bois. Other students had raised the commonplace elitist charge against Du Bois as well as the neoseparatist support for Washington. My response to both issues was that it was not as simple as elitism in terms of Du Bois, who genuinely wanted change in the lived reality of black people, and that it was not some sort of radical separatism on the part of Washington either, who also wanted genuine change. Both men in their essays have a fundamental philosophical difference of opinion about what it takes to bring black people to full citizenship in the United States, and it was this philosophical difference that I was attempting to get students to delineate.

As a way to continue classroom discussion, I had established an Internet discussion board for this African American literature course. I posted topics that I hoped would generate continued discussion from students. I would also occasionally post comments that I hoped would further discussion or bring clarity for all of the students when I found that it was needed. For the Washington and Du Bois discussion, I posted the following topic:

> Examine closely the positions that both Booker T. Washington and W.E.B. Du Bois construct for black people in the United States. Identify the fundamental differences between the approaches that are taken by these two men. In your discussion you should examine where black people ultimately would be situated in the United States under Washington's plan and where Du Bois's ideas about the reconstruction of black life would situate black people within the United States.

On the day following his classroom "correction" of my views concerning Washington, Ryan responded on the forum. His response indicated that the most important concern in this struggle for equality was whether white southerners could view black people as equals, and since white southerners, at that moment in history, could not do this, Washington was acting in the best interest of all southerners by advocating a subordinate position for black people.

I responded to Ryan by restating, in brief, some of the historical contexts for the negative responses to Washington. In my posting I pointed to several historical events that established what I saw as precedents that would cause Du Bois as well as other black people to respond negatively to Washington's ideas, at least eight years after the "Atlanta Exposition Speech" and over twenty years after the founding of Tuskegee Institute in 1881. This forum response emphasized, I believed, telling examples of supremacist ideology which would cast doubt on the notion that the southern power brokers had any real interest in moving, gradually or otherwise, away from a subordinate position for black people and the notion that there was an overwhelming concern on the part of northern power brokers with the material conditions of the formerly enslaved black people.

To make these points I briefly explained the impact of the following historical markers: the 1857 Dred Scott decision of the Supreme Court, which explicitly states that black people are not equal citizens of the United States; the antebellum and primarily northern Black Laws; the principally southern and post-bellum Black Codes, which in their antebellum formation were termed Slave Codes; and the 1896 *Plessy v. Ferguson* Supreme Court decision, which established segregation as national law—commonly referred to as Jim Crow—in the year following Washington's speech.[7]

Ryan's final response to the forum discussion of Washington again focused on the needs and interests of white people while adding an interesting turn toward class concerns. He positioned what were clearly black male voters in conflict with poor white people and white farmers who, Ryan stated, resented these black voters because of the support that they purportedly supplied to conservative power brokers in the South. He suggested that these conservative power brokers maintained their positions through the black vote and essentially continued the dispossession of poor people, a status from which he appears (though his response does not state this explicitly) to exclude the formerly enslaved black people. Ryan then, primarily by shifting the dates that I use to mark the legitimization of Jim Crow laws in the United States, presented a revised narrative to explain these laws, yet in doing this he seemingly supports my assertions that point to the contemporary resistance to Washington's ideas by some black people as a result of the proliferation of exclusionary laws.

The language of Ryan's last post demonstrates that what he actually attempts to do is "correct," as he had done when he intervened in my after-class discussion with Josh, what he perceives as the "wrong" perspective that students may learn from my comments on the historical events of the late nineteenth and early twentieth centuries. Ultimately Ryan takes the position that Washington's gradualist approach—which, Ryan rightly notes, disallows overt displays of dissatisfaction—was the only reasonable way to address the complaints of disgruntled poor white people to and resist the increasing rise of Jim Crow laws, as gradualism provided internal southern solutions to southern problems.

I think that Ryan learned a lot in this African American Literature course, though perhaps not what he or I had anticipated. At this point I can hear numerous colleagues dismissing the concerns that I have in relation to this one incident with Ryan, even while these colleagues recognize that there are subtle cues that can only be interpreted in the moment along with other experiences that preceded as well as followed the exchange on Booker T. Washington. Still, I will begin here: I am not convinced that Ryan would have expressed his disagreement with a male professor, particularly a white male professor, in the same manner as he did with me. I want to be clear that Ryan and I need not agree on Washington's ideas, as I recognize that scholars who focus specifically on Washington's historical moment do not always agree. I am more concerned that Ryan seemed unable to position the concerns of black people on an equal footing with the concerns of poor and farming white people. He seemed to be actively engaged in protecting the race privilege of the dominant culture rather than operating out of a sense of justice. His refusal to analyze Washington's and Du Bois's ideas and his inability to conceptualize equality for black people as a right rather than something that white people must suffer are both problematical. For Ryan, the rights of formerly enslaved black people always seemed, in his responses, to be displaced and subordinated to concerns with issues that would appease angry white people—rather than positioned with issues that located the rights of formerly enslaved people within a context of social and political justice, for instance, or positioned as just the right thing to do regarding fellow human beings.

TEACHING THE TEACHERS (CHARLENE JOHNSON)

The following case study is based on a student's reactions to and interactions with me, taking place primarily through her journal, during the summer session of my introduction to education course. This course is required of all majors in the College of Education and is the gateway course that prepares future educators to address the educational needs of an increasingly diverse student body. I used the *School and Society: Educational Practice as Social Expression* textbook for this course.[8] This book is forthright in its approach to the history of educational policies that have hindered the academic development of African American and Native American students. These policies often are silenced in most teacher education courses. In this course, I place considerable emphasis on students' examining any engrained learning that informs

how they view the world. They also are encouraged to investigate the pedagogical implications that might result from their particular social positioning.
In recent years, courses such as this, which require prospective teachers to
consider the plethora of issues that influence learning—including their own
received attitudes—have become increasingly important in teacher education.

The pedagogical model I employ in my classroom is constructivism.
Jacqueline and Martin Brooks point out that "constructivism is not a theory
about teaching. It's a theory about knowledge and learning. Drawing on a synthesis of current work in cognitive psychology, philosophy, and anthropology,
the theory defines knowledge as temporary, developmental, socially and culturally mediated, and thus, nonobjective. Learning, from this perspective, is
understood as a self-regulated process of resolving inner cognitive conflicts
that often become apparent through concrete experience, collaborative discourse, and reflection."[9] This means that my role in the classroom is that of a
learning community facilitator, someone who helps students learn or construct
knowledge and who ensures that each student is located firmly within the
learning community.

I facilitate learning by first providing students with the primary and supporting materials that are required for them to master the information that they
are presented in the course. Then I encourage them to interact with me and
with their peers in order to construct an accurate understanding of the concepts that they have encountered and are trying to learn.[10]

One approach to classroom interaction that allows me to "hear" the entire
range of student voices is the journal assignment. With journals, all students
are heard, whether they speak out in class or not. Students' written reflections
allow me to gauge how successfully they process and interpret course material and how they react to this material. Journal assignments, unlike formal
papers, are not evaluated for writing mechanics and may be handwritten. I
make these provisions to ensure that students will feel comfortable expressing
their thoughts.

When I read the initial entry by Gretchen, I was taken aback by her candor
and incivility. In her journal, Gretchen refers to me as a "broad" and goes on
to express interest, or perhaps curiosity, in me because she has never had a
"black instructor before." She also remarks on the African pendant I am wearing. Her final comments state that I am creative and fun. This was her initial
entry. Having encouraged students to be open about their reactions to the
class and the material being studied, I accepted her journal entry as a sincere

reaction to me as an instructor and to my style of teaching. Thus, my remarks were not punitive but honest and sincere also. "Excuse me" was my written response to her reference to me as a "broad," for example. I made few additional comments on this journal entry. Gretchen seemed involved in the exchange of ideas that I encourage in the journal, but I was uncertain of her goals. Was she trying to goad me? Or mock my style? I decided to give her the benefit of the doubt and assume that she was unfamiliar with appropriate professor and student etiquette.

As the class progressed that summer session, this student continued in her journal to be contentious with me and to disparage her peers, especially those who displayed any affinity for the ideas in the readings that I presented to the class. Gretchen's troubling journal responses escalated precipitously, as she frequently commented that the subject matter of the course was irrelevant and further analyzed the intellectual and social merits of her classmates, including referring to a classmate's presentation as "interesting shit." I became more direct in my comments on her journal entries. I questioned the appropriateness of her responses and encouraged her to reflect more carefully on the ideas that she was encountering in the course readings and in other students' presentations, instead of on superficial and perhaps unexamined personal issues. I reiterated to Gretchen that her reflection on and analysis of concepts related to teaching and learning should be the major focus of the journal.

Gretchen's last entry in her journal was the culmination of her disregard for the course and for me. She referred to me as a "bitch" and asserted that I had somehow dismissed her as well as her ideas. Gretchen's candid remarks had moved from the realm of putatively sincere feedback into an aggressive, hostile reaction to me as an instructor and a person. When I recounted to administrators of the College of Education my concerns about the level of hostility that I received from Gretchen, my concerns were dismissed, and I was told that other professors had not reported any problems with this student.

Gretchen, like many other students I have encountered, was trying, I believe, to position me within her perception of scholar, a perception which appeared to be contrary to her idea of black women. Over the years, other students, who appeared to me to be struggling with issues related to my presence in the classroom or to the challenging ideas about diversity that we address in the course, have attempted to alleviate their discomfort by telling me about their experiences with or ideas about people of color. One student made a journal entry describing the "nigger raids" his father participated in; this student, even though he condemned his father's action, cavalierly used the above racial epithet, in quotation marks, repeatedly. Another student told me that in her hometown there was a man of African descent whom everyone referred to as "nigger Jake" to differentiate him from a person of European descent with the same name. She explained that this was common in her town and that there was, she claimed, no one in her town who minded this label.

Such encounters with students are typical for me, given my course, its content, and my interactive teaching style. Gretchen remains the best example of a student's obstreperous response to me as "matter out of place." She perhaps was externalizing perceptions that her classmates kept tightly wrapped within their internalized narratives about race. Most students, in fact, reserve their negative responses for the course evaluations. In their evaluations, students regularly accuse me of racism and complain that I am always "harping on" race.

This experience with Gretchen, during my early years as a junior faculty member, served as an initiation into the realities associated with my presence in the academy as well as a powerful reminder of the community admonition that I received as a young woman: "Education is something you should get because it cannot be taken away." I did not take into account that although it could not be taken away the "rights and privileges thereunto appertaining here and elsewhere"—the words imprinted on my diplomas—were questionable. What I in fact found was that others' perceptions of me as "matter out of place" in the academy, given my ethnicity and gender, had implications for instruction. From my encounter with Gretchen, I quickly learned that perceptions about my ethnicity and gender were an integral part of classroom dynamics and had an impact on my interactions with administrators, colleagues in my department, and others within the academy.

Conclusions

In his 1968 treatise *Pedagogy of the Oppressed*, Brazilian scholar Paulo Freire expanded our understanding of pedagogy through his investigation of the ways in which power relations contribute to our acquisition of knowledge.[11] In this book he demonstrates how people who are situated within the power group often find that unless they take care to do otherwise, they have difficulty comprehending and giving legitimacy to the experiences of people who are perceived to be subordinate and thus purportedly located outside of power. As the previous examples indicate, we are currently in an historical moment that has shifted and relocated bodies yet has not caused similar shifts in ideas; thus, many minds still operate out of the old construct that Freire critiques. Classroom interactions—including verbal and written discourse, as well as professional relationships—often are affected, even unconsciously, by paradigms/schema, viewpoints, and worldviews that are shaped before there is an encounter with a black professor.[12] We must be willing to engage these situations with honesty and be willing to recognize the serious implications of the challenges that diversity entails, as these challenges have the potential to place under constant scrutiny and call into question the implicit as well as explicit authority and competence of the black faculty in the position of disseminator of knowledge.

An important purpose for diversifying faculty and curriculum is that diversity enriches students' overall education by allowing them to experience people and ideas that they are likely to encounter as they move further away from their localized comfort zone and into our increasingly heterogeneous society. As educators, we hope that expanding students' perceptions of the world will produce a society in which differences are noted, but do not define. In order to construct such a society, we first must produce the conditions that will allow both systemic and personal change. This means that we must assent to a certain amount of disequilibrium as old ideas begin to shift. We also must acknowledge that cognitive disruptions, which are caused by a perception of "matter out of place," are opportunities for enhancing learning.

In addition to the obvious necessity to increase the number of people of color on many university campuses, we also believe that the following three recommendations serve as an impetus for rethinking what it means to make the university the inclusive place that its name implies.

First, we must be willing to engage in honest and sometimes painful discussions of the issues and problems associated with power and privilege. Moreover, those within the academy whose European ancestry may allow them to be oblivious to this issue must be willing to examine their own perceptions and views and to determine if they are contributing to a climate that resists diversity on their respective campuses. Are you, for instance, so disconnected from the people of color on your faculty or so inimical to the change that their presence represents that you provide a safe and uncritical haven for students who complain about professors of color, the content of their courses, and the manner in which they conduct their classes? Do you seek out this information from students or others instead of talking to your colleague when there are issues that concern you? Why? Given the cultural inheritance of what is now tacit racialism that you might share with these students, your actions have the potential to replicate already existing negative racial attitudes as well as the potential to place you and the students in an alliance that perpetuates the privileges of whiteness and the power of the dominant culture's exclusionary practices. As simple as it sounds, the first step toward tangible diversity involves probing self-examination.

Second, there need to be enforceable policies that address issues of diversity in the academy. These policies require active and vocal support at all levels of university administration. We are referring here to diversity in personnel, opinion, and curriculum as well as to issues such as teaching evaluation instruments, degree and graduation requirements, recruitment initiatives, and hiring practices. Are deans and department chairs evaluated, when appropriate, on the ethnic diversity of student and faculty programs and projects they support or on the strength of their program's inclusiveness in terms of course offerings? Does the teaching evaluation account for courses that challenge students to explore a variety of perspectives? Such measures would demonstrate that the university values and insists on diversity and that it is an issue that is not relegated to one course, to an isolated subject area, or to one person. This step will change behavior, if not personal attitudes, and requires a thorough examination of the ways in which the university may be operating systematically against diversity. It requires proactive measures toward change—measures which must include enforceable sanctions for inefficacious results. Without such measures our discussions of diversity will result in nothing more than palliation.

Finally, periodic assessments of the campus climate should include evaluations of campus diversity. Such assessments must seek responses to this issue from all available alumni as well as all current students and faculty. An assessment of the campus climate also might benefit from the insights of ethnic faculty that choose to leave the university. One administrator from both the university and college level should conduct exit interviews with outbound faculty to determine if they cite problems with diversity as a significant factor contributing to their decision to leave. In a climate that actively supports ethnic diversity, students will be less prone to view faculty of color as "matter out of place" in college classrooms. Instead, they will view them as valued and important members of the academy who, along with their other professors, are regarded highly and accorded "all the honor, rights, and privileges thereunto."

NOTES

1 During the 1967–1968 academic year, San Francisco State University established a Black Studies program, which, in 1969, gained departmental status within the newly formed School of Ethnic Studies, which is now the College of Ethnic Studies at San Francisco State University.

2 John Calmore, "Critical Race Theory, Archie Shepp, and Fire Music: Securing an Authentic Intellectual Life in a Multicultural World," in *Critical Race Theory: The Key Writings That Formed the Movement*, ed. Kimberle Crenshaw et al. (New York: The New Press, 1995), 315–329.

3 Charles R. Lawrence III, "The Id, the Ego, and Equal Protection: Reckoning with Unconscious Racism," in *Critical Race Theory*, 235–257.

4 Stuart Hall, *Race, the Floating Signifier* (Northampton, Mass.: Media Education Foundation, 1996), videorecording.

5 Derrick A. Bell Jr., "Racial Realism," in *Critical Race Theory*, 302–312. While many of the legal, historical, and analytical insights of critical race theory inform our perspective on race in the United States, we do not agree with prominent scholar Derrick Bell's assertion in "Race and Racism" and in his book *Faces at the Bottom of the Well* that black people occupy a permanently subordinate position in the United States. We recognize the permanence of racism, though not the permanence of subordination.

6 Names of students have been changed to protect anonymity.

7 Black Laws, which date back to at least 1804 in Ohio, were enacted primarily as a means by which free people of color in the North were contained and restricted.

8 Steven E. Tozer, Paul C. Violas, and Guy Senese, *School and Society: Educational Practice as Social Expression* (New York: McGraw-Hill, 1993)

9 Jacqueline G. Brooks and Martin G. Brooks, *The Case for Constructivist Classrooms* (Alexandria, Va.: Association for Supervision and Curriculum Development, 1993).

10 Samuel J. Hausfather, "Vygotsky and Schooling: Creating a Scocial Context for Learning," *Action in Teacher Education* 18 (1996): 1–10.

11 Paulo Freire, *Pedagogy of the Oppressed* (New York: Continuum, 1987).

12 On paradigms and schema see Barry J. Wadsworth, *Piaget's Theory of Cognitive and Affective Development: Foundations of Constructivism* (London: Longman, 1996).

BETWEEN A ROCK AND A HARD PLACE:

TEACHING THE BIOLOGY OF HUMAN VARIATION AND THE SOCIAL CONSTRUCTION OF RACE

PHOTO: TIM TRUMBLE, ASU PHOTOGRAPHER

INTRODUCTION: THE SCHOLARS AND THE SCHOLARSHIP

We cannot understand the academy's views on race, and how it presents race in the curriculum, without at the same time understanding the social position of the scientists, sociologists, and historians that make up the faculty within our colleges and universities. Long ago, this social position was made clear to me when a door was slammed in my face. I was only trying to enter a university building. This incident occurred, I believe, simply because the person on the other side of the door didn't think that an African American male had any business entering a biological research building after hours. After all, there were no African Americans in evolutionary biology. Probably every minority scholar can relate such a story.

Unfortunately, things haven't changed much in the academy in the last twenty-five years. The vast majority of university professors are still European American, particularly in the sciences, and, not surprisingly, most of our students are still exposed to a predominantly Eurocentric curriculum. Nowhere is

JOSEPH L. GRAVES JR. is professor of evolutionary biology in the Department of Life Sciences at Arizona State University West and African American Studies faculty at ASU Main. A widely published scholar, his latest work is from Rutgers University Press, titled *The Emperor's New Clothes: Biological Theories of Race at the Millennium.*

Graves describes "Genes, Race, and Society," an interdisciplinary course he developed that focuses on the differences between human biological variation and socially defined racial categories. He argues that such courses should be adopted nationwide as an integral part of any curriculum that seriously addresses race in American society.

this better illustrated than in the way the concept of race is taught. Most university students never take a course that explicitly examines race—from either the biological or sociological perspective—and there are few truly interdisciplinary courses on the subject. Those students who do take a course on race usually encounter various levels of confusion. This is due to the ongoing lack of clarity among scholars themselves about what they mean when they use the term "race." I believe that this in turn stems from deeply engrained beliefs concerning the legitimacy of supposed biological determinants of race still held in the psyche of many academicians. In addition, there are sectors of the academy that are still wedded to biological concepts of race for overtly political reasons. The views of Richard Herrnstein and Charles Murray, as presented in *The Bell Curve*, are precisely such a case.[1] In addition, there seem to be different standards employed in some disciplines when investigating supposed racial characteristics.

For example, studies that report biological differences in races may be published and publicized with standards on inference that would not pass muster if the study were dealing with any other topic.[2] This has led to a situation where false racial notions pervade American society without critical examination. An article on the human genome that appeared in the *New York Times* begins: "Scientists planning the next phase of the human genome project are being forced to confront a treacherous issue: the genetic differences between human races."[3] What is unfortunate about the article is that, after this misleading opening, it goes on to describe precisely why human genome researchers don't use the term "race" when referring to human genetic variation. The reader cannot help but be misled by the first sentence, which implies that human races exist and that scientists will be looking for genome level differences between them. It is small wonder that the public and our students remain confused about the meaning and significance of biological concepts of race.

I submit that the way we treat the concept of race in the curriculum is in urgent need of reform, if not overall revolution. The situation at present is, to use the timeworn metaphor, like the wolves guarding the sheep. In my book *The Emperor's New Clothes*, I discuss the development of biological theories of race in the Western world.[4] I point out that the science of human biological diversity and the social construction of race have deeply influenced each other. Since the nineteenth century, some "race scientists" militantly argued for the importance of biological racial distinctions in explaining human social structure. Not surprisingly, these scholars held privileged positions in the nations that were most responsible for the exploitation of the racial groups that the scholars were studying (for example, Louis Agassiz and Samuel Morton in the United States, Sir Francis Galton in Britain, and Joseph Arthur Comte de Gobineau in France). This intellectual current has, at different times and places, enjoyed varying amounts of private and state support for its research programs. The most obvious example was the support that fascist race scientists received from their states in World War II. A less obvious example are the activities of the Eugenics Record Office in the United States and its educational and propaganda programs that helped to sterilize thousands of supposedly genetically inferior Americans. Today, while these race scientists have been rebuked by the state, they still enjoy significant support from private interests (as in the way the Pioneer Fund supported the research of many of the scientists cited in *The Bell Curve*).

Fortunately, there have been scientists who have studied human biological diversity without themselves adhering to racist preconceptions. In many ways, however, this group has also been intellectually handicapped by its social position. As a result, research on critical questions that might have clarified the relationship between human biological variation and social conceptions of race has been delayed. I believe that this happened in part because the academy has had little vested interest in resolving these issues—particularly with regard to cultural groups who have been historically disenfranchised in the United States, such as African Americans, Hispanics, and American Indians. This lack of interest stemmed from the historical underrepresentation of these populations within the community of scientists. Research and teaching agendas are often influenced by whose interests are served by the knowledge they uncover and transmit. Marginalized groups unlikely to be present during the formulation of the questions could not expect to automatically have their concerns addressed by the research. Neither could they expect dissemination of the resulting information to their communities.

Worse still is that some of the arguments calling for racial justice have been formulated using the same misconceptions about race originated by the racists. Liberation theorists have called this process "the internalization of oppression." Pseudoscientific claims of melanin-producing ancient African astronauts—or of Europeans as warlike barbaric ice people—are no different from claims that climatic differences between Africa and Europe produced large genitalia in the former and large brains in the latter.[5] For example, the following appeared recently in *The Journal of Black Studies*:

Social class designation seems to lead to unexpected variation in human appearance. The Shudras (members of the lowest caste in Hindu India) appear darker than the higher class Brahmins . . . although the two castes had originated from the same Caucasian genetic stock prior to the super-imposed caste system. Males, in general, appear darker than females . . . whereas adults of a group are darker than the young. . . . Presumably, fundamental determinants of human variation do not lie within, but rather without, the persona—that is, one's ecology, going back in time.[6]

Of course, the author is fundamentally wrong about the mechanisms that determine skin pigmentation in this passage. He is confusing Lamarckian (the idea that acquired characteristics may be inherited) and Darwinian (that natural selection determines which variants reproduce differentially) mechanisms of inheritance in this explanation. The rest of the article continues with a number of scientifically erroneous statements.

My experience suggests that, unfortunately, many students are being exposed to pseudoscientific concepts concerning human biological variation when they are enrolled in ethnic (e.g., African American, Chicano/a) studies curricula. This results from the lack of scientific expertise and often anti-scientific attitudes found in even some of the best programs. I recommend that all ethnic studies departments review their curriculum and ask whether they adequately address the history of science and the scientific method, particularly as it relates to their specific discipline. We will gain tremendously by such an approach, since, in the twenty-first century, scientific research will influence society in ways unimagined even twenty years ago. Case in point: few people realize that President Bush's recent moratorium on the use of federal funds to develop stem cell lines is biased against non-Europeans. The bias results from the fact that none of the sixty-four stem cell lines are derived from sub-Saharan Africans or African Americans. Sub-Saharan Africans represent the greatest amount of genetic diversity found within the human species. Thus, the small number of existing cell lines do not reflect the diversity of even the European populations from which they were derived, let alone the rest of humanity. These sorts of issues at the intersection of biology and society must be incorporated into ethnic studies programs also.

THE ROCK

It is imperative that courses on the relationship between the science of human biological diversity and the social construction of race be integrated into the curriculum. I began my own project to achieve this while I was teaching at University of California at Irvine, and the course later matured at Arizona State University. "Genes, Race, and Society" (GR&S), as it is now called, is an explicitly interdisciplinary examination of biological and socially constructed ideas of race in the American context. There are a few courses similar to it in other institutions. However, one of the great advantages of my course is that an African American biologist teaches it. I do not believe that one has to be an ethnic minority scientist to teach such a course. However, integrating such courses into ethnic studies programs and building partnerships with the faculty of those programs will help them to be more effective. My unique experiences facilitated the development of this course. My daily battle with racism in the academy forced me to become an interdisciplinary scholar. For example, when I first began teaching genetics at ASU, there were students who dropped the class because they assumed an African American did not have the expertise to teach such a rigorous course. One student went so far as to write a letter to the provost demanding that I be replaced because she was unhappy about my explanation of mitosis and meiosis in the second lecture of the term. All of this occurred even after the university's newspaper ran an article announcing that I had just been elected a fellow of the American Association for the Advancement of Science for my pioneering work in the genetics and physiology of aging. Experiences such as these taught me that I did not have the luxury of burying myself in the laboratory and focusing on the study of biology that is exempt from its social context.

At ASU, GR&S is now a core course in African American Studies. It is also cross-listed with anthropology, biology, life sciences, and sociology. It satisfies the general studies criteria for cultural competence and historical awareness. There are no prerequisites for the course. The elimination of prerequisites for this course was deliberate. Many students in the humanities have developed a fear of courses that require a facility in science and mathematics. Under the best of circumstances, a course like this one should include a general biology course prerequisite. It would be very helpful ahead of time if the students understood what cells, chromosomes, and DNA were, or if they had some knowledge of population biology. On the other hand, while requiring a general biology prerequisite may have eased my workload, it would have significantly reduced enrollment. GR&S has always been equally enrolled between science majors and humanities students. Both groups of students are challenged by the course—the humanities students struggle with learning the biology behind human variation, while the science students struggle with learning the social and political influences on the science. One of the core goals of the class is to demonstrate that not only are there no biological races in the human species, but that the history of the science surrounding the study of human variation has been profoundly biased. At the same time, the course attempts to familiarize students with the nature of the scientific method and, in particular, with how biology influenced the course of cultural evolution. The greatest difficulty I have encountered teaching this course is that, for most of these students, the material contradicts both their world experience and the subject matter they have been taught in their other courses. The science courses often champion the objectivity of science; the biology courses neglect and marginalize the significance of organic evolution and are still mired in typological thinking. Research biologists still misrepresent the continuity of human biological variation in ways that reify socially constructed racial categories.

We also should recognize that the humanities and social sciences are still strongly imbued with Eurocentric perspectives. Few of the students enrolled in this course have been taught anything about the history of non-European people. Most are shocked and horrified when they are first exposed to this material. Passages describing the enslavement of the Arawaks on Hispaniola or the treatment of African American women in chattel slavery evoke very strong reactions in class. These examples suggest to the students that there are alternative historical experiences that they have never been exposed to in the rest of the curriculum.

The ethnicity of the students enrolled in GR&S over its five years has always been overwhelmingly European American (68 percent, along with 14 percent African American, 2 percent American Indian, 8 percent Asian Americans, and 7 percent Hispanic). These figures result in part from the demographics of the university. We believe that these figures reflect our mission, since the Department of African American Studies has always attempted to engage the entire university community. In addition, it is important that European American students be exposed to this subject material. Without this course many students, particularly the science majors, would not be exposed to any curricular material that analyzed the role of race and racism in American society. An additional strength of this course is that students engage the material with an instructor who is cognizant and critical of their white-skin privilege. Repairing these intellectual deficiencies within one semester—with students of such diverse backgrounds and perspectives—is why I believe this course is situated between a rock and a hard place. Fortunately, my experience suggests that this approach works and transforms our students' views of race and racism in American society.

THE HARD PLACE: DEBUNKING THE REALITY OF RACE

My general pedagogical approach in this course is to allow the students to ask critical questions about their own assumptions concerning race and human biological variation. For this reason, much of the class is driven by student discussion. The course begins with an exercise to gauge the confusion that our students are experiencing over the meaning and significance of race. The students are given a pre-test where they must respond to a series of questions meant to illustrate their views concerning race (see table 1). The students answer the questions before they have begun reading the text or have had any discussion of these topics with the instructor. In the second part of the session, we discuss the individual student responses. I set down the ground rules before discussion begins. In particular, I insist that each student's views will be respected. I suggest to the class that it is okay to criticize a person's views without personalizing the difference of perspective. We have always been able to get a general consensus that these ground rules benefit everyone and contribute to our learning experience. We have managed to maintain this consensus in each of the

TABLE I

GR&S PRE-TEST QUESTIONS

The following are questions concerning what you think about human races. Please justify all of your responses.

1 Please identify your race.
2 How many races can you name in the human species?
3 What features distinguish these races?
4 Where and when did human racial variation originate?
5 Are there well-established differences in racial ability in the following areas?
   a. intelligence, **b.** athletic ability, **c.** reproductive capacity, **d.** predisposition to disease, **e.** anatomical differences, **f.** tendencies toward criminality?

Give examples to justify your views.

TABLE 2

FALL 2001
RESPONSES
TO
PRE-TEST
QUESTIONS

The maximum number of responses for any question is 40.

1 Please identify your race.

Euphemism	19th-Century Race	Geographical Area	Cultural Group	Human	Total
13	11	6	4	6	40

2 How many races can you name in the human species?

1	3	5–9	>10	>30	>50
6	3	19	6	1	3

3 What features distinguish these races?

Physical	Cultural
34	16

4 Where and when did human racial variation originate?

Beginning of time	Pangaea	Prehistory	Ancient history	Recent	Don't know
5	1	20	3	3	7

5 Are there well-established differences in racial ability in the following areas?

Intelligence	Athletic	Reproduction	Disease	Anatomy	Criminal
6	14	5	11	11	3

Note: Only yes answers are recorded in question 5.

courses despite the fact that these discussions have often been emotionally charged.

Table 2 reports a sample set of responses to the pre-test questions. The test is turned in anonymously. The responses to these questions are important to show that we are not dealing with a biased sample of students who already understand the core concepts related to human biological variation or believe that there are no races in the human species. The first question asks students to identify their own race. The written responses were characterized into five categories: euphemism, nineteenth-century anthropological race, geographical area, cultural group, and the human race. The euphemism response included terms like "white," "black," and "brown." The anthropological race category included only two responses, "Caucasian" and "Mongoloid," while the geographical category received responses from all over the world. Some individuals described their race in a way identical to their cultural group, such as Arab or Jewish. Interestingly enough, six students described themselves as members of the human race. This response is best interpreted as representing their belief that no races exist within the human species. Question 2 asks the students how many races they can name in the human species. The number of the responses ranged from one to more than fifty. The most common student response was between five and nine races. This reflected the students' naming the socially constructed groups they were most familiar with in Arizona (white, black, Hispanic, Asian, and Native American). Question 3 is probably the question that best demonstrates the students' confusion concerning the meaning of race. It asks the students to describe what features are used to delineate the racial groups they described in questions 1 and 2. The responses could be broken down into two categories: physical and cultural differences. Most of the students agree that some type of physical differences delineated races (thirty-four out of forty mentioned physical traits), while sixteen students also included cultural differences as race specific. Some students thought that only physical differences were responsible for race identification, while none felt that cultural differences alone were useful in constructing races. Question 4 further illustrates the diversity of perspectives that students initially bring to the class on the subject of race. It asks where and when human racial variation originated. The responses were: the beginning of time, Pangaea, prehistory, ancient history, recent history, and don't know. The most common response of the students was that human racial traits evolved in prehistory. However, three students believed that they were specially created in ancient history—all using the Tower of Babel story from Genesis 11: 1–9 as their source. This illustrates two confusions: first, the significance of the Babel story and, second, whether the Bible ever mentions the creation of racial differences.

The Tower of Babel story recounts how all the people sired after the flood had journeyed from the east. On the plain of Shinar, they began construction of a tower meant to reach heaven. God confused their language and then scattered them abroad upon the face of the Earth. These students are obviously assuming that language is a legitimate racial characteristic. In addition, nowhere in this account is there mention of God changing the physical features of any of the people. Given the account in Genesis, there is no reason to believe that the people who attempted to build the tower were not physically uniform. This example underscores the analysis of Francis Harrold and Raymond Eve, concerning how creationist ideology and pseudoscientific ideas about the human past are still alive and well among our college students.[7] Finally, the students were asked to describe if well-established differences in racial ability existed for intelligence, athletic ability, reproductive capacity, disease predisposition, anatomy, and criminal behavior. Table 2 reports the yes responses for this question (see item 5). The six students who responded "yes" for intelligence all mentioned that they thought Asians were smarter than other races based on their experience in science and mathematics classes. The fourteen students who mentioned yes for athletic ability all cited the supposed superiority of the African American male. The five who mentioned reproductive differences all discussed the supposed greater length of the African American male penis and the hypersexuality of the African American female. The eleven students who mentioned disease predisposition all mentioned sickle cell anemia as a black disease. The eleven students who responded that there were anatomical differences between races gave a range of responses, including epicanthic eye folds, the rounder African American buttocks, and skin color. Finally, three students thought there might be a genetic basis to the greater homicide and incarceration rates in blacks and Hispanics.

These responses have been consistent in character over the five years the course has been offered. Each individual's responses are self-contradictory, and illustrate that the students don't yet understand how they have internalized the social construction of race. They further illustrate that they enter the class knowing very little about human biological variation. I have found that by addressing the core misconceptions embodied in the five pre-test questions, students will begin to think critically about the fallacies embodied in the social construction of race.

Each class session is a mixture of lecture and student discussion on the assigned readings. Much of the lecture is driven by student questions during discussions. The students are responsible for writing a one-page critique of the assigned readings each week. This is graded for the clarity of arguments presented—in particular, how well they support their claims with scientific or historical evidence. There are two essay examinations given in the course that are often take-homes. Finally, each student must write a term paper on some aspect of biological theories of race and their relation to social issues. The students respond well to the term paper assignment because it allows them to do independent research and thinking about race. Several students have built their term paper ideas into honors theses. Table 3 lists some of the term paper topics

TABLE 3

SOME RESEARCH PAPER TOPICS FROM GR&S

1 Renaissance "Race" Theory Reflected in Shakespeare's The Tragedy of Othello, the Moor of Venice

2 HIV/AIDS Cases in African American Women

3 African American Contributions to Medicine During Chattel Slavery

4 Why the Classification of People into Racist to Antiracist Categories Is Racist Itself

5 The Thomas Jefferson Paradox

6 Prometheus's Predicament: T. H. Huxley and the British Eugenics Society

7 Association Studies in the Pima Indians Suggests Strong Genetic Component in the Susceptibility of Type 2 Diabetes Mellitus

8 How Supreme Court Cases Have Dealt with Race

9 Overrepresentation of African American Males in the Criminal Justice System

10 The Inherent Flaw of Using "Race" as Criteria for Contemporary Medical Research

that students have chosen. They reflect the interdisciplinarity of the course—from topics in English literature to molecular genetics.

The range of term paper topics reflects the scope of the lecture topics included in the course (Table 4). This list evolved over eleven years and closely parallels the subjects covered in *The Emperor's New Clothes*. These lectures are designed to identify the core misconceptions that students have about human biological variation and the history of how it was studied. Despite this, these lecture topics are by no means all-inclusive. The readings serve as background information for the course lectures. However, the students require a great deal of supplementary material to allow them to fully grasp the readings. For example, I have found it necessary to provide each class with a thorough overview of African American history up to the Civil War. In addition, most of these students, including the biology majors, require a review and extension of basic Mendelian and population genetics. Recurrent reviews of topics in history and biology throughout the course help the students maintain their interdisciplinary thinking about the subject.

TABLE 4

TOPICS
ADDRESSED
IN GR&S

Topics	Reading assignment Introduction to Graves 2002
Overview and Definitions	Chapter 1
Early Race Theories, Racism Before the "Age of Discovery"	Chapter 2
Colonialism, Slavery, and Race in the New World	Chapter 3
An Overview of African American History to the Civil War	Chapter 4
Nineteenth-Century Anthropology	Chapter 5
Race, Reconstruction, and Social Darwinism	Chapter 6
Race and Immigration	Chapter 7
Early Twentieth-Century Theories of Human Diversity	Chapter 8
Race and Eugenics	Chapter 9
The Second Reconstruction and Race	Chapter 10
Race and IQ in the 90's	Additional Reading
Life History Evolution and "Race"	Chapter 11
Consistent Historical Errors of Race	Conclusion
What Will We Do Without Race?	

Additional Reading:
J. L. Graves Jr., "J. P. Rushton, Life History Theory, and the Pseudoscience of Racial Hierarchy," in *Race and Intelligence: Separating Science from Myth*, ed. Jefferson Fish (Mahwah, N.J.: Laurence Erlbaum Press, 2002).

INTERDISCIPLINARITY: BETWEEN THE ROCK AND THE HARD PLACE

The greatest challenge teaching the relationship between social and bio-logical constructions of race is that success is strongly linked to interdiscipli-nary perspectives. Despite all the rhetoric to the contrary, the academy still doesn't understand what it means by that term. To some, interdisciplinary scholarship means combining subjects such as molecular and cellular biology. To others, it is having the gall to combine European and American writers in the same literature course. The difficulty becomes greater as the disciplines one wishes to combine are further apart in the academic spectrum. At many research universities, colleges of science and humanities don't come in contact in any sort of academic forum. Furthermore, there is an ongoing struggle to understand the methodologies employed to create knowledge in the disparate disciplines. There are still extreme ideologies lurking in the humanities that think that all science is socially constructed.[8] Alternatively, there are scholars who wish to dismiss the idea that social and political forces have any role in shaping scientific research.[9]

Clearly, the truth is somewhere in the middle. This is precisely why, to accurately resolve these questions, real interdisciplinary perspectives must be brought to bear. For example, I argue that both social and political forces influenced our concepts of race, yet they still can be rooted in valid biological phenomena. It is clear that human populations exhibit biological variation. That is a valid observation. Whether such differences can be used to uniquely cluster human beings into legitimate racial groups is what is at issue.

The treatment of African American women by European American masters during chattel slavery illustrates how social and political factors influenced racial characterization. To help the students fully understand this, I present the historical accounts of European American slave masters sexually exploiting African American women. We also discuss this example from the point of view of the various stakeholders within the plantation world. How did the African American and European American women who endured this state of polygamy react? How did this influence the development of African American male psychology? How did European male masters who professed Christian morality and simultaneously saw African American women as beasts justify their actions? How did these actions influence the laws concerning racial identity in the slave states? This discussion can be enhanced if one included the biological questions that naturally arise from these social ones. For example, what is the genetic evidence supporting that these events happened as described in the narratives? How much European admixture is there in people defined as African American? Was this situation different in the Caribbean? How did this change the genetic composition of African Americans relative to Western Africans? Can we ever really suggest that "pure" races exist? Was there some intrinsic feature in male behavior that predisposed slave masters to rape slave women? Why was Harriet Hemings seven-eighth European in genetic ancestry, physically indistinguishable from a European, and yet still considered by Virginia law a Negro and a slave? These questions are very powerful, and through them students reassess what they thought they knew about the link between socially defined race and human genetic variation.

CONCLUSION: MAKING THE ROCK SOFT

In the five years I have been teaching this course, I have seen my students' understanding of race and racism transformed. One student of African American descent wrote concerning the course textbook:

> I can honestly say that Dr. Graves' book has forever changed the way I look at myself. Reading *The Emperor* is more than academic inquiry—it is a rich, emotional experience. Dr. Graves exposes and argues against the flawed, racist science that has prevented the human species from achieving equity within its population. After reading *The Emperor*, you will question everything you've been taught about so-called racial differences. There is one race—the human race.

Still another European American student commented:

> I believe that this book is one of the best books ever written. Its content has the highest potential in changing how we, as a society, view "race." This book intelligently goes into detail in defining just what race is and what it is not. It gives a vast amount of research and data in clearly portraying how multiple "races" got started and it leads the reader in the direction of knowing how to not necessarily change the world's views on racism, but, more importantly, how to change our own. It shows how society views itself and how much of the whole picture we've been too oblivious to even see. In truth, we see too much; we can't even get past the color of one another's skin. This book teaches that it's okay to see a phenotype as long as we learn not to associate a stereotype with the so-called "races" of our society. Lastly, this book taught me that there's no such thing as "race" because, in fact, we are all of the HUMAN race and, therefore, one and the same—not so different as some tend to think.

The GR&S course was made possible, in part, due to my unique academic training. Clearly, everyone isn't familiar and comfortable with teaching topics in science as well as those in the humanities. One could argue that this mediates against the widespread adoption of such courses. Actually, it is a case of whether the glass is half-empty or half-full. If one doesn't have the training to teach all the areas required to make such a course work, there is the option of team-teaching it with a colleague. Or, one might examine the syllabi of one's existing courses and ask whether having a guest lecturer from another department might help to introduce interdisciplinary reasoning. I often guest lecture for colleagues in English and philosophy. What is required for such interdisciplinary courses to really take root is a desire to cooperate with colleagues in different departments—and for academic programs to see such efforts as laudable. Virtually every university has scholars whose expertise touches on some other academic discipline. There are undoubtedly many ways to combine specialties and create interesting interdisciplinary offerings that address the biological and social constructions of race. It is also possible to make practical arguments that present the usefulness of such courses to department chairs and deans. One argument is that these courses are usually well-enrolled, particularly if they are done well. I think that efforts to create such courses will improve the scholarship of those faculty involved in them. There are curriculum reform initiatives in funding agencies—such as the National Science Foundation—that are interested in supporting the development of interdisciplinary curricula. Administrators should be happy when their faculty land external grants to help fuel curricular reform.

I hope that what I have provided is a template to stimulate thinking on how this might be accomplished at other institutions. I also hope that I have illustrated the potential benefits to the curriculum if such courses are implemented. I fear that if we do not make this effort, we will abandon our sheep to the tender mercies of the wolves. Unfortunately, we have too much experience with how that story concludes.

NOTES

1 Richard Herrnstein and Charles Murray, *The Bell Curve: Intelligence and Class Structure in American Social Life* (New York: The Free Press, 1994).

2 For example, a recent study examined the ability of individuals to recognize the same "race" v. different "race" faces utilizing the FFA region of the brain. Their data showed that European American men had trouble identifying African American faces (while African American men had no difficulty recognizing European Americans.) This difference was not reported in the abstract, but the overall race-specific identification was trumpeted even though the study had examined a grand total of eighteen participants from one area. A. J. Golby, J.D.E. Gabrieli, J. Y. Chiao, and J. L. Eberhardt, "Differential Responses in the Fusiform Region to Same-race and Other-race Faces," *Nature Neuroscience* 8, no. 4 (August 2001).

3 Nicholas Wade, "For Genome Mappers, the Tricky Terrain of Race Requires Some Careful Navigating," *New York Times*, July 20, 2001, A17.

4 Joseph L. Graves Jr., *The Emperor's New Clothes: Biological Theories of Race at the New Millennium* (New Brunswick, N.J.: Rutgers University Press, 2001).

5 J. Philippe Rushton, *Race, Evolution, and Behavior: A Life History Perspective* (New Brunswick, N.J.: Transaction Publishers, 1995).

6 Onesphor Kyara, "Variation Within the Black Human Race—Paleoecological Sketches to

the Nonstarted Study: A Theoretical Essay," *Journal of Black Studies* 31 (2000): 812–834.

7 Francis B. Harrold and Raymond A. Eve, *Cult Archaeology and Creationism: Understanding Pseudoscientific Ideas About the Past* (Iowa City: University of Iowa Press, 1995).

8 Michael Ruse, *Mystery of Mysteries: Is Evolution a Social Construction?* (Cambridge, Mass.: Harvard University Press, 1999).

9 Paul R. Gross and Norman Levitt, *Higher Superstition: The Academic Left and Its Quarrels with Science* (Baltimore: Johns Hopkins University Press, 1994).

BONNIE TUSMITH
MAUREEN T. REDDY

CONCLUSION:

TEACHING TO MAKE A DIFFERENCE

We hope we have initiated a dialogue here with our readers. Taken collectively, the essays in this volume tell a heartbreaking story: they indicate that, though we are a purportedly progressive and democratic society, we are far from being colorblind and race-free. Knowing that humans come in different packages—some short, some tall; some big-boned, some small-framed; some light-complexioned, others richly melanined; some XX-chromosomed and thus female, others XY-chromosomed and thus male—should be a source of marvel and wonder. As members of the human race we are, after all, one extended family. So what is racism all about? As our American legacy of slavery and genocide attest, it has something to do with human insecurity and its consequent will to power—the fear of being left behind while other siblings get the goodies. Denial, in and outside the classroom, is a common response in matters of race. The white supremacist tells himself, he is not my brother. The woman with white-skin privilege looks at her dark sister and thinks, she is not like me. It takes an inordinate amount of energy and self-deception to deny what is in plain view: that the Other *is* the Self. Ultimately, being a racist society means that we don't like ourselves very much—for we do not accept ourselves as members of the human race.

The contributors to this volume recognize the irony and self-destructiveness inherent in the social construction of race. We represent those in the teaching profession who have not given up. There is something we can do, we believe, to help pull this country out of the quicksand of racism. As individuals positioned at various educational institutions across the nation, we have independently made the commitment to teach *through*—not *around*—race. Circumventing the racial stereotypes that humans have constructed about one another is not our idea of true education. We know that we have the responsibility to do more than intellectualize the "R" word: we must confront racism and help eradicate it when we teach.

Many college teachers, both experienced and just starting out, find themselves at a loss when confronted with racial issues in the classroom. Doing the right thing isn't always easy and at times seems downright impossible when it comes to the "bottom line" of race. Having been hurt by making the attempt, many professors—including some of our contributors—have come away from an especially negative classroom experience with the thought, "I'll never teach this course again." As editors of *Race in the College Classroom* and veteran teachers, we empathize with this sentiment and wish to state clearly here that we are not calling for martyrs. In our view, no individual should be sacrificed in what is a collective and communal responsibility. So what is a relatively powerless, totally outnumbered instructor, teaching assistant, untenured professor, or even full professor to do in a racially hostile environment? Building a support network is a start.

Identifying trustworthy colleagues with whom to process pedagogical issues of race is a healthy first step. The team-written essays in this volume, for example, provide models for such constructive interaction. Too often, college teachers with no training in teaching—especially, those teaching in racially and culturally diverse classrooms—find themselves suddenly tackling the complex dynamics of race. Being thus unprepared and quickly realizing that negative publicity and potentially low student evaluations may jeopardize their budding careers, they resort to various strategies of survival that actually abet racism. We recognize this pattern as too common to attribute to the weak character of any individual. This is why we recommend open, ongoing discussion and analysis regarding race in our teaching. The crucial point is not to accept the notion that such active exploration reflects poor teaching. Buying into this notion is, in effect, subscribing to the "master narrative" of institutional racism.

We live in an individualistic society; academia not only reflects but also promotes this value system. It's almost ironic for us to agonize over our teaching when universities (which practically every four-year college calls itself these days) advocate self-promotion. Even as administrators and department chairs talk as if teaching counted, the real message to professors is, "Keep up your scholarship and don't worry about your teaching." Devoting time to research pedagogy in one's field of expertise—as we all should to be effective classroom teachers—is often viewed by deans and department heads as frivolous and not valid scholarship. Thus, we're caught in a double bind. To act on the assumption that we have a responsibility to reach our students in spite of this situation should suggest that we are not the problem.

While we could attempt to suggest here some foolproof methods for teaching race, the truth is we don't believe there are any. Experienced teachers know that a strategy that worked beautifully in one class could easily backfire in another. Faculty of color also know that a viable classroom approach for a visibly white professor may not work for them at all. As teachers, our unique subject positions play a significant role in our pedagogy. This means that each of us must develop classroom strategies suited to our specific combination of racial and ethnic designation, field of expertise, and institutional setting. As critical thinkers, researchers, and frontline teachers, we have the ability to achieve this goal. We must keep in mind, however, that incorporating race into our teaching without the support and understanding of others is a difficult proposition. Spending at least a part of one's professional time actively building a community of antiracist educators could very well enhance one's overall effectiveness as a teacher.

Scholarly organizations with annual conferences are increasingly accommodating the need for such professional networking. For example, the national organization MELUS (Society for the Study of the Multi-Ethnic Literature of the United States) is devoting its 2002 annual conference to the theme of pedagogy, praxis, and politics. Similarly, many regional organizations of antiracist educators offer support. In New England, for instance, the Southern New England Consortium on Race and Ethnicity (SNECORE) sponsors two annual symposia, one on scholarship and one on pedagogy. Beyond the traditional scholarly paper, such conferences provide space for impromptu discussions on teaching. Better still, they offer real opportunities for cross-racial, cross-generational interaction. Veteran teachers might share their classroom experiences with younger colleagues as a means of assisting in their training. We urge our readers to get involved with—or start—such a group in their own regions. We should encourage the open exchange of stories to demystify the taboo of race in academic circles. If we teachers can't talk about race, how can we expect this of our students?

Finally, we recommend that socially responsible teachers continue to read relevant discussions on pedagogy and race. Following is a selection of articles and books that we—or at least one of our contributors—have read and thought about. Considering the community of scholars and teachers that these publications and *Race in the College Classroom* represent, it is obvious that a movement is already afoot—so you are not alone.

SELECTED REFERENCES

Adams, Michael Vannoy, *The Multicultural Imagination: "Race," Color, and the Unconscious* (New York: Routledge, 1996).

Adams, Maurianne, ed., *Promoting Diversity in College Classrooms: Innovative Responses for the Curriculum, Faculty, and Institutions*, New Directions for Teaching and Learning, vol. 52. (San Francisco: Jossey-Bass, 1992).

Altbach, P. G. and K. Lomotey. eds., *The Racial Crisis in American Higher Education* (Albany, N.Y.: SUNY Press, 1991).

Anzaldúa, Gloria, ed., *Making Face, Making Soul/Haciendo Caras: Creative and Critical Perspectives by Feminists of Color* (San Francisco: Aunt Lute, 1990).

Bérubé, Michael and Cary Nelson, eds., *Higher Education Under Fire: Politics, Economics, and the Crisis of the Humanities* (London and New York: Routledge, 1995).

Blauner, Robert, "Talking Past Each Other: Black and White Languages of Race," in *Race and Ethnic Conflict*, ed. Fred L. Pincus and Howard J. Ehrlich (Boulder, Colo.: Westview, 1994), 27–34.

Boler, Megan, *Feeling Power: Emotions and Education* (New York: Routledge, 1999).

Bowser, Benjamin P. et al., *Confronting Diversity Issues on Campus* (Newbury Park, Calif.: SAGE, 1993).

Brunner, Diane Dubose, *Inquiry and Reflection: Framing Narrative Practice in Education* (Albany, N.Y.: SUNY Press, 1994).

Butler, Johnnella E., "Transforming the Curriculum: Teaching About Women of Color," in *Transforming the Curriculum: Ethnic Studies and Women's Studies*, ed. Johnnella E. Butler and John C. Walter (Albany: SUNY Press, 1991), 67–87.

Cheng, Anne Anlin, *The Melancholy of Race: Psychoanalysis, Assimilation, and Hidden Grief* (New York: Oxford University Press, 2000).

Collins, Patricia Hill, *Black Feminist Thought: Knowledge, Consciousness, and the Politics of Empowerment*, 2d ed. (New York: Routledge, 2000).

Crenshaw, Kimberle et al., *Critical Race Theory: The Key Writings That Formed the Movement* (New York: The New Press, 1995).

Delgado, Richard and Jean Stefancic, eds., *Critical White Studies: Looking Behind the Mirror* (Philadelphia: Temple University Press, 1997).

Derman-Sparks, Louise and Carol Brunson Phillips, *Teaching/Learning Anti-Racism: A Developmental Approach* (New York: Teachers College Press, 1997).

Eberhardt, Jennifer L. and Susan T. Fiske, *Confronting Racism: The Problem and the Response* (London: Sage, 1998).

Fanon, Frantz, *Black Skin, White Masks* (New York: Grove Press, 1967).

Fiol-Matta, Liza and Mariam K. Chamberlain, eds., *Women of Color and the Multicultural Curriculum: Tranforming the College Classroom* (New York: The Feminist Press, 1994).

Frankenberg, Ruth, ed., *Displacing Whiteness: Essays in Social and Cultural Criticism* (Durham, N.C. and London: Duke University Press, 1997).

Freire, Paulo, *Pedagogy of the Oppressed*, new revised ed. (New York: Continuum, 1993).

Giroux, Henry, *Living Dangerously: Multiculturalism and the Politics of Difference* (New York: Peter Lang, 1993).

Graff, Gerald, *Beyond the Culture Wars: How Teaching the Conflicts Can Revitalize American Education* (New York: W. W. Norton, 1992).

Hill, Mike, ed., *Whiteness: A Critical Reader* (New York: New York University Press, 1998).

Himley, Margaret, ed, *Political Moments in the Classroom* (Portsmouth, N.H.: Boynton/Cook, 1997).

hooks, bell, *Teaching to Transgress: Education as the Practice of Freedom* (New York: Routledge, 1994).

Hune, Shirley, *Asian Pacific American Women in Higher Education: Claiming Visibility and Voice* (Washington, D.C.: Association of American Colleges and Universities, 1998).

Jay, Gregory, *American Literature and the Culture Wars* (Ithaca, N.Y.: Cornell University Press, 1997).

Kanpol, Barry, *Critical Pedagogy: An Introduction*, Critical Studies in Education and Culture Series (Westport, Conn.: Bergin and Garvey, 1994).

Karamcheti, Indira, "Caliban in the Classroom," in *Teaching What You're Not: Identity Politics in Higher Education*, ed. Katherine J. Mayberry (New York: New York University Press, 1996), 215–227.

Kitano, Harry H. L. and Roger Daniels, eds., *Asian Americans: Emerging Minorities*, 3d ed. (Upper Saddle River, N.J.: Prentice-Hall, 2001).

Lipsitz, George, *The Possessive Investment in Whiteness: How White People Profit from Identity Politics* (Philadelphia: Temple University Press, 1998).

Maher, Frances A. and Mary Kay Thompson Tetreault, *The Feminist Classroom* (New York: Basic Books, 1994).

Matsuda, Mari J., *Where Is Your Body? and Other Essays on Race, Gender, and the Law* (Boston: Beacon Press, 1996).

McIntosh, Peggy, "White Privilege and Male Privilege: A Personal Account of Coming to See Correspondences Through Work in Women's Studies," in *Race, Class, and Gender: An Anthology*, ed. Margaret Andersen and Patricia Hill Collins (Belmont., Calif.: Wadsworth, 1995), 76–86.

McLaren, Peter, ed., *Revolutionary Multiculturalism: Pedagogies of Dissent for the New Millennium* (Boulder, Colo.: Westview, 1997).

Memmi, Albert, *Racism*, trans. by Steve Martinot (Minneapolis: University of Minnesota Press, 2000).

Morrison, Toni, *Playing in the Dark: Whiteness and the Literary Imagination* (Cambridge, Mass.: Harvard University Press, 1992).

Noriega, Jorge, "American Indian Education in the United States: Indoctrination for Subordination to Colonialism," in *The State of Native America: Genocide, Colonization, and Resistance*, ed. M. Annette Jaimes (Boston: South End Press, 1992), 371–402.

Omi, Michael and Howard Winant, *Racial Formation in the United States from the 1960s to the 1990s*, 2d ed. (New York: Routledge, 1994).

Palmer, Parker, *The Courage to Teach: Exploring the Inner Landscape of a Teacher's Life* (San Francisco: Jossey-Bass, 1998).

Schoem, David, et al., *Multicultural Teaching in the University* (Westport, Conn.: Praeger, 1993).

Smedley, Audrey, *Race in North America: Origin and Evolution of a Worldview* (Boulder, Colo.: Westview Press, 1993).

Spears, Arthur K., *Race and Ideology: Language, Symbolism, and Popular Culture* (Detroit: Wayne State University Press, 1999).

Tatum, Beverly, *"Why Are All the Black Kids Sitting Together in the Cafeteria?" and Other Conversations About Race* (New York: Basic Books, 1997).

Tayko, Gail and John Paul Tassoni, eds., *Sharing Pedagogies: Students and Teachers Write About Dialogic Practices* (Portsmouth, N.H.: Boynton/Cook, 1997).

Totten, Samuel, "Educating for the Development of Social Consciousness and Social Responsibility," in *Social Issues in the English Classroom*, ed. C. Mark Hurlbert and Samuel Totten (Urbana. Ill.: National Council of Teachers of English, 1992), 9–55.

Trzyna, Thomas and Martin Abbott, "Grieving in the Ethnic Literature Classroom," *College Literature* 18, no. 3 (October 1991): 1–2.

Valverde, Leonard A. et al., eds., *The Multicultural Campus: Strategies for Transforming Higher Education* (Walnut Creek, Calif.: AltaMira, 1998).

Waters, Mary C., "Optional Ethnicities: For Whites Only?," in *Race, Class, and Gender: An Anthology*, ed. Margaret L. Andersen and Patricia Hill Collins (Belmont, Calif.: Wadsworth, 1998), 403–412.

Williams, John A., *Classroom in Conflict: Teaching Controversial Subjects in a Diverse Society* (Albany: State University of New York Press, 1994).

Williams, Patricia J., *Seeing a Color-Blind Future: The Paradox of Race* (New York: The Noonday Press, 1998).

Young, Robert J. C., *Colonial Desire: Hybridity in Theory, Culture, and Race* (London and New York: Routledge, 1995).

FRED ASHE is an associate professor of English at Birmingham-Southern College. His specialty is American literature, and his research interests include African American literature, family memoir, and urban homelessness.

BRENDA BOUDREAU is an assistant professor of English and the director of the gender studies minor at McKendree College in Illinois. Most of her research and teaching focuses on race, class, and gender in contemporary American literature. She also trains students and faculty to recognize and combat bias, bigotry, and racism.

NORMA E. CANTÚ is a professor of English at the University of Texas at San Antonio. She is the editor of the book series Rio Grande/Rio Bravo: Borderlands Culture and Tradition for Texas A & M University Press. She is a member of the Board of Trustees of the American Folklife Center at the Library of Congress, and also serves on the board of the American Folklore Society and the Federation of State Humanities Councils. Cantú is the author of *Canícula: Snapshots of a Girlhood en la Frontera.*

SARIKA CHANDRA is a Ph.D. candidate in English at the University of Florida, where she also teaches courses in American literature and culture. Her research interests include contemporary American travel writing, ethnic literatures, and immigrant literatures. She is working on a dissertation on American travel and immigrant literatures.

PATTI DUNCAN is an assistant professor of women's studies at Portland State University in Oregon. She received her Ph.D. in women's studies from Emory University in 2000. Her current scholarship and activism focus on Asian Pacific American women's resistance to oppression, women of color and third world feminisms, and queer women's histories and movements.

TAMI EGGLESTON is an assistant professor of psychology at McKendree College in Illinois. She received her Ph.D. in social psychology from Iowa State University. Eggleston works with faculty development efforts to encourage effective pedagogy by recognizing issues of diversity and to incorporate technology and community service into the classroom.

KAREN ELIAS became deeply committed to bringing antiracist work to the classroom after attending the National Women's Studies Association conference, Women Confront Racism, in 1981. She has taught at Purdue University, SUNY Oswego, Lock Haven University and, most recently, Philadelphia University.

GĨTAHI GĨTĨTĨ teaches African, African American, Caribbean, Latin American, and comparative literatures at the University of Rhode Island. His work has been published in *The Johns Hopkins Guide to Literary Theory and Criticism, Companion to African Literatures, Current Writing, Paintbrush*, and *Left Curve*. He is also a translator and poet.

JOSEPH L. GRAVES JR. is a professor of evolutionary biology in the Department of Life Sciences at Arizona State University West and African American Studies faculty at ASU Main. A widely published scholar, his latest work is from Rutgers University Press, titled *The Emperor's New Clothes: Biological Theories of Race at the Millennium*.

ROBERTA J. HILL, an Oneida from Wisconsin, is a poet, fiction writer, and scholar. She earned an MFA from the University of Montana and a PhD in American Studies from the University of Minnesota. A professor of English and American Studies at the University of Wisconsin, she is the author of *Star Quilt* and *Philadelphia Flowers*. Her poetry has appeared most recently in the *Beloit Poetry Journal, Luna*, and *Prairie Schooner*. A biography of her grandmother, Dr. Lillie Rosa Minoka-Hill, the second American Indian woman physician, is forthcoming from the University of Nebraska Press.

JENNIFER HO is currently teaching Asian American literature at Mount Holyoke College. Her dissertation, *Feeding Identity: Examining Food and Ethnicity in Asian American Bildungsroman*, looks at the intersections of food and ethnic identity formation in Asian American literature and popular culture. She expects to receive her Ph.D. from Boston University in 2002.

A. YEMISI JIMOH teaches the multiethnic literatures of the United States. Her research interests are in African American literary and cultural studies. Jimoh's book, *Spiritual, Blues, and Jazz People in African American Fiction: Living in Paradox*, is forthcoming from the University of Tennessee Press.

CHARLENE JOHNSON is an associate professor of education at University of Arkansas and teaches foundation courses that focus on the psychology of teaching and learning. Her research focuses on the implications of culture for early adolescent development. She coedited the book *Practicing What We Preach: Preparing Middle Level Educators*, published by Falmer Press.

JUDITH C. JONES has years of experience facilitating diversity work in and out of the classroom. She grew up in a black working-class community in Philadelphia, earning her Ph.D. in political science at Atlanta University. Her experience includes teaching at Central State University, Pennsylvania State University, and Philadelphia University.

GARY L. LEMONS is a professor and the chair of race, ethnicity, and post-colonial studies at Eugene Lang College at New School University. He teaches courses on feminist antiracism, black feminist theory and cultural criticism, and critical pedagogy. He has held two NEH fellowships for college teachers and a Rockefeller post-doctoral fellowship. His work appears in a number of journals and anthologies. He has completed a manuscript on African American men and feminism. Lemons is the founding director of the Memoirs of Race Project.

KAREN J. LEONG is an assistant professor in the Women's Studies Program at Arizona State University. Her teaching and scholarship examine the intersections of gender, race and ethnicity, class, and sexuality in U.S. history, particularly as manifest through women's experiences, social institutions and policy, and popular culture.

DANIEL P. LISTON is a professor in the School of Education at the Universitv of Colorado at Boulder. His areas of interest include radical educational theory, curriculum theory, and teacher education. He is currently completing a book titled *Love and Despair in Teaching*, which will be published by Routledge.

KARYN D. MCKINNEY is an assistant professor of sociology at Pennsylvania State University, Altoona. Her research focuses on race, ethnicity, and gender. She recently coauthored an article for the *Indiana Law Review* and, with Joe Feagin, has written a book titled *The Costs of Racism*, which will be published by Rowman and Littlefield in 2002.

REBECCA MEACHAM is a doctoral candidate at the University of Cincinnati, where she is specializing in fiction writing and ethnic American literatures. Her archetypal study of Amiri Baraka's black arts poetry appears in *Archetypal Criticism*. Since 1992 she has taught literature, women's studies, composition, and creative writing courses.

LOUIS OWENS, currently a professor of English and Native American Studies at the University of California, Davis, is the author of numerous essays, critical studies, works of fiction, and personal narratives. His publications include *Other Destinies: Understanding the American Indian Novel; Mixedblood Messages: Literature, Film, Family, Place; I Hear the Train: Reflection, Invention, Refraction; The Sharpest Sight; Wolfsong; Bone Game; Nightland;* and *Dark River*.

SHARON PACKER, M.D., is a psychiatrist in private practice in New York. She is an ad.junct faculty member at New School University, where she teaches online courses in media, psychology, and cultural studies. Packer has published articles dealing with psychiatry, religion, and culture, and is currently researching racial revelation in the colorblind cyberclass.

PETER KERRY POWERS teaches multiethnic American literature at Messiah College. His book *Recalling Religions*, on religion and memory in ethnic women's literature, was published by the University of Tennessee Press in 2001. He is working on a book concerning race, religion, and masculinity in American culture during the 1920s.

KEVIN EVEROD QUASHIE is an assistant professor in the AfroAmerican Studies department at Smith College. He is coeditor of the anthology *New Bones: Contemporary Black Writers in America* and is currently completing a manuscript entitled *The Love Project: A Cultural Theory of Critical Healing in Contemporary Black Women's Writing*. He writes about and teaches cultural studies.

MAUREEN T. REDDY is a professor of English and women's studies at Rhode Island College. Her other books include *Crossing the Color Line: Race, Parenting, and Culture* and the edited collection *Everyday Acts Against Racism*. She lives with her family in Providence, where she is finishing a book on race and popular fiction.

SIRAT AL SALIM is an African American educator, organizer, and activist. While pursuing his Ph.D. in education at the University of Colorado at Boulder, he directs an outreach project, CU in the House, and serves as educational coordinator and curriculum specialist for the Veterans of Hope Project, based in Denver.

VIRGINIA WHATLEY SMITH is an associate professor of English at University of Alabama at Birmingham, specializing in African American literature. Her work has appeared in *African American Review, Mississippi Quarterly,* and *Approaches to Teaching Native Son*. Her collection of essays, *Richard Wright's Travel Writings,* is published by University Press of Mississippi.

RAJINI SRIKANTH teaches at the University of Massachusetts, Boston. Her coedited collections include *Contours of the Heart,* a book of creative writing and photography by first- and second-generation South Asian Americans and Canadians; *A Part, Yet Apart,* multidisciplinary essays on the ambiguous position of South Asians within Asian America; *Bold Words: A Century of Asian American Writing;* and *White Women in Racialized Spaces,* which explores representations of racialized Others by white women over three hundred years and across four continents.

JOSÉ L. TORRES-PADILLA, associate professor of English at SUNY Plattsburgh, focuses his teaching and research on U.S. ethnic literatures. A published writer of poetry and short fiction, his latest project is a critical anthology of early U.S. Hispanic short fiction.

BONNIE TUSMITH is an associate professor of English at Northeastern University in Boston and President of MELUS, the national multiethnic literary society. Her publications include *All My Relatives: Community in Contemporary Ethnic American Literatures; Colorizing Literary Theory; Conversations with John Edgar Wideman;* and *American Family Album: 28 Contemporary Ethnic Stories.*